W9-CKR-904

GarageBand®

for dummies®
A Wiley Brand

GarageBand

2nd Edition

by Bob LeVitus
Houston Chronicle "Dr. Mac" columnist

Contents at a Glance

Introduction 1

Part 1: Starting on a Good Note 5
CHAPTER 1: Introducing GarageBand for Macs and iDevices 7
CHAPTER 2: Equipping and Setting Up Your Recording Space 25
CHAPTER 3: Introducing Multitrack Recording with GarageBand 49

Part 2: Making Music on a Mac 77
CHAPTER 4: Getting Started 79
CHAPTER 5: Using Loops to Make Music 91
CHAPTER 6: Recording with MIDI and Software Instruments 111
CHAPTER 7: Recording Vocals and Acoustic Instruments with a Mic 137
CHAPTER 8: Recording Electric Guitars and Other Electronic Instruments 157

Part 3: Postproduction: Finishing Songs on a Mac 173
CHAPTER 9: Editing and Polishing Tracks 175
CHAPTER 10: Mixing Tracks into Songs 199
CHAPTER 11: Mastering Mastering 213

Part 4: Making Music with Your iDevice 225
CHAPTER 12: Getting Started 227
CHAPTER 13: Making Music with Live Loops 241
CHAPTER 14: Laying Down Software Instrument Tracks 257
CHAPTER 15: Recording Vocals and Acoustic Instruments with a Mic 273
CHAPTER 16: Recording Guitars and Basses without Mics or Amps 291

Part 5: Postproduction: Finishing Songs on an iDevice 307
CHAPTER 17: Editing and Polishing Tracks 309
CHAPTER 18: Mixing Tracks into Songs 327
CHAPTER 19: Mastering Mastering 341

Part 6: Everything Else You Might Need to Know 347
CHAPTER 20: Playing Live with GarageBand Amps and Effects 349
CHAPTER 21: Jamming with Others over Wi-Fi 357
CHAPTER 22: File Compression and Your Music 365
CHAPTER 23: CD Recording, Reproduction, and Distribution 377

Part 7: The Part of Tens 389

CHAPTER 24: Ten Ways to Improve GarageBand's Performance 391

CHAPTER 25: Ten Ways to Take Your Recordings to the Next Level 401

CHAPTER 26: Ten Useful Websites 411

Index 417

Table of Contents

INTRODUCTION 1

About This Book. 1
Not-So-Foolish Assumptions 2
Conventions Used in This Book. 2
Icons Used in This Book 3
Beyond the Book 4
Where to Go from Here 4

PART 1: STARTING ON A GOOD NOTE 5

CHAPTER 1: **Introducing GarageBand for Macs and iDevices** 7
What Is GarageBand? 8
What Can You Do with GarageBand? 9
What Can't You Do with GarageBand? 9
Checking Your System Requirements 10
The official requirements for Macs 10
The official requirements for iDevices 12
What Else Do You Need to Run GarageBand? 12
Recording with GarageBand: A Few Teasers 15
Sneak peek 1: The recording sequence 15
Sneak peek 2: GarageBand for Mac 18
Sneak peek 3: GarageBand for iDevices. 20

CHAPTER 2: **Equipping and Setting Up Your
Recording Space** 25
Cobbling Together a Studio Without Breaking the Bank. 26
Making the Most of Your Recording Space 27
Deadening the room. 27
Preventing background noise 28
Equipping Your Studio: Must-Have Gear versus
Good-to-Have Gear 28
Choosing a Microphone 29
Dynamic and condenser microphones 31
Microphone polarity patterns 32
Microphone preamps 33
Setting up your microphone 34
Finding the Right Speakers. 34
Listening with Headphones Without Messing Up the Take 36
Adding a MIDI Keyboard to Your Setup 37
Finding a keyboard 37
Connecting a MIDI keyboard to your computer 39

Unraveling the Cable and Connector Conundrum.............39
Adding an Audio Interface to Your Setup 42
    Using an audio interface with GarageBand...................43
    Shopping for an interface................................43
Perfecting Your Mic Setup 45
    Choosing a mic stand 45
    Recording vocals with pop filters and wind screens 47
Boosting Your Hard Drive Space 47
Recording in Tune with a Tuning Device (for Guitarists) 48

CHAPTER 3: **Introducing Multitrack Recording with GarageBand** 49
Understanding the Role of Stereo in Multitrack Recording 50
Strolling through the Recording Process, Quickly 52
Cutting the Tracks ("No Blood on 'em, Mr. Dylan") 53
    Recording tracks on a Mac..............................54
    Recording tracks on an iDevice 57
    Listening to tracks during recording and playback 59
    Changing a track's settings.............................62
    Changing a track's instrument...........................64
    Checking levels during recording and playback 64
    Adjusting levels 65
    Polishing tracks 67
Mix That Sucka..69
    Overview of mixing 69
    Setting the pan......................................70
(Lord and) Mastering.......................................71
Managing Song Files 73

PART 2: MAKING MUSIC ON A MAC 77

CHAPTER 4: **Getting Started**.................................79
General Pane 80
    Software Instrument Recordings section...................80
    Enable the Force Touch Trackpad check box 82
    Reset Warnings button 82
Audio/MIDI Pane 82
    Devices section 82
    Effects section 84
    MIDI section 84
Metronome Pane...84
Loops Pane 86
    Keyboard Browsing setting 86
    Keyboard Layout setting................................87
    Loop Browser setting 88

My Info Pane 88
Advanced Pane 89
    Audio Recording Resolution setting 89
    Auto Normalize setting. 90
    Movie Thumbnail Resolution setting 90

CHAPTER 5: **Using Loops to Make Music** 91
What Is a Loop, Anyway? 91
    Where to find more loops 92
    Spicing up your songs with loops 93
Finding the Right Loop with the Loop Browser. 94
    Viewing loops in button or column view 94
    Seeing more instruments. 96
    Searching for a loop you love 97
    Filtering by loop type 101
    Previewing loops 101
    Keeping your favorite loops at the ready. 102
    Adding third-party loops to the loop browser. 102
Setting a Loop's Tempo 103
Adding Loops to Tracks 104
    Dragging and dropping loops 105
    Undoing and redoing a loop 106
    Extending, shortening, and repeating loops 107
    Editing loops: A preview 108
    Reusing an edited loop in a different song 109

CHAPTER 6: **Recording with MIDI and Software
Instruments** 111
What Is MIDI, Anyway? 112
Controlling Software Instruments with a MIDI Keyboard 112
Choosing Software Instruments 114
Recording Tracks with Software Instruments 117
Altering the Sound of Software Instruments. 119
    Delving deeper into Smart controls 120
    Adding and changing plug-in effects .125
    Compressors and other plug-in effects 129
Drummer Tracks 134
Testing Your Changes. 136

CHAPTER 7: **Recording Vocals and Acoustic
Instruments with a Mic**. 137
Getting Ready to Record. 138
    Setting up your mic and recording track 138
    Tweaking the pan to hear vocals better. 142

       Positioning the microphone.....................................142
       Setting levels 143
       Adding effects 145
       Checking for unwanted noise 146
    Multitrack Recording..149
       Dave Hamilton on multitrack drum recording 149
       Recording with a MIDI drum 151
    Recording the Track 152
    Improving the Sound of Recordings..............................153

CHAPTER 8: Recording Electric Guitars and Other Electronic Instruments..................................157
    Overview from the Top: Direct or Live Recording.................158
    Direct Recording with GarageBand's Virtual Amplifiers...........159
       Setting up to record 159
       Troubleshooting your setup 161
       Making a too soft instrument louder 162
       Setting levels 163
       Recording the track...164
    Recording Live with an Amplifier and Microphones...............165
    Customizing the Sound of Your Guitar Tracks 168
       Changing presets and amp simulators 168
       Editing presets...169
       Making other changes 170

PART 3: POSTPRODUCTION: FINISHING SONGS ON A MAC...173

CHAPTER 9: Editing and Polishing Tracks.......................175
    "When Should I Edit Tracks?" 176
    Editing Software Instrument versus Real Instrument Tracks 176
    Fixing Flubs and Faux Pas 178
       Punching in and out to replace part of a track 178
       Just undo it . . . and then redo it 181
       Splitting and joining regions 182
       Silencing mistakes with the track volume control 184
    Rearranging Regions..185
       The arrangement track and markers 185
    Editing Software Instrument Tracks 188
       Changing the tempo of a song 188
       Changing the tempo of song parts 188
       Changing the pitch 189
       Rearranging notes in a region 190

Sweetening: Add New Material? Or Not?...................195
    Percussion 196
    Backing vocals 196
    Special effects 198
    Horns, woodwinds, and strings.......................198

CHAPTER 10: **Mixing Tracks into Songs** 199
What Is Mixing?.......................................199
Creating a Level Playing Field 200
    Roughing it with a rough mix.........................201
    A fine tune 202
    Level meters: Red = dead.............................203
Panning Tracks Left or Right 204
The Effects of Adding Effects 206
    Equalization or not?..................................207
    Echo and reverb......................................209
    Compressor 209
    Chorus...210
Doubling Tracks.......................................210
    The copy-and-paste method 210
    The re-recording method 211

CHAPTER 11: **Mastering Mastering** 213
What, Exactly, Is Mastering?...........................214
Before You Master.....................................214
The Master Track Is for Mastering Tracks 215
    Applying presets and effects to the master track.........216
    Tweaking effects 217
    Setting the master volume............................221
One More Thing Before You Call It "Done" 222

PART 4: MAKING MUSIC WITH YOUR IDEVICE 225

CHAPTER 12: **Getting Started**...............................227
Global Settings..228
    Allowing GarageBand access...........................228
    Determining knob response 229
    Reducing crosstalk...................................229
GarageBand Settings 229
    Metronome and count-in..............................230
    Tempo, time, and key.................................232
The Control Bar 236
Sharing Projects with a Mac (and Vice Versa) 239

CHAPTER 13: **Making Music with Live Loops** 241

Loop Basics. 242
Find more loops. 242
More about loops 243
Grokking the loop grid 243
Working with Loops 245
Adding Apple loops to cells 245
Finding a loop you love. 246
Listening to loops 247
Keeping your favorite loops at the ready. 248
Types of loops 249
Working with Cells 249
Editing cells. 249
Undoing and redoing a loop 252
Moving cells 252
Recording into a cell 253
Adding remix FX 253
Recording with the Loop Grid 254

CHAPTER 14: **Laying Down Software Instrument Tracks**. 257

What Is MIDI, Anyway? 257
Controlling Software Instruments with a MIDI Keyboard 259
Working with Software Instruments 261
Creating a new software instrument track 262
Selecting a different instrument 263
Recording a software instrument track 264
Working with Tracks 265
Displaying track headers 265
Adding loops 266
Working with regions 267

CHAPTER 15: **Recording Vocals and Acoustic
Instruments with a Mic**. 273

Getting Ready to Record. 275
Preparing to record. 275
Positioning the microphone. 279
Setting levels 280
Adding effects 281
Tweaking the pan to hear vocals better. 283
Checking for unwanted noise 284
Multitrack Recording. 284
Dave Hamilton on multitrack drum recording 285
Recording with a MIDI drum controller 287
Recording the Track 288
Improving the Sound of Recordings. 289

CHAPTER 16: Recording Guitars and Basses without Mics or Amps 291

Overview from the Top: Direct or Live Recording. 292

Direct Recording with GarageBand's Virtual Amplifiers. 293

Setting up to record 293

Troubleshooting your setup 296

Making a too soft instrument louder 296

Setting levels 298

Recording the track 299

Recording Live with an Amplifier and Microphones. 300

Customizing the Sound of Your Guitar Tracks 302

Changing presets and amp simulators 303

Changing and modifying stomp box effects 303

Editing presets 304

Making other changes 306

PART 5: POSTPRODUCTION: FINISHING SONGS ON AN IDEVICE 307

CHAPTER 17: Editing and Polishing Tracks 309

"When Should I Edit Tracks?" 310

Editing Software Instrument versus Real Instrument Tracks 310

Arranging and Rearranging 312

Song sections 312

Fixing Flubs and Faux Pas 313

Punching in and out to replace part of a track 314

Just undo it . . . and then redo it 316

Splitting and joining regions 317

Silencing mistakes with automation curves 318

Editing Software Instrument Tracks 319

Changing the tempo of a song 320

Changing the pitch 320

Rearranging notes in a region 322

Changing a note's velocity 324

To quantize or not 325

Sweetening: Add New Material or Not? 326

CHAPTER 18: Mixing Tracks into Songs 327

What Is Mixing? 327

Creating a Level Playing Field 328

Roughing it with a rough mix. 329

A fine tune 330

Level meters: Red = dead. 331

Panning Tracks Left or Right 331
The Effects of Adding Effects 333
    Equalization or not? 335
    Compressor 337
    Echo and reverb 338
    Chorus 338
Doubling Tracks 339
    The copy-and-paste method 339
    The re-recording method 340

CHAPTER 19: **Mastering Mastering** 341
Before You Master 342
Exporting to a Mac for Mastering 343
Sharing Songs 343

PART 6: EVERYTHING ELSE YOU MIGHT
NEED TO KNOW 347

CHAPTER 20: **Playing Live with GarageBand Amps
and Effects** 349
Playing at Home 350
General Tips for Guitarists and Bassists 351
    Create a practice file 351
    Get to know your amps, pedals, and other plug-ins 352
    Expand your palette with third-party plug-ins 352
Playing on Stage 353

CHAPTER 21: **Jamming with Others over Wi-Fi** 357
Becoming the Bandleader 358
Becoming a Member 360
Working with Jam Sessions 361

CHAPTER 22: **File Compression and Your Music** 365
Understanding Compression 366
    About uncompressed audio files 366
    About compressed audio files 367
Sharing Your Masterpiece 369
    Sharing your songs from a Mac 369
    Sharing your songs from an iDevice 372
How Much Compression Can You Stand? 372
Distributing Your Music 374
    Finding the song file on your Mac 374
    Sending AAC or MP3 files via Mail or Messages 374

CHAPTER 23: CD Recording, Reproduction, and Distribution 377

The Benefits of Burning CDs 378
Getting Ready to Burn Songs on CDs 378
Gathering what you need to burn CDs 378
Setting the cycle area 379
Burning Songs to CDs 380
Burning a song to a CD with GarageBand 381
Burning songs to a CD with the Music app or iTunes 382
Making multiple copies of the same CD 385
Lovely labels for your CDs 386
Distributing Your Music 387
CD Baby and TuneCore 387
More distribution ideas 387

PART 7: THE PART OF TENS 389

CHAPTER 24: Ten Ways to Improve GarageBand's Performance 391

Starting with the Basics 392
Checking on FileVault 393
Paying Attention to CPU and RAM Usage 394
Checking Out Activity Monitor's CPU and Memory Tabs 395
Recording: 16-bits versus 24-bits 397
Minimizing the GarageBand Window While
Playing or Recording 398
Getting More RAM 398
Getting Faster Storage 399
Resetting MIDI Drivers 400
Turn Off Wi-Fi Before Recording or Performing 400

CHAPTER 25: Ten Ways to Take Your Recordings to the Next Level 401

Getting a Better Microphone 401
Making Sure Your Speakers Reproduce Sound Decently 402
Getting Better Headphones 403
Fine-Tuning Mic Placement 404
Improving Room Acoustics 404
Using Quality Cables 405
Adding an Audio Interface (and, Optionally, a Mixing Board) 405
Switch to More Powerful Software 406
Logic Pro 407
Pro Tools 408

CHAPTER 26: **Ten Useful Websites**.................................411

  Learn Songs on Guitar or Bass 411

    Search for free chord charts or tablature 411

    Ultimate-Guitar 412

    GarageBand Karaoke (free MIDI files) 412

  Mix Magazine 413

  MusicRadar..414

  Sweetwater Sound 414

  Musician's Friend 415

  Monoprice 415

  Apple GarageBand Discussion Board........................416

INDEX..417

Introduction

I f you want to make music with GarageBand, you've made the right choice twice — once by choosing GarageBand, which is the easiest way to create your own music on a Mac or iDevice — and again by choosing this book to help you along. Before you know it, you'll be topping the charts and basking in fame, glory, and fortune.

Well, it's possible. By the time you finish this book, you'll possess the knowledge to do so, although I'm afraid it's up to you to provide the talent.

Don't worry. Just sit back, relax, and get ready to have a rockin' good time. That's right. This may be a computer book, but we're going to have a good time together. What a concept!

Whether you're new to music making or a grizzled studio veteran, I guarantee that learning to make music with *GarageBand For Dummies* is going to be fun and easy. Hey, it wouldn't say "Learning Made Easy" on the cover if it weren't true.

About This Book

Of course, *GarageBand For Dummies*, 2nd Edition is going to show you everything you need to get the most out of Apple's amazing GarageBand, which is a complete recording studio and much more.

But I hope to give you much more than that. Here's a quick look at just some of what you can do:

>> Discover how to use GarageBand's numerous (and very cool) features on the Mac and iDevices.

>> Get the lowdown on the equipment you will definitely need, the gear you don't need but may want, and the gear that you don't need — plus all the details on setting up and connecting everything.

>> Find details about creating great-sounding songs all by your lonesome and then distributing them to your friends (or enemies) and (gasp) perhaps even selling them.

>> Be gently introduced to many professional audio recording and engineering techniques that will impress your friends with slick, professional-sounding recordings.

GarageBand For Dummies, 2nd Edition is chock-full of useful information, plus tips and techniques for making good multitrack recordings. If you follow my simple instructions, you'll gain the skills you need to produce great-sounding recordings that are sure to impress your family and friends, not to mention musicians, singers, songwriters, and producers.

Not-So-Foolish Assumptions

Although I know what happens when you make assumptions, I've made a few anyway. The biggest is that you, gentle reader, know nothing about making multitrack recordings or using GarageBand.

I also assume that you know what a Mac, an iPad, and an iPhone are, you know how to turn them on and use them, and you know they have a copy of GarageBand installed. I assume also that you want to understand GarageBand without digesting an incomprehensible technical manual (which, by the way, doesn't exist anyway) and, finally, that you made the right choice by selecting this particular book.

One more thing: I assume you can read. If you can't, please ignore this paragraph.

Conventions Used in This Book

To get the most out of this book, you need to know how I do things and why. Following are a few conventions I use in this book to make your life easier:

>> When I want you to open an item in a menu, I write something like "Choose File ⇨ Open," which means, "Click the File menu and choose the Open command."

>> Stuff that you're supposed to type appears in bold type, **like this.**

>> **Sometimes an entire sentence is in bold,** as you'll see when I present a numbered list of steps. **In those cases,** I unbold **what you're supposed to type,** like this.

>> When I refer to the Mac's menu, I'm referring to the menu in the upper-left corner of the macOS menu bar that looks like an apple (called the *Apple menu*).

>> For Mac keyboard shortcuts, I write something like "press ⌘+A," which means to hold down the ⌘ key (the one with the little pretzel or symbol or both on it) and then press the letter *A* on your keyboard. If you see something like "press ⌘+Shift+A," that means to hold down the ⌘ and Shift keys while pressing the *A* key.

Icons Used in This Book

You'll see little round pictures (icons) off to the left side of the text throughout this book. Consider these icons as miniature road signs, telling you a little something extra about the topic at hand. Here's what the different icons look like and what they all mean.

Look for Tip icons to find the juiciest morsels: shortcuts, tips, and undocumented secrets about GarageBand. Try them all; impress your friends!

When you see this icon, it means this particular morsel is something I think you should memorize (or at least write on your shirt cuff).

This icon signifies something that's not required reading. It could be about pro audio, programming, or progressive rock, but whatever it is, it's not required for you to master GarageBand. (On the other hand, it must be interesting or informative, or I wouldn't have wasted your time with it.)

Read these notes very, very carefully. Did I say *ver-y*? Warning icons flag important information. The author and publisher won't be responsible if your Mac explodes or spews flaming parts because you ignored a Warning icon. Just kidding. Macs don't explode or spew (with the exception of a few choice PowerBook 5300s, which can't run GarageBand anyway). But I got your attention, didn't I? It's a good idea to read the Warning icons carefully.

Beyond the Book

In addition to what you're reading right now, this book also comes with a free access-anywhere Cheat Sheet that provides a handy list of useful keyboard shortcuts as well as instructions for silencing mistakes. To get this Cheat Sheet, simply go to www.dummies.com and type **GarageBand For Dummies Cheat Sheet** in the search box.

I've also created a downloadable GarageBand tutorial with a completed GarageBand project, the finished master track, and a PDF explaining how and why I did what I did in the project, which you can download at www.workingsmarterformacusers.com/blog/garageband.

Where to Go from Here

Go to a comfortable spot (preferably not far from a Mac or iDevice) and read the book.

TIP

I didn't write this book for myself. I wrote it for you and would love to hear how it worked for you. So please drop me a line or register your comments through the Online Registration Form, which you can find by clicking the Customer Care link (under Contact Us) at www.dummies.com.

Did this book work for you? What did you like? What didn't you like? What questions were unanswered? Did you want to know more about something? Did you want to find out less about something? Tell me!

You can send email to me at GarageBandForDummies@boblevitus.com. I appreciate your feedback, and I *try* to respond to all reasonably polite email within a few days.

So, what are you waiting for? Go enjoy the book!

1

Starting on a Good Note

Become familiar with the software and get a high-level overview of digital multitrack recording (which is what GarageBand does).

Determine your recording studio needs and wants (and budget), and then get down to the nuts and bolts of speakers, cables, audio interfaces, and other devices that you can use to achieve better sound.

Explore the process of multitrack recording and the way multitrack recordings are created in GarageBand.

IN THIS CHAPTER

» Finding out what GarageBand is

» Checking out what you can do with GarageBand

» Discovering what you can't do with GarageBand

» Exploring the differences between the Mac version and iOS and iPadOS versions

» Checking requirements

» Taking a sneak peek at the recording sequence

Chapter 1

Introducing GarageBand for Macs and iDevices

W hen GarageBand was introduced at Macworld Expo in January 2004, Apple CEO Steve Jobs informed the audience that one out of two adults play a musical instrument but that almost none of them have recorded themselves playing.

Why not?

Because before GarageBand came along, recording live music decently was just too complicated. It required expensive and hard-to-use software and even more expensive and equally hard-to-use hardware, as well as a basic understanding of audio engineering.

GarageBand changed everything. If you want to record yourself singing or playing an instrument — any instrument — GarageBand lets you do it without spending a lot of time or money. Better still: GarageBand will give you professional-sounding results even if you don't know the first thing about audio recording or engineering.

In this chapter, you begin your acquaintance with GarageBand. First, you learn a bit about what it is and what you can do with it, along with what it is not and what it can't do. You explore the differences between the Mac version and the iPad and iPhone version and review the system requirements for both platforms. Finally, you finish with a quick look at the process of transforming the song in your head into a recording suitable for sharing.

What Is GarageBand?

GarageBand for the Mac is a complete recording studio that includes hundreds of realistic-sounding instruments, effects, and presets configured by experienced recording engineers.

GarageBand for the iPad and iPhone is also a complete recording studio, but the iOS and iPadOS versions are designed for the touchscreen and include realistic-sounding touch instruments you "play" onscreen.

In a nutshell, GarageBand — on either platform — combines everything you need to record, mix, master, and share music with others.

TIP

GarageBand's default settings and templates are a big part of the reason why GarageBand is so great, especially for beginners. The instruments and audio effects sound great right out of the box, and they rarely require much (if any) tweaking. It's kind of like having a crew of professional recording engineers inside your Mac or iDevice.

There has never been a program quite like GarageBand; it's the *perfect* introduction to multitrack audio recording on Apple devices. I mean that. GarageBand is easy, friendly, forgiving, and fun on all platforms and you can't beat the price.

TECHNICAL STUFF

Multitrack recording means recording instruments or vocals with each instrumental or vocal performance recorded on its own track. The sound contained on each track can be adjusted independently of other tracks. Ultimately, the tracks are combined (that is, mixed) in a pleasing manner to create the final product.

I've used 'em all; if you're new to this audio thing, nothing else even comes close to GarageBand. You're gonna love it.

What Can You Do with GarageBand?

GarageBand does things that used to require hours in an expensive recording studio. The following is a fairly comprehensive list of what you can do with GarageBand:

» Record vocals.

» Record acoustic instruments.

» Record software instruments via MIDI (Musical Instrument Digital Interface; more on that in Chapter 2).

» Record electric guitars and basses with GarageBand's virtual amplifier models, so that you can get just the sound you want.

» "Punch in" to a section of an otherwise excellent track to re-record over your mistakes.

» Adjust the sonic (sound) characteristics — volume, equalization, echo, reverb, and so on — for each track individually (all these elements are part of mixing a song, which I cover in Chapter 10) and for the song as a whole (in other words, mastering, which I delve into in Chapter 11).

» Make music using prerecorded loops.

» Combine (mix) multiple tracks of music or loops or both into a two-track (stereo) song file.

» Record a track while listening to (monitoring) one or more other tracks.

This list doesn't cover *everything* you can do with GarageBand, but it at least gives you the gist of the cool stuff you can do.

What Can't You Do with GarageBand?

Well, there's not much GarageBand can't do. When I wrote the first edition of this book, GarageBand's biggest shortcoming (versus more sophisticated recording-studio-type software or an analog recording studio) was that it allowed you to record only one track at a time.

That shortcoming is long gone. Today's GarageBand supports recording on as many tracks at once as your hardware interface (see Chapter 2) and Mac support. Today, its fewer remaining shortcomings are less troubling.

Although you can change the time signature anywhere in a song without missing a beat (pun intended), it's not easy. So, if you tend to write songs with multiple time changes, GarageBand may not be the best tool for you.

Moving right along, some other things you can't do with GarageBand include typesetting a book, removing red-eye from a digital photograph, and sending your mom an email message. But you knew that already (I hope).

Finally, it's possible to create a song that has too many instruments, effects, or tracks for your Mac or iDevice to handle. The older your device (and the less RAM it has), the more likely you'll encounter this issue sooner rather than later. Although this problem can happen when you use higher-end audio software, it happens sooner and with fewer tracks, effects, or instruments in GarageBand.

The next section covers GarageBand's system requirements, so I'll hold the gory details until then. Suffice it to say that newer Macs and iDevices run GarageBand more efficiently than older ones.

Checking Your System Requirements

GarageBand does a lot of intense processing behind the scenes, so it requires more horsepower than some other applications. So, before you go any further with GarageBand, make sure your Mac or iDevice is up to snuff.

The official requirements for Macs

The system requirements for Macs are

- » A Macintosh running macOS 10.13.6 or later

- » At least 8GB of RAM

- » At least 4GB free space on your startup disk for the default install or at least 21GB free space on your startup disk for the full install

Now, please allow me to add *my* two-cents worth regarding what I think is required: GarageBand may run on a 7- or 8-year-old (or older) Mac that meets the preceding requirements, but it probably won't run very well. And 8GB of RAM may not be enough for some advanced productions.

TIP

As a bonus, the more RAM you have in your Mac, the more tracks your songs can have before GarageBand chokes. If you want to know how much of your memory and processor GarageBand is using, open up Activity Monitor (in the Utilities folder inside your Applications folder).

You'll see that even when GarageBand is open but minimized on the dock, as shown in Figure 1-1, it uses more RAM and more processing power than any other program that's running.

But wait! It gets worse. If GarageBand is merely running in the background, as shown in Figure 1-2, it uses three times more processor power than when it was minimized.

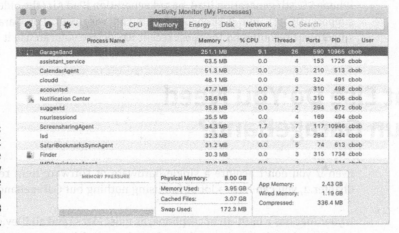

FIGURE 1-1:
GarageBand just minimized on the dock uses nearly 10 percent of the processor and over 250MB of RAM.

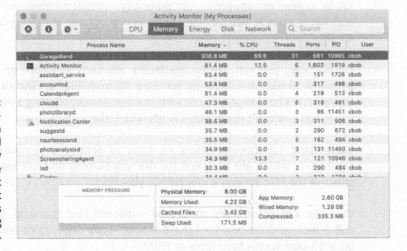

FIGURE 1-2:
When Garage-Band is playing in the background (with Activity Monitor in the foreground), it uses 69 percent of my Mac's processing power.

REMEMBER

Any program or utility that uses that many CPU cycles even when it's minimized or in the background slows down everything else. I recommend that you quit all other apps when you use GarageBand and quit GarageBand (GarageBand ⇨ Quit GarageBand) immediately when you're finished using it each and every time.

The official requirements for iDevices

Following are the system requirements for iDevices:

>> An iPhone, iPad, or iPod touch running iOS 13.0 or later

Here's my one-cent worth: GarageBand may run on an iPhone 6S, iPhone 6S Plus, iPhone SE, 5th generation iPad, or 3rd generation iPad Air (the oldest iDevices that support iOS 13), but it probably won't run very well. For GarageBand to run smoothly, I recommend the most recent iOS device you can use it on.

What Else Do You Need to Run GarageBand?

Even if you don't acquire a single hardware or software item recommended in Chapter 2, you can have a lot of fun using nothing but GarageBand.

If your Mac has a built-in microphone, as most Macs (and all iDevices) do, you can use that microphone to record vocals and musical instruments. The quality will not be as good as connecting just about any external microphone — even a cheap one. But in a pinch, you can use a built-in microphone to capture instruments and vocals.

On the Mac, you can use GarageBand's onscreen keyboard or musical typing keyboard to play the built-in software instruments, as shown in Figure 1-3. However, it's hard to play music with any precision by clicking a mouse or pressing a key, and you can't really play chords with either.

GarageBand for iDevices offers an array of Smart instruments, as shown in Figure 1-4, which are designed for the touchscreen and are easier to use than either of the Mac version's onscreen keyboards.

Pause for a brief interlude about tape — the old kind (cassette, ½-inch, 1-inch, and 2-inch) and the new kind (hard or solid-state drive) in the sidebar, "Recording with tape versus hard drive or SSD."

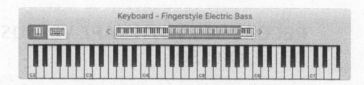

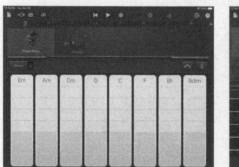

FIGURE 1-3: GarageBand for Mac has a tiny onscreen keyboard (top) and musical typing keyboard (bottom), in case you don't have an external piano-style keyboard handy.

FIGURE 1-4: GarageBand for iDevices has Smart instruments including Smart piano (top left), Smart guitar (top right), Smart strings (bottom left), and Smart drums (bottom right).

RECORDING WITH TAPE VERSUS HARD DRIVE OR SSD

In the old days, you recorded to tape. The more tracks you wanted to record at a time, the more expensive the studio time, equipment, actual tape, and so on. Hobbyists recorded two, four, or eight tracks at a time onto tape that was ⅛, ¼, or ½-inch wide. Professionals tended to record 16 or more tracks at once onto 1-inch or 2-inch tape. The more tracks a studio could record at a time, the more you paid per hour to use that studio.

The specialized equipment used in the professional or semi-professional recording studio — particularly the multitrack tape recorders and mixing boards (or "consoles") with 16 or more tracks, as shown in the following figure — were (and still are) quite expensive.

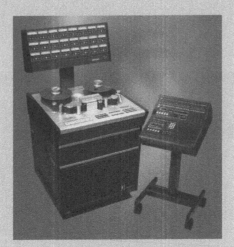

Printed with permission of Studer Professional Audio GmbH (www.studer.ch). Studer is a registered trademark of Studer Professional Audio GmbH.

Luckily, hard drives work as well as tape recorders for storing recorded audio, and big, fast hard or solid-state drives are dirt cheap compared to almost any decent multitrack tape-recording device. Better still, a hard drive doesn't come with a predefined track limit. Put another way, an 8-track tape recorder can record only eight tracks at a time, maximum. A hard drive lets you record (and mix and master) a virtually unlimited number of tracks, software and hardware setup permitting.

Much of the music you hear today has never been anywhere near magnetic audio tape. Instead, it has become cheaper, faster, and easier to avoid tape entirely and record tracks direct to disk — which is precisely what GarageBand is doing when you record a track.

Recording with GarageBand: A Few Teasers

Before I move on to the discussion of your recording space and audio gear, I think you should have a slightly clearer picture of the way this recording-studio-in-a-box works. I cover this material throughout the book in glorious detail, but the following brief "sneak peek" sections should make it easier to grok the big picture.

Sneak peek 1 walks (actually, more like sprints) you through the process of making songs with GarageBand on either platform. Sneak peeks 2 and 3 offer a quick look at the user interfaces for Macs and iDevices, respectively.

Sneak peek 1: The recording sequence

When the folks at Apple say GarageBand contains everything you need to create songs, they aren't kidding. It really does give you everything you need to record, edit, loop, use software instruments, overdub, mix, master, and even make MP3 or AAC audio files (or audio CDs) that you can share with friends or even sell.

I delve further into every step of the process in upcoming chapters. For now, I provide a painless introduction to the process of making a multitrack audio recording:

1. Select or write the material.

I know this seems obvious, but it bears mention just the same. Creating an audio recording, like so many things in life, is subject to the GIGO effect — garbage in, garbage out.

There are, of course, exceptions. If you prefer jam bands, aural soundscapes, random noise, trance music, or Brian Eno, you can probably skip right over this step. As for the rest of you: In my humble opinion, things usually work out better if you have an idea of what you want to record *before* you launch GarageBand.

2. Rehearse, if necessary, recording your rehearsals if desired.

Rehearsal can and will make your recording sessions faster and easier.

TIP

Later in the book, I countermand this advice and tell some of you to record every note you ever play. When I produced the band Vengeance, who were all really good players, I would say: "Tape is cheap. Studio time isn't. I record every note from the moment you plug in until you walk out of the studio. I'm not losing a single usable note just because the tape wasn't rolling."

As for me, I'm such a terrible musician that I never even record a take until I can play the part without mistakes (or at least play the part without a mistake in every measure).

If you have more than a drop of musical talent, though, you might want to record your practice takes. Sometimes, that first or second "practice" take turns out to be the best.

If tape is cheap, disk drives are cheaper, which is a good thing because GarageBand chews up storage space at a rapid clip. My songs range from 30MB for the simplest ones to well over 100MB for more complex numbers. At any time, I may be working on a dozen or more different tunes. The point is, it won't take long to amass gigabytes of GarageBand files on your Mac or iDevice.

TIP

Is your main disk drive (Mac) or internal storage (iDevice) filling up? Mac users can archive files to the cloud or an external hard or solid-state drive. iDevice users can move files to the cloud or an external storage device.

3. **Record tracks.**

When you know what you're trying to do, record the tracks for it. Record as many tracks as the song requires and record them until each performance is as good as it can be.

4. **Edit and overdub.**

As soon as all (or most) of your song's tracks are in the can, it's time to fix what ails them. Most people, including many professional musicians, can't record every track perfectly in a single take. There are often imperfections, major and minor — an unwanted breath in the wrong place, guitar string noise in a quiet passage, a dog barking in the background, or whatever. Listen to your tracks with a critical ear, and then fix or replace anything that doesn't sound right to you.

5. **Mix.**

When all (or most) of your tracks represent the best performance you can possibly create, it's time to begin mixing. When you *mix*, you adjust each track's individual *level* (volume), *equalization* (tone), and *pan* (placement left, right, or center in the stereo sound field), and add audio effects such as echo or reverb, striving for a perfect mix of tracks that blends well and sounds good to your ears.

6. **Master.**

If you've made it through Steps 1 through 5, you're so close to completing the song that you should be able to taste it. But before you break out the bubbly, you probably want to master your masterpiece. In the simplest of terms, *mastering* is the same as mixing, but you adjust audio controls such as level, equalization, compression, expansion, and limiting, applying them to the entire song, rather than any single track.

Mastering isn't rocket science. All you're doing is adjusting the tonal qualities and dynamics of the song the same way you adjusted those things for individual tracks when you mixed. Just play with the mastering effects until the song has the sound you're looking for, and you're done.

This simplistic overview of the process represents the traditional workflow: Rehearse, record, edit and overdub, mix, and master.

7. **Share your work with others.**

If you did a good job on the song, you'll want to share your brilliance with others by creating an MP3 or AAC file of the song and attaching it to an email or text message or making it available on the web. Or, if you want to go old-school, you can even burn the song to an audio CD.

PACKAGING YOUR MUSIC ON A MAC

Technically, the file you create when you use the Save or Save As command on a Mac is a package file. A *package* is a special kind of macOS document that is represented by a document icon but acts more like a folder under certain conditions. In other words, GarageBand's package documents, like folders, contain other files. But when you open a package document (by double-clicking it, choosing File ➪ Open, or using the ⌘+O shortcut), rather than revealing its contents, the package document opens the application that created it. Therefore, when you open a GarageBand package document, it opens in GarageBand.

The secret to seeing inside package documents is to right-click or Control-click the file and then choose Show Package Contents from the shortcut menu, as shown in the following figure.

(continued)

(continued)

Inside a GarageBand document package, you'll find (among other things) a Media folder. Inside the Media folder are the individual audio files that represent the tracks you've recorded for that song, which are selected (highlighted) in the following figure.

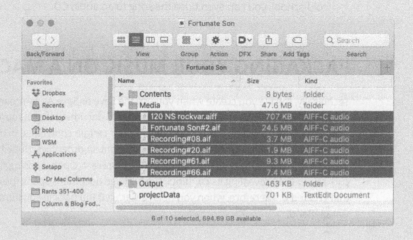

Seven simple steps are all it takes to create and share a magnum opus of your very own from scratch.

Before I close out this chapter, here's a quick gander at the program that makes the magic happen on the Mac and iDevices.

Sneak peek 2: GarageBand for Mac

I start this quick look at GarageBand for Mac with a peek at its main (really, only) window.

TIP

As you get to know GarageBand, you might want to choose Help⇨Quick Help (or click the Quick Help button in the toolbar) and also enable Help⇨Quick Help Follows Pointer (so it displays a check mark). You can now point at most items on the screen to see a brief description what it is and what it does, as shown for the workspace in Figure 1-5.

So that's the user interface — where the magic happens — but that's not what you see after you launch GarageBand. Rather, the first thing you see is the Choose a Project dialog, shown in Figure 1-6.

To open an existing project, click Recent or Open an Existing Project.

Quick Help button   Quick Help

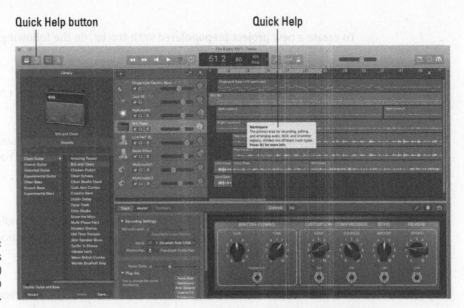

FIGURE 1-5:
GarageBand's
main (only)
window with
Quick Help.

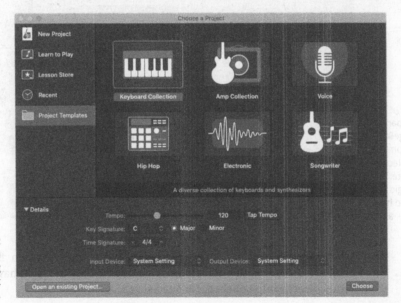

FIGURE 1-6:
The Choose a
Project dialog
offers six project
templates.

To create a new, empty project:

1. Select New Project.

2. Click the Empty Project icon

3. Click the Choose button.

To create a new project prepopulated with tracks, do the following:

1. **Click Project Templates in the sidebar.**

   I delve deeper into the Choose a Project dialog and templates in Chapter 4.

2. **Check out the templates and their prepopulated tracks.**

   By the way, don't worry about that stuff at the bottom of the Choose a Project dialog — namely tempo, time, bpm (beats per minute), and key. You can read all about them in Chapter 4.

3. **Select a template, and then click the Create button.**

   The next thing you see is a GarageBand project (song) with a handful of tracks already created. Figure 1-7 shows the tracks created when you choose the Amp Collection template.

Patch Library   Track headers   Workspace (aka timeline)

FIGURE 1-7:
A brand spankin' new GarageBand project from the Amp Collection template; just add magic and you could have a hit!

That's all you need to know for now. If you can't wait to find out more, Chapters 4–8 have more on laying down tracks; Chapters 9–11 have the scoop on turning tracks into polished, finished songs.

Sneak peek 3: GarageBand for iDevices

I would have started this quick look at GarageBand for iDevices with a peek at its main window, except that GarageBand for iDevices offers two different main windows. When you create a new project in GarageBand on your iDevice, you choose between using live loops mode and tracks mode, as shown in Figure 1-8.

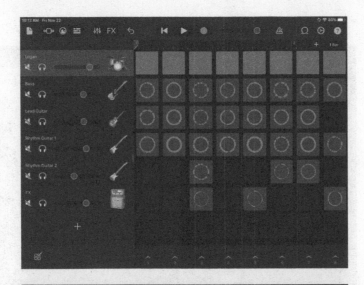

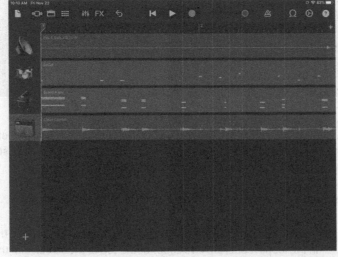

FIGURE 1-8:
GarageBand for
iDevices offers
two ways to
create music: live
loops (top) and
tracks (bottom).

You look at how both modes work and when you might want to use one or the other in Chapter 13 (live loops) and Chapter 14 (tracks).

TIP

Tap the Quick Help icon — the little question-mark-in-a-circle in the upper-right corner of the screen — to see pop-up help and hints, as shown in Figure 1-9.

Now you can tap any note with an angle bracket (>), such as the notes at the top left and bottom right in Figure 1-10, for additional information.

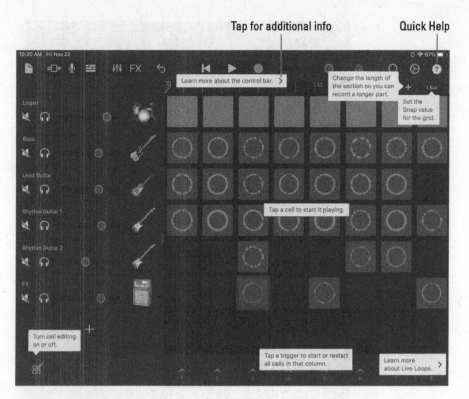

Tap for additional info   Quick Help

FIGURE 1-9:
GarageBand for
iOS's Quick Help.

Although you create music with GarageBand in iDevices in one of two modes, you won't see either when you launch GarageBand. Instead, the first thing you see is GarageBand's Choose a Project screen, shown in Figure 1-10.

From the Choose a Project screen, you can do the following:

>> **Create a project.** Click the + button in the upper-right corner. Then, to work in live loops mode, tap Live Loops at the top of the screen and then tap one of the presets below or on the next page (swipe right to left to see additional presets). Or if you prefer to work in tracks mode, tap Tracks at the top of the screen and then tap the instrument you'd like to record (swipe either way to see additional instruments).

>> **Open an existing project.** Tap the Browse or Recents button at the bottom of the screen, and then tap the project you want to open.

You delve deeper into the Choose a Project screen and creating new projects in Chapter 12.

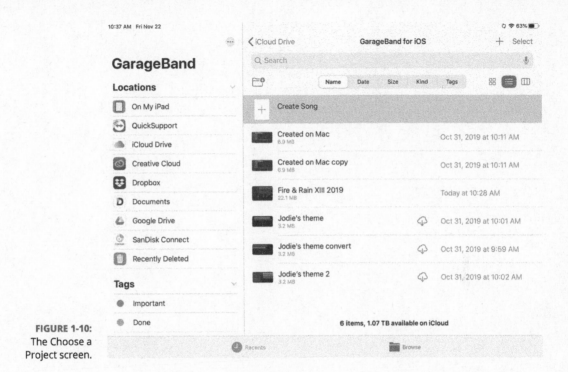

FIGURE 1-10:
The Choose a
Project screen.

That ought to hold you for now. If you can't wait to find out more, Parts 2 and 3 have more on recording on a Mac; Parts 4 and 5 cover the same ground for Garage-Band on iDevices.

Onward!

» Determining your needs

» Working with must-have gear

» Knowing some good-to-have gear

Chapter 2

Equipping and Setting Up Your Recording Space

I have some good news and some bad news. The good news first: Many of you won't have to spend a dime — assuming you have GarageBand installed on your Macintosh or iDevice — to have lots of fun with GarageBand.

All iDevices and many Mac models, including most MacBooks (Pro and otherwise) and iMacs, come factory-equipped with everything you're going to need to use GarageBand. As long as your Mac or iDevice has one or more speakers and a microphone, you have all you need to use GarageBand.

Now for the bad news: Although it's true that you don't need to spend another penny, it's likely your finished song quality will be lacking in some (or many) ways. To make music that sounds fantastic, you'll need to invest at least a few additional bucks (or a few thousand). Although I am about to tell you which gear will have the most effect on your sound (and be easiest on your budget), be prepared to dip into your wallet more than once to get great results from GarageBand.

Cobbling Together a Studio Without Breaking the Bank

You don't have to spend a ton of money on equipment for your studio, especially when you're starting out with GarageBand. The least expensive way to do something is often good enough. And should you outgrow an inexpensive product, you can always find bigger, faster, and flashier ones that are priced accordingly. Here are some tips for assembling a studio to meet your needs but stay within your budget:

>> **When you start out, use the least expensive solution you can find.** The microphones and speakers built into Macs aren't very good for making audio, but they're good enough to use until you're sure that you want to spend some money to improve your recordings.

>> **If you're ready to take your gear up a notch but need to watch your budget, see if you can borrow the gear to test it first or try to find something used.** If you have a friend who records music, see if he or she has an old microphone, keyboard, audio or MIDI interface, or speakers that you can use. Many recording enthusiasts (including yours truly) have a closet full of gear that used to be good enough but isn't anymore. This equipment may be good enough for you.

>> **Remember that the term _better_ is subjective.** For example, a recording microphone is one of the first investments you're likely to make. The free microphones and speakers on most Macs and iDevices are a thoughtful touch and great for computing, making phone calls, and so on. However, if you're making music, these built-in mics just aren't good enough. Is a $1,000 microphone better than a $100 mic? Probably. Is it ten times better? That depends on who is paying. To me, the answer is no. I have no microphones that cost over $150, and they all work fine for the kind of work I do (demo quality recording).

TIP

>> **Purchase your audio gear from vendors with reasonable return policies.** You never know whether a product is right until you use it in your studio. I prefer shopping with vendors that offer a 30-day (or even a two-week) money-back guarantee. That way, I can return a product if I'm not happy with it and receive a refund or a store credit.

Some vendors offer a money-back guarantee but also charge a restocking fee if you return the product. These fees can be substantial — I've seen them as high as 25 percent of the purchase price. On the other hand, while a restocking fee usually isn't such a good deal, it's often better than being stuck with an expensive piece of gear that isn't exactly what you need.

>> **If you're using GarageBand as a primer for more serious recording, don't skimp too much.** This cheapest-first advice is just a guideline. If you're going to record a five-piece band live at some time, consider buying gear that can handle that kind of workload, even if you don't need its capabilities today.

REMEMBER

My advice to most of you: If you're dabbling in audio production for the first time, cheaper is better. Remember that advice, or you might spend way more on audio gear than you need to.

Making the Most of Your Recording Space

Regardless of what you want to accomplish with GarageBand — singing a cappella in the shower, making dance mixes culled from Apple Loops, or creating a band demo — a few truths should be held self-evident.

The first truth is to choose the most appropriate space in which to record. I do most of my recording in my home office. It's not a very good recording space: It has too many hard surfaces that reflect sound and cause echoes and ugly resonation, and it doesn't have enough soft things, such as curtains or pillows, to absorb some of the sound that's bouncing around. But it's the appropriate space for me to record because it's where I have my computer, guitars, keyboards, and other recording equipment. This leads me to my second truth, which is to get rid of extra noise by deadening the room and preventing outside noises as much as possible.

Deadening the room

Unless you're recording an ensemble in a cathedral (in which case the ambient reflected sound might be desirable), it's in your best interest to deaden the room you're recording in as much as you can. Reflected sound is the enemy when you're recording, so if there are curtains, draw them to cover those sound-reflective windows. And set up your mic as far from hard surfaces (walls, windows, artwork, and so on) as possible.

TIP

The middle of a room is a good place to start.

Pillows, blankets, and even sheets can deaden your recording space at little or no cost. But if you're serious about deadening sound, you can spend hundreds (or even thousands) of dollars on special freestanding and wall-mounted sound-absorbing panels.

According to my tech editor for the previous edition of this book, Bryan Chaffin, you can also try the "wall of egg cartons" technique. For this you need a bunch of cardboard egg cartons; the commercial egg cartons used by food service establishments work best. You can often find them at diner-style restaurants, or any restaurant that serves breakfast. Just ask the manager; if one restaurant turns you down, keep trying.

After you've got a stash of egg cartons, string them together in a chain and hang them from the ceiling or attach them to the walls with tape or glue as needed. I've never tried this inexpensive way to baffle your walls, but Bryan swears it works beautifully. He does give a word of warning, though: Throw away any cartons with egg left on them because they will begin to smell bad very quickly.

Preventing background noise

REMEMBER

Always record in the quietest space you can. If you're recording an acoustic instrument or a vocal using a microphone, take extra steps to ensure that the room is as quiet as possible. Here's my routine for preventing background noise:

1. Before I start a recording, I turn off all electronic equipment in my office that isn't involved in the session — television, radio, neon lamp, unused Macs, printer, and so on.

2. I switch off the central heating and air conditioning. When it's running, I can hear it as clear as a bell in my recordings.

3. I silence both of my phones and my iPad.

4. If I'm feeling ambitious, I may even put my dog out in the (fenced) backyard, which is as far from the office as possible. And I've been known to tape a *Please do not ring* sign over the doorbell.

If I do all these things before the first take, I usually avoid having an otherwise perfect take spoiled by background noise.

Equipping Your Studio: Must-Have Gear versus Good-to-Have Gear

Gear falls into two categories: must-have gear and good-to-have gear — especially if you're just beginning to record music. The must-have equipment includes things that you need to record audio and to basically use all features of GarageBand. These must-have items don't need to be expensive or even high quality, and some of them may already be built into your Mac or iDevice.

Here's the bottom line: GarageBand won't be as much fun without the following:

» A microphone

» Stereo speakers (or reference monitors)

» Headphones

» A USB keyboard (MIDI)

» The right cables and connectors

» Gobs of free space on your hard drive(s)

Good-to-have gear includes time- and effort-saving equipment and devices that may be convenient or useful in your setup. Place the following items on your good-to-have list:

» An analog audio interface for connecting guitars, basses, microphones, and such

» More microphones

» A microphone stand

» A pop filter or wind screen (or both) for microphones

I explain what all this equipment does and how you set it up in the following sections. See Chapter 25 for the best ways to take your recording to the next level.

TIP

Two virtual professional audio resources that you should know about are Sweetwater Sound (www.sweetwater.com) and Musician's Friend (www.musiciansfriend.com). Both sites have extensive web catalogs, so you can compare and contrast prices and features of multiple items. If you're not a web shopper and don't already have a favorite pro audio dealer, visit Guitar Center, probably the best-known and largest of the bricks-and-mortar audio stores, which you'll find in most major cities.

Choosing a Microphone

A microphone may be the most critical component that you buy. If you're a singer or want to record almost any acoustic instrument (guitar, piano, flute, and so on), you need a microphone, and the quality of your recording will be greatly influenced by your choice of mic.

My *Merriam-Webster's* Concise Electronic Dictionary defines a microphone as "an instrument for transmitting or recording sound by changing sound waves into variations of an electric current." Technically, that's not a bad definition, but I prefer a simpler one: "A device that captures incoming sound and saves it (as a tape recorder or GarageBand does) or transmits it (as a telephone or walkie-talkie does)."

Musicians and audio enthusiasts often refer to a *microphone* as a *mic* (pronounced "mike").

TIP

I recommend that you begin by using any available microphone. I've made many GarageBand recordings using an old Andrea USB NC-7100, a cheap USB mic that was bundled with speech-recognition software I reviewed more than a decade ago.

If your Mac has a built-in microphone or an audio-input jack or both, you can use the built-in mic or connect a cheap mic to the audio-in jack and make some recordings. If they sound good to you, you just saved yourself a lot of money; if they *don't* sound good, buy or borrow a better microphone and re-record the material. Now compare the two recordings and decide whether the better mic is worth the money.

Microphones vary greatly in price and quality. You can pay as little as $10–$20 for an inexpensive, consumer-quality mic on Amazon.com or at your local Best Buy, or you can spend thousands of dollars for a pro-quality mic at your local or virtual pro audio dealer.

When it comes to microphones, price and sound quality don't necessarily correlate directly. You can find inexpensive microphones that sound as good as (or better than) other microphones that cost even ten times as much. However, you generally get what you pay for, and more expensive microphones usually sound better.

The main things to consider when choosing microphones follow:

>> Type of mic (dynamic, condenser, or ribbon)

>> Polarity pattern (cardioid, omni-directional, figure-8, and so on)

>> Connection to your device (usually USB, XLR, or both)

>> Preamps

>> Price (of course)

In the following sections, I explain these basic considerations and discuss what you need to know about connecting a mic to your computer so that you can start recording.

Dynamic and condenser microphones

Many types of microphones are available, and they use different mechanisms and electronic components. The two types that you're most likely to encounter, though, are *dynamic* and *condenser* microphones. The technical differences in the way that each type works aren't important (at least not in this chapter), but you should know the following nontechnical differences between the two before you consider choosing one kind (or both):

» Dynamic mics are generally less expensive than condenser types.

» Condenser mics generally reproduce vocals and acoustic instruments more accurately and with more warmth. (*Warmth* is a desirable tonal characteristic that might best be described as *mellow* or *not bright*. It refers to a pleasant decrease in mid and mid-to-high frequencies that make a voice or instrument sound smoother when recorded.)

» Dynamic mics can be placed closer to loud bursts of sound — such as drums or a guitar amp — than condenser mics, so dynamic mics may achieve a sound that you just can't get with a condenser mic. Furthermore, a condenser mic is more likely to be damaged by extremely loud sounds than a dynamic mic.

» Many dynamic mics are built for rough use — they better withstand being dropped on the floor or being knocked over with a mic stand. If you're rough on your gear or plan to use it in a live stage setting, a dynamic mic will probably last longer.

» Condenser mics require a power source (known as *phantom power*), so they must contain an internal battery or have the phantom power supplied through the cable by your audio interface or mixer.

WARNING

Not all audio interfaces and mixers supply phantom power to condenser mics. If you plan to use one of these mics, make sure that the device you're going to connect it to — for example, an audio interface, a mixer, or a sound card — provides phantom power for it.

TECHNICAL STUFF

A third type of microphone — the *ribbon mic* — is fragile and expensive ($1,000 and up). And although ribbon mics are prized for a silky response, they don't sound that different from condenser mics. You probably want to avoid ribbon mics unless you're a purist and have deep pockets. I recorded with a ribbon mic in a studio many years ago, and it did indeed sound silky. So does the Neumann U87 (around $3,600), still the gold standard for condenser mics.

If you buy only one microphone, you can't go wrong with a dynamic mic such as the Shure SM57 or SM58. These are two of the most popular dynamic mics around — and have been ubiquitous standards for modern live vocals since their releases nearly half a century ago.

The SM57 and SM58 are similar, but the SM57 has "contoured frequency response for clean sound reproduction of amplified and acoustic instruments," whereas the SM58 is "tuned to accentuate the warmth and clarity of lead and back-up vocals." The SM58 is the ball-shaped mic you see all the time on stage and in videos.

TIP

The differences between the SM57 and SM58 are small and you may not even be able to hear them. Either is fine for both vocals and instruments. If you're buying only one, decide whether recording vocals or recording instruments is more important, and choose accordingly. You can buy either one from online music vendors such as Sweetwater Sound (www.sweetwater.com) and Musician's Friend (www.musiciansfriend.com) for under $100.

Microphone polarity patterns

Each microphone is designed with a specific *polarity pattern*, which means they pick up sound from certain locations better than others. The three polarity patterns you're most likely to encounter follow:

>> **Cardioid (directional):** *Cardioid mics,* as you can see in Figure 2-1, reject sound from the rear and sides, making them excellent for recording an instrument or a vocal with little or no extraneous sound leakage.

>> **Omni-directional:** *Omni-directional mics* pick up sound from all directions equally, as you can see in Figure 2-2. That feature makes them a fine choice for recording a large ensemble or orchestra but not the best choice for recording individual voices and instruments, which is what you do in GarageBand most of the time.

>> **Figure-8 (bi-directional):** *Figure-8, or bi-directional, mics* pick up sound from the front and back equally while rejecting sound coming from either side, as shown in Figure 2-3.

Figures 2-1, 2-2, and 2-3 are polar graphs that show how well the mic picks up sound from the front, rear, and sides. The specification sheets for most microphones will include a polar graph of its polarity pattern.

TIP

The three flavors of cardioid are so similar that you won't notice much (if any) difference between them for the kind of recording you're likely to do when working with GarageBand. I merely include this information so you won't be confused when you start seeing these terms in brochures and reviews.

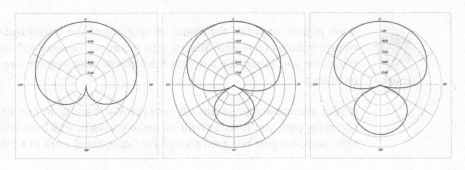

FIGURE 2-1:
Cardioid patterns come in three flavors: cardioid (left), super cardioid (middle), and hyper cardioid (right).

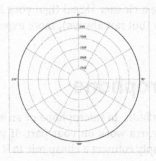

FIGURE 2-2:
The omni-directional pattern picks up sounds from every direction.

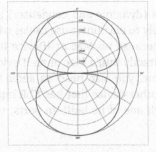

FIGURE 2-3:
The figure-8 pattern is perfect for recording two instruments or vocalists.

Finally, my favorite mic at the time of this writing is a Blue Yeti Pro, a great sounding condenser mic with both USB and XLR connectors as well as four polarity patterns. It's not cheap, at around $250, but it has been superb for almost everything I've recorded with it.

Microphone preamps

You have one last thing to consider if you're buying a microphone: Your mic preamps have a tremendous effect on how your mic will sound.

A *mic preamp* amplifies the sound coming out of the microphone to the higher voltage known as *line level*. Mixers, tape recorders, GarageBand, and almost anything else you might use a decent microphone with require line level input for recording.

If your microphone plugs directly into the Mac's audio-in port or your iDevice's Lightning port, you're using built-in audio preamps, which are lower quality than most outboard gear but good enough for GarageBand work in a pinch.

If you purchase an external audio interface, chances are it will tout its own pre-amp circuits; all of these will provide a cleaner signal than your Mac or iDevice's built-in audio-in subsystem. Usually (but not always), more expensive interfaces offer higher-quality preamps.

Setting up your microphone

Many Macs and older iDevices have a built-in microphone or an audio-input jack or both. A built-in mic requires no extra work on your part. If you have just an audio-in jack, you may be able to simply connect a cheap mic to it and make some recordings.

However, most quality microphones (dynamic and condenser) as well as many other pieces of audio gear you're likely to encounter use cables with XLR connectors (shown later in Figure 2-11). Because no Mac or iDevice has built-in XLR ports, you can't plug an XLR cable directly into a Mac or an iDevice. If you choose a microphone with an XLR connector, you also need an audio interface (or an internal sound card), a mixer, or another device that has XLR inputs. This device sends its output to your Mac through one of its built-in ports, such as USB, PCI (Power Macs only), or Lightning.

I cover cables, jacks, plugs, ports, and connectors in the "Unraveling the Cable and Connector Conundrum" section, later in this chapter. For more on audio interfaces, see the "Adding an Audio Interface to Your Setup" section, also later in this chapter.

Finding the Right Speakers

Choosing the speakers you use to listen to your GarageBand work is almost as important as selecting the right microphone. The perfect recording will never sound good in your car, on your home stereo, or on your iDevice if you don't use speakers that accurately reproduce the sound produced when you mixed and mastered.

You don't have to spend a bundle on speakers. The built-in speakers in your Mac or iDevice may be good enough for the kind of work that you plan to do.

If the built-in speakers aren't good enough, almost any set of computer multimedia speakers will be a major improvement. With my MacBook Pro, I'm currently using the Audioengine A2+ (www.audioengine.com) premium speaker system (see Figure 2-4), a pair of small desktop speakers that deliver amazing sound for a reasonable price. They are not inexpensive— around $250 a pair— but they sound better than some speaker systems costing three times as much.

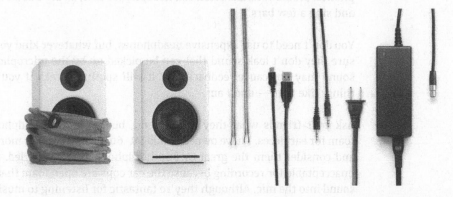

FIGURE 2-4:
What's in the box:
Audioengine A2+.

Speaking of spending more for better sound, if you're serious about recording, you'll probably want studio-style speakers, which reproduce audio so accurately that they're known as *reference monitors* or *near-field reference monitors*.

I also have a pair of Tapco's S-5 Active Studio Monitors (now discontinued) on my desk with an A/B switch so I can switch between the S-5s and the A2+s to ensure that my recordings sound good on both.

The S-5s are designed by Mackie, one of the most famous manufacturers of mixing boards and other professional recording gear, and feature dual high-precision internal amplifiers. It's no surprise that the S-5s sound better than many reference monitors costing significantly more.

Although the S-5s cost more than the A2+s (the S-5s were around $400 when I got them a decade ago), they sound spectacular and may be a better choice, depending on your needs and budget.

TIP

If you want to hear your music reproduced as accurately as possible, you should probably spend a bit more for a pair of near-field reference monitors rather than plain old stereo speakers.

Listening with Headphones Without Messing Up the Take

If you intend to use any kind of microphone while you record a voice or an instrument, you can't use your speakers or reference monitors while you sing or play because doing so would almost certainly cause ear-shattering feedback.

When you use microphones to record, you listen to the other tracks through headphones. Studio veterans often call headphones *cans,* as in "Put on that pair of cans and sing a few bars."

REMEMBER

You don't need to use expensive headphones, but whatever kind you choose, make sure they don't leak sound that can be picked up by the microphone. The leaked sound may not cause feedback, but it will spoil the track if you're picky about things like that — and I am.

Ask your friends what they recommend, but avoid any headphones with open foam for earpieces. I have owned Grado SR-60 headphones for more than a decade and consider them the greatest $80 headphones I've ever tried. Sadly, they are unacceptable for recording because the ear cups are open foam that leak too much sound into the mic. Although they're fantastic for listening to music, they're unfit for recording.

I used to do a radio show from my home office, and the engineers at the station (CNET, before it went off the air) recommended Sony headphones. Mine are the MDR-7506 (around $125), which have leather-like earpieces that seal in the sound nicely, sound darned good, and are super comfortable for extended periods.

TIP

If you own an iDevice, try using the earbuds that came with it. If you don't set the listening level of the tracks too high, these "free" earbuds are serviceable, but almost any other in-ear headphones will probably sound better. Look for ones with different-sized rubber or silicone ear caps, which not only ensure a snug fit but also seal in more of the sound than the one-size-fits-all-ears hard plastic ones on Apple EarPods shown in Figure 2-5.

Finally, although it's necessary to use headphones when you record, you shouldn't rely on headphones to mix or master unless you have no other choice (that is, speakers or studio monitors are unavailable).

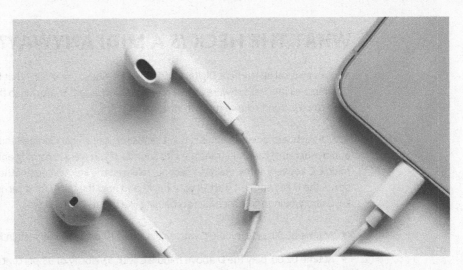

FIGURE 2-5:
Earbuds like these Apple EarPods are headphones that fit almost entirely inside your ear.

Adding a MIDI Keyboard to Your Setup

If you play the piano or organ and want to record GarageBand's software instruments well, you should buy a MIDI controller, or keyboard. A MIDI keyboard can send information about what you're playing in a format that your computer can understand. (See the sidebar "What the heck *is* a MIDI anyway?" for details.)

Finding a keyboard

TIP

You may already have a MIDI keyboard. Look around your house and the houses of close friends for anything that has piano-like keys. I discovered an old Miracle Piano that my kids used in the '90s had MIDI-in and -out ports. Sadly, it was a little too grimy and missing a bunch of keys. But I could have used it with Garage-Band (with the proper cables) in a pinch.

I have an M-Audio Keystation 49e — a decent 49-key, velocity-sensitive MIDI keyboard (since superseded by the Keystation 49 MK3 shown in Figure 2-6). If you're short on space, check out smaller MIDI-controller keyboards such as the Keystation Mini 32 MK3 shown in Figure 2-6.

I'm not trained as a keyboard player, but the Keystation feels like a keyboard to me, even though the keys are not weighted and are made of plastic. My musician friends tell me that it doesn't compare to their expensive keyboards, which have special weighted keys made from the same material as real piano keys. But even they agree that an inexpensive USB MIDI controller such as the M-Audio Keystation is good enough and a great value for non-keyboardists.

WHAT THE HECK *IS* A MIDI ANYWAY?

MIDI, or Musical Instrument Digital Interface, is an industry standard that has been used by almost all musical software and hardware. A device that conforms to the MIDI standard can send and receive musical information.

A MIDI keyboard doesn't send sound; it sends messages that GarageBand (or other audio programs) can then translate into sounds. If you were recording and pressed the middle C key very softly, waited 1 second, released the key, waited another second, then struck the D key above it with all your might and held the D key for 4 seconds, your MIDI keyboard would send a message something like this to GarageBand:

- At time 00.00, play middle C with a velocity of 17 percent and sustain it for 1 second.

- At time 02.00, play the D above middle C with a velocity of 98 percent and sustain it for 4 seconds.

That's a gross oversimplification. The MIDI standard lets a device send and receive much more information than just pitch, velocity, and sustain. But that's all you need to know for now — you play the MIDI keyboard, and GarageBand memorizes what you played.

FIGURE 2-6:
M-Audio Keystation 49 MK3 (top) or Keystation Mini 32 MK3 (bottom) are inexpensive and perfectly adequate MIDI keyboards.

Prices for MIDI controllers range from well under $100 to well over $1,000 based on features, number of keys, and bundled software, so it pays to shop around. You'll find the best selection of them at sites such as Sweetwater and Musician's Friend and Amazon.com.

Connecting a MIDI keyboard to your computer

Most modern MIDI keyboards connect to your Mac via a USB port or Bluetooth; older MIDI devices use special MIDI ports and cables. (Macs and iDevices have never included these special MIDI ports.)

The solution to this problem is a small box called a *MIDI interface.* You plug a thick, expensive, old-school MIDI cable (or cables) into the MIDI port(s) on the interface, and then plug the interface's USB cable into your Mac.

Fortunately, most modern MIDI devices (typically keyboards, but many instruments including MIDI guitars and MIDI drums can send and receive MIDI) have their own USB port or use Bluetooth, with some also including one or more MIDI ports.

WARNING

My advice is to use the more common, more reliable, and less-expensive USB or Bluetooth connections if possible.

Finally, you can use many USB MIDI controllers (and other USB devices) with your iDevice, but you'll need an adapter. Cheap adapters are available, but I've found many third-party offerings unreliable. I recommend Apple's Lightning-to-USB camera adapter ($29) in spite of it being grossly overpriced.

Unraveling the Cable and Connector Conundrum

Nothing is more frustrating than having a cool new toy and not having the proper cable to connect it to your Mac. Your Mac has only so many holes (that is, ports) that you can stick things into — and most iDevices have only one hole — the Lightning connector.

Unfortunately, the holes in your Mac or iDevice don't always accept cables that fit the holes in your audio gear. But with a little cable-and-connector know-how, hooking up your gear should be fairly easy. Table 2-1 gives you an overview of common connectors and cables and indicates how to plug them into your Mac or iDevice. The rest of this section explains how to recognize each cable and connector and describes what you need to know about them.

TABLE 2-1   ## Sorting Out Connectors, Cables, and Ports

Connector	Typically Found On	To Connect It to Your Mac or iDevice
Mono	Anything that sends audio to your computer, such as microphones, and electronic instruments such as guitars and basses.	Insert the ⅛-inch plug into your Mac's audio-in port or into your iDevice's Lightning port using a Lightning-to-3.5 mm headphone jack adapter. If the device uses ¼-inch plugs, you'll also need a ¼-to-⅛-inch mono converter (available at Amazon.com).
Stereo	Any gear that plays audio coming out of your computer, such as headphones and speakers.	Insert the ⅛-inch plug into your Mac's headphone (or audio-out) port. If the device uses ¼-inch stereo plugs, you'll need a ¼-to-⅛-inch stereo converter (available at Amazon.com). For iDevices, connect the ⅛-inch plug to a Lightning-to-3.5 mm (⅛-inch) headphone jack adapter and then plug it into your device.
XLR	High-quality audio gear, such as microphones and mixing boards.	Plug the XLR connector into an audio interface with XLR inputs, then connect the interface to your Mac via USB or Thunderbolt or to your iDevice via a compatible audio interface with XLR inputs. See the "Setting up your microphone" section, earlier in this chapter, for details and don't forget that some microphones with XLR connectors require phantom power to operate (so make sure your audio interface supplies phantom power if you need it).
RCA	Consumer audio and video products, such as receivers, DVD players, audio amplifiers, or CD players.	Plug the RCA connector into an audio interface with RCA inputs, then connect the interface to your Mac via USB or Thunderbolt or to your iDevice via a compatible audio interface with RCA inputs. See the "Setting up your microphone" section, earlier in this chapter, for details.

TIP

Note that if you have a newer iDevice, you will need Apple's Lightning-to-3.5mm headphone jack adapter ($9) to use ⅛-inch plugs and a Lightning-to-USB camera adapter ($29) to use USB. And while 3.5mm is not exactly ⅛ inch, it's close enough for rock and roll. So, 3.5mm and ⅛ inch are the same when it comes to ports, plugs, and adapters.

Moving right along, *mono plugs* and *stereo plugs* can be confusing for two reasons: They look almost alike, and they come in two different sizes. Note the following examples:

» The audio-out port (for most headphones and speakers) mates with a stereo minijack plug, known as a ⅛-inch stereo plug.

» The audio-in port (for microphones and instruments) mates with a mono minijack plug, known as a ⅛-inch mono plug.

» Electric guitars and other electronic instruments use a ¼-inch mono plug.

» Many good headphones and other electronic devices use a ¼-inch plug as well, but they use a stereo (not mono) ¼-inch plug.

The size difference is fairly easy to figure out: ⅛-inch plugs are smaller and fit into your Mac's existing ports and ¼-inch plugs don't. But how do you tell the difference between mono and stereo plugs? Stereo plugs have two rings, and mono plugs only have one.

Compare the ¼-inch mono plug and the stereo plug in Figure 2-7. Note the two rings on the stereo plug and the single ring on the mono plug. The two-ring/one-ring deal applies to the minijacks (⅛-inch plugs) as well. Always make sure that the plug you shove into a given port is the right one for the job.

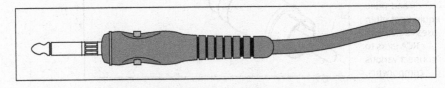

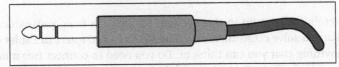

FIGURE 2-7:
A ¼-inch mono plug (top) and a ¼-inch stereo plug (bottom).

TIP

Want a trick to remember which plug to use? Stereo comes out of two speakers and stereo plugs have two rings.

You're also likely to encounter *XLR cables* and *XLR connectors*, particularly if you use higher-quality audio gear such as microphones and mixing boards. Two XLR connectors are shown in Figure 2-8.

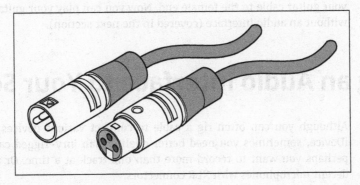

FIGURE 2-8:
Male (left) and female (right) XLR connectors.

**TECHNICAL
STUFF**

XLR cables are quieter than other types of analog cable and are less likely to add hiss, static, or hum to your recording.

Finally, many consumer audio products, as well as some computer audio products, use *RCA jacks*. In the old days, these jacks, shown in Figure 2-9, were also known as phono plugs.

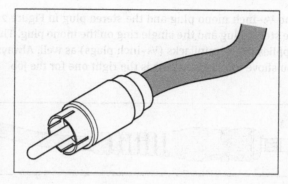

FIGURE 2-9:
Consumer audio and video equipment often uses cables with RCA jacks to connect various components.

TIP

Here's the best tip in this section: RadioShack (www.radioshack.com) is a great place to solve cable dilemmas. The Shack has adapters or cables that do just about anything that you can think of. Do you need to connect two mono ⅛-inch cables to a single ⅛-inch stereo jack? RadioShack sells cables and adapters for that. Do you need a male connector when all you have are female connectors? No problem; Amazon.com has gender switchers for most plugs. Do you need a cable with one type of plug on one end and a different connector on the other? Chances are Amazon.com or Monoprice.com has it.

TIP

Every guitarist should have at least one adapter — a ¼-inch-mono female-to-⅛-inch-stereo male minijack. Plug the male end into your Mac's audio-in port or your iDevice's Lightning-to-3.5mm headphone jack adapter and connect your guitar cable to the female end. Now you can play your guitar in GarageBand without an audio interface (covered in the next section).

Adding an Audio Interface to Your Setup

Although you can often rig a cable to connect various devices to your Mac or iDevice, sometimes you need better quality than jury-rigged cables provide. Or perhaps you want to record more than one track at a time. Or you want to use decent microphones with XLR connectors.

The answer is an external device known as an audio interface.

Using an audio interface with GarageBand

With GarageBand, an *audio interface* is most commonly used for microphones (or other devices with those pesky professional XLR connectors) as well as electric guitars, basses, and the like. An audio interface acts as a bridge between the XLR or ¼-inch cable port your Mac doesn't have and the USB port that it does have. An analog audio interface can also help you use other connectors that your Mac doesn't have a port for — for example, ¼-inch mono or stereo plugs and several other types of plugs, depending on the interface you choose. (See the "Unraveling the Cable and Connector Conundrum" section, earlier in this chapter, if you're not sure what all these plugs are for.)

Audio interfaces come in all shapes and sizes and many combinations of inputs and outputs. The three main types available follow:

>> *Thunderbolt audio interfaces,* which plug into a Thunderbolt port on your Mac

>> *USB audio interfaces,* which plug into a USB port on your Mac

>> *Lightning audio interfaces,* which plug in the Lightning port on your iDevice

Thunderbolt interfaces are the most expensive, but are faster than USB interfaces and capable of handling more channels. That said, USB interfaces can handle up to 24 channels in and out, which is more than most users will need.

Shopping for an interface

If you would like to use an interface with GarageBand, think about how serious you are about recording and how many tracks you hope to record at the same time. Buying the right interface for your needs will save you a ton of money. Keep the following points in mind:

>> If you're just starting out, choose the least expensive audio interface that does what you need. Otherwise, you'll end up paying for features and capabilities you may never need or use.

>> If you're on a tight budget, make do with microphones and instruments you can plug into the audio-in jack or into the USB or Lightning port on your device. Doing so eliminates microphones with XLR connectors from consideration, which is probably best if you're trying to spend as little as possible to get decent results.

>> The price of the interface is determined primarily by the number of inputs and outputs it has and the quality of its microphone preamplifiers. If you're using GarageBand just for fun, don't buy more interface than you need.

For example, if you intend to play guitar and sing, you don't need more than two inputs. On the other hand, if you plan to someday move up to more sophisticated recording software, a more capable (and more expensive) audio interface with more inputs and outputs may be worth considering.

My current audio interface is a Focusrite Scarlett Solo (USB) that sells for around $130. It has one XLR input with phantom power (for a microphone), and one ¼-inch mono input (for a guitar or bass). Its preamps sound darn good to me, and because I record myself playing guitar or singing alone in a room, two inputs is all I ever need.

Here's one last shopping tip: You'll find audio interfaces bundled with a dizzying array of "free" software and hardware as well. For example, my Focusrite Scarlett came with all this bundled stuff:

>> Ableton Live Lite

>> Pro Tools First Focusrite Creative Pack

>> Softube's Time and Tone Bundle

>> Focusrite Red Plug-In Suite

>> Access to the Focusrite Plug-in Collective (free software downloads and generous discounts)

>> One free Addictive Keys virtual instrument

It's interesting and potentially useful stuff, but I never use most of it. Don't be dazzled by the software bundle. Buy the interface that does what you need at the price you want to pay. If it comes bundled with software, great. But chances are you'll need little or none of it and won't be much worse off without it.

That said, sometimes you see audio interfaces with hardware bundles that include a microphone, studio earphones, desktop monitors, mic stands, or more. These bundles can save you a bundle (ha ha), but shop carefully. These days, there's no excuse for not Googling products before you buy and reading what buyers say in the reviews (at reliable sites such as Sweetwater, Musician's Friend, and Amazon).

The more reviews you see the better; avoid buying products with only a handful of reviews (which could be bogus).

Perfecting Your Mic Setup

If you're using microphones to record, supplementing your mic setup can help you get a better recording. The obvious addition to your mic is a mic stand. If you're recording vocals, pop filters and wind screens can also help you get a better take.

Choosing a mic stand

I have four mic stands, and they are all cheapies — bought on sale at one of Guitar Center's Super Savings Spectacular Sale-a-Thon promotions. Figure 2-10 shows a boom-style mic stand on the left and a straight stand on the right.

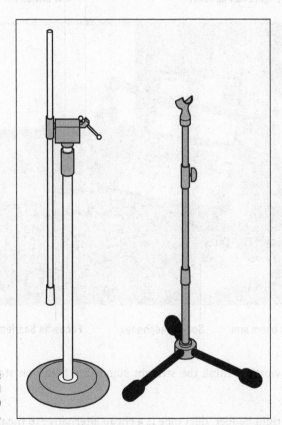

FIGURE 2-10:
Boom (left) and
straight (right)
mic stands.

I prefer a boom because it's more flexible when placing the mic. When you're recording using a microphone (and you're going to hear me say this time and again), mic placement is critical. Placement 2 inches one way or the other could mean the difference between an award-winning take and a pile of garbage. Boom stands make it a lot easier to place the mic exactly where you want it. The downside is that they tip over easily. (I've tipped them over more times than I care to remember.) I've also whacked myself in the head with both ends of the boom — more than once. So be careful; those mic stands are inherently unstable critters.

I do a lot of recording standing behind my desk, and I also record voiceovers for presentations and video chats. My favorite boom stand is the Blue Compass ($99) shown in Figure 2-11, which has whisper-quiet internal springs and built-in cable management. Its smooth, quiet operation and rock-solid stability are so good I drilled a hole in my desk and mounted it permanently.

Tapco S-5 speaker

Audioengine A2+ speaker

Blue Yeti Pro mic

A/B switch (for speakers)

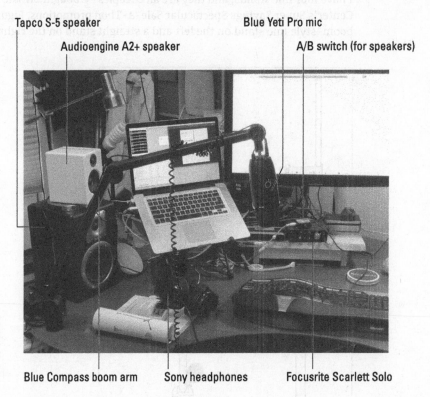

FIGURE 2-11:
My Blue Compass boom arm, which is permanently attached to my desk.

Blue Compass boom arm   Sony headphones   Focusrite Scarlett Solo

For what it's worth, I think the straight stands are better on stage than in the studio.

TIP

If you're on a tight budget, duct tape is a cheap alternative to the mic stand. Tape your mic to an object that's big and heavy enough so that it doesn't vibrate while you're recording. Or prop the mic on pillows piled on a chair and point the mic at the sound hole of your acoustic guitar. You can also dangle a mic from the ceiling. (It's not good for the cable, but it might sound cool.) When it comes to how and where to position a mic, anything goes. Use your imagination. It couldn't hurt and the result might just sound spectacular!

Recording vocals with pop filters and wind screens

Two more tools that pros use for their recordings are pop filters and wind screens.

A *pop filter* is a thin piece of cloth (usually nylon) stretched over a frame slightly larger than the microphone itself. The idea is that the pop filter minimizes the popping sound created when you pronounce certain letters, such as P. Place the filter 4 to 6 inches from the mic, and even the most plosive p-poppin' vocalist will sound less percussive.

You can make a pop filter from a wire coat hanger and panty hose, or you can buy a ready-made filter at most music stores for about $25. Make them or buy them, but use them for most vocals. These filters almost always improve your sound, even if your vocalist doesn't pop his or her Ps.

Along the same lines but less important in studio work are wind screens. Like pop filters, *wind screens* keep unwanted noise from entering the mic. When a television newscaster shoves a microphone in someone's face, the foam ball that you see is the wind screen that covers the microphone.

A wind screen can help with plosive Ps, but a pop filter usually works better. A wind screen may also muffle more than a pop filter what you're recording. I use the pop filter for all vocals and rarely use a wind screen, but if you have a wind screen, try it and see if you like it.

Boosting Your Hard Drive Space

Something you can't do without is plenty of free space on a hard or solid-state drive — internal or external. iDevice users need to be mindful of how much space their GarageBand compositions are consuming because there's no easy way to add storage.

GarageBand and its attendant files are huge, and a single song can use from a handful to hundreds of megabytes of space. The more files you create with Garage-Band, the faster your will run into space issues.

Mac OS X doesn't like it when the startup (boot) drive is nearly full. This condition may slow your Mac's performance, affect your ability to record in GarageBand, or both. My guideline is to leave at least 10 percent of my boot drive free; bad things can happen if you let the hard drive get much fuller.

If your Mac startup disk gets too full, one option is to purchase an external drive. Following are my top reasons why external drives are better than replacing your internal drive with a higher-capacity disk:

>> If an external drive has problems, you don't have to open your Mac to get or replace the drive. With a USB device, you merely connect the replacement drive to your Mac and plug in its power supply (if necessary), and you're back up and running.

>> External drives can be bootable, so you can use one drive with more than one Mac and have all your stuff just the way you like it. If you use more than one Mac — such as a MacBook and an iMac — being able to easily use (or even boot from) the drive with either computer is a plus.

>> If you compose or record with friends, you can take the external drive containing the GarageBand session files to their house instead of lugging your Mac.

TECHNICAL STUFF

I know I'm getting ahead of myself, but you should probably hear this while I'm talking about drives. Audio applications other than GarageBand strongly recommend that you save your project files on a drive other than your startup (boot) drive. You get better performance from many audio applications by storing your projects on a non-boot drive, and GarageBand is no exception. So, if you another drive connected to your Mac, try saving your GarageBand projects to it instead of to your startup drive.

Recording in Tune with a Tuning Device (for Guitarists)

Last but not least, if you're a guitarist or you play a tunable instrument, you should use a digital tuner before every recording. If you record a piece when your instrument is out of tune, it's never going to sound as good as if you had tuned first, no matter how hard you try, because GarageBand's software instruments never play off-key.

TIP

GarageBand includes an onscreen tuner that works pretty well (as I explain in Chapters 8 and 17). But if you have a tuner you prefer, such as the little clip-on Snark tuner (under $20) on my guitar's headstock, use it before you even launch GarageBand to record.

» **Recording tracks**

» **Mixing tracks into a song**

» **Mastering a song when it's finished**

» **Managing your song files**

Chapter **3**

Introducing Multitrack Recording with GarageBand

There's no getting around it: Making a song with GarageBand uses pretty much the same process that musicians and producers use to make hit records in multimillion-dollar recording studios. GarageBand is easier and a lot less expensive, but the process is much like the one the pros use.

And so, to use GarageBand well, you need to understand the multitrack recording process that lies beneath it. After you understand multitrack recording, you can plan and produce better recordings with GarageBand. If you're ignorant of the process, you're likely to flail about hopelessly, without ever composing anything good enough to listen to more than once. It's that simple.

Even if you're a grizzled old studio vet who has been overdubbing and sweetening tracks since I was in diapers (unlikely), you may want to read the chapter anyway. You may think you know the multitrack recording process, and you probably do, but I guarantee that you don't know GarageBand like I do.

Have you ever been inside a multimillion-dollar recording studio or mixed audio on a 48-channel console? Recorded songs on a 24-track tape machine that costs more than many houses? Produced demo recordings for rock bands? Mixed audio for television and radio commercials? Well, I did all that and more before I gave up the advertising and audio engineering games to become a full-time Mac geek way back in 1985.

But I digress.

Here, I try to kill two birds with one chapter. This little chapter expands on the sneak peeks back in Chapter 1, but this time you stroll through the process of multitrack recording in GarageBand.

This chapter is a road map at 20,000 feet. As such, it foreshadows many techniques, terms, features, and other things that I cover in more detail throughout the rest of the book.

Understanding the Role of Stereo in Multitrack Recording

The way I see it, listening to music has had three major paradigm shifts over the ages:

>> **The Age Before Recorded Music:** I won't even attempt to put dates on it, but this was the time before the invention of recorded audio.

>> **The Age of Monaural Music:** During this period, audio was recorded onto many types of media, using all kinds of strange devices (wire recorders, rotating drum recorders, and tape recorders, to name a few). During the Monaural Age, though, everything recorded had something in common: It played out of a single speaker. Or, to be a bit more technically correct, even if multiple speakers played back the sound, you heard a single track, or channel, of audio.

This era could have easily been known as The Age of One-Channel, but for reasons that will become apparent in just one second (or one sentence, whichever comes first), the monaural metaphor works better here.

>> **The Age of Stereo:** One day, probably before I was born (my tech editor said it was 1933), the recording industry noticed that audio sounded dramatically better when it came out of *two* speakers, with each speaker playing a discrete track (or channel) of music.

Stereo caught on by the late 1950s and has been the way we listen to music ever since (although popular songs continued to be released as monaural recordings well into the 1960s).

STEREO VERSUS MONO (VERSUS QUADRAPHONIC VERSUS 5.1 VERSUS 7.1)

In the simplest terms, stereo sounds great because it plays two tracks of music from two speakers — and you have two ears. With stereo sound, your ears receive sound waves from any source at different times. Each ear hears overtones, echoes, harmonics, and everything else about that sound at different times.

Stereo recordings create the illusion that a stage exists between your speakers, with the music coming from the stage (well, a sonic illusion, if not a visual one). When you listen to a well-produced stereo recording on a good sound system, some instruments sound as if they're in the very back of the stage, all the way over on the left side, while others sound like they're just right of center in the front row, playing loudly.

As a producer of stereo recordings, you can create this illusion, too. When you mix and master a multitrack recording, you can assign each instrument or voice a position on the *sound stage* (sometimes called the *sound field*). In recording lingo, you assign the amount of each track that you want to hear coming out of each speaker with a control known as *pan* (for *panorama*). In most systems, pan is controlled with a knob, and GarageBand is no exception. Turn the Pan knob to the left, and you hear more of the track on the left. You get a similar effect by turning the Pan knob to the right.

As far as making one instrument or vocal sound more up front than others, you adjust the track's *level,* which is how loud that track is in relation to other tracks. You can use other tricks to emphasize a single track over others, but level is the one that you'll probably use the most.

By the way, many people now have fabulous 5.1 and 7.1 audio systems (also known as *surround sound*) and awesome home theater setups. But guess what? Although some music is still released in the 5.1 surround sound format, stereo — 50 years after its introduction — is still the way most music is heard, and I don't see that changing anytime soon.

Quadraphonic sound — four channels of audio played through four speakers — was introduced in the late 1970s but never caught on. I used to think quad failed because humans don't have four ears. My 5.1 system shoots that theory all to heck.

The Who's *Quadrophenia*, released in 1973, was one of the first pop albums in the quadraphonic format, and songwriter/guitarist Pete Townshend and associate producer/engineer Glyn Johns spent many hours recording ambient sound effects for the album — waves crashing, rain falling, and such — because few quadraphonic recordings of that sort were available. For what it's worth, Pink Floyd's *The Dark Side of the Moon,* an album that has spent most of my life on the Billboard Hot 100, was also released in quadraphonic form.

It still didn't catch on.

Although the way we listen to music — stereo playback — has not changed much in over 50 years, the way we *record* that music has changed dramatically many times. Paradigm shifts happen, and in the world of audio recording, they've happened frequently. We made the leap from monaural to 2-track to 4-track to 8-track recording (all on tape); from ¼-inch tape to 1-inch tape to 2-inch tape (still tape); from tape to disk (no longer tape); and from million-dollar studios to hundred-dollar pocket-sized recorders to free software such as GarageBand.

If you have the chops, you can create music with GarageBand that sounds almost as good as (or even better than) music made in million-dollar studios 30 years ago. But regardless of how many tracks, channels, machines, tape decks, instruments, outboard gear, or microphones you have, your songs *always* end up mixed down to just two tracks, or channels (also known stereo mix). Figure 3-1 is worth at least a thousand words.

In Figure 3-1, the four tracks at the top represent three instrument tracks and a vocal track that will be mixed together to create the final two-track master. The two tracks at the bottom (L and R for left and right) represent the final mixed and mastered product — a two-track (stereo) mix.

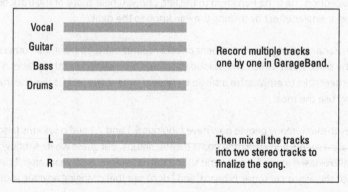

FIGURE 3-1:
In the simplest of terms, this is how multitrack recording works.

So now you know what that song in your head will look like after you record all the parts in GarageBand.

Strolling through the Recording Process, Quickly

After you've rehearsed (ha), the multitrack recording process begins. Here's a quick overview of each step:

1. **Get all the tracks down on tape (or disk in the case of GarageBand).**

   In studio-speak, this is called getting the tracks *in the can*. Be careful here; studio-speak can be confusing. In another chapter, I mention that *can* is studio-speak for *headphones*. Here, *in the can* means all the tracks you need for this song are finished. In this instance, the *can* is a metal or plastic container used to store tape (or film). The plural form (cans) still means *headphones*. I told you studio-speak can be confusing.

   REMEMBER

   Tracks are the basic building blocks of multitrack recording. You record tracks, enhance tracks, mix tracks, put tracks in the can, and so on.

2. **Adjust each track's settings — level, pan, equalization, echo, reverb, effects, and so on — so that everything sounds just right to you.**

   This step is called *mixing* or *postproduction*.

3. **Add effects to the song as a whole.**

   This step is called *mastering* — you add echo, reverb, equalization or other effects to the whole project, and add a fade-in, fade-out, or both.

4. **Export your *mastered project* as a two-channel (stereo) audio file.**

I discuss tracks, mixing, and mastering in GarageBand in just a moment, but first, I want to be sure you're ready to rock and roll.

Cutting the Tracks ("No Blood on 'em, Mr. Dylan")

As you may remember from a page or two ago, the *track* is the basic building block of a song; each song is made up of one or more tracks.

TECHNICAL STUFF

The maximum number of tracks is a function of the speed of your Mac's processor, the amount of memory (RAM) it has, and the speed of your disk drive(s). If your Mac is old and its guts are slower, the number of tracks you can have in a project may be limited. On the other hand, most modern Macs are capable of handling heaven-only-knows-how-many tracks. You'll usually see a warning dialog when your project exceeds your device's capabilities. If that happens, you'll need to reduce the number of tracks (or the number of effects on tracks) to proceed.

This section explains how to begin the multitrack recording process by laying down tracks in GarageBand. I explain how to record tracks and how you use a few of GarageBand's features to make each track sound its best before you mix and master those tracks into a song.

In GarageBand, I usually record one track at a time. Although you *could* record your entire band playing a song live, or record yourself singing and playing the piano at the same time, unless you have a powerful Mac and a multichannel audio interface, you'll be limited to recording one or two tracks at a time. Just remember to record each instrument or vocal on a separate track, so you can adjust the instrument or vocal track separately from the rest of the song's tracks.

Recording tracks on a Mac

To record a track on your Mac, follow these steps:

1. **Launch GarageBand.**

If you don't see its icon on the dock, look in your Applications folder; if you don't see it in the Applications folder, search your Mac for *GarageBand*. If you don't find it, open the Mac App Store (from the dock or the Applications folder), search for *GarageBand,* and download a copy.

The Choose a Project dialog appears.

2. **Click New Project in the sidebar, as shown in Figure 3-2.**

Note that if a project was open when you quit GarageBand, that project will reopen when you launch GarageBand. To close that project and start a new one, choose File ➪ New.

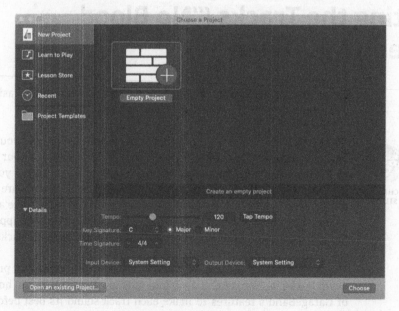

FIGURE 3-2:
You see this dialog when you launch GarageBand on your Mac.

The settings in the Details section at the bottom of the dialog are the default for new projects. Accept them as they are, or adjust them to your liking as follows:

- **Tempo:** Use this slider to adjust the project's tempo expressed in beats per minute (BPM). Or click the Tap Tempo button in time with your song to set the tempo manually.

- **Key Signature:** Use this pop-up menu to adjust the project's key.

- **Time Signature:** Use this pop-up menu to adjust the project's time signature.

- **Input Device and Output Device:** Use these pop-up menus to change your input and output devices.

Don't fret (pun intended) too much about these options at this time. Just leave the Tempo, Key Signature, and Time Signature settings alone if you aren't sure, at least for now. You can always change them later if you like.

3. **Create a new project by clicking Empty Project and then clicking the Choose button.**

The Choose a Track Type dialog shown in Figure 3-3 appears.

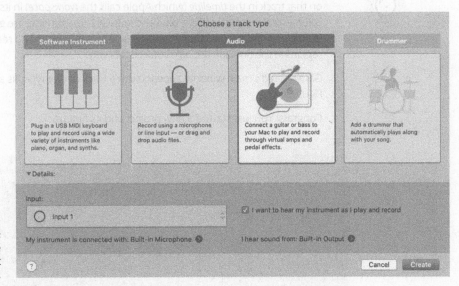

FIGURE 3-3: Specify the type of track to start with.

4. **Select a track type for the first track in this project.**

GarageBand offers four kinds of tracks for recording: software instrument, audio (mic), audio (guitar/bass), and drummer. Here's how to choose the right type of track for the instrument or voice you want to record first:

- **Software instrument track:** Record using GarageBand's built-in software instruments with either a MIDI keyboard connected to your Mac or one of GarageBand's two onscreen keyboards.

- **Audio (microphone) track:** Record using a mic connected to your Mac, a mic connected to an audio interface connected to your Mac, or your Mac's built-in mic.

Your Mac's built-in mic sounds worse than almost any other microphone in the world. Use it only if no other options are available.

WARNING

- **Audio (guitar/bass) track:** Record an instrument connected to your Mac or an instrument connected to an audio interface connected to your Mac.

- **Drummer track:** Create a virtual drummer track for your song. Each virtual drummer includes a unique drum kit and playing style, both of which can be edited at will.

Nice touch: After you record a track, the region you just recorded appears on that track in the *timeline* (which Apple calls the *workspace*) in its proper color — real instruments are blue and software instruments are green. Tracks even glow their proper color when you select them. Loops and real audio regions in the timeline are also colored this way.

TIP

GarageBand's main window appears with a track of that type, as shown in Figure 3-4.

Congrats! You just started a new project and its first track.

FIGURE 3-4: GarageBand's main window after choosing an Audio (guitar/bass) track for the first track.

TIP

GarageBand for the Mac doesn't automatically save your work, so I recommend that you save your project with a descriptive name by choosing File⇨ Save before you record. Furthermore, to avoid losing work if your Mac crashes or freezes, make a habit of saving your projects (File⇨ Save or its keyboard shortcut ⌘+S) every few minutes while you work.

Recording tracks on an iDevice

In this section, you create a new project with one track on your iDevice. Simply do the following:

1. **Launch GarageBand.**

Tap the + button to create a new song project. The screen shown in Figure 3-5 appears.

Note that if a project was open when you quit GarageBand, that project will reopen when you launch GarageBand. To close that project and start a new one, tap the new project icon in the upper-left corner (and shown in the margin).

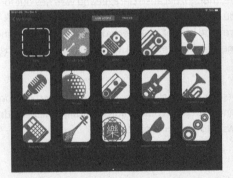 

FIGURE 3-5:
Create a new song using live loops (left) or tracks (right).

2. **Tap Tracks at the top of the screen.**

You're going to work in tracks mode for this exercise; you explore live loops mode in Chapter 13.

3. **To choose a preset for the first track, swipe left or right and then tap the preset you want to use.**

Your choices are Audio Recorder, Strings, Bass, Guitar, Amp, Keyboard, Drums, World, or Drummer. What you see next depends on which item you just tapped. Suffice it to say that your song appears and you're ready to record.

Congrats! You just started a new project and created its first track.

LOOPS AND TRACKS

You may be wondering where loops fit into the scheme of things (*things* being tracks), and that's a darn good question. The darn good answer is that *loops* are premade snippets of music and sound that come with GarageBand. You can use them to build an entire song or use them with your own singing and playing. When you want to use a particular loop, you drag it onto a track.

Loops come in two flavors: Some are software instrument loops, which you put on software instrument tracks, and the others are real instrument loops, which you put on real instrument tracks.

You may have as many different loops on a track as you like, but they all have to be the same flavor. In other words, you can have an unlimited number of software or real instrument loops, but you can't have both kinds on the same track. Don't worry if this isn't making sense yet. It will soon.

Loops can be combined with your performances on any track as long as the loop and performance are both the same flavor — real instrument or software instrument.

These rules are no biggie, though, because GarageBand watches out for you behind the scenes. For example, you can't drag a loop onto the wrong kind of track — GarageBand doesn't allow it. And here's the best of all: When you drag a loop from the loop browser onto the workspace (timeline), GarageBand automatically creates the right kind of track for it.

To recap: Loops can be either real or software. They can be used only on the appropriate kind of track, and that kind of track is created automatically when you drag and drop a loop from the loop browser to the workspace.

You can tell which kind of loop you're looking at in the loop browser by its icon (a green musical note for software instruments or a blue sound wave for real instruments). You can them apart in the timeline by the color and shapes they contain (green with dots and dashes for software instruments and blue with sound waves for real instruments). If this book were printed in color, you would know instantly that software instrument loops are greenish and real instrument loops are bluish, in the workspace and loop browser.

Whether you like it or not, GarageBand for iOS autosaves your song when you close the app, when you open a different song, and when idle.

TIP

I recommend that you become familiar with your iDevice's undo feature (shake the device and then tap the Undo button) and remember to use it if you don't want GarageBand saving the song after you delete a region or track or make a change you're not happy with.

Listening to tracks during recording and playback

Creating a multitrack recording is an iterative process. You record a track (or multiple tracks); when that's done, you listen to make sure it's okay before you move on. When you're certain that track sounds okay, you record more tracks and listen to them. Then you listen to all the recorded tracks together. You record more tracks and then listen to all of them together as well as in different combinations.

Later, during mixing and mastering, you add effects to a track (or to the entire song) and listen again. Or you might change an instrument sound — and listen again.

And so it goes — you record a bit, you listen a bit, you adjust a bit, you listen a bit, you tweak this and that, and then you listen some more.

To play or record your project, you use GarageBand's *transport controls,* which move the playhead much like the controls you'd find on a tape recorder, audio CD player, iPod, or DVD player. These controls can be seen in Figure 3-6 (Mac) and Figure 3-7 (iDevices).

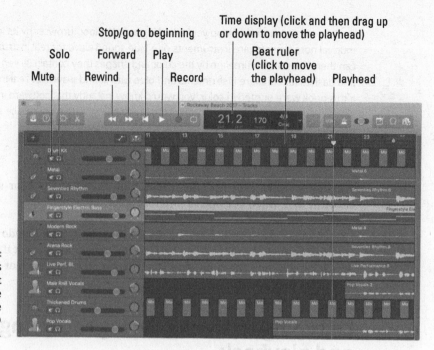

FIGURE 3-6: GarageBand's transport controls on the Mac work like the controls on a CD player.

Mute
Solo
Forward
Rewind
Stop/go to beginning
Play
Record
Time display (click and then drag up or down to move the playhead)
Beat ruler (click to move the playhead)
Playhead

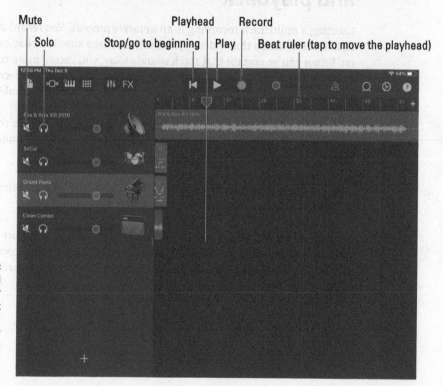

FIGURE 3-7: GarageBand offers fewer transport controls on iDevices, but they still work like the controls on a CD player.

Mute
Solo
Stop/go to beginning
Playhead
Play
Record
Beat ruler (tap to move the playhead)

With all that playing, recording, and listening, it would behoove you to memorize the myriad ways you can move the playhead hither and yon:

>> Click or tap the play icon (or use the Mac keyboard shortcut, the spacebar) to play or stop the song.

>> Click or tap and drag the playhead to a new position in the beat ruler.

>> Click or tap anywhere in the beat ruler to move the playhead to that point.

>> Click or tap the stop/go to beginning icon to move the playhead to the start of the song.

>> (Mac only) Click the rewind icon (or use the keyboard shortcut, the ← key) to move the playhead backward one measure at a time.

>> (Mac only) Click the forward icon (or use the keyboard shortcut, the → key) to move the playhead forward one measure at a time.

>> (Mac only) Click the number in the time display and then drag up or down without releasing the mouse button to move the playhead to that point in the song. Or double-click the time display, type a new number, and then press Return.

Choosing which tracks you hear

The mute and solo icons are opposite sides of the same coin. You use them to determine which tracks you hear (or don't hear) during recording and playback. The mute icon mutes (that is, silences) the track; the solo icon mutes all tracks but tracks with soloing enabled. So, for example, if you had four tracks numbered 1 through 4 but wanted to hear only tracks 1 and 3, you would either mute tracks 2 and 4 or solo tracks 1 and 3.

REMEMBER

Having both the mute and solo options is convenient as you begin to have more and more tracks in your song.

The icons light up when enabled. For example, in Figure 3-6, the mute icon is enabled for the Fingerstyle Electric Bass track.

You may mute or solo as many or as few tracks as you like (or none or all) during playback or recording.

Deciding a track's fate: Scrap bin, editing room, or mix?

After you play back a track, you may notice that it has some flaws. If you want to correct those flaws, you have several options:

>> **Punch in and re-record over the mistake.** See Part 3 (Mac) or Part 5 (iDevice) for details on editing and tweaking.

>> **Delete the region you just recorded and start over.** Do this if you want to re-record the entire part you just recorded. To delete the part (which GarageBand calls a *region*):

- **Mac:** Click the region in the timeline and press Delete (Backspace on some keyboards).

- **iOS:** Double-tap the region in the timeline and then tap the Delete button that appears above it.

Now move the playhead to the appropriate spot in the song and re-record that part.

>> **Delete the entire track.** If you decide the track just isn't working and probably never will, you can delete it:

- **Mac:** Click its name and press ⌘+Delete (⌘+Backspace on some keyboards).

- **iOS:** Double-tap slowly on the track's icon and then tap Delete. If you double-tap too quickly, the track's Smart instrument controls will appear instead of the Delete button. If that happens, try again but tap more slowly.

Changing a track's settings

You can change the settings of a track as follows:

>> **Mac:** Double-click the track's icon on the left, or select it (with the mouse or the arrow keys) and then click the Smart controls icon, as shown in Figure 3-8.

>> **iOS:** Double-tapping its icon on the left or tapping the Track Controls button, as shown in Figure 3-9.

Library

Smart controls

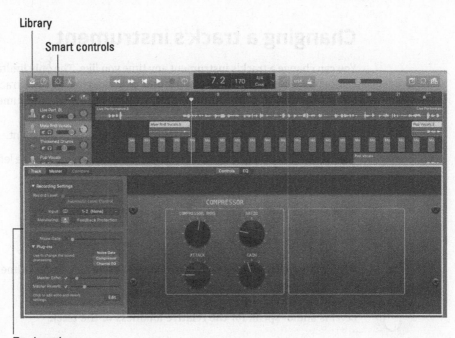

FIGURE 3-8:
Track settings for
the Male RnB
Vocals track
(Mac).

Track settings

Tap to change instruments

Track settings   Track controls

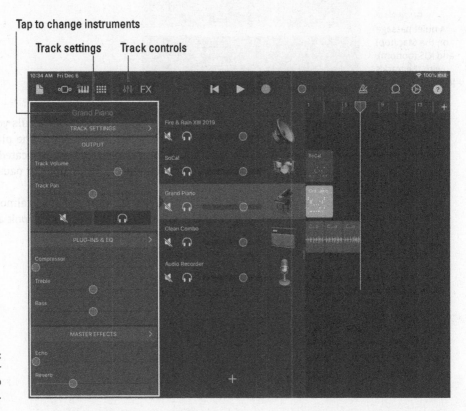

FIGURE 3-9:
Track settings for
the Grand Piano
track (iOS).

Changing a track's instrument

You can change a track's instrument any time you like. The only limitation is that you can't change a real instrument track into a software instrument track, or vice versa. Other than that little hiccup, do the following to change the instrument on a track:

>> **Mac:** Click the library icon and then select a different instrument.

>> **iOS:** Tap the instrument's name above the track settings on the left.

Checking levels during recording and playback

A simulated LED display shows the level of the track in real time as you play or record, as shown in Figure 3-10.

Level is audio-speak for the relative loudness of the track.

FIGURE 3-10:
A quiet passage on the Mac (top) and iOS (bottom), with the track's level display unlit.

So, when you play or record, the level display for each track tells you that track's record or playback level at that precise point in your song. The playhead always shows that point on the timeline. Wherever the playhead is located, that's where the song will resume playing or recording if you've stopped or paused.

Figure 3-10 was captured during the playback of a very quiet (almost silent) passage. As you can see, the level display is unlit. Now take a look at Figure 3-11, which was taken during a much louder passage.

FIGURE 3-11:
A loud passage on the Mac (top) and iOS (bottom) with the level display fully lit (and red on the right).

The red LEDs on the right end of the level display are your enemies. You want to see as little of them as possible when you record a track. If you see too much red, the track is too "hot," and will sound broken up and distorted when you play it back. An old studio saying goes like this: "If you see much red, your track is dead." Believe it.

TIP

If you notice that this dot is lit after you record a track, listen to the track very carefully. The track may have been spoiled if you recorded it in the red — or hot — zone.

If a track is too hot when you're rehearsing or recording, adjust its level so you see little or no red, and then record (or re-record). The following section provides further details on adjusting levels.

Adjusting levels

When you record, you mostly use the level faders to keep tracks from being recorded too hot, which can ruin the take. Later, during mixing and mastering, you use the level faders to mix all your tracks so each instrument and voice is heard clearly.

You can adjust the track level in two ways:

» **Adjust the level of the entire track with the fader control.** *Fader* is a pro audio term for a sliding control. The fader for each track is located under its name on the left side of the screen, as shown in Figure 3-12.

FIGURE 3-12:
The level faders
for Mac (left) and
iOS (right).

» **Adjust only part of a track with the track volume control.** When you want to make part of a track louder or softer than the rest (or adjust its level in more sophisticated ways), you use a track volume control, which appears below the track when automation is enabled. No pro-audio term for the track volume control exists; it's strictly a computer innovation. If you've used iTunes or Final Cut Pro, you know how to use the track volume control; if not, you find out how a little later in this section.

You start with the faders, which you click and slide to the left to lower the level or slide to the right to raise it. For example, in Figure 3-12:

>> The Grand Piano track is silent.

>> The Male Rock Vocals track is set to a modest recording level.

>> The Fingerstyle Bass track is set at 100 percent. (Don't do that.)

So that's about it for the level fader control, but you have a second way to adjust the level of a track that's often better, and here's why: The fader lets you choose only one level for the entire track. The method that I'm about to show you lets you change the level anywhere you like — and as many times as you like. For example, a track could start very quietly and build to a normal level (a fade-in), play at that level until a really loud passage occurs, drop the level for the loud part, bring the level back to normal again, and then fade-out.

To use the track volume control (officially known as the *track volume automation control*), follow these steps:

1. **Display the track volume control as follows:**

    ● **Mac:** Choose Mix ⇨ Show/Hide Automation (or press the A key).

    ● **iOS:** Tap the track's icon and then tap Automation.

2. **Click the track volume control and drag the resulting dot up or down to raise or lower the level at that point in the song.**

    Figure 3-13 shows the track volume control for a Mac track (top) and iOS track (bottom).

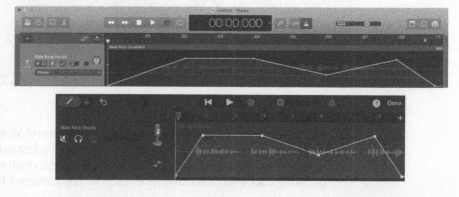

FIGURE 3-13:
The track volume control tells this track, "Fade-in, play a few seconds, get softer, get louder, and fade-out" for the Mac (top) and iOS (bottom).

Here's a blow-by-blow description of what happens to the level for the Male Rock Vocals track in Figure 3-13:

Time (Seconds)	Action
0	Silent
0–2	Increase the level from 0% to 75% (fade-in)
2–4	Remain at the 75% level
4–6	Decrease the level from 75% to 50%
6–8	Increase the level from 50% to 75%
8–9	Decrease the level from 75% to 0% (fade-out)

The track volume control method gives you more precise control than using the fader, so you'll probably use the former on most of your tracks during mixing and mastering.

TIP

I recommend against using the track volume control when recording. It can be done, but it's tricky and more likely to hurt your efforts and waste your time. Instead, I highly recommend that you use the level faders when you record and use the track volume control when you mix. I discuss mixing in great detail in Parts 3 (Mac) and 5 (iOS).

Polishing tracks

So you now know enough to lay down some tracks. After you have most or all of your tracks in the can, you can polish and embellish your song. You may want to redo a vocal part that isn't as good as it could be, add the gentle strains of a string ensemble in your choruses, or insert some handclaps or the sound of a tambourine. You can trim noise at the beginning or end of a track, cut out and delete mistakes, and more, all of which comes under the heading of "editing" your tracks and is covered in Parts 3 (Mac) and 5 (iOS).

One of the greatest things about multitrack recording is that it's not over until you say it's over. If you decide that something doesn't sound right, even months after mixing and mastering the song, you can go back to your original GarageBand file and change it to your heart's content and then remix and remaster, and you're off to the races with a new version of your song.

Two things that you can do to polish your songs are overdubbing (redoing) any part of a track that isn't as good as it could be and sweetening, which is adding new tracks to fill out the sound of your song. I describe these terms briefly in the following sections and in more detail in Parts 3 (Mac) and 5 (iOS).

Overdubbing

Overdubbing is re-recording a part of a track to fix mistakes that were made in its performance or recording.

In the old days, you couldn't overdub unless you had fairly sophisticated high-end tape machines that let you "punch in and punch out." You would listen to playback, and right before the bad part of the track, the engineer would "punch" the Record button. As soon as you finished singing or playing the replacement part, he or she would punch the Record button again. What came before and after the replacement part remained intact, but the replacement track was grafted into the middle like magic.

Overdubbing doesn't sound convincing if the replacement part sounds much different from the original part, so try to use the same setup that you used when you recorded the original track — the same microphones, room, instrument, audio interface, level and other settings, and so on — when you record overdubs on that track.

One last thing: If you flub an overdub take (or any take, for that matter), Garage-Band is forgiving. Just undo the flubbed take by choosing Edit ⇨ Undo (or pressing ⌘+Z), and try again.

TIP

You learn an even easier way to record multiple takes in Chapters 4 (Mac) and 12 (iOS), but for now, just get your head around the concept of recording a part more than once in your quest for the perfect take.

MULTIPLE TAKES VERSUS OVERDUBS

You can reduce your need to overdub by recording multiple takes of a part. When you finish recording a take and you're relatively happy with it, create a new track just like it and then mute the original track. Record the part again on the new track. If you like the new track, repeat the process; if you don't, use the Undo feature and try again.

When you have three or four good takes in the can, you can usually select pieces from them and use them in place of overdubs to create one superb take. Because the takes were recorded at the same time on the same setup, they should naturally sound the same so you don't have to worry about whether the overdub matches the original.

Sweetening

Another way that you can make your song sound more professional and finished is by *sweetening* it by adding tracks after your primary recording is completed. Sometimes, you listen to a semi-finished mix and realize that what this song needs is one or more embellishments, such as the following:

>> Handclaps

>> Bells

>> Whistles

>> Violins and cellos (a.k.a. *a string pad*)

>> Tambourines or other percussion

You can sweeten a song anytime you want. If you've already mastered it, go back to the GarageBand file that you mastered from, add the new track or tracks, and remaster the song. Sweetening is covered in detail in Chapters 9 (Mac) and 18 (iOS).

Mix That Sucka

When you've finished recording tracks, and performed any overdubbing or sweetening your song needs, you're ready to mix. When you mix a song, you're doing two things:

>> Adjusting the level for each track until all the tracks blend beautifully together, with none too loud and none too soft

>> Setting the pan position for each track to place it on the sound stage — left, center, or right

Overview of mixing

Here's an overview of how I work through the mixing process:

1. **I usually start mixing by using the fader level controls until the relative level of each track is close to what I want to hear.**

    I call this a rough mix, but it's a fast and easy way to get this far.

2. When I need better control over a track's level throughout the song, I use the track volume (automation) control.

3. After I get the individual track levels set to my liking, I adjust the pan location of each track.

4. Finally, I turn on and adjust effects (if necessary) for each track and then check all my levels and pans again.

After I do all that, I'm ready to move on to the final step, mastering.

Setting the pan

For everything — turn, turn, turn — there is a season — turn, turn, turn. And, for every track, there is a pan knob — turn, turn, turn.

Turn the knob to the left to make more of that track come out of the left speaker; turn it to the right to do the reverse. Figure 3-14 (Mac) and Figure 3-15 (iOS) show a track with its pan set to hard left (top), dead center (middle), and hard right (bottom).

FIGURE 3-14:
A Mac track panned hard left (top), dead center (middle), and hard right (bottom).

In the top version, the track is panned all the way to the left so that all the sound comes from the left speaker. In the middle version, the track is panned dead center, and you can hear equal parts of it from the left and right speakers. And the bottom version shows the track panned all the way to the right.

Note that the top and bottom versions in Figure 3-14 have only one of their two rows of LED level display lights lit, but the middle version has both rows lit. The level displays are showing you the stereo output for the track. The top row of simulated LEDs tells you the level of the left channel; the bottom row shows the level for the right channel.

So, to make a track sound like it's coming from slightly to the left of center, you would turn the pan control slightly to the left of center. And so on.

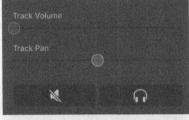

FIGURE 3-15:
An iOS track panned hard left (top), dead center (middle), and hard right (bottom).

(Lord and) Mastering

After you're satisfied with your mix, heave a big sigh of relief — the end is near. All that's left is to master that puppy and be done with it.

Mastering is setting the song's level and equalization and create a fade-in or fade-out. But mastering is useful also for emphasizing a quieter passage or deemphasizing a louder one.

All it takes is a few clicks. . .

TECHNICAL STUFF

. . . which makes it nothing like mastering a stereo recording in the real world. The art of changing a two-track mix into a fantastic-sounding Red Book Audio CD (the type of CD you buy at a music store) is just that — an art. Only a few hundred truly great mastering engineers exist in the world today, each an artist who can take a decent-sounding stereo mix and master it so that it sounds absolutely brilliant when you play the CD.

On the other hand, mastering your song with GarageBand on a Mac couldn't be easier. (Sadly, the iOS version of GarageBand doesn't have a mastering step.)

Here are the steps to master a song on a Mac:

1. **Enable (show) the master track by choosing Track ⇨ Show/Hide Master Track or pressing ⌘+Shift+M.**

REMEMBER

   If the master track is displayed, the ⌘+Shift+M command hides it; if the master track is hidden, the command displays it. So, if you don't see a master track at the bottom of your workspace, press ⌘+Shift+M now.

2. **You may have to scroll down to see the master track; it always appears as the last track on the list, as shown in Figure 3-16.**

FIGURE 3-16:
The Master Track is always at the bottom of the track list.

Master track   Fade-in   Fade-out

3. **Choose Mix ⇨ Show Automation or press the A key to display the master track volume control so you can adjust the song's level that way if you care to.**

TIP

   Using the volume control on the master track is the easiest way to create the fade-in or fade-out effect at the beginning or end of your song.

   In Figure 3-16, I've set up the volume control to fade-in quickly at the beginning of the song and fade-out slowly at the end. I've also made the first chorus a little louder than the rest of the song, because it had some quiet, delicate guitar work under the vocals. (Yeah, sure.)

4. **Click the library icon to display the mastering presets.**

5. **Click a preset.**

I chose Slick Pop in Figure 3-16. Try a few presets and see how you like them — or maybe you did such a superb job mixing the song that it doesn't need any master effects.

6. **When you're satisfied with the sound you're hearing, choose Share ⇨ Song to Music (or Song to iTunes) to export the song to the Music (or iTunes) app.**

In a few moments, you can open the Music or iTunes app and listen to your masterpiece.

And that's that. You've now laid down the tracks, and then produced, mixed, and mastered your song.

If you want to get the best possible song, you still have a bit more work ahead of you:

1. **Listen critically to the song.**

Play the song on your favorite audio systems: in your car, your portable speakers, with headphones, and on a boom box.

2. **Take notes on what you hear, don't hear, and think you'd like to hear.**

3. **Remix and remaster according to your notes.**

4. **Repeat until you're totally satisfied with the song.**

Now the song really is done.

For details on tweaking the master volume, applying presets, and more, see Chapter 11 for Mac and Chapter 19 for iDevices, which cover mastering in loving detail.

Managing Song Files

Don't delete your GarageBand project files after you finish (master) a song. You might decide to remix, sweeten, or remaster the song in the future, and you can't do that if you don't have the GarageBand file.

When and if you remix or remaster a song, add a number or a descriptive word or two to the new version. If you added some tambourine and handclaps to a song named Bliss, for example, name the revised version something like Bliss2 or BlissT&C. Then you'll have a better chance of finding the version that you want a few months from now.

When a song is absolutely perfect, you can add something like GoldenMaster (for example, BlissGoldenMaster). I've never finished a song that was even close to being absolutely perfect, but I'll probably add GoldenMaster to its name if I do.

WHY AND WHEN TO CONSIDER SAVE AS RATHER THAN SAVE (ON YOUR MAC)

One last thing: If you think your song is pretty good, it behooves you to save early and save often while you work on it. I save every few minutes. If I get out of the chair while a project is open, I save the file before I walk away from my desk.

And if your song is really, really good — or really, really important — consider using the Save As command to create backup copies, too.

I prefer to use Save As (choose File ⇨ Save As or press ⌘+Shift+S) to save songs on a different disk than the original (or to iCloud or another cloud-based storage). But even if you don't have an extra disk or cloud-based storage, using the Save As command to create a backup copy of your song file — even one saved to the same disk or folder as the original — may be the most important thing you do all day.

If you have only one copy of your song file, it can be lost in a heartbeat. If you use the Save As command to create a backup copy, however, you'll have a copy that's frozen at that moment in time. You can always use the backup if something awful happens to the original. The more important the song, the more often you should stash away a backup copy of it.

Warning: After you perform a Save As command, the version of the song on your screen is the new one that you just saved (as). You may (or may not) want to close it and reopen your original song file. You should know which file you're working on and where that file resides (so that you can reopen it and work on it again after you quit GarageBand). For this reason, you should always use descriptive names.

Another way to determine which version of a file is which is to append a number (or date) after its name. Adding the date and time is superfluous these days (click the file in the Finder and choose File ⇨ Get Info and you'll see why).

If you don't see a Date Modified column in your Open dialog box, click the View button and choose List. Now click the words *Date Modified* in the column header to sort by modification date; click the words *Date Modified* again to reverse the sort order (that is, to sort from A to Z or from Z to A). Neat!

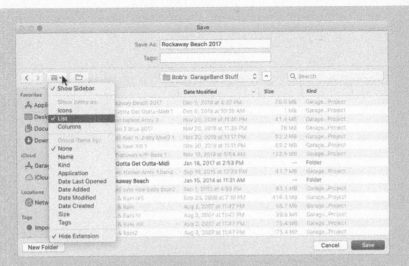

Trust me: Save As can be a lifesaver if you totally screw up a song, if you delete tracks that you didn't mean to delete (and didn't undo), if your Mac or hard drive or both are damaged, or if the file becomes corrupted. Many fates can befall a song file, and most of them have unpleasant consequences if you don't have a backup.

2
Making Music on a Mac

Walk through GarageBand's global preferences with recommendations and tips for getting the results you desire.

Become acquainted with Apple loops, which are song snippets you can assemble into an almost-frighteningly professional-sounding tune in minutes.

Delve into MIDI (Musical Instrument Digital Interface), which lets you record music using GarageBand's built-in software instruments and a MIDI keyboard (if you have one) or GarageBand's onscreen keyboard (if you don't).

Record vocals and acoustic instruments with a microphone.

Discover the ins and outs of recording guitar, bass, and other amplified instruments without amps, microphones, or stomp boxes.

IN THIS CHAPTER

» Using the General pane

» Working with the Audio/MIDI pane

» Keeping time with the Metronome pane

» Learn about loop options in the Loops pane

» Adding your own info to the My Info pane

» Gaining experience with the Advanced pane

Chapter **4**

Getting Started

Before you work and play with GarageBand, you should familiarize yourself with its six preferences panes and their settings. These settings are global and generally affect every project you create.

You probably don't know how you like your preferences, at least not yet. But you will in just a few short pages. This chapter helps you adjust each item in every preferences pane, accompanied by the usual wit and wisdom and whatever else that I think you may find helpful.

Some of you may think that I'm putting the cart before the horse by covering preferences in Chapter 4, because some of the features that these preferences affect are not introduced until later in Part 2 and Part 3. But there's a method to my madness.

You're going to take a quick look at every one of the little critters (that is, the preferences panes) so that you know what they are, where they are, and how to configure them appropriately. For many of you, I'm hoping to do this *before* you try to make music.

General Pane

Using the General pane is generally painless. In this section I examine each option, starting at the top.

To get to the General pane (and the other preferences panes), choose Garage-Band ⇨ Preferences (or press ⌘+,) and click the General tab at the top of the Preferences window. The pane shown in Figure 4-1 appears.

FIGURE 4-1:
The General Preferences pane.

Software Instrument Recordings section

The first section of the General Preferences pane governs what happens when you record over an existing software instrument recording, known as a *region* in GarageBand parlance. To understand the Cycle Off and Cycle On pop-up menus, you first have to understand the cycle area and cycle mode, labeled in Figure 4-2.

You use the cycle area to play a specific part of your project over and over. It's handy any time you need to hear part of a song repeatedly, such as when you want to practice a challenging passage before recording it; record multiple takes without pausing; listen critically to a specific part of the project while mixing or mastering.

To enable the cycle area, do one of the following:

>> Click the cycle mode icon in the toolbar.

>> Click and drag in the top part of the ruler.

>> Press the C key on your keyboard.

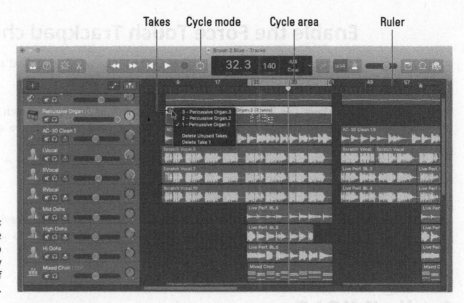

Takes   Cycle mode   Cycle area   Ruler

FIGURE 4-2:
Use the cycle
area to
continuously
replay a part of
your project.

To adjust the start and end points of the cycle area, click and drag its left or right edge. To move the entire cycle area, click in the middle of the cycle area and then drag left or right.

Now that you know about the cycle area, let's dig into the pop-up menus on the General pane.

The Cycle Off pop-up menu determines what happens when you record a software instrument track over an existing region with cycle mode off:

>> Choose Replace to overwrite previously recorded regions when cycle mode is off.

>> Choose Merge to merge your performance with previously recorded regions when cycle mode is on.

The Cycle On pop-up menu determines what happens when you record a software instrument track over an existing region with cycle mode on:

>> Choose Create Takes to record multiple takes on a single track. You can then choose which take is active by clicking the take number for the track and choosing a take from the drop-down menu, as shown in Figure 4-2.

>> Choose Merge to merge your performance with previously recorded regions on that track.

Enable the Force Touch Trackpad check box

Enabling the check box labeled Enable the Force Touch Trackpad adds additional gestures you can use with your Force Touch trackpad.

This check box is disabled if your Mac doesn't have a Force Touch trackpad. (It's disabled in Figure 4-1 because my MacBook Pro doesn't have a Force Touch trackpad.)

Reset Warnings button

Use the Reset Warnings button to reset all warnings and alerts previously set to Do Not Show Again. Put another way, click the button if you'd like to see those warnings and alerts again.

Audio/MIDI Pane

Many Macs have built-in microphones and speakers as well as audio input and audio output. If you have a USB or Thunderbolt audio interface, the interface has at least one audio-in and one audio-out port. The Audio/MIDI Preferences pane lets you specify which device you want to use for output (listening) and input (recording).

The Audio/MIDI pane, shown in Figure 4-3, is where you select the input and output that you want GarageBand to use. It's also where you optimize GarageBand's performance. Last but not least, this pane tells you how many MIDI devices GarageBand recognizes at the moment (it recognizes one in Figure 4-3).

To open this pane, choose GarageBand⇨Preferences (or press ⌘+,) and click Audio/MIDI at the top of the Preferences window. The following sections explain your options.

Devices section

The first section in this pane is Devices, which contains the Output Device and Input Device menus. If your Mac has more than one audio input (for example, the built-in audio-in port plus a USB or Thunderbolt audio interface) or output (for example, the built-in headphone port or a USB or Thunderbolt audio interface), choose the one you want to use from these menus.

FIGURE 4-3:
The Audio/MIDI
Preferences
pane.

That's it. If you see only one input and output choice in either menu on your Mac, wave bye-bye. You won't have to use them much until you add a new audio device to your setup, and you can ignore the upcoming warning.

If you see two or more input or output choices, read the upcoming warning carefully.

TIP

If you see two or more choices in either menu *and* you like to plug and unplug your audio devices with reckless abandon (like yours truly), you should read this warning even more carefully, because it's even more likely to apply to you.

WARNING

When you don't hear what you expect to hear; the sound is not coming from the speakers or headphones that you expected; or your microphone or instrument doesn't play through, don't panic. GarageBand has a maddening tendency to change the inputs and outputs you've selected for no apparent reason and without permission. So, if the music isn't coming or going where you expect it, check these two menus first.

Here's another tidbit: If you unplug the current input or output, GarageBand, always the model of politeness, informs you of the change. I disconnected my Scarlett Solo audio interface and saw the warning dialog shown in Figure 4-4.

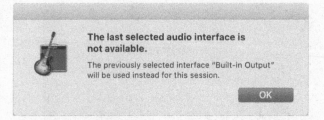
Effects section

The Effects section has a single check box that determines whether or not Garage-Band will recognize third-party plug-ins known as audio units. If you have never downloaded or purchased a plug-in, feel free to leave the Enable Audio Units check box deselected. But, if you do have plug-ins, you won't see them in Garage-Band unless audio units are enabled here.

MIDI section

The last section in the Audio/MIDI pane is MIDI. In this section, you see the MIDI Status item, which reports how many MIDI devices GarageBand believes are connected to your Mac at the moment. So, MIDI Status isn't a preference; it just displays a bit of information.

In Figure 4-4, you can see that my device (a MacBook Pro) has one MIDI device connected to it.

Now wave bye-bye to this feature. You probably won't need to look at it again.

Metronome Pane

Before I talk about the Metronome Preferences pane, let me explain what a metronome is and why you will probably need to use it.

It's important to keep time with your song so you can play the right notes at the right time. To do that, you need to hear a steady beat. GarageBand's built-in *metronome* plays that steady beat (sometimes called a *click track*) to help you play and record in perfect time at the project tempo you've specified.

You can turn the metronome on or off at any time — while recording, playing back, mixing, or mastering. But you'll probably find it most useful while recording tracks.

To make a choice that suits you, here are some tips to keep in mind:

>> **To play or sing in time with a song's time signature, tempo, and other tracks, use the metronome every time that you record a track.** Just remember that YMMV (your mileage may vary). Some musicians have perfect time and can play entire pieces without missing a beat. I'm such a lousy musician that I have trouble staying in time, even with the metronome clicking away.

>> **You may prefer to toggle the metronome on and off, which I do often.** To do so, click the metronome icon in the toolbar (and shown in the margin) or press the K (for *klick*) key. You can tell whether the metronome is on (without listening) because the icon is highlighted in purple. If it's on and you click the icon (or press the K key) again, the button turns gray and the metronome shuts up.

When I start a new project, I use the metronome during playback to rehearse parts without recording them and to try out different tempos for a piece. But as soon as I have drum and bass tracks — and maybe a guitar or keyboard part or two — I turn the metronome off and leave it off. By this point, the other tracks should be in time with each other, so I should be able to keep time with them when I'm playing or singing, without hearing the annoying tick of the metronome.

As the song's track count increases, it gets harder to hear the metronome anyway. That's why you may want to record your rhythm tracks — mostly drums and bass — first.

Just know that the metronome is there if you want it, during recording or playback. It can be turned on and off in a heartbeat by pressing its keyboard shortcut (K)— that is, unless that heartbeat happens to beat while you're playing or recording.

If you're playing or recording, follow these steps to toggle the metronome on or off:

1. **Press the spacebar (to pause recording or playback).**

2. **Click the metronome icon (or press the K key) to turn the metronome on or off.**

3. **Press the spacebar to start playback or press R to start recording.**

Now, here's the scoop on the two controls in the Metronome Preferences pane, which is shown in Figure 4-5:

>> **Tone slider:** Move this slider left or right to change the sound of the metronome. Play with various settings to determine which tone works best for you.

>> **Volume slider:** Move this slider left to make the metronome quieter or to the right to make it louder.

FIGURE 4-5:
The Metronome
Preferences
pane.

Loops Pane

The Loops Preferences pane has three little settings, as you can see in Figure 4-6.

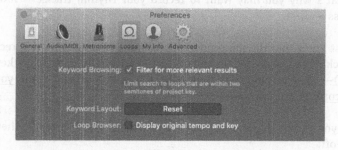

FIGURE 4-6:
The Loops
Preferences
pane.

Keyboard Browsing setting

In the first setting, the Filter for More Relevant Results check box does exactly what it says: If you deselect this check box, you see more loops, but many of them won't sound good in your song.

It may seem that finding more loops would be a good thing, but it's not — so resist the temptation. Try it if you have the time, and you'll see my point.

I always keep this check box selected. You can deselect yours if you like, but if you do, I hope you don't waste too much time with loops that sound lousy in your composition.

'Nuff said.

Keyboard Layout setting

The loop browser (which I cover in detail in Chapter 5) uses keywords to describe the sounds in loops. The keywords appear on buttons in the loop browser's button view (shown in Figure 4-7) and can be customized by clicking and dragging a button to a different position.

The Reset button in the Loops Preferences pane will set your mess back to the original layout when you decide that you hate what you've created.

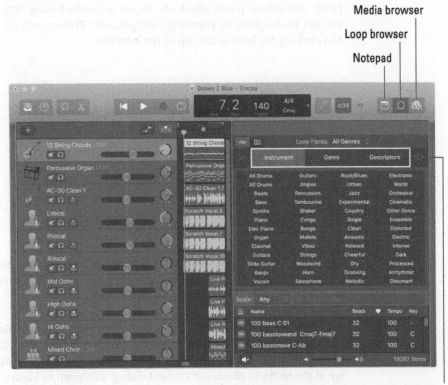

FIGURE 4-7:
Click the loop browser icon and then click Instrument (shown here), Genre, or Descriptors, each of which presents a different set of buttons.

Media browser

Loop browser

Notepad

Display keywords by instrument, genre, or descriptor

Blowing away these customizations isn't a big deal; you don't lose sounds or settings. Only the positions of the keywords in the loop browser's button view are changed.

Loop Browser setting

Last but not least, enable the Display Original Tempo and Key check box to see the tempo and key for each loop in the loop browser (refer to Figure 4-7). If you don't care to see the tempo and key for every loop, leave it deselected and leave more room onscreen for the loop's name.

My Info Pane

You use the My Info pane, shown in Figure 4-8, to set your desired playlist, composer, and album name when you export a finished song into iTunes. As usual, you get to the pane by choosing GarageBand⇨ Preferences (or by pressing ⌘+,) and clicking My Info at the top of the window.

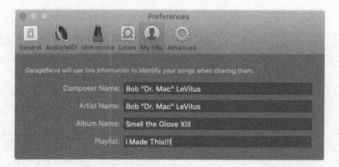

FIGURE 4-8:
The My Info
Preferences
pane.

When you're ready to export a song, GarageBand uses the information in the four text fields shown in the pane: Composer Name, Artist Name, Album Name, and Playlist.

So, when I export a finished song by choosing Share⇨ Song to Music (or iTunes on Macs running macOS Mojave or earlier), the song arrives in the Music app (or iTunes) with the information that I typed in the My Info pane already entered for me in the Share to Music (or iTunes) dialog, as shown in Figure 4-9.

That's nice, but what's nicer is that the app also picked up the title of the song — which I never typed into the preferences pane!

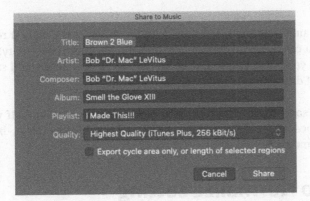

All the fields are editable, so you can make changes before you click the Share button and send the song to Music (or iTunes).

Advanced Pane

The Advanced pane, shown in Figure 4-10, doesn't contain anything advanced. My guess is that Apple is trying to keep you from changing these settings unless someone else tells you to.

Audio Recording Resolution setting

GarageBand can record audio at two resolutions (kind of like quality levels). The default is to record higher quality 24-bit audio, but you can disable the 24-bit check box if you want to record smaller, lower quality 16-bit files instead.

TIP

In my humble opinion, you should always record at the highest resolution available. You can always compress (shrink) the file later if necessary. If you record at 16 bits, your song will sound worse than at 24 bits. Sure you'll save a few megabytes of disk space, but it's usually not worth it.

Record something in 24 bits, then record it again in 16 bits. If you don't hear a difference, or the difference doesn't bother you, disable the 24-bit check box and save some space.

Auto Normalize setting

The Export Projects at Full Volume check box is selected by default, so GarageBand automatically exports your project at the optimum loudness — the highest volume level at which no distortion occurs. If you've set your track or master levels imperfectly, Auto Normalize does a great job of making them sound better when you export them, which is why I recommend keeping this check box enabled. Unless, like yours truly, you prefer to manage final volume levels manually when you master.

One last thing: This setting has no effect on the volume level of tracks playing back in GarageBand; it comes into play only when you share (export) your song.

Movie Thumbnail Resolution setting

If you use GarageBand to add a soundtrack to a movie, this setting governs the size and resolution of the movie thumbnails displayed as you compose.

Now you know how every control in GarageBand's six preferences panes works, and my recommendations for their settings.

Are you ready to rock and roll? In Chapter 5, you start making music without playing a note by using GarageBand's loops.

IN THIS CHAPTER

» **Understanding loop basics**

» **Finding the right loops**

» **Knowing what the loop browser can do for you**

» **Adding loops to your song**

» **Tinkering with loops**

Chapter **5**

Using Loops to Make Music

Even if you can't play or sing a note, you can have lots of fun using GarageBand's loops, which are prerecorded bits of music that require absolutely no talent on your part to sound great. In many cases, the fastest and easiest way to get a song started is to use one of the thousands of loops included with GarageBand.

We're starting our Mac recording journey with loops for a reason. I have no idea whether you're a talented musician or someone who can't play a note on any instrument. With loops it doesn't matter.

In this chapter, you create a song using only the prerecorded loops that come with GarageBand. (You're free to add an audio track and sing your masterpiece if you like, but that's optional.)

What Is a Loop, Anyway?

A *loop*, in its simplest form, is a piece of music that can repeat (loop) seamlessly. Loops are designed this way; a good one can be repeated without missing a beat. When you repeat a loop, it's called *looping*. To use a loop, you drag it onto a track (or onto the workspace, where a track is created for it automatically). But I'm getting ahead of myself.

Anyway, the thousands of little pieces of sound that come with GarageBand are called loops. If you repeat a loop seamlessly, the loop is looped. The act of doing so is called looping.

TECHNICAL
STUFF

The term *loop*, which indicates a repeating segment of music, stemmed from the fact that the first artists doing this (Eno and Fripp come to mind) would cut the magnetic recording tape and paste it back together in a loop that played continuously. The process required multiple tape players and must have been awkward, but that's how looping got its start.

GarageBand has two kinds of loops:

>> **Software instrument loops:** These are recorded using a MIDI keyboard, drum machine, or another MIDI controller.

>> **Real instrument loops:** These are recorded from an analog (real) source, that is, electric guitars, basses, horns, wind instruments, and of course, vocals.

Where to find more loops

Many loops are samples of music created by other artists. Other loops, including the loops that come with GarageBand, are original work.

You don't have to confine yourself to the loops that Apple provides with Garage-Band. First, you can download additional sounds and loops for free by choosing GarageBand ➪ Sound Library ➪ Download All Available Sounds, and then clicking Get in the resulting dialog.

GarageBand includes a passable selection of software instrument sounds and loops by default, but if you download all additional sounds and loops, you'll have over 2 more gigabytes of sounds and loops!

TIP

I encourage you do that right now — unless your SSD or hard disk is almost full. Even then, I encourage you to archive some files from the almost-full disk to another disk to free up space for the free additional sounds and loops. If you're going to use GarageBand, you might as well stock it with everything you can that's free — you never know what's going to come in handy in a recording session.

Bottom line: GarageBand is great by default, but it's even greater when you add thousands of additional high-quality sounds and loops without paying a penny.

You can also find thousands of free GarageBand-compatible loops on the Internet. Just search for *"GarageBand Free Loops"* (include the quotation marks to avoid a lot of unwanted hits) and you'll find dozens of sites offering free content.

TECHNICAL STUFF

The format for the loops used by GarageBand is known as *Apple loops*. Other programs, including Apple's Logic Pro ($199.99) and MainStage ($29.99), also use the Apple loop format. You can find Apple Loops in your Library/Audio folder; they have the .caf (core audio file) file extension.

Spicing up your songs with loops

Entire music genres — dance, electronica, house music, rap, and many others — have made an art form out of using loops. But don't let these genres limit your perception of how loops are used. In GarageBand, loops don't have to be looped. In fact, many GarageBand loops sound better as a one-shot accent than in repeated in a loop.

Here are just a few ways you can use loops:

>> **As a background groove or as the central, driving theme of a song:** You can use a drum loop to provide the backbeat to your song or maybe just to keep the beat while you build other tracks with loops, instruments, and vocals.

>> **As musical punctuation marks:** You can make a horn part lurk in the chorus, or a funky guitar riff chug along in the verse. For better or verse (groan), a loop can be the perfect tool for your song, regardless of the sound that you seek (or think you're seeking).

>> **To spice up a single chorus, bridge, or verse and make it just a little bit different than the other ones.** You might add a shaker or other percussion loop in the last verse and find that the addition was exactly what was missing in the song. Alternately, perhaps you need a bridge to break up a song. With a few loops, you can make a bass line, drum fill, and horn riff that punch up your song to the next level.

That's enough background on loops. Now let's dig in and start playing with them!

Finding the Right Loop with the Loop Browser

The loop browser is GarageBand's tool for managing the thousand(s) of loops in your loop library. It's where you find GarageBand's built-in loops, downloaded All Available Sounds loops (GarageBand ⇨ Sound Library ⇨ Download All Available Sounds), and loops you've picked up from other sources. You use the *loop browser* to find, preview, and select loops from your collection so you can add them to tracks.

You can make the loop browser appear on the right side of the main window in several ways:

>> Click the loop browser icon (shown in the margin) near the upper-right corner of the GarageBand window. Click it again to hide the loop browser.

>> Choose View ⇨ Show Loop Browser. Choose View ⇨ Hide Loop to (you guessed it) hide the loop browser.

>> Press the 0 key. Press it again to hide the loop browser.

Regardless of which way you make the loop browser appear, when it does, the right side of the GarageBand window transforms into the loop browser.

Viewing loops in button or column view

The loop browser offers two convenient views so that you can always find the right loop without working too hard:

>> **Button view:** This view provides three tabs — Instruments (shown in Figure 5-1), Genres, and Descriptors — each of which displays buttons for filtering your loops.

>> **Column view:** If you're not the button type, GarageBand also offers column view. In column view, you can browse your loops by genre, instruments, moods, or favorites. Select a category in the leftmost column, a subcategory in the middle column, and (if you want), a sub-sub category in the third column, as shown in Figure 5-2.

In either view, the list below displays only loops that match your choices. So, if you don't see the loop you want, try selecting different buttons or categories and subcategories.

Button view

FIGURE 5-1:
The loop browser
in button view.

Column view

FIGURE 5-2:
The loop browser
in column view.

To toggle between the two views, click the button view or column view icon in the upper-left corner of the loop browser (labeled in Figures 5-1 and 5-2).

Seeing more instruments

When you open the loop browser in button view, as shown in Figure 5-1, the Instrument tab may display only six or seven rows of buttons, about half the instrument buttons in GarageBand. The other half are inexplicably hidden.

To see more rows of buttons in your loop browser's Instruments tab, follow these steps:

1. **Open the loop browser.**

2. **Click the Instrument tab.**

3. **Hover the cursor over the dividing line between the buttons and the list until you see the resizer cursor.**

   When you're in the correct spot, your cursor will turn into a *resizer cursor,* as in Figure 5-3 (and in the margin).

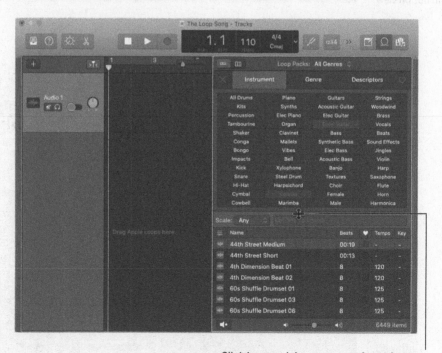

FIGURE 5-3:
Click the dividing line and drag downward to reveal more instrument buttons.

Click here and drag up to see fewer buttons

4. **Click and drag downward to see more rows of buttons or upward to see fewer.**

In Figure 5-3 I've dragged downward to reveal 13 rows of buttons (versus the 7 rows in Figure 5-1).

You can't scroll the top (button) area in the loop browser, so using the resizer is the only way to see all buttons in the Instrument tab.

All buttons on the Genre and Descriptors tabs are displayed, so using the resizer trick on these tabs is kinda pointless.

Searching for a loop you love

Finding the right loop is the hard part, especially when you have thousands to wade through. But, as you've just seen, GarageBand has two views to help you. These views conveniently divide GarageBand loops into instruments, genres, and descriptors, as shown in the previous figures.

In other words, Apple has done the heavy lifting for you. All you have to do to find the right loop is click a button or buttons, or an item or items in columns to filter your loops. GarageBand, marvel that it is, does the rest, filtering out loops that won't sound right in your song, based on the key and tempo that you chose when you started the project and your choices in the loop browser.

Although you probably don't know the names of loops you like best just yet, over time you'll come to know some loops by name. When you do, you can bypass the buttons and columns and type your query in the Search Loops field, as I describe shortly.

Until then, here's how you use GarageBand's button and column views to find just the right loop for your song.

Searching in button view

The following steps walk you through a loop search in button view:

1. **Start out in button view by click the button view icon at the top of the loop browser.**

The button view icon is labeled in Figure 5-1.

2. **Click the Loop Packs drop-down menu at the top of the loop browser and choose All Genres to ensure that you're working with all the loops.**

   Use the resizer cursor as described in the previous section to make sure you are seeing all the buttons.

3. **Click a button.**

   I clicked Beats. Figure 5-4 shows the 1,796 loops in that category.

TIP

That's cool but here's something even cooler: GarageBand has eliminated choices that don't fit your selection. I have 6,449 items in my loop collection, so GarageBand is hiding 4,653 loops (6,449 minus 1,796 is 4,653). You have to love that.

4. **Now that GarageBand has narrowed your choices to only loops that can work in this context, click another button (or buttons) to narrow your search further.**

   Clicking the Beats button alone yielded 1,796 loops. Clicking the Urban button in the Genre tab alone yielded 124 loops. But clicking both the Beats and Urban buttons narrowed the field to a more manageable 12 loops, as shown in the lower-right corner of Figure 5-5.

FIGURE 5-5:
In this image, I've narrowed the selection to only loops that are in both the Beats and Urban categories.

5. **If you want to refine your choices, use the Scale pop-up menu below the buttons in the loop browser.**

   The Scale menu options are Any, Minor, Major, Neither, Good for Both.

6. **When you've narrowed your search enough to be manageable, listen to some of the loops, as described in "Previewing loops," later in this chapter.**

7. **When you find the appropriate loop or loops, drag them to the location on the workspace labeled *Drag Apple Loops Here*.**

To clear your button selections and start over, click the big X below the button and column view icons to the left of the Instrument tab.

Searching in column view

Moving on to the loop browser's other view, the column view is a lot like the Finder's column view, so you should feel right at home using it.

The following steps explain how a search in column view works:

1. **Start out in column view by click the column view icon at the top of the loop browser.**

   The column view icon is labeled in Figure 5-2.

2. **In the leftmost column, choose All (to see all loops), Favorites, Genres, Instruments, or Moods.**

   The appropriate choices become available in the adjacent column to the right.

3. **Choose from the choices that appear in the second column.**

   More choices become available in the third column.

4. **Choose one of the items in the third column.**

   Loops that match that criteria appear in the rightmost column. For example, in Figure 5-6, I chose Genres, Electronic, and then Vinyl and found nine DJ vinyl record scratches.

FIGURE 5-6: It won't make you an honorary Beastie Boy, but this scratch might hit the spot.

Using the search field

Another tool you can use to find loops is the search box. If you type a generic term such as *Blues* in the Search Loops field at the bottom of the loop browser, you see a list of every loop Apple designated as blues-like.

To see your recent searches, click the magnifying glass icon on the left side of the Search Loops field.

TIP

I don't use the search tool much because I find it unpredictable. Filtering my loop collection with the button or column view works well for me, so they're my tools of choice when I need to find just the right loop for a project.

Filtering by loop type

Another way to limit your search results is by the type of Apple loop. Click the loop types icon and the choices shown in Figure 5-7 appear. Select the check box or boxes for the types you want. Your choices are All Loops, Audio, MIDI, and Drummer.

Loop types icon

Speaker icon (loop is playing)

Previewing loops

After you find a loop that you think may fit the bill, you want to hear it, of course. So, when you click a loop in the list in the loop browser, a speaker icon appears before its name to indicate that the loop is currently playing. (Refer to Figure 5-7 to see the speaker icon.)

Click the speaker icon again to stop playing the loop.

Alternately, you can click the little green speaker icon at the bottom of the loop list to start or stop playing the selected loop.

Either way, you can quickly hear a loop without dragging it into your song, listening to it there, and deleting it if you don't like it.

TIP

To audition many loops quickly, use the up and down arrow keys to navigate the list while a loop is playing. You don't even have to wait for the current loop to finish; just press the up or down arrow key and the next (or previous) loop will start almost immediately. Use this wonderful technique when you find a loop with a promising name — and too many similarly named variations.

Keeping your favorite loops at the ready

Most people have particular loops that they really like or ones they want to be able to find quickly while they're working on a song. GarageBand has a favorites list built into the loop browser, and it couldn't be easier to use:

REMEMBER

» **Add a loop to your favorites.** When you find a loop that you like, simply select the Fav check box at the far right of the loop browser. The loop is added to your favorites list, which you can access through the button or column view in the loop browser.

If you don't see a Fav column in the loop browser, use the scroll bar below the list of loops or click the green gumdrop at the upper-left corner to fully expand the GarageBand window.

TIP

» **Remove a loop from your favorites list.** Just find the loop and deselect the Fav check box.

To find the loop you want to delete, looking in your Favorites category is usually fastest. However, you can also find the loop by the other search method (buttons, columns, search box).

TIP

The favorites list is particularly handy when you find a loop that you like a lot, but the loop isn't quite right for the current project. Adding it to your favorites list makes that loop easy to find when you're working on another project where it will work perfectly.

Adding third-party loops to the loop browser

As I mention in the section, "Where to find more loops," earlier in this chapter, you can find tons of free GarageBand loops on the Internet and in third-party packages. The question is, how do you make those loops appear in the loop browser?

But because GarageBand offers no Import command, you may be at a loss as to how you add Apple loops to your loop library. The process is easy. Simply drag the loop into the loop browser and drop it there, as shown in Figure 5-8. The loop is automatically placed in the appropriate folder (Library/Audio/Apple Loops folder).

If the loop is a properly made Apple loop, it will be categorized automatically; if it's not, it won't.

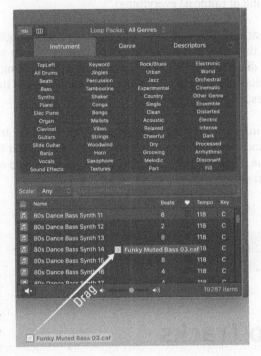

FIGURE 5-8:
Drag the loop file from the Finder (the gray desktop below the GarageBand window here) and drop it onto the loop browser to add it to your personal loop library.

TIP

You can drag multiple files, a folder, or even a disk full of loops into the loop browser. All loops in all subfolders will be added.

Setting a Loop's Tempo

Each loop is created with its own tempo, which you can see in the Tempo column of the loop browser. (If you don't see the Tempo column, select the Display Original Tempo and Key in Loop Browser check box in the Loops tab of GarageBand's Preferences. See Chapter 4 for details.)

TIP

If you can't see all contents in the Name, Beats, Favorites, Tempo, or Key column, you can resize the column. Just hover the mouse pointer over a column divider (between column names). The resizer cursor appears when you're hovering in the proper spot. When you see the resizer, click and drag to resize the column.

GarageBand changes the tempo of any loop that you add to your song so that it matches the song's tempo. Even more intuitively, when you preview a loop in the loop browser, GarageBand plays the loop at the tempo of your song. Those crazy folks at Apple think of (almost) everything!

TIP

You can get an entirely different feel from a loop just by changing the tempo or, rather, by using that loop at a different tempo than what you see in the Tempo column. A slow, dirge-like drum loop may turn into something Latin-tinged or jazzy when you double its tempo. Think of the default tempos in the Tempo column as guidelines, and don't be afraid to experiment!

To change the tempo of your project, click the tempo indicator in the toolbar and drag upward to increase the tempo or downward to decrease it (see Figure 5-9). The number in the tempo indicator updates in real time; drag up or down until you hit the tempo you desire.

FIGURE 5-9:
Click the tempo indicator and drag up or down to change the project's tempo.

Adding Loops to Tracks

You add a loop to your song by dragging it from the loop browser to the workspace. For example, Figure 5-10 shows the very tasty Blue Jazz Organ Riff 01 after I dragged it from the loop browser onto its own track on the workspace.

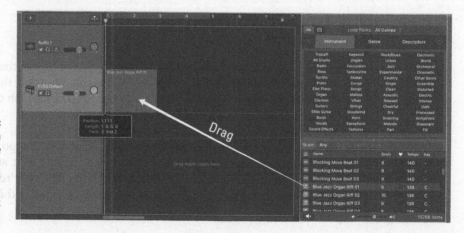

FIGURE 5-10:
Drop a loop into a blank spot on the workspace and GarageBand creates a track to hold it automatically.

TIP

I recommend laying down software instrument loops and tracks first, before you begin recording real instrument tracks. That way, if you decide the tempo is too slow or fast, or the pitch is too high or low, you can change software instrument tracks without re-recording them. But if you record real instrument tracks first, and then decide a song is too slow, fast, high, or low, you'll have to re-record all those real instrument tracks.

Some loops are short and others are long, but most are 4, 8, or 16 beats. Don't worry much about length now because, as I explain the following sections, loops can be looped (repeated indefinitely).

Dragging and dropping loops

You can drag and drop a loop in a few different ways:

>> **Place a loop on its own track:** Drag the loop into any empty spot on the workspace, where a track of the appropriate type (real or software) is created for the loop automatically.

>> **Insert a loop into an existing track:** Drag the loop onto that track, and GarageBand leaves it wherever you dropped it on the track.

>> **Move a loop within or between tracks:** Drag the loop to its new destination and release it.

REMEMBER

The only restriction is that you can't drag a blue (audio) loop onto a green (software instrument) track. If you try, GarageBand gently scolds you in words and with the "not allowed" cursor, as shown in Figure 5-11.

FIGURE 5-11:
Drag a blue (audio) loop onto a green (software instrument) track and GarageBand provides a gentle reminder that you can't do that.

You can drag a green (software instrument) loop onto a blue (audio) track, but when you do, the loop changes from an editable MIDI instrument loop (green) to a not-editable real audio loop (blue).

You discover how to edit software instrument regions and loops in Chapter 9. For now, just tuck that little tidbit away in the back of your mind.

No correct or better way to add loops to your songs exists. If you have a track of the proper type already created, you may want to drag the loop onto it to keep your track count down. If you're just starting a song, you may want each loop to create a new track. If the loop is being used as punctuation, you may want to drag it onto existing audio and replace that audio with the loop. It just depends what you're doing and the effect you're trying to achieve.

WARNING

If something is on the track when you drop it, you will replace all or part of that something.

You can drag as many loops onto one track as you like, but only one loop at a time can play in any single track. If you want multiple loops to play at the same time, you must put each loop on its own track.

You can construct an entire song using nothing but loops. For those following along at home, drag a few loops onto the workspace and then click the play icon (or slap the spacebar) to hear your all-loop song.

Undoing and redoing a loop

If you drop a loop onto a track that has been recorded previously or has other loops in it, the loop segment that you're dragging replaces what you drop it on. In other words, if you drag a loop that's 4 beats long into the middle of a screaming guitar solo that you finally nailed after 56 attempts, the loop replaces 4 beats of your solo.

TIP

That's why GarageBand has an undo feature — choose Edit➪Undo or press ⌘+Z. I'm not sure how many actions you can undo GarageBand, but it's more than a handful, though I hesitate to call it unlimited. And did you notice the Redo command up there on the Edit menu? Choose Edit➪Redo or press ⌘+Shift+Z to redo something you've undone.

You can step forward or backward by repeating either command, which is useful for listening to something the way it sounded before you did whatever you just did, and then the way it sounds after you did it.

As with any Mac program, the Undo and Redo commands are linear, so pay attention lest you undo something you didn't want to undo.

Extending, shortening, and repeating loops

Not every loop works perfectly as is. When you drag a loop into your song, it's short — a lot shorter than your song unless you write extremely short songs. And, as you've heard several times, loops are designed to repeat (all together now) *seamlessly*. So, the next thing you need to know is how to loop a loop in a track. I start with that and then look at how you can make a loop longer (or shorter) without affecting that seamlessness. I also explain how to extend and shorten loops.

Before trying this exercise, it will be easier if you zoom in a little or a lot by sliding the zoom controller (labeled in Figure 5-12) to the right. It's harder to locate the correct area to click in when you're zoomed out (with the slider to the left).

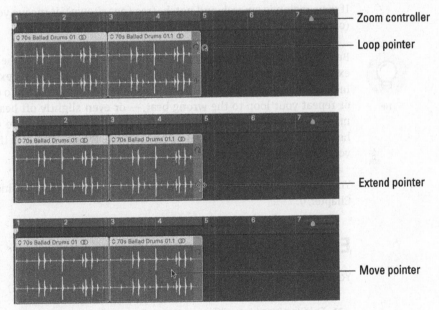

Zoom controller

Loop pointer

Extend pointer

FIGURE 5-12:
The loop pointer (top), extend pointer (middle), and move pointer (bottom).

Move pointer

Depending on where you click in a region, you see one of three pointers, or cursors, as shown in Figure 5-12.

When you click any part of the region (either type — software or real) except the right edge, you see a move pointer. The move pointer is the one that you want when you're moving regions around within a track or moving them to other tracks.

When the pointer is over the right edge of a loop region, it changes into one of two pointers, as follows:

>> If you click in the top half of the right edge of a loop region, the loop pointer appears.

>> If you click in the bottom half of the left or right edge of a loop region, the extend pointer appears.

As you probably guessed, the loop pointer (the circled arrow) is the control for repeating (looping) a loop; the extend pointer (the straight arrow) is used for extending or shortening the length of a loop.

When you see the appropriate pointer, just click and drag. You'll know that you are repeating your loops if the outline of the track repeats and you see notches in the region denoting the repetitions (as shown in all three images in Figure 5-12).

If your region is smooth and notch-free (not shown), it means you are extending (or shortening) your loop.

TIP

Be careful when you extend, shorten, or repeat loops. Some loops can't be extended, but all loops can be shortened. Other loops can be extended but may include only empty space when you extend them. It's also easy to extend, shorten, or repeat your loop to the wrong beat — or even slightly off beat. Use the guide marks in the ruler and the Snap to Grid feature (Edit ➪ Snap to Grid or ⌘+G) to help you keep everything lined up and in time. Finally, listen to the results before you do additional work on the project.

You can also edit loops in the same way you edit tracks. To find out more, see Chapter 9.

Editing loops: A preview

You can perform simple edits on any loop by

>> Splitting loops into different parts

>> Deleting part of a loop

>> Moving sections of a loop

>> Rearranging the notes in a software instrument loop

But you should also know that you can get creative with loops by using all the techniques you might use on non-loop tracks.

I describe all these techniques in Chapter 9.

Reusing an edited loop in a different song

Sadly, you can't save edits to a loop in the loop browser, but you can reuse your lovingly edited loop by following these steps:

1. **Open the song that contains the edited loop you want to reuse.**

2. **Copy the edited loop region to the clipboard.**

   Click the loop region and choose Edit ⇨ Copy or press ⌘+C.

3. **Open a different (or new) song and create the appropriate type of track for the loop (software or real instrument).**

4. **Paste the copied loop region onto that track.**

   Choose Edit ⇨ Paste or press ⌘+V.

The process is cumbersome but makes sense with GarageBand's consumer-friendly approach to recording music all in one window. And it also means you'll never screw up one of the loops that came with the program (because you can't).

Onward!

IN THIS CHAPTER

» **Finding out what MIDI is**

» **Choosing software instruments**

» **Recording tracks with software instruments**

» **Altering the sound of software instruments**

» **Dealing with drummer tracks**

» **Testing your changes**

Chapter **6**

Recording with MIDI and Software Instruments

GarageBand is more than just a recording-studio-in-a-box; it also includes an orchestra full of high-quality musical instruments. It's chock-full of pianos, guitars, drums, horns, synthesizers, and even a chorus of heavenly voices, all available to use in your musical compositions for free.

In this chapter, you first learn about MIDI and MIDI controllers, and why they matter. That topic is followed by pretty much all you need to know to play and record using GarageBand's massive collection of software instruments.

What Is MIDI, Anyway?

MIDI stands for Musical Instrument Digital Interface and is pronounced "middy." The term covers a lot of ground, as you can see from this description by the MIDI Manufacturer's Association (www.midi.org):

The Musical Instrument Digital Interface (MIDI) enables people to use multimedia computers and electronic musical instruments to create, enjoy and learn about music. There are actually three components to MIDI, which are the communications Protocol (language), the Connector (hardware interface) and a distribution format called Standard MIDI Files.

In other words, MIDI is a language, a hardware interface, and a file format. The language of MIDI allows different devices to talk to each other. The hardware interface sends and receives MIDI information between devices that speak MIDI. Music made with MIDI can be saved in a file format that can be understood by other MIDI devices.

The upshot is that many kinds of devices that you may use in audio (or video) production — such as keyboards, computers, mixing boards (control surfaces), and even lighting gear — can talk to each other in a common language called MIDI.

Controlling Software Instruments with a MIDI Keyboard

Although MIDI is a multiheaded beast, in the context of using GarageBand, I focus on using a MIDI keyboard to control GarageBand's software instruments.

REMEMBER

Note that word *control*. MIDI keyboards are appropriately referred to as *MIDI controllers* because you're using an interface — a piano-like keyboard — to control the software instruments on your Mac.

And, in fact, a pure MIDI keyboard is just that — a controller —incapable of making sounds of its own. All it can do is send MIDI information to a MIDI host (in this case, GarageBand on your Mac or iOS device), which translates the information into sound.

To further complicate things, many MIDI keyboards are *also* synthesizers, which *can* produce sound on their own. For the purposes of this chapter, think of your MIDI keyboard as just a MIDI controller, even if the keyboard can make sounds all by itself.

TECHNICAL STUFF

In the pre-MIDI era, when you played a device such as synthesizer, an electric piano, or an electric organ, the device didn't control anything but its own internal circuitry. So each keyboard device produced only the sounds that its internal circuits knew how to make. For this reason, an Arp synthesizer sounded like an Arp, a Moog sounded like a Moog, and a Prophet 5 sounded like — you guessed it — a Prophet 5. Any artist worth his or her salt had a rack of different synthesizer keyboards for producing different sounds.

We've come a long way since then; that rack of keyboards and much, much more are built right into GarageBand at no extra cost.

By the way, if you have an older sound-making keyboard, it might support MIDI and be usable with GarageBand. If it is, you'll see either a USB port or one or two large round ports, probably labeled MIDI in and MIDI out. If you don't see a USB port, you'll need a MIDI interface — a small, reasonably priced piece of hardware — to connect those round MIDI in and MIDI out ports on the keyboard to a USB port on your Mac.

Here's the bottom line: When you play a MIDI keyboard (controller), the keyboard isn't producing sound. It's noting the keys that you press, and how hard and how long you press them, and then sending that information to your Mac, where GarageBand translates it and plays that sound with a software instrument.

Conversely, when you strike a drum, the sound occurs when the drumstick hits the drumhead. When you play an electric guitar, the sound occurs when the pick or a finger strikes the strings and is captured by your Mac (or an audio interface connected to your Mac as discussed in Chapter 8), or is fed through an amplifier. And, when you play a piano, the sound occurs when the hammers hit the strings.

MIDI controllers can be used also to control other keyboards or anything dedicated to working with the MIDI protocol. For example, *MIDI work surfaces* look like miniature versions of a big-time mixing board, complete with sliding faders, rotating knobs, and VU meters with needles. You use these work surfaces to control audio applications such as Logic, Pro Tools, and even GarageBand. You can also use MIDI drum pads to tap out drum patterns with your fingertips. In addition, you can find MIDI stage lighting controllers and many other types of controllers that speak MIDI. The list of things you can do with MIDI is almost endless.

I highly recommend using a MIDI keyboard if you're even half-serious about recording with GarageBand. For purposes of this chapter, I assume that you're using a USB keyboard such as the M-Audio Keystation 49 MK3 keyboard ($99; www.m-audio.com), shown in Figure 6-1, which is a direct descendant of the MIDI keyboard John Mayer demonstrated when Steve Jobs introduced GarageBand at Macworld San Francisco in 2004. You may be able to find an even cheaper MIDI keyboard, but you can't go wrong with the Keystation 49 MK3 for around $100.

FIGURE 6-1:
This 49-key M-Audio MIDI keyboard is inexpensive and perfectly adequate for GarageBand's software instruments and my meager keyboard skills.

REMEMBER

If you're not sure that you want to spring for a keyboard yet, don't forget that you can control software instruments by using the onscreen keyboard (choose Window ➪ Show Keyboard) or the musical typing keyboard (choose Window ➪ Show Musical Typing or press ⌘+K).

TIP

To avoid confusion, for the rest of the book I refer to the keyboard on which you type letters and numbers as the *QWERTY keyboard*. Keyboards that have black-and-white piano-like keys will be referred to as plain old *keyboards*.

Choosing Software Instruments

To record a software instrument, you create a software instrument track and then choose the instrument to record on it.

REMEMBER

A software instrument may be more than one instrument. Drum kits, for example, contain 50 or 60 different drum, cymbal, and percussion instrument sounds, each triggered by a different key. So, for example, playing middle C triggers the sound of a kick drum, D triggers the sound of a snare drum, and D-sharp triggers the sound of a closed hi-hat.

Even though a drum kit contains 50 or 60 different instrument sounds, it's considered a single software instrument. In any case, a track *may* contain the sounds of many instruments, but they all have to be part of the same software instrument, like those 50 or 60 different drum sounds.

WARNING

Make sure that the type of software instrument you use matches the track you're recording on. When you select a software instrument for a track, that instrument will play the MIDI notes on that track, even if they're not the right notes for that instrument. In other words, you can do horrible things to a song if you're not paying attention and, for example, drag a drum region onto a track assigned to a piano. The notes will play on the piano and it'll sound bloody awful. Hey, it's just a dumb machine. It does only what it's told, and you told it to play a drum track with a piano.

So, don't do that!

To set up a software instrument track for recording, follow these steps:

1. **Create a new empty project (if you haven't already) by choosing File ⇨ New.**

   The Choose a Project dialog appears.

2. **Click New Project in the sidebar, click the empty project icon, and then click the Choose button.**

   The Choose a Track Type dialog appears.

3. **Choose Software Instrument for your track type and then click the Create button.**

   A new software instrument track with the Classic Electric Piano instrument assigned is created and the musical typing window appears in front of the project.

   If the musical typing window didn't appear, choose Window ⇨ Show Musical Typing or press ⌘+K.

4. **Type F, F, F, W, E, E, E, A on your QWERTY keyboard.**

   Congratulations! You just played the opening notes of Beethoven's *Fifth Symphony*.

5. **(Optional but highly recommended) Choose File ⇨ Save, name your project, and save it to disk.**

As I mention in Chapter 3, it's always a good idea to save early and often.

Go ahead and play around with your electric piano by typing on your QWERTY keyboard or your MIDI keyboard (if you have one).

You now have a project with a software instrument track that uses the Classic Electric Piano patch. But what if you don't want to record a Classic Electric Piano? No worries! GarageBand has hundreds of other instruments and sounds you can assign to a software instrument track.

Let's change the Classic Electric Piano to something more appropriate for Beethoven:

1. **If the Library isn't displayed on the left side of the window, choose View ⇨ Show Library or press the Y key.**

2. **Choose a category in the first (leftmost) column, choose a subcategory in the second column, and then choose an instrument in the third column.**

TIP

If you don't see all three columns (but would like to), hover the mouse pointer over the line between the library and the track list. When it turns into a resizer cursor, click and drag right to widen the library so you can see more columns.

When you choose a software instrument, note that the icon to the left of the track's name changes. Each instrument has a different icon. These features should help you keep track of what's on a track.

You can change the icon by right- or Control-clicking it in the track list. When the pop-up window of alternate icons appears, click the icon you want to appear on this track.

3. **To hear the instrument you just selected, play a few notes on the musical typing keyboard or your MIDI keyboard.**

TIP

You can use the up-, down-, left-, and right-arrow keys on your QWERTY keyboard to quickly change instruments when an instrument is selected (highlighted) and the library is active (surrounded by a thin blue outline), as shown in Figure 6-2.

Alternately, you can hover the pointer over the instrument's icon in the library and click the left arrow (previous instrument or category) or right arrow (next instrument or category) to quickly check out various instruments.

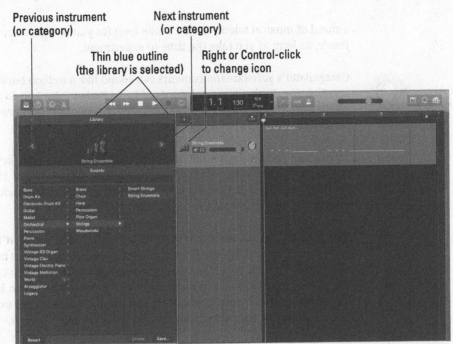

Previous instrument (or category)

Next instrument (or category)

Thin blue outline (the library is selected)

Right or Control-click to change icon

FIGURE 6-2: The library with the String Ensemble instrument selected.

You're now ready to record a track with this instrument. You can find the details about recording tracks in the next section. Or, if you decide that you want to try a different software instrument (even if you've already recorded on the track), just select it in the library.

TIP

The change occurs as soon as you click the new instrument name. Your track instantly sounds different — perhaps completely different.

Recording Tracks with Software Instruments

After you create a new track and select a software instrument (see the preceding section), you're ready to move on to the fun stuff — recording some music with that software instrument.

The funny thing is, this is either the hard part or the easy part, depending on your musical chops. If you know your way around a keyboard, you'll probably find it easy to record a software instrument in GarageBand. Or if you simply have a bit of theoretical knowledge, the process will likely be a snap. But even if you don't have a shred of musical talent, it won't take long for you to figure out enough to make music, as long as you take the time to experiment.

TIP

GarageBand's software instruments can sound like a million bucks — or a million cats fighting. In the immortal words of Peter Parker (also known as Spider-Man), "With great power comes great responsibility." You hold the power of an orchestra in your hand; try not to abuse it.

To practice (before laying down a new track), just play your keyboard with the appropriate track selected. You can either play solo (without clicking the play icon), or you can click the play icon to play along with other tracks or loops in the project or the metronome (also called the *click track*).

TIP

The selected track is the track that will be recorded. If you don't hear what you expect, make sure the proper track is selected and that no tracks have their solo or mute icon activated (see Figure 6-3). If you don't hear what you expected to hear, the solo or mute icon is often the culprit. If a track's solo icon is activated, you hear only that track during recording and playback; if a track's mute icon is activated, you do not hear that track during recording and playback.

Mute (enabled)   Mute (disabled)

Solo (enabled)   Solo (disabled)

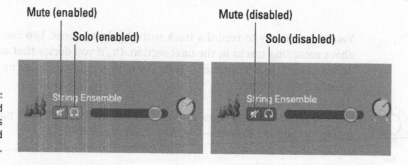

FIGURE 6-3:
The solo and mute icons enabled (left) and disabled (right).

GarageBand offers two features to help you record: the metronome and count in. With the metronome on, you hear a soft click marking the beat of your song. Note that the sound of the metronome is never recorded.

REMEMBER

You hear the metronome during playback and recording.

The second useful feature for recording is count in. When you have it turned on, an additional measure (or two) is counted before GarageBand starts recording.

To record a track, follow these steps:

1. **Move the playhead to the point in your song where you want to record.**

   To move the playhead, click and drag it. To move the playhead to the beginning of the song, press Return or Enter.

2. **If you want to hear the metronome, click the metronome icon in the toolbar (and shown in the margin).**

   The metronome icon is a toggle; it's gray when disabled and purple when enabled.

3. **If you want to use the Count In, click the Count In icon in the toolbar (and shown in the margin).**

   You can also choose Record ⇨ Count In ⇨ One Measure or Two Measures to enable count in. Choose None to disable it. Like the metronome icon, the count in icon is a toggle and is gray when disabled and purple when enabled.

4. **Click the record icon (the red dot) or press R, and recording begins.**

That about covers it. When you click the record icon or press R, GarageBand counts in (if you've enabled the feature) and begins recording what you play on your keyboard.

When you're finished, click the play/pause icon or slap the spacebar to end the recording.

Altering the Sound of Software Instruments

Apple made GarageBand incredibly powerful for a so-called consumer application. Although the company could have simply provided just the instrument patches, it included the power to edit software instruments. Ergo, GarageBand lets you edit software instrument patches to your heart's content to get a different sound.

Some users will be happy with every software instrument just the way it sounds out of the box, never even opening the Smart controls for that instrument. But for the rest of us, Apple makes it easy to twiddle the sound of almost every software instrument, and that's a good thing. If your drum track lacks bass, you can add more bass by using an equalizer. If your piano doesn't sound like a piano, you can add echo, reverb, compression, and equalization effects until it sounds perfect.

Almost anything you can think of doing to change the sound of an instrument can be done with the Smart controls built into GarageBand.

Following is a bird's-eye view of how to make the magic happen, for those of you who just can't wait. Don't worry if the process seems daunting; you learn all about using Smart controls and effects in just a moment (and it's easy — all you need are your ears):

1. **Click the name of the track you want to alter to select it.**

2. **Open the Smart controls.**

    You can choose View ➪ Show Smart Controls; press the B key on your QWERTY keyboard; click the Smart controls icon in the toolbar (and shown in the margin); or double-click the gray area surrounding the track name and icon.

3. **Adjust the Smart controls to change the sound of the instrument.**

   Each instrument has a different selection of controls (as shown in Figure 6-5). Some instruments have more or fewer knobs, buttons, and faders, and they probably have different names than the ones you see in Figure 6-5. Don't worry if you don't know what the labels mean. Just play back your recorded track(s) or MIDI (or onscreen) keyboard while you listen closely to the changes as you rotate each knob (or slide each slider or enable and disable each button).

As soon as you make a change to a Smart control, the Compare button is enabled. Click it when you want to compare your changes to the original factory patch. Click it again to return to your edited version of the patch.

Delving deeper into Smart controls

Smart controls are the foundation of every software instrument. If you change the Smart controls for a software instrument, you can dramatically alter the sound of that instrument. If you're looking for an unusual sound, one that you may not otherwise come across in GarageBand, changing a software instrument's Smart controls is a good place to start.

But you knew that, so let's dig a bit deeper into Smart controls and how to use them.

At the top of the Smart controls section you'll find six buttons (left to right): Track, Master, Compare, Controls, EQ, and an inverted V that enables the Arpeggiator menu, as shown in Figure 6-4.

DON'T BLOW AWAY YOUR ALTERED INSTRUMENTS!

TIP

If you make changes to an instrument patch and then click another instrument, you'll see the following warning dialog.

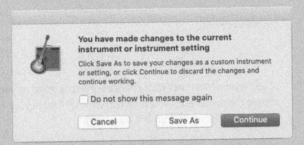

This warning is enabled by default with good reason — it's important. That's why I advise never clicking the Do Not Show This Message Again check box.

Why? After I spent an hour working to perfect my modifications of the Steinway Grand Piano by adjusting equalization, echo, and other settings until it sounded superb, I accidentally clicked another instrument. Fortunately, that lifesaving warning saved my bacon.

The warning dialog wouldn't have been any help if I weren't paying attention. Continue is the default button in the warning dialog. If you aren't paying attention and click this button (or press Return or Enter), you'll lose all changes you've made to the original instrument.

Because I liked the way my Steinway Grand Piano sounded, I did want to save my settings, so I clicked the Save As button, and a standard Save dialog appeared. You should proceed with caution in the Save dialog too. The default button is Save. If you click the Save button (or press Enter or Return) without typing a new name, you could confuse your modified instrument with the fantastic Grand Piano that came with GarageBand — the one configured by a professional musician or producer and one of the nicest things about GarageBand. I really like GarageBand's Grand Piano. My piano may sound good to me now, but I don't want to replace that trained professional's Grand Piano.

Always rename modified instruments before you click the Save button. As shown in the following figure, I appended a descriptive word or two (BL Bright) to the instrument's original name, so I can tell what the modified instrument is supposed to sound like.

(continued)

(continued)

If you later decide that your changes aren't as good as you thought, you can always delete the modified instrument (which you'll find in your Home ⇨ Music ⇨ Audio Music Apps ⇨ Patches ⇨ Instrument directory).

You may not know much about altering an instrument yet (I'll tell you more in upcoming sections), but this is another time when the sooner you develop good habits, the less likely you are to lose good stuff to carelessness, inattention, or accident. Blowing away a modified instrument isn't the end of the world, but it can be a hassle to redo your modifications. Unfortunately, the Undo command doesn't work after you click the Save button in the Save Patch dialog box.

The good news is that you can work around this minefield of dialog boxes: When you've painstakingly tweaked the settings for an instrument and everything is just the way you like it, save your settings right away by clicking the Save button at the bottom of the library (or clicking another instrument and then clicking Save As in the warning dialog). Although we all lose useful stuff occasionally, you'll lose less good stuff if you save it immediately each time you tweak a patch and are happy with the result.

Bottom line: Save your modified instruments early and often.

TIP

Figure 6-4 shows the Smart controls for a Mallet instrument called Aurora Bell. This instrument sounds more like an old clavinet or organ than any kind of bell, at least to me. The point is that you should listen to every patch, even ones with dorky names that don't tell you much. You never know which patch is going to be "the one," but it's frequently the one with a dorky, less-than-descriptive name.

Every instrument offers Smart Controls specific to that instrument, as shown in Figure 6-5.

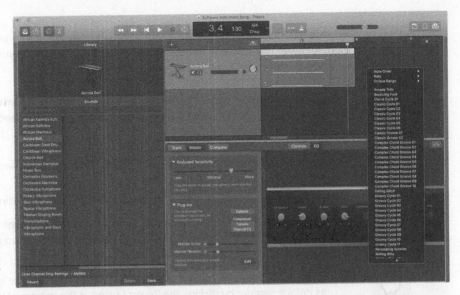

FIGURE 6-4:
Smart controls
for the Aurora
Bell instrument
with the
Arpeggiator
menu enabled.

FIGURE 6-5:
Smart controls
for the String
Ensemble (top),
Baroque Organ
(middle), and
Hard Rock Guitar
(bottom).

Because each instrument has different controls, and there's no way I could cover them all here, my advice is to listen to as many instruments as you can and adjust as many knobs and sliders as you can whilst listening closely.

TIP

Sadly, software instruments don't have a favorites feature, so when you find one you love, either remember its name or save a descriptively named version of it as a user patch.

Let's go back to those buttons at the top of the Smart controls section:

>> **Track:** Click to work with the selected track's Smart controls settings.

>> **Compare:** This button is enabled only when you've made at least one change to the Smart controls. When enabled, you can click this button to compare your customized instrument settings to the default settings.

TIP

If you're not happy with your customizations, you can return the instrument to its default settings by clicking the Revert button at the bottom of the library (or clicking another instrument and clicking Continue in the warning dialog).

>> **Master:** The Master track contains effects applied to the entire project (as opposed to a specific track). I spend an entire chapter on mastering. For now, realize that mastering is the last (or next-to-last) step in the recording process.

>> **Controls:** These are the main controls — mostly knobs — for the selected instrument.

>> **EQ:** This button applies equalization to the selected instrument track. A section on equalization appears later in the chapters so I'll leave it at that for now.

>> **Arpeggiator:** When the Arpeggiator is enabled, chords you play on your keyboard are *arpeggiated*, or played one note at a time rather than all at once.

When the Arpeggiator is enabled, the Arpeggiator pop-up menu appears next to the Arpeggiator icon (refer to Figure 6-4). From this pop-up menu, you can:

● Choose an Arpeggiator's preset.

● Change the Arpeggiator's note order.

● Change the Arpeggiator's note range.

● Choose the Arpeggiator's octave range between 1 (the default) and 4.

Now that you know what all the buttons do, let's look at another way to alter the sound of your software instruments — by adding plug-in effects.

Adding and changing plug-in effects

Each instrument has a unique set of plug-in effects and settings. And each plug-in has a unique set of controls.

Dozens of plug-in effects are built into GarageBand, such as compressor, tape delay, limiter, and noise gate. However, three effects are always available (though they may not be enabled by default): equalizer, master echo, and master reverb.

WARNING

The following sections concern modifying and saving custom settings for plug-ins — please be careful! If you forget to save changes you make to a plug-in's settings, you will lose all the tweaks you just made. And don't forget to rename your tweaked version for clarity.

So, please be as careful about saving modified settings (which I also call presets or patches) as you are about saving modified instruments. (You did read the "Don't Blow Away Your Altered Instruments!" sidebar earlier in the chapter, didn't you?)

First let's look at the three always-available plug-ins.

Equalizer

The *equalizer* effect is like EQ in your home stereo (or iTunes or the Music app): It enables you to adjust the relative loudness of different parts of the sound spectrum. For example, if the cymbals on your drum track don't sizzle and hiss enough, try the Brighten High Hat or Brighten Overheads patch, which emphasizes the high frequencies on the track. Or if your software instrument guitar sounds wimpy, check out the Guitar Sweetener patch, which reduces the emphasis on low and low-mid frequencies while slightly increasing the mid-high and high frequencies.

To enable EQ for a track, first make sure the Smart controls are enabled by clicking the Smart controls icon in the toolbar (labeled in Figure 6-6). Now click the EQ button (next to the Controls button in the Smart controls menu bar). The Smart controls are replaced by a graphic equalizer.

You can tweak the equalizer manually, as I show you in a moment, but it's almost always easier to begin by choosing a custom setting from the Equalizer Settings drop-down menu, as shown in Figure 6-6.

In recording terms, brightness and high(s) usually mean treble; fullness and richness usually refer to sounds in the middle ranges; bass, low, and bottom refer to low frequencies; and flat means neutral equalization for all frequencies.

The preset names for EQ patches are mostly descriptive.

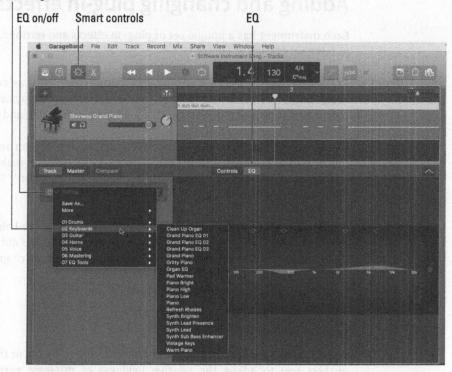

Settings menu

EQ on/off   Smart controls   EQ

FIGURE 6-6:
You can choose
from a variety of
patches for the
EQ on your
software
instrument.

The best way to understand what each patch does to the sound of an instrument is to apply it to a track. If you don't like the sound it creates, either choose a different patch or click the little power button to the left of the drop-down preset menu to turn off EQ.

If none of the patches does the trick for you, GarageBand also lets you make manual adjustments, as shown in Figure 6-7.

The eight icons across the top represent the eight frequency bands of the equalizer. Click an icon to enable control over that frequency band. Then click and drag that band's control point, as shown in Figure 6-8 for band 5.

Finally, click the Analyzer button while your song is playing to see changes to its frequency curve as shown by the squiggly lines in the lower part of Figure 6-8.

Move the control points around and watch the changes to the song's frequencies in real time.

WARNING

Turn off the analyzer unless you're using it because it chews up a lot of CPU cycles and may slow down other things.

Band 1 on/off   Band 2 on/off   Band 3 on/off   Band 4 on/off   Band 5 on/off   Band 6 on/off   Band 7 on/off   Band 8 on/off

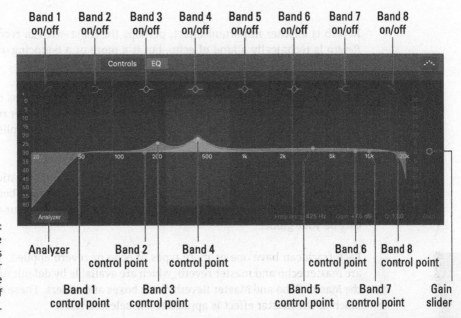

FIGURE 6-7:
You can create manual settings on your equalizer by clicking the eight on/off buttons.

Analyzer   Band 2 control point   Band 4 control point   Band 6 control point   Band 8 control point

Band 1 control point   Band 3 control point   Band 5 control point   Band 7 control point   Gain slider

FIGURE 6-8:
Band 5 is enabled and configured to slightly boost all except the highest highs and lowest lows with the Analyzer enabled.

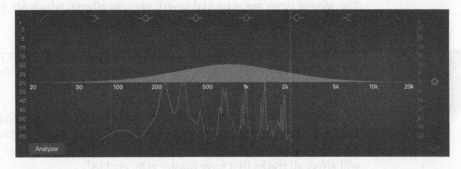

TIP

There's a lot more to the equalizer effect than I have space for here. I hate to use a "weasel-out," but if you're interested in more information on using the equalizer as a high or low pass, shelving, or parametric bell filter; changing the Q or Gain/Slope parameters; and other equally exciting equalizer esoterica, all you have to do is open GarageBand Help (⌘+?) and search for *EQ*. I was surprised at the level of detail; I think you'll be pleasantly surprised as well.

Master echo and reverb

What what exactly exactly is is master master echo echo??

Hey, is there an echo in here? Okay, it's a groaner, but I couldn't resist. It's the easiest way that I know to explain the sound of echo.

Reverb is another important effect, perhaps the most-used in recording history. *Reverb* is technically a kind of echo, but it's more of a bouncing-off-the-walls-all-around-you sound than the repeated sound of echo.

When used judiciously, echo and reverb are potent effects. And, as usual, Garage-Band makes using them simple. Enable the master echo or master reverb effect by selecting its check box. Then adjust the amount of the effect applied to the track by sliding its slider.

Echo (and reverb) make your tracks sound more lifelike and realistic. By adjusting echo (and reverb) you can simulate the sound of the instrument being played in a spacious cathedral or a sound-deadened recording studio. It's your call — let your ears be your guide.

Each track can have one or more types of echo or reverb applied. The first types are master echo and master reverb, which are available by default for all tracks via the Master Echo and Master Reverb check boxes and sliders. These determine how much of the master effect is applied to the selected track.

The second types are echo and reverb plug-in effects, which are exclusive to the track they're assigned. You can use either, neither, or both.

Note that the Master Echo settings in the Effects tab apply to every track, and the Master Echo slider determines how much (or how little) of that master echo will be applied to this track.

To change the settings for master echo on all tracks, click the Edit button below the Master Echo and Master Reverb sliders, or click the Master button in the Smart controls toolbar and then click the Effects tab. Either way, changes you make here will affect all tracks that have master echo enabled.

You explore mastering, master echo, master reverb, and the master track in full and loving detail in Chapter 11. Until then, this brief description should hold you.

The other type of echo and reverb are plug-ins, which, unlike master echo and master reverb, apply to only the current track.

You delve into enabling and using plug-ins in the Other Effects section up shortly.

Weird Al Yankovic recorded "Another One Rides the Bus" in a bathroom with just his accordion. In fact, recording engineers love bathrooms for recording because their hard surfaces give the recording a rich, warm, natural reverb. You can get the bathroom effect with GarageBand by cranking up the echo and the reverb.

The first electronically produced reverb effects used springs to create the reverberation effect. The effect was like listening in an enclosed room (such as the aforementioned bathroom, only springier, or more accurately, more metallic). In fact, many early guitar amps had springs to provide that spring reverb sound. And many engineers use a bathroom as an isolation booth for a guitar amp. They run a long microphone cable into the bathroom and record the amp sitting in the middle of this very live room with all its hard surfaces and reverberation.

Now let's look at a few of the useful plug-in effects that are included with GarageBand.

Compressors and other plug-in effects

Each patch can also have up to four plug-in effects, which appear above the Master Echo and Master Reverb sliders, as shown in Figure 6-9.

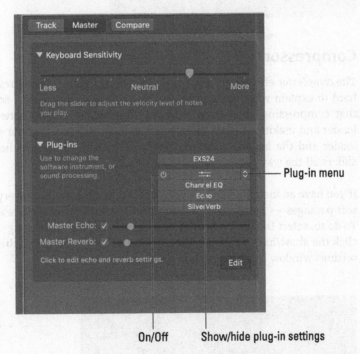

FIGURE 6-9:
A patch can have up to four plug-ins enabled.

This area is where you choose effect plug-ins for the patch, enable or disable them, reorder them (by dragging up or down in the list), or remove them (by choosing No Plug-In from the menu, shown in Figure 6-10).

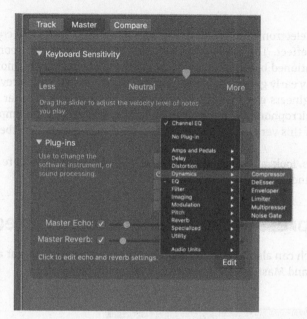

Compressor

The *compressor* effect does just what its name suggests: It compresses sound. It's hard to explain what something sounds like using only words, so suffice to say that compressing an instrument track does something in between making it louder and making it more intense. Technically, it's making the softer passages louder and the loudest passages less loud. Unless you crank the Compressor's sliders all the way up, its effect will be subtle.

If you have an instrument track with a lot of dynamic range — very loud and very soft passages — you should probably add at least a little compressor effect to it. To do so, select Dynamics ➪ Compressor from the drop-down Plug-in menu. Next, click the show/hide plug-in settings icon (labeled in Figure 6-10); the plug-in's settings window appears, as shown in Figure 6-11.

FIGURE 6-11:
Settings for the
compressor
plug-in with the
Pop Piano preset
selected.

Settings differ greatly from plug-in to plug-in, so it's best to experiment by sliding all the sliders one by one while you listen carefully. If you're following along at home, click the solo icon for the track and play it while you click the Settings menu (which says Pop Piano in Figure 6-11) and select various presets.

When you find a preset that's close to what you want, you can adjust the intensity of its four parameters (Threshold, Ratio, Attack, and Gain) by moving each slider to the right for more of that parameter or to the left for less.

TIP

Make small adjustments and listen closely. You may have to lower the overall volume level of the track as you increase the compression; keep an eye on the track's LED lights and take the level down a notch or two if you start seeing red.

When the settings are perfect (hah!), you can close the settings window and use these perfect settings in only this project. Or you could save the settings and have them available in all tracks and projects evermore.

When you have the settings just the way you like them, click the Settings menu, choose Save As, name your file, and then click Save.

TIP

If you use generic names you'll never remember which custom settings do what. Instead, name your patches descriptively by including the instrument name and something specific about the settings, such as My Perfect Piano or My Great Lead Guitar Compressor. That way, you can more easily remember what that patch is when you come back to it later.

To reuse your saved settings on another track or project, click the Settings menu and select it, as shown in Figure 6-12.

FIGURE 6-12:
If you save your perfect preset, you can then reuse it on other tracks or projects evermore.

Other plug-ins

Dozens upon dozens of other plug-ins are available, and you can have up to four enabled for each instrument.

When you choose a software instrument, between zero to four of its plug-in slots will already be populated. For example, in Figure 6-13, the Steinway Grand Piano instrument has three effects enabled by default — channel EQ, compressor, and tape delay.

FIGURE 6-13:
The Steinway Grand Piano instrument has three plug-ins enabled by default: channel EQ, compressor, and tape delay.

Now check out Figure 6-14, which shows additional plug-ins that can fill that fourth plug-in slot or replace any of the three plug-ins enabled by default.

You can choose from the presets that each effect includes, or you can click the show/hide plug-in settings icon and create your own settings.

As with Smart controls, the settings for each plug-in effect are specific to that particular effect, and some effects have fewer options than others.

For laughs, I added the distortion II plug-in's Biting Distortion Heavy preset to Steinway Grand Piano, as shown in Figure 6-15.

If necessary, I can tweak the Biting Distortion Heavy preset by adjusting the sliders.

FIGURE 6-14:
A handful of the dozens of plug-ins you have available.

FIGURE 6-15:
I added the distortion II effect with the Biting Distortion Heavy preset in the fourth plug-in slot for the Steinway Grand Piano.

Look for a reason to leave things alone! Too many effects or too much of an effect on an instrument can ruin it by making it sound muddy — or just plain stupid. Most of the software instruments sound quite good using the built-in presets without additional tweaking. If you want to add something but aren't sure what, try adding a little reverb, chorus, or echo.

Finally, remember that you don't need to add or alter the effects for every instrument on every track; sometimes it's best to just leave things alone.

Drummer Tracks

Drummer tracks are a special type of software instrument track that add a virtual drummer to your project. You can choose from a variety of different drummers, each with its own genre, drum kit, and playing style.

To create a drummer track, choose Track⇨ New Track, click Drummer Track, and then click Create. Now, to fine-tune your drummer's performance:

1. **Choose a genre.**

   I chose Rock.

2. **Choose a drummer and a subgenre.**

   I chose Max as my drummer and Punk Rock as the subgenre.

3. **Choose a drum kit.**

   I chose East Bay.

4. **Choose a preset.**

   I chose Mudslinger. See Figure 6-16.

Now try different drummers, genres, subgenres, drum kits, and presets until you find the sound and style that suits your project. Then, if necessary, use the XY pad, drum kit controls, and performance controls to fine-tune your drummer even further.

Here's how:

>> **XY pad:** Adjust the complexity and loudness of the selected drummer region. Drag the big yellow dot up to make your drummer play louder, down to play softer; left to make the drummer's playing simpler; and right to make the playing more complex.

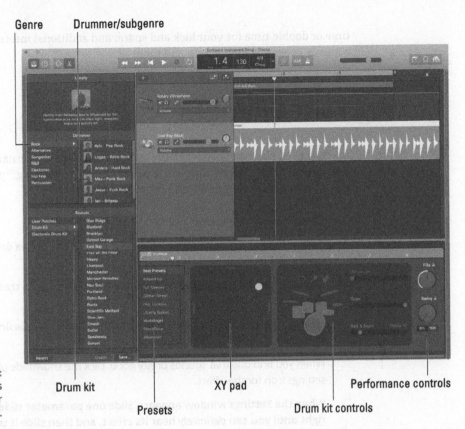

Genre　　Drummer/subgenre

XY pad

Drum kit controls

Performance controls

Drum kit

Presets

FIGURE 6-16:
Use these options
to create your
drummer track.

TIP

Drag the dot a tiny amount and wait to hear the result before moving it further, and then repeat until you're satisfied.

>> **Drum kit controls:** Click an instrument to enable or disable it. Slide the sliders to add more or less Percussion, Hi-Hat, or Kick & Snare.

>> **Performance controls:** Adjust the number and length of fills with the Fills knob; adjust the shuffle feel with the Swing knob.

Fiddle with these controls until you achieve the drum sound you're looking for.

One last trick: In the drum kit controls area, enable the Follow check box for Kick & Snare and then choose a track from the pop-up menu that appears. Now your drummer will play in time with that track!

TIP

There's much more to drummer tracks than I have space for here. If you care to dig deeper into drummer track features, search for *Drummer* in GarageBand Help. The coverage of drummer tracks is extensive and includes such diverse topics as using a brush kit to adjust the snare brush technique with drummers; using half time or double time for your kick and snare; and additional information on all the controls I cover in this section and more.

Testing Your Changes

It's easy to be overwhelmed by all the sliders and their esoteric names in plug-ins, instruments, and effects. Here's my prescription for creating "perfect" settings quickly and easily without tearing out your hair:

1. **Click the track's solo icon to listen to only that track.**

2. **Turn off the effect in question by deselecting its check box or by clicking its on/off button.**

3. **Click the play icon or press the spacebar and listen to the track without the effect.**

4. **Turn on the effect, and listen to the track again while choosing different presets.**

   When you find one that sounds pretty good, click the show/hide plug-in settings icon for the effect.

5. **When the Settings window appears, slide one parameter slider to the right until you can _definitely_ hear its effect, and then slide it to the left until you can _barely_ hear the effect.**

   You'll find the perfect setting somewhere between those two points.

Repeat the above for each parameter and you'll get the sound you like quickly and with a minimum of overwhelming-ness!

Chapter **7**

Recording Vocals and Acoustic Instruments with a Mic

his chapter cuts to the heart of audio recording — using a microphone or microphones to record vocals and instruments. As usual, Apple has done much of the heavy lifting already by including several dozen presets that you can use to change the sound of your recorded vocals and acoustic instruments. You, as the recording engineer, don't have to worry as much about what type of microphone you should use to record which instrument or how much echo to apply to a grand piano, for example. The presets do it all for you — and quite nicely I might add.

And so, when you record with GarageBand, you can use almost any microphone that you have handy and then apply a preset to get a more professional and polished sound out of it.

That said, the type of microphone you use does have an effect on the quality of your recording. And some mics work better for vocals and instruments than others. You can find details about choosing a mic in Chapter 2. In this chapter, you find out how to set up and position microphones for recording, followed by advice, tips, and hints for making better recordings with said microphones.

Before you start, though, keep in mind that recording with microphones is an art, a science, and a skill; don't expect to master it all at once. Many, many things can affect the sound you record, and understanding how these things interact and affect your recordings will take time.

You have a lot to cover, so let's rock.

Getting Ready to Record

I'm going to assume that you have some kind of microphone at hand and are ready to commence recording with it. But before you record a single note, you need to attend to a few things if you want to end up with great-sounding tracks.

The two things that you need to master first are microphone placement and level setting. If you nail those two first, you'll always get better results.

At this point, I wouldn't recommend spending a lot of time trying to deaden the room (see Chapter 2 for details). Rather, I suggest that you place the microphone and record the sound (or monitor it through headphones). Now decide whether you have too much room sound coloring the track and adjust accordingly.

I guarantee that you'll record better-sounding real audio tracks after reading this chapter.

Setting up your mic and recording track

When your room setup is as good as it gets, it's time to set up your mic or mics. Perhaps the most important factor in what ends up being recorded is the position of the microphone during recording. Your job is to position the microphone where it sounds the best to your ear. But to do that, you need to make the microphone live so that you can hear the effect of repositioning it.

To set up your mic so that it's live and then create the track to record on, follow these steps:

1. **Mute or disconnect your speakers.**

   Most Macs have a mute key on the keyboard as well as a volume control slider in the menu bar, which you can slide to its lowest setting to mute your speakers.

If your speakers are connected to an audio interface that's connected to your Mac, you're on your own as to how to mute your speakers. Try turning the audio interface off if you can; some bus-powered interfaces are always on as long as they're connected to a USB or FireWire port on your Mac.

2. **If your Mac has a built-in microphone, as most modern Macs do, choose ◆ ⇨ System Preferences, click the Sound icon, and then click the Input tab. Now make sure that Internal microphone is *not* selected for input.**

Should you not follow Steps 1 and 2, you will hear awful high-pitched howling, known as *feedback,* as soon as you monitor your real instrument track.

You have to tell GarageBand which input and output device to use in the Audio/MIDI Preferences pane. Otherwise, you may not be able to hear or record.

3. **Connect your headphones to your input source, which is often the headphone jack on your Mac.**

4. **To double-check that you won't sear your ears with feedback, test your setup *before* you connect your mic by playing an existing track in GarageBand.**

   If you hear the track through anything but the headphones, review the previous steps to mute or disconnect the speakers (or your Mac's built-in mic) before you continue.

   When the only sound you can hear comes out of the headphones, you're good to go.

5. **Open a GarageBand project, or create one.**

   Choose File ⇨ Open (⌘+O) or File ⇨ New (⌘+N). See Chapter 4 for details on creating new projects.

6. **Create a new track:**

   a. *Choose Track ⇨ New Track or press ⌘+Option+N.*

   b. *At the top of the Choose a Track Type dialog, click the mic icon.*

   c. *Click Create.*

7. **In the left column of the library, choose the appropriate category.**

   You want to choose the category that best describes the instrument or vocal part you're recording. The categories are self-explanatory: Choose Voice to record vocals; choose Acoustic Guitar to record acoustic guitars; choose Electric

Guitar or Bass to record (gasp) electric guitars and basses. Or choose Legacy ⇨ GarageBand for additional options, including the following:

- *Acoustic Guitars:* Record an acoustic guitar.

- *Band Instruments:* Record horns (trumpet, trombones, saxophone), flutes, violins, or other orchestral instruments you might find in a performing band.

- *Basic Track:* Record a basic track with no effects applied. You'll rarely want to use a basic track without effects in a song. Instead, you'd usually choose this category to start from scratch and specify and apply all the effects for the track yourself.

- *Bass:* Record instruments such as a bass guitar, string bass, electric string bass, and so on.

- *Drums:* Record drums or percussion instruments.

- *Effects:* Use strange treatments that make your voice or instrument sound weird or unearthly. My favorite effect preset is Telephone Lines, which makes your voice sound like it's coming through the earpiece of a very bad telephone. Way cool.

- *Guitar Track:* Record your guitar as an electric guitar (connected directly or played through an amp and captured with a microphone, as explained in Chapter 8) or acoustic guitar (played into a microphone).

- *Vocals:* Make your vocals sound like a million bucks.

  Note that if you've installed third-party plug-ins or instruments, you might see additional categories and presets.

8. **In the rightmost column, choose a preset for the selected category.**

The presets are subcategories. Choose the one that best describes the instrument or vocal you're about to record. Figure 7-1 shows some legacy Guitar Track presets you can use for guitar parts.

TIP

To audition presets, play (and pause) your song.

9. **In the Input pop-up menu in the Recording Settings section, select an input channel.**

In plain English, this means select the port or device that the instrument is currently plugged into. The input channel is 1 (Yeti X) in Figure 7-1.

TIP

If you plugged a microphone or instrument directly into your Mac, the correct choice is almost always Channel 1. My Yeti X is plugged into a USB port, so it appears on Channel 1. If your mic or instrument is plugged into an audio interface, you'll see the interface name rather than the microphone name. Either way, make sure the correct device is selected here; otherwise you won't be able to record.

FIGURE 7-1:
Crystal Arpeggios
to Memphis
Clean (and the
presets above
and below them)
are different
sounds for
recording guitar
tracks.

10. **Click the Monitoring button below the Input pop-up menu.**

This way, you can hear yourself play or sing as well as hear backing tracks through your headphones.

11. **Make sure the proper track is selected, and then click the play icon.**

You should hear your project — the tracks recorded previously — and your mic should be live with this track ready for recording.

With headphones on, speak into the mic. If you hear yourself, you're golden. If you don't hear yourself (and the track's level-meter LEDs light up), consider the following (in no particular order). Make sure that

- >> All your cables are firmly connected.

- >> The correct devices are selected for input and output in GarageBand's Preferences pane. (Open GarageBand Preferences, click the Audio/MIDI tab, and choose the appropriate input and output devices from the Audio Input and Output menus.)

- >> The proper track is selected (you can't record a track unless it's selected).

- >> The track you're recording doesn't have its mute icon illuminated.

- >> No other track has its solo icon illuminated.

- >> The track's volume slider isn't all the way to the left.

» The mic is turned on (not all mics have on/off switches).

» The audio inputs in System Preferences or your audio interface or both are turned up.

» The selected output device is not muted or doesn't have its level set too low for you to hear.

» You can hear other sounds through the selected output device to see whether the problem is with your headphones (and not your mic setup).

If none of these solve the problem, try a different mic or a different input.

Tweaking the pan to hear vocals better

The *pan settings* control where a sound is coming from in the stereo field — that is, from the left or right. Although it's more effective to wait and fine-tune pan settings for each track when you mix and master, a simple tweak to the pan settings may help you hear vocals better in your headphones.

Here's how it works: Pan a track or more than one track hard left or right and pan the track that you're recording hard to the opposite side. This way, you hear the previously recorded instrument or voice tracks in one ear and the track that you're currently recording in the other ear. Some musicians and singers find this less confusing than hearing everything in both ears. Try it and see if it works for you. I find it particularly helpful for recording harmony vocals.

Positioning the microphone

Assuming that you can hear the input from the microphone in your headphones (as described in "Setting up your mic and recording track" earlier in the chapter), it's time to adjust the mic's position for optimal recording. Most vocals are recorded using a classic close mic technique, where the microphone is 6 inches or less from the vocalist's lips. For other sound sources, the optimal distance from the sound to the mic can range from 6 inches to 2 feet or more.

Many mics pick up sound in a cardioid pattern (see Chapter 2), which is the preferred pattern for vocals and most single-instrument recordings. The closer you move a cardioid pattern mic to the sound source, the more bass response you hear, which is known as the *proximity effect*. You can really hear this effect in your cans (headphones) as you move the sound source and microphone closer together or farther apart.

WHEN USING AND NOT USING A MICROPHONE

When you're not using a microphone, store it somewhere cool, clean, and dry. Put it in a pouch or cover it with a piece of cloth or an upside-down plastic bag. (Don't seal the bag; just let it hang over the mic.) If you keep dust and airborne gunk away from your mic, it will perform better and last longer.

Use a pop screen to minimize the amount of saliva that gets onto the mic. Saliva isn't a good thing where delicate electronic devices are concerned, so dry your mic gently with a soft cloth as soon as possible. Do not try to blow a mic dry with a hair dryer or compressed air in a can; either can render the mic inoperable.

Because cardioid-pattern mics pick up sound directly in front of them better than from the back or sides, changing the orientation of the mic can dramatically change what you hear. So don't just move it closer or farther away — change the angle or direction in which the mic is pointed, too.

And by the way, the 6 inches to 2 feet guideline isn't etched in stone. If your oboe sounds fantastic when the mic is exactly 3.75 feet away, fantastic! You can find the sweet spot for a mic only by experimenting with its placement.

After you're happy with your mic's placement, you're ready to set the levels. See the next section for details about how to do this.

Setting levels

When the mic is positioned and sounds its best to you, fine-tune your recording level for the track. Because you're recording real audio (and not a software instrument), you can't change the recording level later. If you record the track too hot or too cool (with too much or too little level), the track will be distorted or too quiet.

TIP

If you spike into the red zone once or several times during a performance, don't lose hope. You may be able to use the track volume control to lower the volume during those hot passages. If you don't have too much distortion in the recording (from being too hot) and with other tracks blended in, your track may be fine.

REMEMBER

It's always better to record at the right level, though. If you record a track too hot or too cool, you risk losing a great performance or, at best, having to work extra hard in post-production to salvage it.

So pay close attention to track levels and master levels when you record and also when you mix and master.

To set the levels before you record a take, play or sing a bit of the song that you want to record and watch the levels on the LED display, which you find in the Mixer column for that track. What should you look for to get a proper recording level? Check out Figure 7-2 to find your answers. The top LED meter shows levels that are too cool (quiet/indistinct); the middle pair of meters represent a good range of recording levels; the bottom meter is too hot (loud/distorted).

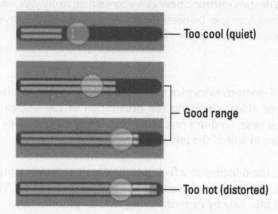

Too cool (quiet)

Good range

FIGURE 7-2:
The range
of good and
bad levels.

Too hot (distorted)

You want the recording level as green as possible, without much (or any) yellow and little or no red. An occasional spike near the red, as shown in the second image in Figure 7-2, won't hurt, but don't let it stay that hot for long. If both red LEDs are lit, like they are in the bottom picture in Figure 7-2, your recording will almost certainly be distorted and may be unusable.

If your tracks are too cool or too hot, first try adding a bit of compression, which I discuss in more detail in the next section. Then play a bit of your song again to see whether that puts it in the green. If that doesn't work, try adjusting the level by sliding the level fader to the left. Keep tweaking compression and levels until you find the right amount of level that gives you a useable track. If you're using an audio interface, try increasing its gain (level). You can find more details about adjusting levels in Chapter 4.

Finally, memorize my late, great Uncle Yogi's mantra for recording levels, and things will be fine:

Lots of green, it's sweet and clean;
Too much red, your track is dead.

Adding effects

One way of making a track sound different or better is to add effects to it.

TECHNICAL STUFF

In the past, the rule was to use as few effects as possible during recording. The object was to keep what was on tape as pristine as possible. If you recorded a track with echo and reverb, for example, and later decided that you didn't want echo and reverb or wanted less of it, you were stuck. The track on tape had the echo and reverb in its DNA. Sometimes it was necessary to add some compression or equalization to a track during recording, but most other effects were added later, giving you the option of using them or not.

With GarageBand, you have no such limitation because it uses *nondestructive* effects — meaning that you hear the effects in real-time, but they're not applied to your tracks until you export the project. And that, my friends, is a really good thing.

The upshot is that you no longer have to worry about spoiling a take by adding an effect. If you don't like the effect, you can remove it without affecting your track. No harm, no foul.

If you're a veteran of analog recording, this feature probably seems like a miracle. In the old days, effects were usually outboard hardware devices that were filled with strange DSP chips capable of such real-time shenanigans. Today, our Intel processors are more than powerful enough to add effects such as these on the fly.

It's nice to know that you can add effects at any time. So add 'em or not as you like — you won't hurt anything. Knock yourself out choosing different presets and adjusting the EQ, reverb, and echo — whatever rocks your boat.

That said, with most effects, you don't gain a great advantage adding them before recording. But compression is a special case. Even in the old days, sometimes it was best to add a bit of compression to an instrument or voice before committing it to tape. And the same holds true for GarageBand.

REMEMBER

When you have a track with a few (but not too many) hot spots, you may be able to bring the loudest and softest parts closer together by adding a bit of compression. I almost always add some compression to my vocals, guitar, bass, and drum tracks. There's not much I don't compress at least a small amount. So before you lower the level of the entire track or enable automation and use the track volume control, try adding a small amount of compression. You should see less yellow and red in the LED level displays, and you should be able to hear softer passages better than before. A bit of compression can free you from having to "ride the faders" (or "diddle the track volume rubber band controls," in GarageBand parlance) to compensate for loud and soft portions.

The *small amount* is key. Although a little compression can make a track that's too hot in some parts and too cool in others sound better, too much compression can make it sound artificial and even robotic.

To add just the right amount of compression for a vocal or acoustic instrument track, follow these steps:

1. **Begin playing your song by clicking the play icon or pressing the spacebar.**

2. **Select the track you want to alter by clicking its name.**

3. **Open the Smart controls.**

   To do so, choose View ➪ Show Smart Controls, or press the B key on your QWERTY keyboard, or click the Smart controls icon in the toolbar (and shown in the margin).

4. **Enable (click) the Track and Controls buttons in the Smart controls toolbar.**

   One of GarageBand's Compressors will appear in the Controls area.

5. **Twist one of the Compressor's knobs while listening closely.**

   You may want to click the solo icon for the track so you can hear it more clearly.

6. **Repeat with other knobs until you like what you hear.**

7. **Use the Compare button to compare your current settings with the default settings for this patch.**

8. **Check your levels again.**

   For details, see the "Setting levels" section, earlier in this chapter.

You may have to slide the track's level slider to the left or right by a small amount to achieve the best level for the track after you've added compression or changed your compression settings.

TIP

Checking for unwanted noise

Before you start recording your tracks, listen carefully once more for extraneous noise. Is the air conditioner or refrigerator running? (Better catch it before it runs away.) If you live in the South, listen for those ceiling fans; if you're a Northerner, listen for steam pipes or oil heaters clanging; no matter where you live, listen for jet planes flying overhead and big trucks driving by outside your window.

PROOF OF NONDESTRUCTIVE EFFECTS

In the old days, you had to be careful adding compression to tracks because the compression couldn't be removed. GarageBand and other modern recording software break that rule in a big way by making all of their effects nondestructive. Here's how to see it for yourself:

1. **Create a new project and record a track using a preset that adds a distinctive sound.**

   If you play guitar, try one of the Crunch Guitar presets, which add easily discernable fuzz tones; for vocals, try the one that alters the sound of your voice dramatically, such as Telephone or Fuzz Vocal presets.

2. **Save the project and exit GarageBand.**

3. **Locate the file on your hard drive, right-click (or Control-click) it, and choose Show Package Contents from the contextual menu, as shown in the following figure.**

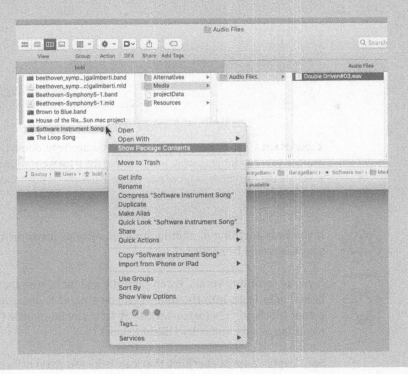

(continued)

(continued)

4. Open the Media folder, and then open the Audio Files folder.

You'll see at least one file with a name related to the track you just recorded. I used a Crunch Guitar preset called Double Driven, so it's named DoubleDriven#03.wav, as shown in the figure.

This file is the saved version of the track you just recorded — or more accurately, what GarageBand wrote to your hard drive when you recorded.

The easiest way to hear the recording is to select the .wav file and press the spacebar to open a QuickLook window. Now, click the Play button in the QuickLook window to hear what was recorded, as shown in the following figure.

It sounds just a wee bit different than it did in GarageBand, doesn't it? The effects you heard in your headphones while you recorded the track were added on the fly but not written to the hard drive — proof that GarageBand effects are nondestructive.

WARNING

If you hear anything in addition to your voice or instrument in the headphones, your take could be spoiled.

TIP

If you're recording vocals, listen carefully and make sure that no sound from your headphones leaks into the mic when you sing. If it does, reduce the headphone output (the better choice) or back away from the mic a little (which may hurt your recording quality and is less likely to work).

See Chapter 2 for a checklist that can help you prevent background noise from showing up on your tracks.

Multitrack Recording

Recording one track at a time with one microphone can be a drag. If you need to record a band live, several performers simultaneously, or live drums, you'll want to use a separate microphone and track for each player, instrument, or drum.

I'll use drums as an example of multitrack recording, but know that the techniques described here work just as well for recording an entire band live, three acoustic guitarists and a singer, or almost any recording scenario you can think of with more than one audio source.

Alas, I am not a drummer and don't even play one on TV, so I asked my friend and colleague Dave Hamilton to help me out. Dave is the drummer for the greatest garage band you never heard, the Macworld All-Star Band; he's also the CEO of BackBeat Media and president of the *Mac Observer*. He's played and toured with members of the Dave Matthews Band, cats who have played in the horn section for Phish, and members of David Letterman's CBS Late Night Orchestra. So he's the real deal.

Dave is also an underrated writer whose work has appeared in *MacAddict* and the *Mac Observer* as well as other Mac publications (but not often enough, if you ask me).

Now, without further ado, here's Dave's take (pun intended) on recording drums with GarageBand.

Dave Hamilton on multitrack drum recording

The one place where GarageBand falls short is in recording live drums. Garage-Band's limitation of recording one track at a time (without an expensive multi-channel audio interface and enough microphones) leaves many would-be home engineers scratching their respective (drum)heads. Recording drums properly requires a minimum of three microphones (although you can use more if you want), and GarageBand is not built to accept that many mics unless you buy a bunch of additional gear. Don't fret — I have two solutions, depending on your needs.

One track at a time

One option is to let GarageBand dictate the way you record — that being one track at a time. Because you'll be recording one instrument at a time, make sure you have your song mapped out (either in your head or on paper) from start to finish.

Choose your first instrument — the hi-hat, for example — and place your microphone accordingly. Then get your song set up in GarageBand, set your tempo (you'll want to record using GarageBand's metronome as a guide), put on a pair of headphones, and fire away. When you have that track the way you want it, move on to the next instrument. Get your bass drum miced the way you want it, put the headphones back on, and go for it. Then do the snare, and so on.

This process is tedious, but the result will be clean and pristine tracks. These tracks can be individually equalized and effected in GarageBand, giving you complete control over the mix. The trade-off is that you may lose some of the feel of having a live drummer playing all the parts at once.

Don't want to make that trade-off, you say? Well, you have two other choices: Use a mixer to record multiple mics to a single track, essentially recording as above, or use a multichannel audio interface to record multiple tracks at once.

Multiple tracks at once

To record multiple tracks at once, you must purchase a USB-connected audio interface with enough XLR inputs to match the number of microphones you want to record simultaneously. The Focusrite Scarlett 18i20 allows eight microphones to be connected and is available for less than $500.

After you've procured your audio interface and connected it to your Mac, you're ready to start. Follow these steps to record with a mixer:

1. **Position your microphones.**

   I prefer a minimum of three mics (one on the bass drum and then two overheads to get a stereo image of the sound) for decent results. You can, of course, move on past that and mic the snare (top and bottom!), toms, and individual cymbals if you're so inclined. Make sure to get a cowbell mic, too.

2. **Connect the microphones to the microphone inputs on the mixer, and head into GarageBand.**

3. **Add one audio track for each microphone you've plugged in, and select the input to match.**

   If the bass drum mic is plugged into the first input, choose Input 1 for that track. Then choose Track ⇨ New Track and create the next track, choosing the next input to match.

4. **After all your tracks are in, choose Track ⇨ Configure Track Header and ensure that the Record Enable box is selected.**

   This is the trick that will allow GarageBand to record multiple tracks simultaneously.

5. **Click the newly added red circle in each drum track (but not your other tracks). Only flashing tracks will be recorded.**

6. **Click the record icon and bash away, playing the drum track naturally!**

   You may find that you need to adjust the gain levels on the audio interface if one drum is recording too loudly or softly. This process, by its nature, is one of trial and error, so don't record your masterpiece first. Just test it, adjust, and test again until you have a setup that captures your sounds the way you like.

Whichever option you choose, you end up with a decent drum sound that you can tweak to your heart's content with GarageBand's effects.

Happy recording!

To which I say, "Thanks, Dave!"

For what it's worth, Dave sent me an MP3 file of some drumming that he recorded using the three-microphones-and-a-mixer setup described in this section. It sounded just like drums (which is just what it should sound like).

Recording with a MIDI drum

You have one more option for recording drums: Use a MIDI drum controller such as the Korg nanoPAD2 Slim-Line USB MIDI Pads to tap out your drum part on 16 velocity-sensitive pads, as shown in Figure 7-3.

FIGURE 7-3:
Korg nanoPAD2
Slim-Line USB
MIDI Pads sends
touch-sensitive
MIDI information
to your Mac.

Remember the MIDI keyboards I've been talking about throughout the book? Think of the Korg nanoPAD2 as serving the same purpose with a twist: Instead of sending MIDI information when you press a key, the nanoPAD2 sends MIDI information when you tap one of the 16 touch-sensitive pads with your finger.

Any drummer will tell you how hard it is to play drums using a MIDI keyboard. Although I'm not a drummer, I've used nanoPAD2 for many tracks and they sound significantly more realistic than ones I create on a keyboard.

Priced at around $50, nanoPAD2 is an outstanding value if you need to record drums that sound reasonably realistic on a tight budget.

You can spend more on MIDI drums that look and play like a real drum set, such as the Alesis Drums Nitro Mesh Kit (under $400), shown in Figure 7-4.

Recording the Track

Okay then, now that you have everything ready to record, all that's left is to actually record. No worries — it's a snap.

Here's how:

1. **Move the playhead to the point in your song where you want to begin recording, or press Return or Enter to move the playhead to the start of the song.**

    GarageBand has two features to help you record — a metronome and a count-in.

2. **If you want to use the metronome, click the metronome icon in the toolbar (and shown in the margin) or press the K key on your QWERTY keyboard.**

   The metronome is a toggle; it's on when the icon lights up (turns purple), and off when the icon is gray. See Chapter 6 for details on the metronome.

3. **If you want to use count-in, click the count-in icon in the toolbar (and shown in the margin), or choose Record ⇨ Count In.**

   When count in is turned on, you get an additional measure counted out before GarageBand starts recording. Count-in, like the metronome, is a toggle; it's on when the icon lights up (turns purple), and off when the icon is gray. See Chapter 6 for more information.

4. **Click the record icon (red dot) or press R, and the recording begins.**

   Remember to watch your levels while you record.

5. **When you've finished recording, click the play/pause icon or press the spacebar to end the recording.**

   Wasn't that simple?

Improving the Sound of Recordings

If you've been paying attention and haven't killed the tracks that you've recorded (remember Uncle Yogi's mantra: *Too much red, your track is dead*), you can tinker with the sound to your heart's content.

Remember the nondestructive feature, described earlier in the chapter? You can add and subtract effects without affecting the quality of your original track — until you export it, that is.

So listen to what you've recorded now, and pay particular attention to both the sound of the instrument or voice and the performance itself. Now add some effects or change some presets (see Chapter 6 for details), and then listen some more.

Are some parts too loud or too soft? Add a bit of compression, or use the track volume control to reduce the level. As shown in Figure 7-5, I played three chords way too loud for this part of the song. The track volume control let me reduce the level smoothly before the first loud chord and increase it smoothly after the third one. See Chapter 9 for details on using the track volume control.

Track volume control   Three loud chords

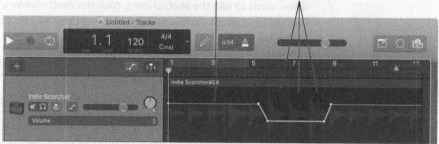

FIGURE 7-5:
Changing the
level (riding
the fader) with
the track volume
control.

TIP

If you hear other problems on a recording, don't worry yet — small problems can be fixed in several ways without redoing the entire track:

» **If you hit a wrong note — or even three or four — read the section in Chapter 9 about fixing flubs.** You can find several techniques for editing out mistakes and replacing mistakes with better performances.

» **To fatten up the sound of almost any instrument or vocal track, try double-tracking, which is an age-old production technique.** GarageBand gives you two ways to do this; each has pros and cons:

• *Way 1:* Duplicate the original guitar track (choose Track ➪ Duplicate Track or use the shortcut, ⌘+D) and copy and paste the original guitar region onto the new track. This technique is fast and easy, but unless you're careful, it will sound mechanical because both tracks will be exactly the same. One way to soften the effect is to change one of the tracks by adding effects; try a bit of Chorus and the doubled track sound sounds ethereal. Or choose a preset with lots of distortion for one track and choose a cleaner-sounding preset for the other.

• *Way 2:* Create a new track and record the part a second time, playing or singing along with the original track. You want to repeat your performance as precisely as you can, but because you're only human, the second recording will have small differences from the original track. Although this technique can take you more time, the differences between the two takes can make this sound better than copying and pasting the same performance.

» If you hear pitch problems in your vocals, try using the Antares Auto-tune pitch-correcting plug-in; it's nothing short of a miracle. (See Figure 7-6.) In a nutshell, this plug-in puts your voice or certain instruments back on pitch if they wander off.

There's one more thing: I created a downloadable GarageBand tutorial with a completed GarageBand project, the finished master track, and a PDF explaining how and why I did what I did in the project.

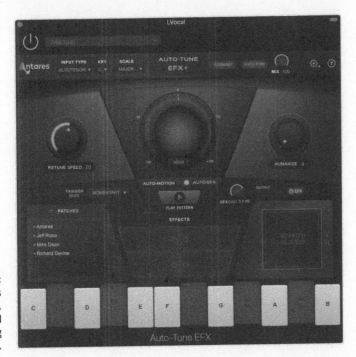

FIGURE 7-6:
With the Antares
Auto-tune plug-in,
even I sound
"pitchy" and sing
on key.

One of the things I did was to use Antares Auto-tune on every one of my vocal tracks (since I'm a mediocre singer at best). I included two finished masters — one with Auto-tune and one without — so you can hear the difference yourself.

The download is free and you find it here: `www.workingsmarterformacusers.com/blog/garageband`.

Chapter **8**

Recording Electric Guitars and Other Electronic Instruments

n Chapters 6 and 7, I explain how to record software instruments and vocal and acoustic instrument tracks. In this chapter, I explain how to record another type of instrument: an amplified instrument, most notably an electric guitar.

REMEMBER

Throughout this chapter, I use the electric guitar as an example because that's the instrument I happen to own and play. However, the electric guitar is just one of many electronic or amplified instruments you might record directly. So, if you play another electronic instrument, such as an electric piano, synthesizer, violin, bass, or whatever, merely substitute the name of your instrument wherever you see the word *guitar*.

For the most part, electric instrument tracks are the same as vocal and acoustic instrument tracks (discussed in Chapter 7). The big difference is that you can record electronic instruments without a mic by plugging the instrument directly into your Mac (or audio interface) instead of placing a microphone in front of the instrument's amplifier.

For those who prefer recording the old-school way, I also cover recording guitars and other electronic instruments with a mic in front of their amplifiers.

Finally, I show you how to customize the sound of your electronic instrument track to make it sound even better.

Overview from the Top: Direct or Live Recording

Recording an electronic instrument with GarageBand is easier than with some other recording software because, once again, Apple did the heavy lifting for you. This time Apple has included built-in guitar amplifier and stomp box emulations with presets designed by professional guitarists and recording engineers. By merely choosing a different preset, you can give your guitar a vintage British Invasion sound, the overdriven distortion of Chord Burner, the dulcet tones of Cool Jazz Combo, and other guitar and bass presets too numerous to mention. Just pick a preset and record your masterpiece.

Recording electronic instruments with GarageBand is easy also because Garage-Band doesn't require you use an amplifier. Instead, you plug the instrument into your Mac (or into an audio interface connected to your Mac), and GarageBand emulates the sound of the amplifier and stomp box effects. The result sounds like an amp and stomp boxes. It's slick.

TIP

Even if you're not a guitarist, if you have a guitar available — even if it's a crummy one that sounds like garbage through an amplifier — try some of GarageBand's guitar presets. I think you'll be pleasantly surprised.

In the recording industry, plugging an electric guitar (or other electronic instrument) directly into your computer is called *direct recording*. I recommend direct recording if possible. Unless you have a lot of time to experiment with amplifier and microphone placement, you'll almost always get better results this way — and it's faster.

However, I realize that some purists, pros, recording engineers, and producers prefer to capture the unique interplay of guitar and amplifier by recording the guitar and amplifier *live*, using a microphone or microphones. If you want to record your guitar live, I cover most of what you need to know about setting up and recording with microphones in Chapter 7. Amplifiers are notoriously difficult to record well, so I have a few tips and hints for those of you who insist on recording with an amp and microphone(s).

When I worked in recording studios in the 1970s, the technology wasn't good enough to record directly. The only way to record electric guitar and bass tracks was with a mic and an amp. Today, amp-modeling and sound-shaping software is so spectacular sounding that many popular artists play through modeled amps on stage and in recording. A few years ago, I played two sets with the Macworld All-Star Band sans amplifier, using GarageBand for all amp and effects sounds, with my Mac connected directly into the house sound system! It sounded great and, as a pleasant side effect, the sound level onstage was lower than usual, which meant we could hear ourselves playing and singing better.

TIP

I show you how to use GarageBand to play live without an amplifier in Chapter 20.

My Marshall amp died a few years ago and I didn't bother to replace it. These days, if I want to play, I just open GarageBand and use one of its fine guitar presets (without recording) instead of an amp and stomp boxes.

Direct Recording with GarageBand's Virtual Amplifiers

When you record directly, you bypass amplification and plug your instrument directly into your Mac. When you play, the sound comes out of your Mac speakers (or selected monitoring source). You can change your instrument sounds by selecting a different instrument or preset.

Setting up to record

Before you begin, you need two things: your instrument and the appropriate cable or cables to connect it to your Mac or audio interface. (See Chapter 2 if you're wondering what an audio interface is.)

TIP

You can buy an adapter (see Chapter 2) that lets you plug your guitar into the audio in port on your Mac (if it has one) for under $20. It's worth having an adapter even if you have an audio interface; that way, if you have a problem with the audio interface, you can just plug your guitar into your Mac instead. An adapter is also great for recording your guitar on the road without having to carry additional devices or boxes or cables or power supplies.

With your instrument plugged into your Mac, follow these steps to record your guitar (or other instrument) directly:

1. **Open GarageBand Preferences by choosing GarageBand ➪ Preferences or pressing ⌘+ (⌘+comma). Click the audio/MIDI icon, and then click the Input Device drop-down menu.**

2. **Click the input that your guitar is plugged into.**

   In Figure 8-1, I'm choosing my Focusrite Scarlett Solo audio interface (connected to my Mac via USB).

WARNING

If your Mac has a built-in microphone, as most Macs do these days, make sure Built-in Microphone is *not selected* before you proceed. Select either Line In (if your Mac has a Line In port) or your audio interface (if your instrument is plugged into an audio interface). Should you not heed this warning, you'll hear the awful high-pitched howling known as *feedback* as soon as you monitor any real instrument track.

Now you need to establish whether GarageBand "hears" your instrument.

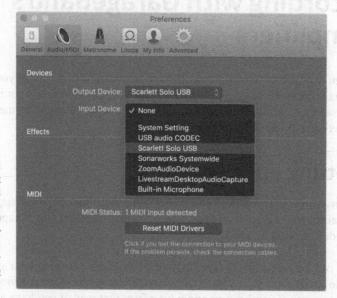

FIGURE 8-1:
Choose the input
your guitar is
plugged into
(Scarlett Solo USB
here); *don't*
choose Built-in
Microphone or
your ears will get
a nasty surprise.

3. **Open a GarageBand project by double-clicking it in Finder. Or create a project by choosing File ➪ New or pressing ⌘+N.**

4. **When the Choose a Track Type dialog appears, click the connect a guitar icon and then click Create.**

5. **Select the new track (if it's not already selected) and choose an instrument category in the first column of the library, and a subcategory in the second column (if necessary).**

If you're playing a guitar or bass, choose the Electric Guitar and Bass category. If you're playing an acoustic guitar, choose the Acoustic Guitar category. If you're playing another type of electronic instrument, choose a category that sounds appropriate.

TIP

If you see a category called Legacy, you should definitely explore it because it features presets from earlier versions of GarageBand that are no longer bundled with it but can still be used.

6. **In the right column, choose a preset for the category.**

You just want to ensure that GarageBand can hear what you play, so you can choose any preset for now. Chapter 7 unravels how these categories and presets work.

7. **Set the input to the channel to which your instrument is connected.**

8. **Click the monitoring button to enable monitoring (so you can hear what you play).**

9. **Strike a chord or play a riff (or do whatever it is you like to do with your instrument).**

Did you hear what you played from your output source (usually your computer speakers)? And did you see activity in the track's level meter and the master level meters?

If you heard your instrument loud and clear and answered both questions with a resounding "yes," you're good to go. Feel free to skip ahead to the "Setting levels" section. If you answered "no" to either question, see the next section, "Troubleshooting your setup."

Troubleshooting your setup

If you followed the steps in the preceding section and the setup didn't work quite right, here are some quick fixes (in no particular order):

>> **Make sure all your cables are connected firmly.**

>> **Make sure the correct devices are selected for input and output in GarageBand's Preferences.** Open GarageBand Preferences, click the audio/MIDI icon, and choose the appropriate input and output devices from the Audio Input and Output menus. See Chapter 3 for more details about preferences.

>> **Make sure the proper track is selected in the main GarageBand window.**

>> **Make sure the mute icon for the track you're recording isn't illuminated.** If you mute the track you're recording, you won't hear yourself play.

>> **Make sure the solo icon for another track is not illuminated.** If you solo any track but the one you're recording, you won't hear yourself play.

>> **Make sure the volume slider for the track isn't all the way to the left.**

>> **Make sure the volume control on your guitar is turned up.**

>> **Make sure the audio inputs in System Preferences or on your audio interface cards are turned up.**

>> **Make sure your Mac speakers aren't muted (if that's the output you're using).** Choose ⌘ System Preferences, click the Sound icon, and choose the Output tab. If the Mute check box contains a check mark, clear it to unmute your Mac.

>> **Make sure you can hear other sounds through the selected output device.**

>> **If none of this works, try switching to a different input.** If you have an audio interface available, use it. If it's an audio interface that's giving you trouble, try using your Mac's line in port instead.

Making a too soft instrument louder

If you get a signal from the guitar — you can hear it and see activity in its volume meter — but it's not loud enough, even with the volume slider slid all the way to the right, you can do a few different things.

First, make sure the volume knob on your guitar is cranked up all the way. Temporarily use the same cable to plug into an amp or a headphone amp to check. I know I just mentioned this earlier, in the list of things to check, but I want you to double-check before I suggest spending money to resolve the problem.

If checking the volume didn't do the trick, an audio interface can make your instrument louder without adding noise (hissing, buzzing, crackling, and the like). If your guitar still doesn't put out a loud enough signal and you've turned up the input levels everyplace you can, you need an audio interface with preamps.

My Scarlett Solo USB audio interface (shown in Figure 8-2), for example, has two inputs with preamps and suits my needs perfectly at a reasonable price (around $150).

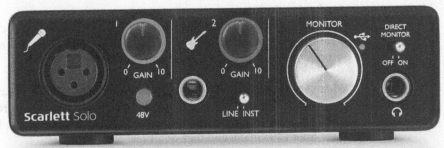

FIGURE 8-2:
Scarlett Solo USB
(front and back) is
an audio interface
and preamp,
which makes
instruments and
microphones
louder without
adding unwanted
noise.

In addition to a pair of ¼-inch guitar inputs, the Scarlett Solo also offers an XLR port, which can supply phantom power to microphones. The interface is super quiet (it doesn't add noise) and boosts the level of my guitars and microphones quite nicely for GarageBand.

An audio interface with preamps can be used with almost any instrument or microphone you use to record — electric guitars and basses, acoustic guitars, microphones with XLR connectors, or other electronic instruments that require additional amplification to provide a sufficient signal to GarageBand.

Most audio interfaces include at least one input with a preamp. Many also offer one or more XLR inputs with phantom power. Read the specifications carefully to make sure your choice has the features you need before you buy, and buy this kind of stuff from a trusted vendor with a reasonable return policy.

TIP

I mention a few of my go-to online audio gear vendors in Chapter 26.

Setting levels

Because you're recording on a real instrument and not a software instrument, you won't be able to change the recording level after a track is laid down. So if you record the track *too hot* or *too cool*, meaning with too much or too little level, that's the track you're stuck with.

To ensure that you're making a useable track, remember to check your levels before you begin recording. You do this by playing a bit of the song you want to record and watching the LEDs next to the track.

What should you look for? Take a gander at Figure 8-4 for the answer. You want to see as much green as possible without much or any yellow or red. An occasional spike near the red, as shown in the third picture in Figure 8-4, is fine as long as there aren't too many and they don't last too long.

WARNING

If *both* red LEDs light up at once, as shown in the bottom picture in Figure 8-4, your recording will almost certainly be distorted and is likely to be unusable.

For more on checking and adjusting levels before you record, see Chapter 4.

By the way, if Figure 8-3 looks familiar, that's because it's also in Chapter 7. But it's so important that I felt obliged to include it here, too, for your convenience.

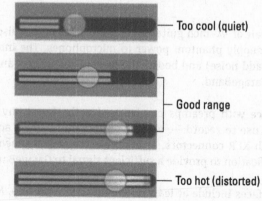

Too cool (quiet)

Good range

FIGURE 8-3:
The top picture is too cool, the two middle pictures are in the just-right range, and the bottom picture is too hot.

Too hot (distorted)

That's pretty much it. Just remember this mantra when you record guitars (or anything else, for that matter): *Lots of green and it's sweet and clean. Too much red and your track is dead.*

Recording the track

There's really not much to recording a track after GarageBand hears your guitar and you've set the levels. Because you've already created the track, all that's left to do now is to turn on the metronome and count-in features if you want them, and then record. (See Chapter 7 for the specific steps.)

Even if you checked the levels before recording, you still need to pay careful attention to the levels while you record, too.

TIP

If only one or two brief passages were recorded too hot or cool (as opposed to a track that's too hot or cool from start to finish), you can try lowering or raising the level of the hotter or cooler passages using the track volume control. (See Chapter 7 for details.) If there's not too much distortion in the recording (from being too hot) and you have other tracks playing simultaneously, you can often make it good enough to get by. Still, it's better to record at a proper level in the first place.

Let your ears be your guide. If it sounds good, it's a keeper. If it doesn't sound good, re-record it.

Recording Live with an Amplifier and Microphones

As I mention earlier in the chapter, recording an electric guitar (or other electronic instrument) *live* means that you hook your guitar up to a traditional guitar amp and record the amp (and room sound) with a mic, rather than plugging your guitar directly into your Mac and using GarageBand's amp simulators.

The key to a good amplified electric guitar recording is patience. You need to experiment with mic positions, amp positions, microphones, rooms, and surfaces before you begin to understand how to achieve just the sound you want. If you think you're just going to simply plug in a mic, hang it near an amplifier, and get a great guitar sound, you've got another think coming 'cause it ain't that easy. But if you're not averse to a bit of work, the results can be outstanding, just like (well, almost like) Jimmy Page, Eric Clapton, or Gary Clark Jr.

All the details in Chapter 7 apply to recording an amplified electric guitar with a microphone. Here are additional tricks and tips to help you capture the sound you desire as it leaves the amplifier:

>> **Mic placement is key.** You need to experiment and find the best location for the mic you're using. No single right way exists; you have to find the sweet spot for your combination of microphone, guitar, and amp. Start with the mic about an inch from one of the amp's speaker cones. Move it off-axis, to the left and right. Swivel it at different angles. Move it away from the speaker

cabinet in small increments. If your amp has an open back design, try micing the back of the cabinet instead of the front. Move the mic around as before.

Microphone stands are a must in situations like this where precise positioning of the mic is necessary.

>> **Loud isn't always good.** If you're trying to get an overdriven or distorted guitar sound, set the levels of your amp and guitar as low as you can and still achieve the effect you desire. Playing louder will just muddy the recording (make it sound distorted and buzzy). This effect may be the one you're looking for, but you'll usually get a better recording if you play at the lowest level you can.

>> **A small practice amp is often better than a big old Marshall double stack for home recording.** If you have both, try your little amp — you'll be surprised at how nice it sounds when recorded.

>> **Consider room acoustics.** If you're going for that reverb/echo/distortion sound, a lively room with many hard surfaces will add natural echo and reverb. For a more jazz-like passage, you might prefer that the room add as little color as possible, with soft surfaces to absorb reflected sound waves before they leak back into the mic.

If you play too loudly, you'll end up with echo-and-reverb-laden mud instead of a sweet rock-and-roll guitar sound.

Try this experiment: Record something three times with the amp set to three different levels — quieter than usual, normal, and louder than heck. You'll find that the louder-than-heck version rarely sounds as good as either of the others.

Many engineers like to record guitar amps in the bathroom. All you need is a long mic cord and guitar cable. The effect is interesting, to say the least.

If you try the bathroom trick, remember to experiment with mic position. It's a time-consuming chore but worth it if you want the best sound. I've heard more than one recording engineer say that setting up guitar mics (or drum mics) properly often takes longer than the recording session itself.

Conversely, if you're getting too much room sound in the track, try using pillows or blankets in front of the amp to reduce reflected sound. Move the amp around the room, too, and point it in different directions if you think that will help.

Finally, if you're trying to record an acoustic guitar, you may have more luck with an electrified acoustic guitar, such as the J.R. Beck 9861EQ acoustic/ electric guitar shown in Figure 8-4. It's a standard acoustic guitar with three additions: a pickup inside (think little baby microphone), a hole to plug a guitar cable into, and a

4-band equalizer and volume controller. It plays and sounds like an acoustic guitar, but you can plug it into an amplifier, an audio interface, or a Mac and record it without a microphone.

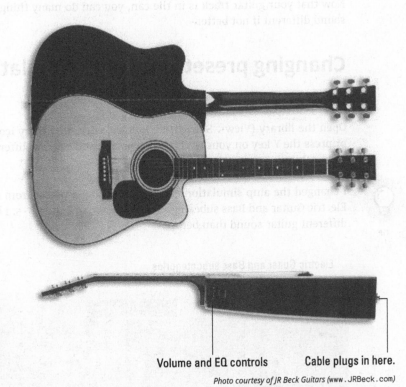

FIGURE 8-4:
This acoustic guitar can be recorded as though it were an electric guitar!

Volume and EQ controls   Cable plugs in here.

I can't tell you how much easier it is to record my 9861 than it is to record my older Yamaha acoustic with a microphone. Also, the sound is much better, with less unwanted noise and other crud. If you plan to record a lot of acoustic guitar tracks, an electric/acoustic will save you hours of setup and microphone placement and adjustment. It will also almost certainly sound better.

TIP

J.R. Beck was a small guitar manufacturer that used the Dell model to offer great guitars at amazingly low prices on the web. The 9861 in Figure 8-4, for example, cost me around $200 but plays and sounds better than other electric/acoustics costing much more. Sadly, J.R. Beck went out of business.

Customizing the Sound of Your Guitar Tracks

Now that your guitar track is in the can, you can do many things to it to make it sound different if not better.

Changing presets and amp simulators

The first and easiest task is to choose a different amp model.

Open the library (View ➪ Show/Hide Library, click the library icon in the toolbar, or press the Y key on your QWERTY keyboard) and select a different preset in the right column.

TIP

I changed the amp simulation effect by choosing a preset from one of the seven Electric Guitar and Bass subcategories, as shown in Figure 8-5. I heard an entirely different guitar sound than before.

Electric Guitar and Bass subcategories

FIGURE 8-5:
Choose one of these seven subcategories and then choose a preset to achieve a new sound on your track.

TIP

If you're looking for an unusual sound, try some of the bass, vocal, drum, or even band instrument presets, which may (or may not) sound great laid on your guitar track. Don't be afraid to try different presets; you can always undo (⌘+Z) if you don't like it.

Editing presets

If you still haven't found the sound you want among the amp and instrument presets, find the one that's the closest to the sound you desire and edit it to your specifications. Here's how:

1. **If the Smart controls for your guitar track aren't displayed, choose View ⇨ Show Smart Controls; click the Smart controls icon in the toolbar; or press the B key on your QWERTY keyboard.**

GarageBand has a wide variety of amplifiers, stomp boxes, and plug-in effects. The Smart controls and plug-ins you see will differ for each preset, as shown in Figure 8-6.

FIGURE 8-6: Smart controls and plug-ins for the Burnin' Tweed (top), Clean Studio Stack (middle), and Indie Scorcher (bottom) guitar presets.

Note that each of the three different amps has a unique set of Smart controls. And although the plug-ins look almost the same for all three presets, if you were to open them up, you'd find they have different settings for each preset.

2. **Adjust the Smart control knobs until you like what you hear.**

You can play (or record) while you're adjusting these controls. That way, you can try a bunch of settings before settling on the ones you want to record.

3. **If you're still not satisfied with what you hear, click a plug-in and tweak its settings. Repeat (if necessary) for the other plug-ins.**

Don't forget that occasionally turning off a plug-in is more effective (and faster) than trying to tweak it.

4. **If you like the sound enough to want to reuse it someday, click the Save button at the bottom of the library and save it with a descriptive name.**

When you're asked to name a preset or instrument, choose a name other than the instrument or preset's original name. If you use the original name when you save, you run the risk of confusing your preset with the Apple-configured version, which is never a good thing.

Making other changes

When you're satisfied with the sound of your guitar track, here are some more tricks to try:

>> **Double tracking:** Double tracking is an age-old technique to fatten up the sound of a guitar (or voice or other instrument). See Chapter 10 for details.

>> **Finding additional amp models:** Many third-party amp modeling plug-ins are available, but my favorite is AmpliTube (see Figure 8-7). Its assortment of amps, speakers, preamps, stomp box effects, and presets is virtually endless. Even a mediocre guitar sounds better when you play it through an AmpliTube preset.

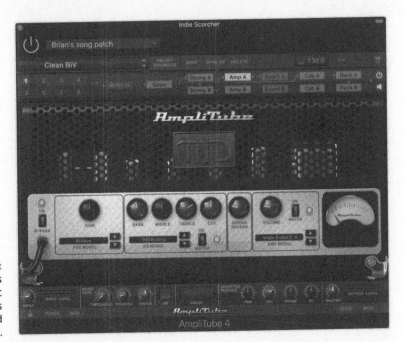

FIGURE 8-7:
AmpliTube offers
dozens of realistic
amp models, plus
stomp boxes and
myriad presets.

3

Postproduction: Finishing Songs on a Mac

Discover the joys of editing your tracks or, as I see it, the joys of fixing your mistakes quickly and easily.

Marvel at the macrocosm known as mixing — that alchemistic undertaking in which you adjust the level and tonal characteristics of each individual track so they all blend together harmoniously.

Uncover the deep, dark secrets of mastering, replete with those fabulous finishing touches that make your recordings sound like the real thing.

IN THIS CHAPTER

» Figuring out when to edit tracks

» Editing software instrument versus real instrument tracks

» Fixing mistakes

» Rearranging regions

» Sweetening

Chapter 9

Editing and Polishing Tracks

This chapter covers the details of editing tracks, which is your last sanity check before you mix and master your song. Here, I ask you to think about editing, arranging, and sweetening your song — all the things you do to give it that little something extra that makes some songs more special than others.

First, I explain some basics: the best time to edit and the important differences between editing software instrument tracks and real instrument tracks. Then, I cover easy ways to fix mistakes without re-recording the entire track. You also discover all-purpose editing techniques that can be used to improve an imperfect track as well as things that you may (or may not) want to add to the song before you mix.

TIP

If you plan to do heavy experimentation on a song, save a copy of it (by choosing File ⇨ Save As) before you begin editing. Then, if your experiment goes awry, you can always go back to the way the song was, even if you've saved again and again while you experimented.

"When Should I Edit Tracks?"

The acts of editing and sweetening aren't time sensitive and can take place at almost any point in production or postproduction. In other words, you don't have to wait until the tracks are in the can to edit, arrange, or sweeten them.

You can do anything any time you like. I prefer to do my editing, arranging, and sweetening (hand claps, tambourines, shakers, and so on) after all (or most) tracks are in the can.

REMEMBER

It's okay to edit or sweeten at any point in the process, but you should try to do all the editing and sweetening *before* you mix and master. If you edit or sweeten a song after you mix and master it, you'll have to go through at least one more cycle of remixing and remastering. Because remixing and remastering can be a huge time sucker, I try to avoid these tasks whenever possible by doing as most editing and sweetening before I even begin a rough mix.

Editing Software Instrument versus Real Instrument Tracks

Not too surprisingly, software instruments offer you the greatest control when it comes to changing almost anything, including individual notes. As you've heard before, real instrument tracks contain recorded song but software instrument tracks contain information about the note you played. Because software instrument tracks contain information rather than recorded sound, you can do things to them that you can't easily do to a real instrument recording, such as changing the intensity, pitch, duration, and sustain of a note or notes, or changing the song's tempo — a little or a lot — without sacrificing sound quality. You can't do most of these things to real instrument tracks.

When editing software or MIDI instruments, you have all sorts of options. Here are just a few examples:

>> **Change the tempo.** If you feel the song is too fast or too slow, you can change the tempo a little or a lot and your software instrument tracks will adapt to the new tempo instantly and sound wonderful most of the time.

>> **Change the pitch.** If you attempt to sing the song but can't reach the highest notes, you can transpose the song into a lower key as long as it doesn't yet contain real instrument tracks.

TECHNICAL STUFF

You can try to correct the pitch of real instrument tracks without third-party plug-ins (with the Pitch Correction control in the editor). But I've never been pleased with the results. Even if you use a high-quality plug-in such as AutoTune, many (if not most) real instrument tracks will sound lousy if you correct or change their pitch.

» **Rearrange the notes.** You can get away with some drastic edits in a software instrument track. For example, moving a note to the left or right changes when it is played, and moving a note up or down changes which note (or, in the case of some instruments including drums, which instrument) is played. You can change the duration of a note by grabbing either edge and dragging to extend or shorten it. To duplicate a note or notes, select them and then Option-drag them to another location in the region. Or copy them (Edit ⇨ Copy or ⌘+C) and then paste them (Edit ⇨ Paste or ⌘+V) into a different part of the track (or a different software instrument track).

TIP

Lay down as many software instrument tracks as you can before recording real instrument tracks. That way you'll have the option of changing the tempo or key for the project. After you add real instrument tracks, you're locked into the key and tempo unless you re-record the real instrument tracks in the new key or tempo.

I explain all the details of editing tempo, pitch, and individual notes in the "Editing Software Instrument Tracks" section, later in this chapter.

You have less control over fixing boo-boos in a real instrument (which includes vocal tracks). Although you can't change sour notes or make them play longer, you still have options. You can do what the pros call a punch-in and punch-out. A *punch-in* and *punch-out* is the act of recording over a section of a track, without touching the rest of the track. So, if you have a mistake in your bass line, guitar line, or even your vocals, you can punch-in over the mistake and fix it.

I made it sound easy to punch-in and -out, but the process is often hard to do properly. When you have a recorded session and try to replace part of that session at a different time or location, the ambient sounds are likely to be different. Or the track might have a particular room sound that would make replacing part of it difficult or impossible anywhere but in the same room with the same microphones — and even then it might not sound quite right.

WARNING

If you have a mistake of that magnitude, you may just have to re-record the entire track.

Fixing Flubs and Faux Pas

GarageBand lets you disguise and fix mistakes in tracks in a number of different ways. I'm a terrible musician and a worse singer, so fixing and disguising mistakes after the fact is almost always faster and easier than re-recording the entire track, at least for me. So the next time you lay down a track that's almost perfect, or find a flaw that you hadn't noticed before in a track, don't delete the track until you've tried some or all of the following techniques.

TIP

Every so often a track has problems that can't be fixed or disguised. In the beginning, you won't know until you try, so check out some of the techniques discussed in this chapter before you press Delete. After a while, you'll have a sixth sense about whether a mistake is fixable the moment that you make it.

Punching in and out to replace part of a track

If you make a mistake when you record a track, you can sometimes fix the mistake by re-recording the part with the mistake. As mentioned, in recording parlance, this process is called *punching in* and *punching out*.

In the olden days, punching in and out was an exotic process that was done only in the best studios using the highest of high-end audio gear. If you were recording at home, your gear was too noisy to get away with punching in much if at all. So if there was a mistake in a track, you either masked it as best you could with the available tools or re-recorded it. As time marched onward, the technique trickled down to consumer recording equipment; today, punching in and out has become a checklist item, available in almost every audio program.

REMEMBER

Punching in using GarageBand is easy; doing it well enough to fool your ears is challenging.

When you punch-in and -out in GarageBand, you use the cycle area to choose which part to re-record.

REMEMBER

When the cycle area is turned on, every time the playhead reaches the end it loops back to the beginning of the cycle area. So the region plays (or records) continually until you click the stop icon or press the spacebar.

To punch-in and -out on a track, follow these steps:

1. **With your song open, click the cycle icon (shown in the margin) or press C to activate the cycle area.**

A yellow ruler appears under the beat ruler showing the cycle area, as shown in Figure 9-1. The first time you use the cycle area, it appears at the far left end of the beat ruler. But if you move the cycle area, it will reappear where you moved it the next time you turn it on.

Record icon   Cycle icon   Cycle area   Zoom slider

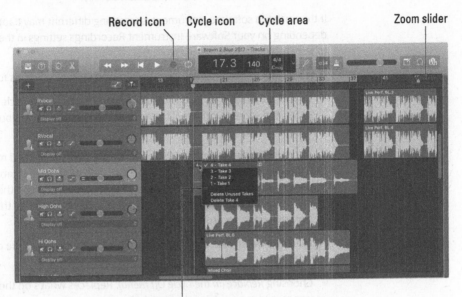

Take folder pop-up menu

FIGURE 9-1:
Click the cycle icon to turn on the cycle area.

2. **Select the track that needs to be fixed.**

3. **Find the precise part that you want to re-record by moving the playhead and listening to the track.**

4. **Position the cycle area over the part that you want to re-record.**

   Click and drag the middle of the yellow cycle area to move it; click and drag on either end to extend or shrink it.

   Use the zoom slider in the upper-right corner of the ruler to zoom in (or out) on the timeline if you need to.

   TIP

5. **It's almost impossible to perform a decent punch-in without using GarageBand's count-in feature, so choose Record ⇨ Count In and select 1 Bar or 2 Bars.**

   TIP

6. **Click play or press the spacebar to play the contents of the cycle area:**

   • *If the area contains the exact part you want to re-record, proceed to Step 7.*

   • *If not, continue to move, expand, and contract the cycle area until it contains only the precise portion of the track you want to re-record, and then proceed to Step 7.*

7. **To start recording, click the record icon (labeled in Figure 9-1) or press R.**

8. **Record the part one or more times.**

   If the track is a real instrument, each time you record the part with the cycle area enabled, a take will be created automatically.

   If the track is a software instrument, something different may happen, depending on your Software Instrument Recordings settings in the General tab of Preferences, shown in Figure 9-2.

   When the cycle area is turned on, punching into a track works as follows:

   - *Choosing Create Takes (in the Cycle On menu):* Turns on the cycle area, which works the same as on a real instrument track, and enables you to record multiple takes.

   - *Choosing Merge (in the Cycle On menu):* Records each take and merges it with the previous takes. For example, you can play snare drum on the first pass, the hi-hat on the second pass, and the ride cymbal on the third pass. Then, when you click the stop icon or press the spacebar, all three passes will have been recorded on the same track. Neat, eh?

   You can also determine how punching into a track works with the cycle area turned off:

   - Choosing *Replace (in the Cycle Off menu):* Replaces what's on the track when you record over previously recorded regions.

   - Choosing *Merge (in the Cycle Off menu):* Records each take and merges it with the previous takes.

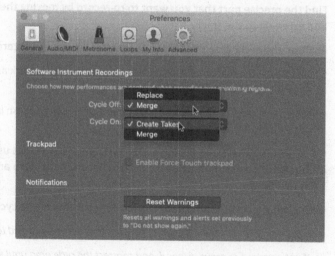

FIGURE 9-2:
Preferences General tab with both Software Instrument Recordings pop-up menus popped up.

If punching in doesn't behave as you expect for a software instrument track, double-check your settings in the General tab's Software Instrument Recordings section.

9. **When you've finished playing the part, stop recording by clicking the play icon or pressing the spacebar.**

10. **Click the little numeral in the upper-left corner of the region and then select the take you want from the Take folder pop-up menu.**

   The numeral represents the number of takes (4 in Figure 9-1). The selected take plays while the other takes are muted.

   Use the solo icon, if necessary, to listen critically to your takes and then choose the best one or record additional takes.

11. **Click the cycle icon or press C to turn off the cycle area.**

Just undo it . . . and then redo it

With GarageBand, it's easy to undo many mistakes immediately. You can undo the last thing that you did. But did you know that you can undo the next-to-last thing you did, and the thing before that one, and the thing before that, and so on?

The first time you use the undo feature, it reverses the last change that you made. But tell GarageBand to undo a second time, and it undoes the action before that. You can continue to use undo as needed.

Here's a quick list of undo and redo commands:

» **To undo the previous action:** Choose Edit ⇨ Undo or press ⌘+Z.

» **To redo what you just undid:** Choose Edit ⇨ Redo or press ⌘+Shift-Z; what you undid will be redone.

» **To get the ultimate undo:** Choose File ⇨ Revert to Saved, and your song goes back to the way it was the last time you saved it.

The undo and redo features are linear, so pay close attention. It's easy to undo something good — something that you *didn't* want to have undone — if you just keep pressing the shortcut without watching what happens each time. Don't rely too heavily on undo and redo. I recommend you save a copy of your song before you begin undoing or redoing by choosing File ⇨ Save As.

If you're not sure what you're about to undo or redo, the Edit menu is your friend, as shown in Figure 9-3.

| File | **Edit** | Track | Record | Mix | Share |

Undo Drag	⌘Z
Redo Delete	⇧⌘Z
Cut	⌘X
Copy	⌘C
Paste	⌘V
Paste Replace	⇧⌘V
Delete	
Delete and Move	
Select All	⌘A
Split Regions at Playhead	⌘T
Join Regions	⌘J
✓ Snap to Grid	⌘G
Alignment Guides	⌥⌘G

FIGURE 9-3:
The Edit menu
tells you what
you're about to
undo or redo.

Splitting and joining regions

You can take any region on any type of track and divide it into two or more parts. This technique has many practical uses, but the one you'll probably use most is deleting part of a region.

From a cough to a sour note, splitting a region is the most direct, easiest, and often the best way to edit out a part of a track that you no longer need.

TIP

If you trim out dead space in live instrument tracks, your songs will have a brighter, cleaner sound. For example, if you start recording 12 seconds before the guitar plays the first note, you should trim out those 12 seconds of dead space. The same goes for vocals — if you recorded air, trim it out because that dead space has noise in it. Deleting the dead space lowers the overall noise level for your song. So if you want the cleanest, brightest mix possible, delete dead space longer than 2–3 seconds on any real instrument track. It's a hassle, but your song will sound better for your trouble.

To split a region, follow these steps:

1. **Click the region once to select it.**

   To split regions on multiple tracks, click and drag a box to select them or hold down Shift and click to add additional regions.

2. **Move the playhead to the precise point where you want the split to occur.**

3. **Choose Edit ➪ Split Regions at Playhead or press ⌘+T.**

4. **Click to select the part of the region that you want to delete and then press Delete or Backspace.**

In Figure 9-4, I selected the first region on six tracks — Bright Country, AC-30Clean 2, LVocal, RVocal, RVocal2, and Punk Bass — and split them. My goal is to remove the approximately 2 seconds of silence before the instruments (and voices) begin.

The regions were first split at the playhead. I then selected the silent parts (the left half of the split, as shown in the top image in Figure 9-4). With the left part of all six regions selected, I pressed Delete (or Backspace) to remove them from their tracks (bottom).

Go ahead and try it out. I have all the time in the world.

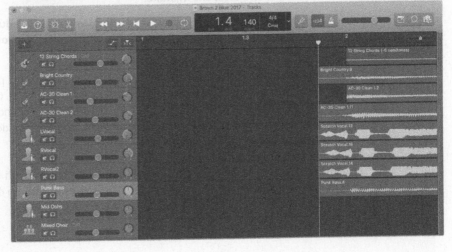

FIGURE 9-4:
Six regions split at the playhead before (top) and after deleting the left part of each split region (bottom).

You can split a region into as many regions as you want. If you're cutting out part of a track, you may need to add a second split to isolate the section that you want to delete. After you do that, select the section of the track that needs to go and delete it by pressing Backspace or Delete.

Silencing mistakes with the track volume control

Some tracks just can't be fixed. But if nothing else so far in this chapter has helped, you can try one more tool: the track volume control, which you use to make the mistake fade out gradually so that no one knows that the mistake was ever there.

Here's how to use the track volume automation control to erase a mistake:

1. **Click the automation icon at the top of the track list (shown in the margin).**

   The track volume control is now enabled.

2. **Select the track that you want to adjust and choose Volume from the Automation Parameter pop-up menu.**

   Listen to the track and find the mistake.

3. **Click the track volume control's rubber band to create a control point one or two seconds before the mistake.**

4. **Add two more control points in the middle of the mistake, and another a second or two after the mistake.**

5. **Now drag the two middle control points downwards to reduce or eliminate the sound during that portion of the track, as shown in Figure 9-5.**

TIP

   To find the precise location to start fading out and in, move the playhead back and forth and click the play icon or press the spacebar to listen. Or use the cycle area to listen to a small segment repeatedly. When you find the mistake, begin your fade out before the mistake occurs and end your fade-in after the mistake ends.

This trick won't work every time, but if your song has enough other stuff going on, you can usually fade a mistake right out of the mix, with no one (except yourself) the wiser.

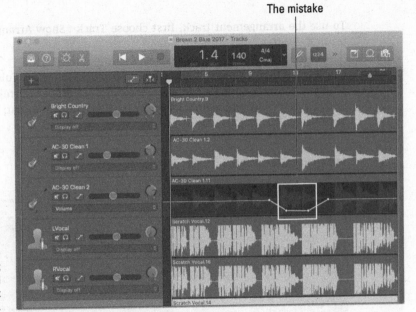

The mistake

FIGURE 9-5:
I played the wrong chord, but the rubber band cheat removes it from the mix.

Rearranging Regions

It's important to remember that with digital recording, you can easily move anything to anywhere. You can take any region and drag it anywhere on the timeline, even to an entirely different track. You can also copy and paste regions anywhere on any track.

REMEMBER

You can move real instrument and software instrument regions anywhere on the timeline with just one proviso: Software instrument regions can go only on software instrument tracks; real instrument regions can go only on real instrument tracks.

The arrangement track and markers

GarageBand offers an *arrangement track* and *arrangement markers* to denote different sections, such as an intro, verse, or chorus. You can then move the sections around the tracks area to rearrange your project.

Arrangement markers can be particularly useful when you add material (recordings, loops, or media files) to the project and want to try out different arrangements, such as repeating the bridge later in the song or repeating a chorus more than once.

To use the arrangement track, first choose Track⇨Show Arrangement Track or press ⌘+Shift+A.

You'll see a thin strip above the track names just below the ruler. Click + in the strip to add your first arrangement marker at the start of the project; click + again to add the second arrangement marker to the right of the first; continue adding arrangement markers as needed, as shown in Figure 9-6.

Add arrangement marker Arrangement markers   Arrangement track

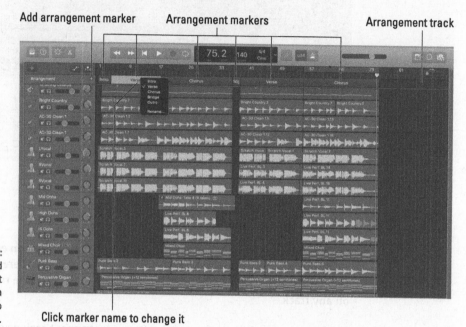

Click marker name to change it

FIGURE 9-6: Click + to add arrangement markers; click a marker's name to change it.

To change a marker's name, click it and select a new name from the drop-down menu (Verse in Figure 9-6).

You can resize or move a marker the same way you resize or move the cycle area, as described earlier in this chapter. Click and drag on either side of the marker's name to move it left or right; click and drag on either end to extend or shrink it.

You might find three other attributes of the arrangement track useful. First, when you move an arrangement marker, all regions on all tracks move with it. Think about that for a moment. In my experience, moving regions often requires tweaking every track to make the transition sound decent.

Pay close attention when you drag arrangement markers around in the arrangement track and remember to use undo if you make a mess of things.

TIP

Second, if you press the Option key on your QWERTY keyboard before clicking and dragging an arrangement marker, you'll create a copy of the marker, as shown in Figure 9-7. This feature is especially useful if, for example, you decide you want the last verse to repeat twice but you recorded it only once.

FIGURE 9-7:
Press Option before you click and drag an arrangement marker to create an identical copy.

Finally, if you create arrangement markers before you add a drummer track, that drummer track will create a separate region (and drumming pattern) for each marker, which is pretty sweet.

For what it's worth, I find that last attribute the most useful. But if I'm not planning to use a drummer track, I don't usually bother with the arrangement track. I'm old-school when it comes to editing tracks, and I'm still more comfortable splitting, duplicating, copying, and pasting regions by hand.

That said, *you* should definitely try the arrangement track. Even though I don't use it much, you might love it.

Editing Software Instrument Tracks

Software instrument (green) tracks offer the greatest flexibility for editing. You can, of course, choose a different instrument, but you can also change the pitch or tempo (and not just by a little), without ill effect. You can't do those things to real instruments. If you alter their tempo or pitch very much, they'll sound unnatural — or worse.

REMEMBER

As I've said before, I recommend laying down software instrument tracks before you begin recording real instrument tracks. That way, if you decide the tempo is too slow or too fast, or the pitch is too high or too low, you can make the appropriate changes to the software instrument tracks without re-recording them. If you record real instrument tracks first and then decide that a song is too slow, fast, high, or low, you will have to re-record all the real instrument tracks.

Changing the tempo of a song

GarageBand lets you change the tempo of an entire song but not the tempo of an individual track. If you change the tempo of one track, you have to change the tempo of all the tracks.

If that's what you want to do — change the tempo of the song — click the Tempo readout on the digital display in the toolbar and drag upward to increase the tempo or downward to decrease it.

Changing the tempo of song parts

You can also change the tempo for just part (or parts) of a song with the tempo track. To enable the tempo track, choose Track⇨Show Tempo Track or use its keyboard shortcut, ⌘+Shift+T. Now you can create tempo changes by double-clicking the tempo track rubber band to add a tempo point. You can then edit a point's values by either

>> Clicking and dragging the tempo point up or down

>> Pressing ⌘+Option+Control and clicking the target time position, and then typing a new bpm value and pressing Return

To create a *tempo curve* to transition smoothly between two tempo points, select the two tempo points and then click and drag the tip of the right-angle line (corner) above or below the second tempo point. The *Move Tempo Curve Automation Point* help tag appears when you click in the right spot, as shown in Figure 9-8.

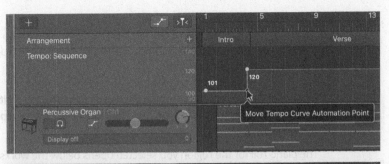

FIGURE 9-8:
Click the corner
of the second
tempo point (top)
and drag it to
create a tempo
curve (bottom).

You can adjust the range of values for the tempo track by either

>> Grabbing the maximum or minimum values (140 and 90 in Figure 9-8) in the tempo scale and dragging vertically

>> Double-clicking either value and entering a numeric value in the field

Finally, you can delete a tempo point by either

>> Clicking the tempo point or the line to the right of it, and then choosing Edit ➪ Delete or pressing the Delete key

>> Double-clicking the tempo point

And that's how you change a project's tempo for the entire song or parts of it.

Changing the pitch

If you can't sing the highest notes or, as often happens to me, you can play the part more easily in a different key, you can change the pitch of any software instrument track at any time and it won't affect the rest of your tracks.

But as I mention earlier in this chapter, changing pitch works well only with software instrument tracks.

If you want to change the key of the entire song, you have to do the following for each instrument (except drums and percussion instruments). To change the pitch of a software instrument track:

1. **Double-click the region for which you want to change the pitch, or single-click to select the region and then click the editors icon (shown in the margin).**

   The piano roll for the region you selected opens below the workspace (timeline), as shown in Figure 9-9.

2. **Move the Transpose slider (on the left side of the piano roll) to the left or right to make the pitch of your loop rise or fall.**

   The number that's changing is the number of half steps from the original pitch.

TIP

You may want to change the pitch by a little or a lot, depending on your intent. If you can't quite hit the highest note in a song, dropping the song's pitch by one, two, or three half steps ought to do the trick.

TIP

I often make my software instrument tracks sound different by transposing them up or down a full octave, which is 12 half steps. Sometimes when I double-track an instrument, I'll transpose one of the tracks up or down an octave for a fuller sound. A benefit of transposing by a factor of 12 is that you don't have to change the pitch of any other instrument tracks.

3. **Listen to the track by clicking the play icon or pressing the spacebar on your keyboard.**

   Click the solo icon if necessary to listen to only the transposed track.

4. **Adjust the Transpose setting some more if necessary.**

5. **(Optional) Click the editor icon again to hide the editor portion of the timeline window.**

REMEMBER

Be careful if you change the pitch of just one loop or track. The new pitch needs to be in the same key as other loops and tracks, or it will sound icky. Without getting into a bunch of musical theory that is beyond the scope of this book (plus, I couldn't explain it to you anyway), just remember to listen and confirm that everything sounds right after you adjust the pitch — or after you adjust most things, for that matter.

Rearranging notes in a region

Now, without further ado, here's how to fine-tune a software instrument region by rearranging the notes. Remember, in the track list, mixer, and regions in the timeline, blue denotes a real instrument and green denotes a software instrument.

REMEMBER

Before undertaking any major surgery on your song, it's a good idea to save a copy of the song by choosing File ⇨ Save As and entering a new name for the file before clicking the Save button. That way, if you screw things up totally, you can go back to where you were before you made the changes by opening the original (and un-screwed up) song file.

To edit a software instrument track, follow these steps:

1. **Double-click the region whose notes you want to edit, or single-click to select the region and then click the editors icon.**

   I recorded a take using the Classic Rock Organ software instrument from the Vintage B3 Organ category. The notes I played are represented by a series of dashes on a grid in the editor.

2. **Expand the editor.**

   To do so, hover the cursor over the dividing line between the workspace (timeline) and the editor, as shown in Figure 9-9. When the cursor turns into a resizer (as shown in the margin), you're over the right spot to drag upward and expand the editor area.

Resizer cursor   Dividing line

FIGURE 9-9: Use the resizer cursor to click the dividing line, and then drag up to enlarge the editor or down to reduce it.

TIP

Each dash represents a single note in your region. By default, GarageBand displays software instrument (MIDI) notes as dashes, which it calls a *piano roll*. If you prefer the more traditional staff and notation, click the Score button at the top of the editor, as shown in Figure 9-10.

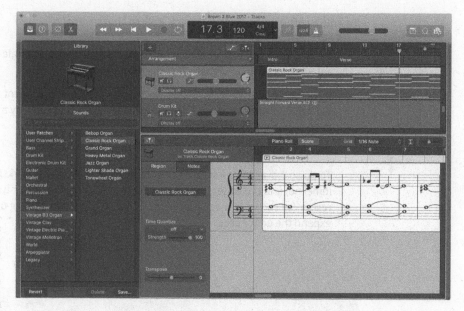

FIGURE 9-10:
To edit a traditional score instead of dashes, click the Score button.

I use the piano roll for this example not because it's better but because I prefer it to notation. If you would rather work with notation, substitute the word *note* for the *dash* in the following description.

Dashes of various lengths displayed in a green track are the notes, and each horizontal line in that graph represents a different note on the musical scale or instrument or both, depending on the software instrument.

TIP

If you don't see the dashes after you record, use the scroll bar to scroll up and down in the editor until you find them, or click the dividing line and expand the editor (refer to Figure 9-9).

3. **Change the zoom in the editor so that you can see the notes that you want to edit, as shown in Figure 9-11.**

TIP

The editor has its own zoom control at the right edge of its toolbar. It works just like the timeline zoom control — slide it to the right to zoom in on the notes in the editor. You see fewer notes but have finer control over the individual notes that you do see. Conversely, slide it to the left to zoom out. You see more notes at once, but they're smaller and harder to drag around.

Each dash represents a measure, and the size of each dash grows when you zoom in. The top picture shows 65 measures of MIDI information, the middle picture shows 17 measures, and the bottom picture shows less than 4.

TIP

If you've recorded many higher and lower notes, you might have to scroll up or down in the editor to see them all.

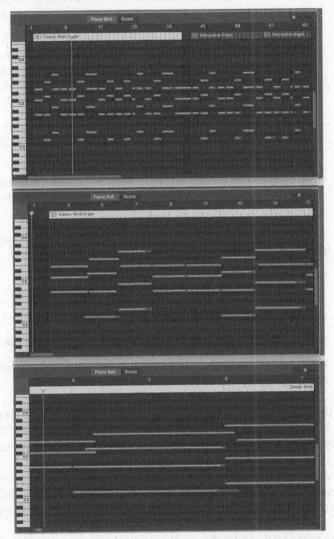

FIGURE 9-11:
Editing the software instrument track at three zoom levels: least (top), more zoom (middle), and most zoom (bottom).

4. **To edit the notes in the editor, click one of the dashes to select it.**

   Do you hear that? When you click a dash, you're "playing" the note that it represents. To select multiple notes, either click them while holding down the

Shift key or drag a selection rectangle around them. With the note or notes selected, you can start making changes.

Here's a quick list of edits you can make to notes:

- **To move a note or notes:** Slide the note to the right or the left on the same horizontal line, and you change *when* it is played. Slide the note up or down to a different horizontal line and you change the *pitch* of the note. It's that simple! When you move a dash, you change when the note is played, the pitch of the note, or both.

- **To change the length of a note:** Click the note that you want to change; then grab the right edge and drag it to the right or the left. Dragging the edge to the right lengthens the note, and dragging it to the left shortens the note.

- **To duplicate a note:** Option-drag the note to another spot on the grid. You can do the same thing with multiple notes by Shift-clicking or dragging a selection rectangle around as many dashes as you want.

- **To delete a note:** Select the note (single-click it) and press Delete (or Backspace). Again, you can select multiple notes and delete them the same way.

5. **To create a new note without touching the keyboard (the music keyboard, that is), press ⌘ and click anywhere in the editor grid.**

   When you press ⌘, your cursor changes to a little pencil.

   As always, listen to your changes by clicking the dash you just created, clicking the play icon, or pressing the spacebar on your QWERTY keyboard.

6. **When you're satisfied, you can close the editor by clicking the editor icon.**

7. **When you're absolutely sure you're satisfied, save your changes by choosing File ⇨ Save.**

Use the Time Quantize drop-down menu and slider to move notes to the nearest beat in the grid. If no notes are selected, the drop-down menu affects all notes in the region; if notes are selected, the menu affects only those notes.

Quantization is a great way to perform a quick-and-dirty fix on some tracks. For example, if you have a MIDI drum track with some beats slightly out of time, quantizing the region to the nearest 1/8 or 1/16 note may fix the beats that were off.

Listen to the track, and if the results aren't what you expected, choose Edit ⇨ Undo or use the shortcut ⌘+Z, choose a different value from the Time Quantize menu, and try again. Repeat the process until you're satisfied.

TIP

The grid scale affects the amount of correction applied. A scale set to 1/1 Note moves the note more than a scale set to 1/32 Note.

TIP

Be careful when using the quantize feature. If you have pickup notes or anything funky or off-beat, you may mess up your track by *fixing* its timing. If you don't like the results, undo the fix immediately, lest you lose your chance by saving or crashing before you do (undo).

Finally, to change the velocity (loudness) of a note, click the note (or Shift-click multiple notes) and then slide the Velocity slider. The velocity scale runs from 0 (silent) to 127 (loudest). To increase the velocity of all notes in the region, click anywhere in the editor and choose Edit⇨Select All (or use its keyboard shortcut ⌘+A) before moving the Velocity slider all the way to the right (to 127).

Sweetening: Add New Material? Or Not?

Now that you've seen how to edit tracks and remove excess gunk, you should consider one last thing before you're ready to mix and master: Does this song need anything else? If it does, that's called *sweetening,* which is otherwise known as adding one or more tracks during postproduction.

Why would you want to add something else to your song at this point? If the song needed it, you would have recorded it, right?

Well, one truism about producing music is that less is usually more. The fastest way to wreck a perfectly good song is to add one more track to it.

That is, unless you actually need that track.

Deciding when to sweeten a track is subjective. But a time will come when you'll need to add that track to your song to take it from good to great, so in this section I provide you with food for thought.

REMEMBER

An old poker maxim says, "Look for a reason to fold." It means that you should not look for reasons to pay more money to stay in the game, but rather you should look for a reason to stop wasting money on the hand and lay down your cards. I am going to rejigger that phrase with a musical twist and tell you that when you're recording a song, you should look for a reason to leave it alone. Make it your mantra, and say it along with me now:

Look for a reason to leave it alone.

Okay, now that you have the right frame of mind, you're ready to look at some of the times when you may be better off *not* leaving a song alone and adding one or more tracks before you mix.

Many songs recorded during the last several decades have been comprised of one or two guitars, drums, a bass, some keyboards, a lead vocal, and maybe background singers. But many more hit songs had all that plus one other memorable thing, such as percussion, backing vocals, special effects, horn, woodwinds, or strings.

In the sections that follow, I talk about some familiar examples (familiar to me, at least) of songs with worthwhile extras, and I give you tips for adding them to your song with GarageBand.

Percussion

Think about the Beatles song "I Wanna Hold Your Hand." What's the best part of the song? The handclaps are it for me.

What about the cowbell part in Blue Oyster Cult's "Don't Fear the Reaper"? An entire *Saturday Night Live* sketch was dedicated to that cowbell! (I also have a love/hate relationship with the sound of the cowbell in "Mississippi Queen," by Leslie West's Mountain.)

From maracas to a guiro and from a tambourine to a triangle (can you say, "Comfortably Numb"), sometimes just a whack or two on a percussion instrument is what a song needs.

REMEMBER

Don't forget your loops. If you can't play what you want to hear or you can't find the right instrument to play it, try your loops. You can find a loop or part of a loop for almost every occasion. Chapter 5 is all about loops.

Backing vocals

Does your song have backing vocals? Does it need them? Are you capable?

A backing vocal can often be the backbone of a song. Heck, in some songs, I find myself singing along with the backing vocal instead of the lead part. The chorus of "What I Like about You," by the Romantics, leaps to mind, or maybe the "oohs" in "All My Loving," by the Beatles.

Many of the songs in your music library probably have compelling backup vocals.

I wouldn't presume to tell you how to write music, but I will tell you that the best way to find that magic is to experiment. So if you think your song might benefit from backing vocals, create a new track and sing a few "oohs" or "la-la-la-la-las." Or hum. Or click. There's no telling what may come out. Who knows, the killer counter-melody might come rolling off your lips.

Greek chorus

Or how about the Greek chorus approach? Edwin Starr had a huge hit in the '70s with his anthem "War." The backing vocals are a classic Greek chorus school of backup vocals.

On paper it would look like this:

> War! Huh! Good God, ya'll!
>
> What is it good for?
>
> Absolutely nothing!
>
> Say it again!

But here's how it's sung:

> Everyone: "War! Huh!"
>
> Edwin: "Good God ya'll!"
>
> Backup singers: "What is it good for?"
>
> Edwin: "Absolutely"
>
> Backup singers: "Nothing!"
>
> Edwin: "Say it again!"

It all flows together, and I bet when you sing it, you sing it as if it were one person singing the whole thing. But if that were the case, it wouldn't sound like it does. Most songs wouldn't work with a back-and-forth Greek chorus background vocal like that, but you never know.

Harmony vocals

Some parts of the song may beg for a harmony vocal, and the right harmony track can make a great song out of what was merely a good one.

TIP If you don't know how to sing harmony, take some vocal classes.

Again, when it comes to harmony, less is more. Using a harmony vocal throughout your entire song is usually a bad idea (with "Bye Bye Love," by the Everly Brothers, being one possible exception). If you think that your song needs a harmony vocal, try adding it on just the verse, or the chorus, or even just one verse or chorus.

Special effects

Producers have been adding sound effects to popular music for as long as people have been listening to music. From the spooky Theremin floating throughout the Beach Boys' classic, "Good Vibrations," to the toll of the bells in Pink Floyd's "Time" or the cash register in "Money" — or even the crying tires and the busting glass in J. Frank Wilson's "Last Kiss" — the right sound effect at the right place in the right song can make all the difference in the world.

On the other hand, a wrongly placed sound can make your serious attempt sound like a song parody. So once again, look for a reason to leave it alone.

If you feel you must, you can create interesting sounds using many different software instruments including most of the synth presets. Or record the sound to a real instrument track using a microphone. The only limit is your imagination.

Horns, woodwinds, and strings

Once upon a time, it would have cost tens of thousands of dollars to add horns or strings to a song, but today a full orchestra is at your command, just a MIDI keyboard away. You can lay down a layer of sophisticated musical goodness underneath your song — from an upright bass to a string ensemble.

This is another example of something you need to experiment with to know whether it's going to work in a song. Don't be afraid to try anything. You never know what will sound totally cool, and you can always delete your change if it doesn't.

Unless you know how to arrange a song for woodwinds, horns, or strings, you may want to keep it simple. In other words, playing a single horn or string part is easier than building an entire marching band or string ensemble arrangement.

As awesome as synthesized and sampled horns, woodwinds, and strings are with modern technology, real musicians often sound better. It's hard to mimic all the nuances and subtle sounds live musicians coax from their instruments, but you can come pretty darn close using software instruments.

Of course, this is *GarageBand For Dummies* and not *Million Dollar Recording Studios For Dummies*, so use those software instruments and try adding strings or horns to your project.

If it sounds good, nobody will notice (or care) that you didn't use real violins or trumpets.

IN THIS CHAPTER

» **Finding out what mixing is**

» **Setting levels**

» **Panning tracks left or right**

» **Adding effects**

» **Doubling tracks**

Chapter **10**

Mixing Tracks into Songs

he tracks are in the can. You've edited, tweaked, and cleaned each track until it's the best it can be, and added a few more to sweeten your project. Now you're ready to convert that pile of individual tracks into a song. I'm talking, of course, about mixing.

In this chapter, you learn what mixing is, and then you discover how to mix a song. You conclude with an age-old studio trick that can make your mix better with little effort.

What Is Mixing?

When you've done all you can with individual tracks, it is time to blend them harmoniously by mixing the tracks together to create a stereo track you can master and then export, listen to, and share with others.

Here's how mixing works. Play each track and do the following:

1. Set its level so it blends harmoniously with the others.

2. Set its pan (left/right) to place this instrument (or vocal) in its place in the imaginary stereo sound field.

3. **Add effects, such as echo, reverb, and compression (if needed).**

TIP

Not every track needs effects. In fact, adding too many effects is a common mistake, particularly when the producer is new to multitrack recording. Forewarned is forearmed; don't overdo it. Remember your mantra: "Look for a reason to leave it alone."

I mix my songs in the same order as the preceding steps — set the levels, set the pan, and then add effects. But that order isn't ironclad; if you want to add effects before you set your pan positions, go for it. The point is that three fairly discrete components make up the mixing process. You need to pay attention to all three if you want the final song to sound its very best.

REMEMBER

When you master your song (which you explore in the next chapter), you pretty much repeat the mixing process. But rather than tweaking individual tracks, you set levels, pan, and so on for the entire song all at once on the master track.

TIP

Take your time mixing your songs. Experiment and try different combinations of levels, pan, EQ, and effects. The mix is where the magic occurs; I often spend more time on mixing than recording.

You don't need a degree in musicology or even audio engineering to mix. All you really need are ears. There is no right or wrong mix; the perfect mix is the one that sounds right to you.

To me, mixing is the most creative part of the production and postproduction process — and the most fun. Mixing is where you add that special something that makes your song "music" and not just a collection of recorded tracks.

Now relax, get comfortable, and let's mix.

Creating a Level Playing Field

In general, you're shooting for a mix in which no instrument or voice overpowers the others, and each instrument or vocal can be heard clearly. So, the first step in mixing is usually to create a rough mix, where you set the level of each track relative to the other tracks. Then you can fine-tune the levels of each track. All the while, keep an eye on both individual track levels and the master level to make sure they all stay out of the red.

The following sections have the details.

Roughing it with a rough mix

Before you do anything else — before you touch the pan control or add effects — you create a rough mix for each track so that no instrument or vocal track is dominant and all the tracks can be heard clearly. Create your rough mix by following these steps:

1. Play your song by clicking the play icon or pressing the spacebar, and then listen closely to the levels.

Is any instrument or vocal far too loud or soft? Are you hearing every instrument and vocal track?

2. Adjust the level of each track that seems too soft or too loud by moving its slider control to the left or right in the Mixer column.

TIP

Keep an eye on the master level meter near the upper-right corner of the timeline window; it represents the level of your stereo mix. If you make a track too hot, you'll probably overload the master level meter and see some red. If you keep an eye on the meter now, you won't have to readjust your levels later to prevent clipping.

In addition to watching for red LEDs on your track level meters, also watch out for those red LEDs on the master level meter. Your goal is to keep track levels set so that you see little or no red on the master level meter.

3. Listen to the song again to see how adjusting the level affected the rough mix. If the levels still aren't quite right, keep tweaking using the level sliders.

I usually spend a few minutes adjusting level controls for any tracks that are too loud or soft. I then listen and adjust any tracks that are still too loud or soft. When I have a reasonably good balance and nothing is horribly loud or soft, I move on to the next step, knowing that I can always make additional adjustments later if necessary.

And that's all there is to the first step in the process. You now have a rough mix of your song.

TIP

You can use the mute and solo icons in the Tracks column to enable or disable tracks when you're working on your rough mix. I usually mute the vocal tracks until I have a rough mix of the instrument tracks. Then I unmute the vocal tracks and mix them in.

When you're satisfied with your rough mix, it's time to begin mixing in earnest by fine-tuning your levels, which is what the next section is all about.

A fine tune

Now you'll give your song a more critical listening, this time searching for *parts* of tracks that are too loud or too soft. If you have a wonderful vocal that sounds perfect during the verses but overloads the level meters during the louder choruses, you can fine-tune the track so that its level is perfect all the way through.

The track volume automation control is the key. You use it to lower the level of the vocal during those overly loud choruses so that the entire track plays without seeing red in the meters.

TIP

You can use this technique also to emphasize a solo or disguise a flubbed part.

Figure 10-1 shows a mix that's been fine-tuned by using the track volume control on two of the four tracks. The acoustic guitar (Acoustic Harmonics) is louder during the introduction and chorus and quieter during the verse; the electric guitar (Big Brute Blues) is softer during the intro and chorus and louder during the verse. Note how the chorus begins at measure 5, with the acoustic guitar getting louder and the electric guitar getting softer.

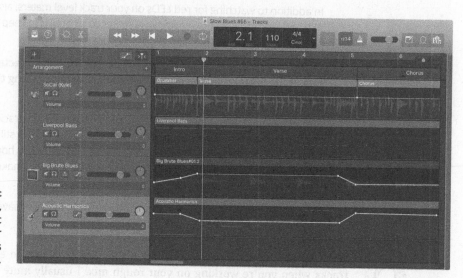

FIGURE 10-1:
A fine-tuned mix, with the acoustic and electric guitar part levels automated.

TIP

I almost always mix drums and bass (the rhythm section) first, and I rarely use the track volume control for either. The rhythm section usually remains at a constant level throughout the entire song — except when it doesn't. (Every rule has exceptions.)

To use the track volume automation control for a track, follow these steps:

1. **Enable automation by choosing Mix ⇨ Show Automation or pressing the A key on your QWERTY keyboard.**

2. **Select Volume from the Automation Parameter pop-up menu for the track you want to tweak (if it's not already selected).**

3. **Find the point in your track where you want to raise or lower the level.**

   To find the right spot, move the playhead and click the play button or press the spacebar.

4. **Click the track volume control (rubber band) to create your first control point.**

   It's best to start your adjustment a little before the part where you want the level adjustment to occur.

5. **Click near the beginning of the part, near the end of the part, and several beats after the end of the part to create three more control points.**

6. **Drag the two control points in the middle upward or downward to increase or decrease the sound for that part.**

7. **Listen to what you've done and make any adjustments.**

   If it doesn't sound smooth and natural, try dragging the control points around a little — up or down to change the level, or left or right to change the duration.

Level meters: Red = dead

Each track has a pair of level meters for its left and right channels. Be sure and pay attention to them as you mix your song. If the level of any track is too hot (that is, too high), you'll introduce distortion and other undesirable crud to your song — something you should avoid at all costs.

If a track's level is too hot, you'll see red LEDs on the right side of its level meters. In a nutshell, no track should be red for more than a second, and it's better if you see no red at all.

The most important level meters of all are the master level meters near the upper-right corner. These indicate the level for the left and right channel of the stereo mix. If *they* go into the red, you risk ruining the entire song. So although it's important to keep individual tracks out of the red, it's even more important that the master levels aren't too hot.

The master levels reflect the combined levels of all the tracks. If your master levels are hot, reduce the level of one or more tracks. Ideally, you want to see as much green and yellow as possible and little or no red.

Panning Tracks Left or Right

When you're satisfied with your levels, it's time to look at panning your tracks. *Pan* determines how much of each track is sent to the left and right speaker. The object of panning is to create an imaginary stereo sound field and to place instruments on the virtual stage.

For example, suppose that the acoustic guitar player is on the far right side of the stage, the singer and drummer are smack dab in the middle, the bass player is just to the right of the drummer, and the electric guitarist is on the far left side. Figure 10-2 shows tracks that are panned to create the illusion that I just described.

FIGURE 10-2: Drums (SoCal Kyle) and vocals (Bright Vocal) are panned dead center; acoustic and electric guitars (Acoustic Harmonics and Big Brute Blues) are panned hard right and hard left, respectively; bass (Liverpool Bass) is panned soft right.

You can even create the illusion that one instrument is closer to the front of the stage than others with effects such as delay, reverb, and echo. For more on these terms, see "The Effects of Adding Effects," later in this chapter.

The ear is less sensitive to the direction of low frequencies such as a bass guitar or kick drum, so bass and drums are usually panned dead center. All other instruments and voices, though, are candidates for panning.

REMEMBER

Another objective in mixing is to separate different but similar-sounding instruments so that you can hear that they're two different instruments. To that end, you should avoid panning instruments in the same frequency range to the same side. Here's an example: If your song has guitar and harmonica tracks (both occupy the midrange), you should pan one to the left and the other to the right. If you panned them both the same way, they blend, and neither will sound as clear and distinct as when they're panned to opposite sides.

Pan positions range from no pan, or dead center, to all the way to the left or right, known as panning the track hard left or hard right, respectively. The other positions are described as if the knob were a clock face. So a track panned halfway to the right, such as the bass track in Figure 10-2, is panned right to 2 o'clock.

As I said earlier, mixing is not an exact science. However, if you're trying to create a song that sounds like what you hear on the radio, here are some suggestions for panning particular instruments and vocal parts:

>> **Drums:** If the drums are a loop and contained on a single track, I pan them dead center. But if I have separate drum tracks for different drum parts, I may pan the kick drum and snare dead center and the tom-toms and cymbals a little off-center, say to 11 o'clock and 1 o'clock, respectively.

>> **Bass:** Remember what I said earlier about low frequencies being less directional? I usually pan the bass dead center or possibly slightly off-center (no farther than 11 o'clock or 1 o'clock).

>> **Guitar:** There's no hard and fast rule here. I sometimes pan the lead guitar hard left or hard right and the rhythm guitar hard to the opposite side. Other times, I pan the lead guitar a little to one side and the rhythm guitar a little to the opposite side — say, 2 o'clock and 10 o'clock.

>> **Keyboards/organs/pianos/synths:** Again, there's no set rule about where keyboard instruments sound best in a mix, so they might go left or right or even center if the drums and bass aren't completely filling the center of the mix. If you have guitar parts and keyboard parts, it's usually best to pan guitars one way and keyboards the other. In this case, the lead guitar might be panned left to 2 o'clock, the rhythm guitar panned hard left, and the keyboard panned somewhere on the right.

>> **Lead vocal:** This vocal is usually panned dead center or slightly off-center. If I double a vocal track, I pan one track slightly left, to about 10:30, and the doubled vocal to the right, at about 1:30.

WARNING

>> **Background vocals:** I almost always double background vocals and usually pan one track hard left and the second track hard right. If I want an even thicker harmony vocal sound, I sometimes add a third instance of the track panned dead center but with a lower level than the left and right ones. This gives a kind of Beach Boys effect to the background vocals.

Be careful: The middle of the sound field gets mighty crowded in most songs, so adding more tracks panned dead center can muddy the mix rather than make it clearer.

>> **Handheld percussion (tambourine, shakers, washboards, and so on):** Pan it anywhere you think it sounds good. If you have cymbals panned left or right, you might want to pan the percussion instrument the opposite way.

Let these suggestions be your guide, but remember that there are no absolute rules for setting a track's pan. If you pan each track where it sounds best to you, regardless of what anyone (including me) suggests, your songs will come out sounding just fine.

The Effects of Adding Effects

Using effects in the studio could be the subject of a book even bigger than this one. Not only are there so many different effects, but you can use them in so many different ways. In this section, I offer you a quick glimpse of a few of the effects that you'll likely be using the most.

Using effects on your tracks isn't mysterious or technical: You basically turn the effect on, twiddle with the settings, listen to the track, and decide whether the effect helps or hurts the song.

Turn on an effect and listen to the difference. Tweak its settings, and listen to what happens. After a while, you'll know what each effect does and what it sounds like when applied to a track. It won't be long before you find yourself listening to a song on the radio and thinking, "I love the chorus effect on that guitar."

I'll say it one more time: "Just trust your ears."

TIP

To modify or add effects, first select the track, and then click the Smart controls icon. When the Smart controls appear, make sure the Track and Controls buttons in the Smart controls toolbar are enabled, as shown in Figure 10-3.

In the next section, I show you some of the effects that come into play (pun intended) most often.

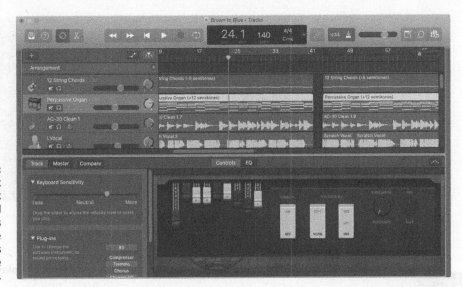

Equalization or not?

Equalization (also known as *EQ*) lets you control specific frequencies within a track (or song) and increase or decrease the volume for those frequencies to impart different sound characteristics to a track. Want to brighten an acoustic guitar? EQ can do that. Want to make a cymbal sound less hissy? That's another issue you can fix using EQ.

Words aren't the best way to understand the effect of EQ, so let's try a little experiment:

1. **Open GarageBand, and create a new song project with a software instrument track.**

   Choose a piano for the track if one isn't already assigned to it.

2. **Record a few measures of piano.**

   You can use your MIDI keyboard; the onscreen keyboard (Window ➪ Keyboard); or the musical typing keyboard (Window ➪ Show Musical Typing or ⌘+K).

3. **Turn on the cycle area (click the circular arrow or press C) and stretch it to cover the region that you just recorded so that it plays continuously, as if it were a loop.**

4. **Select the track (if it's not already selected), click the Smart controls icon (if necessary), and then click the EQ button in the Smart controls toolbar, as shown in Figure 10-4.**

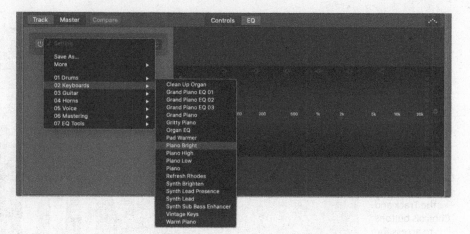

FIGURE 10-4:
Click the EQ
button in the
Smart controls
toolbar to
add or adjust
equalization.

5. **Listen to the music by pressing the spacebar or clicking the play icon.**

   Listen once or twice to get a feel for what it sounds like before you add any EQ.

6. **Adjust the EQ (as described in Chapter 6) or use the Setting pop-up menu to choose a preset. Then press the spacebar to listen.**

7. **To compare the track with and without EQ, click the on/off icon (to the left of the Setting pop-up menu).**

   When the on/off icon is lit (as shown in Figure 10-4), EQ is being applied; when it's dark, EQ is off.

And that's how you add EQ to (and remove EQ from) a track.

TIP

My advice is to use the presets first and diddle with the buttons and control points only if none of the factory-supplied presets work. And, if you like what you hear after you mess with the buttons and control points, remember to choose Save As in the Setting pop-up menu and give your new preset a descriptive name.

The following sections give brief descriptions of several more frequently used effects.

Buying effects

If you want more effects than those that came with GarageBand, all you need is cash. GarageBand supports industry-standard audio unit plug-ins, of which there are thousands, including organs, pianos, synthesizers, orchestral instruments, postproduction effects, and amp modelers.

One of my favorite third-party plug-ins is AmpliTube (www.amplitube.com). (AmpliTube packages start at $99.) It runs beautifully in GarageBand, and I have more than a thousand guitar and amplifier configurations based on some of the best modern and vintage amps and effects ever made. These are amazing, high-quality amp simulations. They're so good, in fact, that Queen's guitarist (Brian May) raves about AmpliTube, as do producer Steve Levine (the Clash, Beach Boys, and Culture Club) and plenty of other guitarists and producers (as opposed to poseurs like yours truly).

Download the free demo, and you'll be hooked. (I just got the Brian May package and it rocks.)

Another favorite plug-in of mine is Auto-Tune EFX+ (www.antarestech.com), which magically fixes sour notes I sing and transforms a subpar vocal into one that's nearly perfect pitch-wise.

Echo and reverb

Echo (also known as *delay*) copies the original sound and plays it back later in time, with enough of a time lapse to be heard distinctly from the original.

Reverb (short for *reverberation*) is an effect that re-creates the sound of an acoustic space by playing back many copies of the original signal, at slightly varied times and volume levels.

It's hard to explain when and how to use these effects, so just turn them on, crank them up, and listen to the results. Some tracks sound much better with a little echo or reverb or both; other tracks sound better with none. Once again, trust your ears. See Chapter 6 for additional info on applying echo and reverb to tracks.

TIP

If you don't use echo or reverb on a track or tracks, you can still apply echo or reverb to the entire song. But that's part of the mastering process, which I cover in Chapter 11.

Compressor

The *compressor* effect decreases the difference between the loudest and the softest parts of a song or track. Compression adds punch and focus to a song and can make it sound better when played on a cheap audio system or on the radio. Many hit songs have a bit of compression applied to compensate for the limited frequency response of most radio speakers.

See Chapter 6 for additional info on applying compression to tracks.

TIP

If you don't use the compressor on a track or tracks, you can still apply compression to your entire song. Again, that's part of the mastering process, which I cover in Chapter 11.

Chorus

The *chorus* effect plays copies of the original sound later than the original, with each copy slightly out of tune, so one voice or instrument sounds like several voices or instruments playing in unison. (Actually, the instruments or voices play *close to* unison, which is not quite *in* unison.)

To use the chorus effect, choose Modulation ⇨ Chorus from the pop-up menu of one of the audio effects slots. Try this effect on vocals or instruments, but only use it a little. Don't forget to try the presets — some of them are pretty cool.

Doubling Tracks

Doubling tracks is one of my favorite pro mixing tips. When a track sounds wimpy, try *doubling* it to thicken the sound a bit. This means you have two copies of the same track, which you can create by copying and pasting or by re-recording the same part on a new track.

The copy-and-paste method

The copy-and-paste technique is fast and easy. Those are its pros. The con is that unless you're careful, it will sound mechanical because both tracks are *exactly* the same.

Following is the copy-and-paste method:

1. **Copy the contents of the track that you want to beef up by clicking the region and then choosing Edit ⇨ Copy or pressing ⌘+C.**

2. **With the track still selected, create a new track with duplicate settings by choosing Track ⇨ New Track With Duplicate Settings or by pressing ⌘+D.**

3. **Paste the contents of the original track into the new track by selecting the track and then choosing Edit ⇨ Paste or by pressing ⌘+V.**

Applying a different instrument to the doubled track worked wonders — it now sounds like a wall of guitars instead of one wimpy one.

4. **Make the track even better by first turning off GarageBand's grid (choose Edit ⇨ Snap to Grid or press ⌘+G).**

   The drop-down menu is a toggle, so double-check the menu for a check mark next to Snap to Grid. I didn't find one, so I knew the grid was turned off.

5. **Slide the zoom control to the right to zoom in and then move the duplicated guitar part to the right ever so slightly, as shown in Figure 10-5.**

6. **Now move the doubled track to the left or right in tiny increments until your ears tell you it sounds good.**

FIGURE 10-5: Slide the doubled track (Big Brute Blues) to the right a tiny amount so it's slightly out of sync with the original track (Clean Studio Stack).

Use this technique to make a single guitar track sound as if a pair of blazing-hot guitarists played it. Perfect!

The re-recording method

Alternatively, you can double the track by creating a new track and recording the part a second time, playing or singing along with the original track. You want to repeat your original performance as precisely as you can, but because you're only human, the second recording will have small differences from the original track.

Although this technique can take you more time, the differences between the two takes can result in a better sound than copying and pasting the same performance. If you're a consistent enough player or singer, the minor differences between the two performances may sound spectacular when played together; just ask the Beatles.

REMEMBER

To achieve a different kind of depth, offset one of the tracks just a bit by turning off the grid, zooming all the way in on the timeline, and sliding one of the tracks slightly to the left or right (refer to Figure 10-4).

TIP

You get a richer, fuller sound if you pan one of the doubled tracks left and pan the other track right by an equal amount. Try different combinations of panning and offsetting the doubled tracks until you find the combo that's perfect for your song.

Chapter **11**

Mastering Mastering

There's no mystery about mastering — you already know how to do it; you just don't know that you know yet. You see, mastering is nothing more than applying familiar effects, such as EQ, echo, reverb, and compression, to your entire song instead of individual tracks.

Mastering is the final step in the multitrack recording process; it's the last thing you do before you distribute your work for others to hear. In big-time major-label music production, mastering is a specialized art performed by a handful of highly paid mastering engineers with state-of-the-art mastering studios and the highest-of-high-quality audio-processing hardware and software.

Fortunately, you don't have to go to that trouble or expense: The plethora of presets in GarageBand's built-in mastering harnesses the knowledge of a roomful of mastering engineers.

I'm only half-kidding. The GarageBand mastering presets are excellent and can give most people the results they want and expect most of the time. However, if you plan to have your song professionally duplicated in quantity, you might want to enlist a good mastering engineer to ensure that what ends up on the discs (or digital files) sounds exactly the way you want it to — or, perhaps more importantly, the way that radio programmers expect it to.

Mastering your masterpiece in GarageBand can be as easy as choosing a preset. If you're not sure what your song needs, let that room full of experienced mastering engineers do the mastering for you, and don't touch those dials. Or, if you prefer the hands-on-the-knobs approach, start with the preset that sounds closest to your ideal and then tweak its individual settings until your fingers bleed. Either way, you'll end up with a song that sounds darned good to most people most of the time.

Without further ado, it's time to master mastering!

What, Exactly, Is Mastering?

In the simplest of terms, *mastering* is adjusting the overall tone and level of the final stereo mix. When you master in GarageBand, you're merely using on the entire song the same effects you've used before on individual tracks — such as echo, reverb, equalization, and compression.

Mastering is adding effects *judiciously* to improve overall tonal balance and dynamic range. A song with too many low frequencies sounds boomy, boxy, and muddy; a song with too many high frequencies sounds screechy, shrill, and brittle. Your goal in mastering is to balance the highs, mids, and lows and refine the overall sound to make the song sound smooth, relaxed, and professional.

In addition to judiciously adding effects, you can adjust a song's dynamic range — the difference between the loudest and softest parts. Adding compression and other effects can make your song sound punchy and radio friendly, but too much can make it sound artificial and icky.

If you're creating a complete album to be pressed on vinyl or CD, mastering also accomplishes the following:

>> Determines the order of the songs on the vinyl or CD

>> Levels the songs so that they all play at roughly the same loudness and that no song is louder or softer than the others

Before You Master

Mixing and mastering are different sides of the same coin, so GarageBand makes it easy to switch between these two chores. This is a good thing, because everything you do to the master track affects the mix.

REMEMBER

You can always go back and change anything you like in the mix, but it's best to have your mixing as close to complete as possible before you master. If not, you may end up spending more time than necessary remixing and remastering.

Before you begin mastering, double-check that you are happy with the following:

>> Relative loudness (level) of each track

>> Ronal characteristics (equalization) of each track

>> Spatial positioning (pan) of each track

You did all these things when you mixed, which I cover in great detail in Chapter 10.

TIP

You should also trim noise or extraneous sound at the head or tail of any or all tracks (if you haven't done so already); your final product will sound better for it. The easiest way to get rid of dead space is to create a split where you want the song to begin and then delete the dead space after it's split from the song. Check out Chapter 9 for details.

Having checked and double-checked your mix and ensured that it's as good as it's going to get, it's time to master it — and (I hope) make it sound even better.

The Master Track Is for Mastering Tracks

When you master, you use the same effects and controls that you've been using on tracks, which makes mastering familiar and easy. GarageBand uses a special track, called the *master track*, for mastering. Any settings and effects that you apply to this track affect your entire song.

Here's a brief overview of what you can do with the master track (where the mastering magic takes place):

>> **To show or hide the master track:** Choose Track ➪ Show/Hide Master Track or press ⌘+Shift+M. The master track appears below the last track in your workspace.

>> **To adjust the tonal characteristics and add effects to the whole song:** Select the master track and then choose View ➪ Show Smart Controls; click the Smart controls icon; or press the B key on your QWERTY keyboard.

>> **To choose a preset:** Choose View ⇨ Show Library; click the library icon; or press the L key on your QWERTY keyboard. Now, you can simply apply a preset and move on; apply a preset and then customize its effects; or start from scratch. See the next section for details.

>> **To change the song's level, make part of the song louder or softer, or add a fade-in or fade-out:** Enable automation (Mix ⇨ Show Automation or press the A key on your QWERTY keyboard) and use the master volume automation control. (This control works just like the one you use for individual tracks.) You find out more about the master volume automation control in the "Setting the master volume" section, later in this chapter.

TIP

If you're going to use the master volume automation control, you should apply it last.

Applying presets and effects to the master track

Your goal here is to improve the overall sound of the song by judiciously adding effects. So start by selecting the master track and opening the library.

Using presets

The current release of GarageBand offers 11 mastering presets by default, as shown in Figure 11-1.

FIGURE 11-1:
The master track offers 11 presets by default.

TIP

If you've installed earlier versions of GarageBand (as I have), you may see dozens of additional legacy mastering presets (as shown in Figure 11-1). Alas, there's no way to install or reinstall them if you don't see them, so you either have them or you don't. If you have them, by all means try them out.

Now click different presets in the library to hear how they affect your song. (Click the play icon first, of course.) Listen critically for the perfect blend of instruments and voices that pleases your ear.

TIP

Try out the different categories and presets regardless of their name. Just 'cause a preset is called, say, Classical doesn't mean that it won't sound fabulous when applied to your pop ballad. Try it — you never know what's going to sound awesome to your ears.

TIP

In a hurry? Or don't have the patience for the "listen, adjust, listen, adjust, repeat until satisfied" cycles that it usually takes to master a song? If so, browse through the presets until you find one you like, and don't worry about tweaking the effects. You can add a fade-in or fade-out if you like (see the section "Setting the master volume," later in this chapter); other than that, you're done with your mastering.

Tweaking effects

Sometimes you'll find a preset that sounds almost perfect, but you think to yourself, "If only it had. . ." Well, you can probably add whatever is missing by adjusting any or all master track effects: echo, reverb, equalizer, or plug-ins.

If you decide to tweak the effects, here are some points to keep in mind:

WARNING

» The echo and reverb effects for individual tracks are relative to the echo and reverb effects in the master track. If you turn off the echo or reverb effects in the master track, they will no longer be available to individual tracks.

» If you have a track panned all the way to the left or the right and apply effects to the master track such as echo, reverb, or EQ, some sound from that panned track may still be heard in the other speaker because master track effects are applied in stereo.

TIP

Most instruments and vocals sound better with a little echo, reverb, and compression. So even if you added some of these effects to individual tracks during mixing, try adding a bit more to the whole song here in the master track.

Now let's explore how to tweak those effects.

Tweaking master EQ

To adjust overall equalization for your project, do the following:

1. **Select the master track.**

2. **Display the Smart controls for the master track.**

   To do so, click the Smart controls icon, choose View ➪ Show Smart Controls, or press the B key on your QWERTY keyboard.

3. **Click the EQ button in the Smart controls toolbar.**

At this point, I recommend choosing a preset from the Settings pop-up menu on the left side of the equalizer controls, as shown in Figure 11-2.

FIGURE 11-2: Don't overlook the Settings menu's EQ Tools category.

Now give your track a listen and try to determine if any particular range of frequencies is too loud or too quiet. If the EQ is not quite what you're looking for, try another preset or fiddle with the equalizer's buttons and control points (as described in Chapter 6) until you find the settings that sound best to your ear.

TIP

Try the presets in the Mastering category first, but don't limit yourself; try presets from the other categories as well. Although the EQ Tools category (refer to Figure 11-2) is not designed for mastering, it often contains useful presets.

Tweaking master echo and master reverb

To adjust the master echo and master reverb for your project, follow these steps:

1. **Select the master track.**

2. **Display the Smart controls for the master track.**

   Click the Smart controls icon, choose View ➪ Show Smart Controls, or press the B key on your QWERTY keyboard.

3. **Click the Effects button in the Smart controls toolbar.**

4. **In the Echo/Reverb pop-up menu, choose Master Echo (or Master Reverb).**

I usually recommend trying a preset first. As I've said before, Apple put a lot of time and effort into providing presets that sound pretty darned good under most conditions. And in this case, because you've already selected a factory mastering preset, chances are the echo and reverb settings associated with that mastering preset will work nicely for your project.

So, before you start sampling presets, try sliding the master echo or reverb slider (to the right of the Smart controls) or twisting the knobs in the Master Echo or Reverb panel to the left of the slider and pop-up menus (or both). If that doesn't do it for you, try other presets.

Tweaking the compressor and other master effects

If you can't resist the urge to tweak the sound of your tune even further, you can fine-tune the compressor and other plug-in by clicking the Output button in the Smart controls toolbar.

The controls for master track plug-ins are the same as controls for the compressor and plug-ins on other tracks, as shown in Figure 11-3 and described in Chapters 6, 7, and 8.

Finally, if you still aren't getting the sound you're looking for, you can add a new effect or replace an existing effect with a different one. The plug-in effects available for mastering are the same ones available for other tracks; they work as described in Chapter 6.

As you may recall, blue plug-ins (Channel EQ, Multipressor, and Limiter in Figure 11-3) are enabled; gray plug-ins (Compressor, Gain, and Exciter in Figure 11-3) are not. In a nutshell:

>> Enable disabled plug-ins by clicking the power on icon to the left of its name.

>> Choose a different plug-in by clicking the little up-and-down arrows to the right of the plug-in's name.

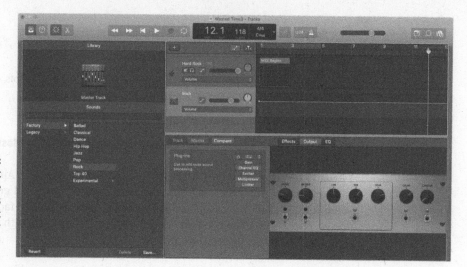

FIGURE 11-3:
Click the Output button in the Smart controls toolbar to adjust the compressor and plug-in effects.

» Change a plug-in's settings by clicking its name; its controls appear in a new window. In Figure 11-4, I clicked the Noise Gate plug-in and the Output 1-2 window appeared.

» Choose a preset from its Settings pop-up menu or slide its sliders.

REMEMBER

Most plug-ins have their own presets, as shown in Figure 11-4. You might want to try one or more presets by sliding sliders or changing numerical values.

FIGURE 11-4:
Click a plug-in's name to open its settings window.

WARNING

Some of these effects, such as overdrive and distortion, are inappropriate for mastering. Be careful if you use extra effects because an effect that sounded great on another track may sound awful when applied to the master track.

Setting the master volume

You should always double-check the master volume for your project before you call it done. Use the master volume slider in the toolbar to change the volume of your now mixed and mastered project all at once.

REMEMBER

The final level of your track should be as high as possible without showing red in the level meters.

To reset the volume slider to 0, option-click it.

TIP

If your song sounds okay at the same level from start to finish, and if the master volume doesn't go into the red, and if the entire song sounds fantastic, you can skip the rest of this section and go directly to the final section.

However, if you want your song to fade-out at the end or, less frequently, fade-in at the beginning, or if you find that part of your song sounds louder than the rest, you need to use the master track volume control.

Creating a fade-out at the end of a project is easy: Choose Mix⇨Create Volume Fade Out on Main Output. The volume control's rubber band appears with the fade-out created for you, as shown in Figure 11-5.

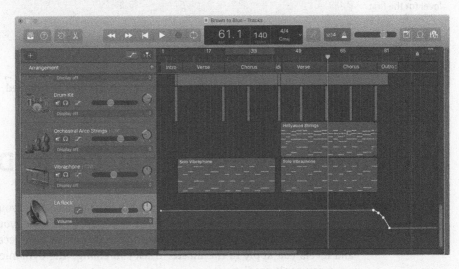

FIGURE 11-5:
The master track volume control with its default fade-out control points.

If the song sounds okay, you're done. If you want to change something — make the duration of the fade-out longer or shorter, add a fade-in, or raise or lower the volume for part of the song — I have good news. You simply use the track volume control techniques described in Chapters 9 and 10.

For example, I made the fade-out in Figure 11-5 much longer by moving its starting control point to the left by a few seconds. The result is shown in Figure 11-6. I also added a fade-in (the three leftmost control points on the volume control's rubber band), and lowered the level of the first chorus, which sounded a tad too loud to my ear.

FIGURE 11-6:
The master track volume control customized with a fade-in, a slightly lower level for the first chorus, and a longer, gentler fade-out.

When everything sounds just right, you may think you're finished, but there's still one more thing to do — and it's not optional.

One More Thing Before You Call It "Done"

After you've set the effects and volume for the master track, you should have a project that's nearly finished, but before you can call it done, you need to listen critically several more times. You should take this extra step because the effects and levels you apply to the master track can change the dynamics of the mix in ways you can't predict.

So, now that you've applied master track effects and set the levels, give the song another listen and pay particular attention to instruments or vocals that are too prominent or too quiet, drums that aren't crispy or are too crunchy, guitars that sound muffled or artificial, or anything else that *could* sound better.

Fix what needs fixing, and then export the final song to the Music app (or iTunes) and sync it to your iPhone or other device. (Or burn it to a CD if you're old-school; Chapter 23 walks you through the process of creating a CD of your song.)

The following may be the most important part of mastering: Listen to the song in your car, at your home, in your office, on a boom box, in the shower, using earphones, and anywhere else you might listen to music.

TIP

As you listen, take notes about your song. For example, "Lead vocal louder during second verse and chorus," "Drums too loud in break between chorus and third verse," or "Overall mix muddy; can't hear brass."

After you have a feel for what's right and what's wrong, go back into GarageBand, remix, remaster, export, and do it again. Only when you no longer hear anything that needs to be changed is your song *really* done.

TIP

As soon as you export a song to the Music app (or iTunes), change its name to something that allows you to discern between versions. Each time I remix and remaster, I give the song name a suffix (for example, GM-01, GM-02, GM-mayBfinal). Then, when I'm absolutely, positively, without any question done with my remixing and remastering, I delete all but the final version of the song from my Music library.

4

Making Music with Your iDevice

IN THIS PART . . .

Get an overview of GarageBand and how it works on iDevices (iPad and iPhone).

Create songs in the live loops grid, which lets you assemble song snippets into an almost frighteningly professional-sounding tune in mere minutes.

Discover the ins and outs of laying down tracks using GarageBand's exclusive touch-controlled Smart instruments.

Record recording vocals and acoustic instruments with a microphone.

Record guitar, bass, and other amplified instruments on your iPad or iPhone without an amp, a mic, or a stomp box.

Chapter **12**

Getting Started

B efore you work and play with GarageBand on your iDevice, you should familiarize yourself with its settings. These settings are found in two places: Global settings are in the Settings app, and settings specific to the current project are in GarageBand's Settings menu.

You probably don't know how you like your preferences, at least not yet. But you will in just a few short pages. This chapter helps you adjust each item in both places, accompanied by the usual wit and wisdom and whatever else that I think you might find helpful.

Some of you may think that I'm putting the cart before the horse by covering preferences in Chapter 12, because some of the features these preferences affect won't appear until later in this Part 4 or in Part 5. But there's a method to my madness.

You're going to take a quick look at every one of the little critters (settings) so you know what they are, where they are, and how to configure them appropriately when you need them.

Global Settings

To adjust GarageBand's global settings, tap the Settings app. Then scroll down the Settings list on the left side of the screen and tap GarageBand, as shown in Figure 12-1.

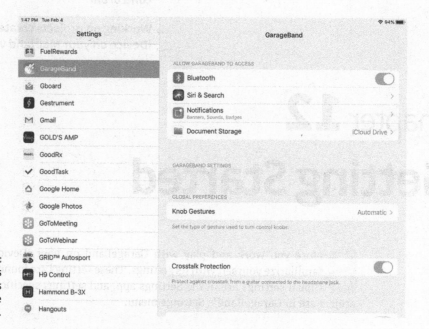

FIGURE 12-1: GarageBand's global settings are found in the Settings app.

Allowing GarageBand access

The first four items control GarageBand's access to external devices and other iDevice apps and services.

» **Bluetooth:** Use an external Bluetooth keyboard or other Bluetooth device with GarageBand.

» **Siri & Search:** Reveal the following four settings:

• **Learn from this app:** Allow Siri to learn how you use GarageBand and make suggestions across apps.

• **Show in Search:** Allow Search and Look Up to display information or shortcut suggestions or both for GarageBand.

- **Suggest Shortcuts:** Receive shortcut suggestions based on how you use the app.

- **Show Siri Suggestions:** Receive shortcut suggestions on your lock screen (based on how you use GarageBand).

» **Notifications:** Reveal the standard iOS (or iPadOS) Notifications settings screen. As usual, you can enable or disable notifications from GarageBand; enable or disable sounds and badges; and specify the behavior of notification previews and grouping.

» **Document Storage:** Choose a destination for saved projects. You can choose iCloud Drive, On My iPad (or iPhone), or any other cloud-based storage app on your device, such as Dropbox, Google Drive, or OneDrive.

Determining knob response

Tap Knob Gestures to choose how knobs respond to your touch. It's hard to describe how they work, so try them one at a time so you can determine which feels most natural. To do that, tap Knob Gestures, and then tap Linear. Switch to GarageBand and swipe some knobs, noting how it feels.

Switch back to the Settings app, tap Knob Gestures, and then tap Circular. Switch to GarageBand again and swipe more knobs. Compare that to Linear and choose the one that feels most natural.

Or choose Automatic and let your iDevice determine what to do based on how you swipe the knob.

Reducing crosstalk

If you plug a guitar into your iDevice's headphone port or Lightning port (using an appropriate plug adapter), enable the Crosstalk Protection setting to reduce noise (crosstalk) that could affect other tracks.

GarageBand Settings

To access GarageBand's project-specific settings, tap the settings icon in the toolbar. The menu shown in Figure 12-2 appears.

FIGURE 12-2:
GarageBand's
Settings menu.

Metronome and count-in

Before I talk about metronome settings, let me explain what a metronome is and why you'll probably need to use it.

It's important to keep time with your song so you can play the right notes at the right time. To do that, you need to hear a steady beat. GarageBand's built-in *metronome* plays that steady beat (sometimes called a *click track*) to help you play and record in perfect time at the project tempo you've specified.

You can turn the metronome on or off at any time — while recording, playing back, mixing, or mastering. But you'll probably find it most useful while recording tracks.

TIP

To make a choice that suits you, here are some tips to keep in mind:

>> **To play or sing in time with a song's time signature, tempo, and other tracks, use the metronome every time that you record a track.** Just remember that YMMV (your mileage may vary). Some musicians have perfect time and can play entire pieces without missing a beat. I'm such a lousy musician that I have trouble staying in time, even with the metronome clicking away.

>> **To toggle the metronome on and off (which I do often), tap the metro-
nome icon in the toolbar.** You can tell whether the metronome is on or off
(without listening) by the metronome icon's color — white is off and blue is on.

When I start a new project, I use the metronome during playback to rehearse parts
without recording them and to try out different tempos for a piece. But as soon as
I have drum and bass tracks — and maybe a guitar or keyboard part or two — I
turn off the metronome and leave it off. By this point, the other tracks should be
in time with each other, so I should be able to keep time with them when I'm
playing or singing, without hearing the annoying tick of the metronome.

TIP

As the song's track count increases, it gets harder to hear the metronome anyway.
That's why you may want to record your rhythm tracks — mostly drums and
bass — first.

Just know that the metronome is there if you want it, during recording or playback. It can be turned on and off with a single tap of the metronome icon.

Now, here's the scoop on the metronome and count-in settings shown in
Figure 12-3:

The first two settings involve count-in:

>> **Count-in:** Enable this setting to hear one measure of clicks before recording
begins (after you tap the Record button). This feature helps ever so much
when you need to start a song (or an overdub) in perfect time with either the
metronome or with other tracks.

>> **Visual Count-in:** When Count-in is enabled, you can also enable this setting to
see a numerical countdown onscreen in time with the clicks.

Moving right along, the next five items are your options for the metronome's click
sound — Click, Woodblock, Hi-Hat, Rimshot, and No Sound. To try them, enable
the metronome and tap the play icon. Now try them all and choose the one you
prefer.

If you're wondering why there's an option for No Sound, that's so you can enable
Visual Count-in without hearing the metronome, because you must enable the
metronome before you can enable Visual Count-in.

Finally, use the Metronome Level slider to set the volume level of the
metronome.

FIGURE 12-3:
Metronome and
count-in settings.

Tempo, time, and key

The Tempo, Time Signature, and Key Signature settings are where you specify the (duh!) tempo, time signature, and key for your project.

Tempo

The Tempo setting determines this project's beats per minute (bpm). Before you adjust it, you should probably enable the metronome and tap the play icon if you want to hear clicks at the selected tempo, which you almost certainly do.

Now, to change the tempo, press the number (110 in Figure 12-4) and drag up or down, or tap the little up or down arrows.

FIGURE 12-4:
Set the tempo
numerically or
by tapping with
your finger.

If you don't know the precise number of beats per minute you seek, start at 110 and work your way up or down until you nail it.

Or, tap out the tempo with your finger on the Tap to Set Tempo button and let GarageBand figure out how many beats per minute you want.

To tap a tempo with your finger, do the following:

1. **Enable the metronome.**

    Trust me, you want to hear clicks while you do this.

2. **Tap the play icon.**

    The metronome starts clicking at the current tempo.

3. **Tap the Tap to Set Tempo pad rhythmically at the tempo you desire.**

    The numerical value and time between clicks is updated in real time as you tap; keep tapping until the metronome clicks are playing at the tempo you desire.

And that's how you set the tempo for the current project.

Time and key signatures

Setting the time signature is easy as long as your song is played in 4/4, 3/4, or 6/8 time. Those three are the only time signatures available, so I hope you weren't planning to record any Dave Brubeck or Emerson, Lake, and Palmer tunes.

You have pretty much unlimited options for choosing your project's key signature, as shown in Figure 12-5. Just tap the button for the key you desire, and then tap Major or Minor. If you're not sure, leave the key set to C and enable Follow Song Key, which transposes touch instrument recordings to match the key in other tracks.

Other settings

The remaining settings are Edit Chords, Fade Out, Note Pad, Jam Session, Advanced, Restore Purchase, and Help. Here's how they work:

>> **Edit Chords:** You won't discover the joys of the Smart Guitar until Chapter 15. For now, merely note that the Edit Chords setting lets you specify the chords you want the Smart Guitar to play (as shown in Figure 12-6).

>> **Fade Out:** Enable this setting to have your song gradually fade-out at the end.

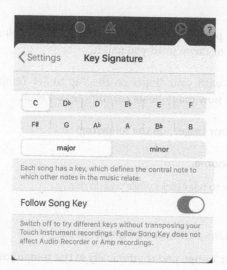

FIGURE 12-5:
Any key signature
you like, major or
minor.

> » **Note Pad:** Tap Note Pad to add a note to your project. For example, you
> might want to remind yourself to re-record the harmony vocal or add a third
> guitar part (or whatever). If you're the type who likes to keep notes on your
> projects, this is a good place to keep them.

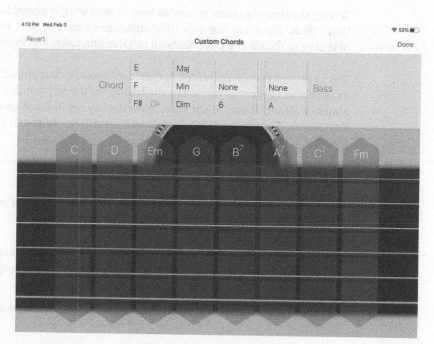

FIGURE 12-6:
This is how you
assign a chord
(Fm) to the Smart
Guitar's rightmost
chord strip.

>> **Jam Session:** Enable this setting to jam with other users over Wi-Fi. I wrote an entire chapter about this topic (Chapter 21), so I'll leave it at that for now.

>> **Advanced:** Tap Advanced to reveal five settings you'll rarely (or never) need:

- **Multitrack Recording:** Enable this setting if you want to record more than one track at a time. Note that when you connect an audio interface with more than one channel, GarageBand should allow multitrack recording regardless of this setting. It's here because GarageBand doesn't always recognize multi-input interfaces; if you plug one in and can't record on multiple tracks at once, check this setting.

WARNING

- **24-bit Audio Resolution:** Enable this setting to record, mix, or export higher-quality recordings.

  Note that enabling this setting causes your saved projects to require as much as three times more storage than a project saved at the default resolution of 16-bits.

- **Run in Background:** Enable this setting if you want GarageBand to continue running in the background while you use other apps.

WARNING

  Be careful. Enabling this setting may deplete your battery faster.

- **Bluetooth MIDI Devices:** Tap this item to select a Bluetooth LE MIDI device (usually a keyboard or other MIDI controller) to use with GarageBand.

- **Send MIDI Clock:** You may need to enable this setting to sync your Bluetooth- or Lightning-connected MIDI device with your project. If your MIDI controller doesn't perform as expected, enable this setting and try again.

>> **Restore Purchase:** Tap this item to redownload any purchased (or free) sounds, presets, instruments, or other GarageBand add-ons.

>> **Help:** I don't know why this useful item is hidden away at the bottom of the Settings menu. Tap it to see the extensive GarageBand Help documentation (shown in Figure 12-7).

And that's pretty much all you need to know about GarageBand's global and project-specific settings.

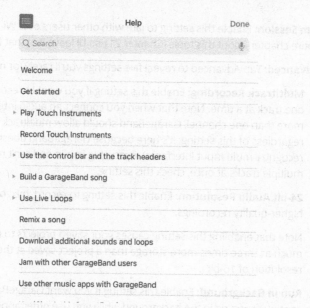

Help   Done

Q Search

Welcome

Get started

▸ Play Touch Instruments

▸ Record Touch Instruments

▸ Use the control bar and the track headers

▸ Build a GarageBand song

▸ Use Live Loops

Remix a song

Download additional sounds and loops

Jam with other GarageBand users

Use other music apps with GarageBand

FIGURE 12-7:
The result of tapping the semi-hidden Help item in the Settings menu.

The Control Bar

The strip of icons that runs across the top of the GarageBand screen is known as the control bar. I cover these controls in greater detail throughout this part and Part 5. Following is a gentle introduction to each of its controls (from left to right):

>> **My Songs:** Tap the my songs icon to save the current song and open the My Songs browser, which is where you create, save, and share your songs.

>> **Browser:** Tap the browser icon to open Sound Browser (shown in Figure 12-8, top), where you can select a touch instrument or open the live loops grid. Swipe left or right to see other instruments; tap the Live Loops button at the top of the screen to switch to the live loops grid.

Press and hold down on the browser icon to choose a different instrument, as shown in Figure 12-8 (bottom).

TIP

>> **Tracks view:** The tracks view icon lets you switch between the current touch instrument and tracks view.

Note that the tracks view icon appears only after you make at least one touch instrument recording in tracks view. Also note that the icon transmogrifies into an icon reminiscent of the selected track whilst in tracks view. Tap the instrument-looking icon to play the Smart instrument; tap the tracks view icon (shown in the margin) to return to tracks view.

You get the skinny on using tracks view in Chapter 14.

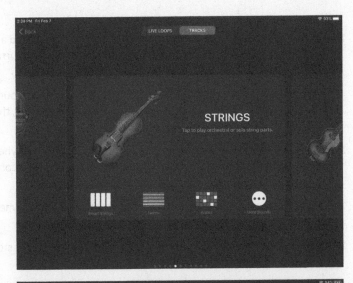

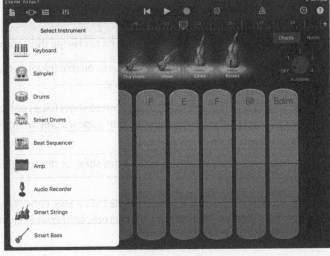

FIGURE 12-8:
Swipe left or right
(top), or press
and hold down
the browser icon
(bottom) to select
a different
instrument.

 » Grid: Tap the grid icon to switch between the current touch instrument and the live loops grid. You'll see this icon only if a live loops grid has been created for this song. You can get the scoop on live loops and grids in Chapter 13.

 » Track controls: Tap the track controls icon to see the controls for the selected track.

 » FX: Tap the FX icon to show or hide the remix FX controls, which you learn about in Chapter 13.

>> **Undo:** Tap the undo icon to undo the last thing you did. Deleted a region and want it back? Tap undo. Edited a take and don't like the way it turned out? Tap undo.

The undo icon is context sensitive, which means it appears in your toolbar only if you do something that can be undone. If you don't see it, there's nothing to be undone at the moment.

>> **Go to beginning:** Tap the go to beginning icon to move the playhead to the beginning of the song. If a song is playing, the go to beginning icon turns into a square stop icon.

>> **Play:** Tap the play icon to begin playing your song from the playhead's current position. Tap it (or the square stop icon) to stop playing.

>> **Record:** Tap the record icon to begin recording. Tap the play or stop icon to end your recording.

>> **Master volume slider:** Slide the master volume slider to the right to make your song louder and to the left to make it softer.

You can use your iDevice's volume buttons to change this setting, too.

>> **Metronome:** Tap the Metronome button to enable (blue) or disable (white) the metronome while playing or recording.

>> **Loop Browser:** Tap the Loop Browser icon to show (blue) or hide (white) Loop Browser. Note that the Loop Browser icon appears only when you're in track view.

>> **Settings:** Tap to adjust the settings for this song, as discussed earlier in the chapter.

>> **Info:** Although I'd call this icon *help,* Apple calls it *info.* Either way, tap this icon to see coaching tips for what's on your screen, as shown in Figure 12-9 for tracks view.

And that, my friends, is your GarageBand control bar.

Before we move on to making songs, you need to know one more thing, namely, how to share projects with GarageBand on a Mac. Although you might think the process is as simple as sharing and opening a file, sadly, it's not.

So, up next I describe what you need to know to share a project with your Mac (or share a Mac project with your iDevice).

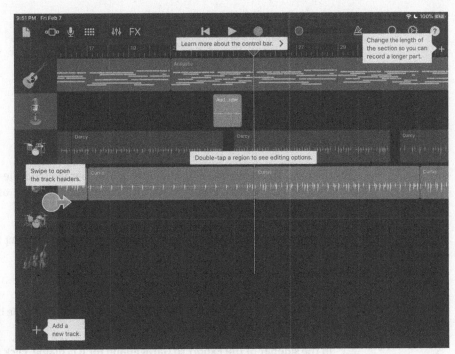

9:51 PM Fri Feb 7   100%

Learn more about the control bar. ›

Change the length of
the section so you can
record a longer part.

Acoustic

Aud...rder

Darcy   Darcy   Darcy

Double-tap a region to see editing options.

Swipe to open
the track headers.

Curtis   Curtis   Curtis

Add a
new track.

FIGURE 12-9:
Tap the info icon
to see coaching
tips, shown here
for tracks view.

Sharing Projects with a Mac
(and Vice Versa)

If you're hoping to work on projects on both your Mac and iDevices, this section
will save you a bunch of heartache.

If you start a project on your iDevice, when you first open the file on your Mac
GarageBand asks you to resave the file (and optionally rename it, which is not a
bad idea). The project then opens on your Mac and everything is more or less
identical to the project on your iDevice.

Note that if you added a remix FX track to the song on your iDevice, that track will
appear as an automation on the master track when you open the file on your Mac.

If you want to share a Mac project to an iDevice, however, things aren't quite so
easy. If you try to open a GarageBand for Mac project on your iDevice, you'll see
the error message shown in Figure 12-10.

FIGURE 12-10: This is what you see if you try to open a Mac GarageBand file on an iDevice.

Don't panic. Although you can't just open a Mac GarageBand file on an iDevice, you can share a special GarageBand for iOS-compatible version of your Mac file and work on that file on your Mac.

Here's how to share an iDevice-compatible version of your project from your Mac to your iDevice:

1. **Choose Share ⇨ Project to GarageBand for iOS.**

   The Export to GarageBand for iOS dialog appears. Rename the file before the next step if you care to.

2. **In the sidebar of the Export to GarageBand for iOS dialog, click iCloud Drive and then click the GarageBand folder to select it.**

3. **Click the Save button.**

   Your project will now appear in the My Songs browser on your iOS device as a new song with a single track containing a mix of the entire GarageBand (Mac) project.

You can add, edit, and arrange new tracks in GarageBand for iOS, and then share the updated song back to iCloud. When you reopen the project in GarageBand on your Mac, the new tracks will be added to the original project.

Finally, it should go without saying that sharing a project to GarageBand for iOS requires an active Internet connection and iCloud login.

Now let's start making some music!

» Finding the right loops

» Knowing what the loops browser can do for you

» Adding loops to your song

» Tinkering with loops

Chapter **13**

Making Music with Live Loops

E ven if you can't play or sing a note, you can have lots of fun using GarageBand's *live loops*, which are prerecorded bits of music that require absolutely no talent on your part to sound great. In many cases, the fastest and easiest way to get a song started is to use one of the thousands of loops included with GarageBand.

Unlike GarageBand for Mac, which offers only a traditional multitrack interface, GarageBand for iDevices offers two paths to making music: a traditional multitrack interface similar to the Mac version and live loops, which use a grid of touch-sensitive pads to trigger sounds.

You start your iDevice recording journey with live loops for a reason. I don't know if you are a talented musician or can't play a note on any instrument. I also don't know if you have an instrument handy or a way to connect an instrument to your iDevice (topics I describe in Chapters 16 and 17, respectively). None of these issues matters with loops — all you need is GarageBand and one or more fingers.

In this chapter, you create music using only the prerecorded loops and templates included with GarageBand. Of course, you're also free to add an audio track with a vocal or guitar solo to your masterpiece.

Loop Basics

A *loop*, in its simplest form, is a piece of music that can repeat (loop) seamlessly. Loops are designed this way; a good one can be repeated without missing a beat. When you repeat a loop, it's called *looping*. To use a loop, you drag it onto a track (or onto the workspace, where a track is created for it automatically). But I'm getting ahead of myself.

Anyway, the thousands of little pieces of sound that come with GarageBand are called loops. If you repeat a loop seamlessly, the loop is looped. The act of doing so is called looping.

TECHNICAL
STUFF

The term *loop*, which indicates a repeating segment of music, stemmed from the fact that the first artists doing this (Eno and Fripp come to mind) would cut the magnetic recording tape and paste it back together in a loop that played continuously. The process required multiple tape players and must have been awkward, but that's how looping got its start.

Find more loops

You don't have to confine yourself to the loops that Apple provides with Garage-Band. First, you can download additional sounds packs for free by tapping the loops browser icon on the control bar, and then tapping Go to Sound Library.

In the sound library, you can tap a sound pack to see additional information, tap the Preview button to hear it play, or tap the Get button to download the sound pack to your device.

GarageBand comes with a passable selection of software instrument loops and live loops templates. If you also download all additional sounds, packs, and loops, you'll have 2 more gigabytes of raw material (for free)!

TIP

I encourage you download the free material right now — unless your iDevice is almost full. Even then, I encourage you to get rid of some stuff to make room for these free sound packs. I mean, if you're going to use GarageBand, you might as well stock it with everything you can that's free — you never know what's going to come in handy.

Bottom line: GarageBand is great by default, but it's even greater when you add thousands of additional high-quality sounds and loops without paying a penny.

More about loops

Entire music genres — dance, electronica, house music, rap, and many others — have made an art form out of making music with loops. But don't let these genres limit your perception of how loops are used. In GarageBand, loops don't have to be looped. In fact, many GarageBand loops sound better as a one-shot accent than when repeated in a loop.

Here are just a few ways you can use loops:

>> **As a background groove or as the central driving theme of a song:** You can use a drum loop to provide the backbeat to your song or maybe just to keep the beat while you build other tracks with loops, instruments, and vocals.

>> **As musical punctuation marks:** You can make a horn part lurk in the chorus, or a funky guitar riff chug along in the verse. For better or verse (groan), a loop can be the perfect tool for your song, regardless of the sound that you seek (or think you're seeking).

>> **To spice up a single chorus, bridge, or verse:** You might add a shaker or other percussion loop in the last verse and find that the addition was exactly what was missing in the song. Alternately, perhaps you need a bridge to break up a song. With a few loops, you can make a bass line, drum fill, and horn riff that punch-up your song to the next level.

That's enough background on loops. Now let's dig in and start playing with them!

Grokking the loop grid

 You work with live loops on the loop grid. To follow along, open GarageBand, tap the my songs icon on the control bar, tap the + icon to create a new project, tap Live Loops at the top of the My Songs screen, and then tap Rock to select and open the Rock template.

The loop grid appears, populated with rock-oriented loops, as shown in Figure 13-1.

The *loop grid* is comprised of cells arranged into rows and columns. The bottom of each column has a trigger, and each row represents loops featuring a single instrument.

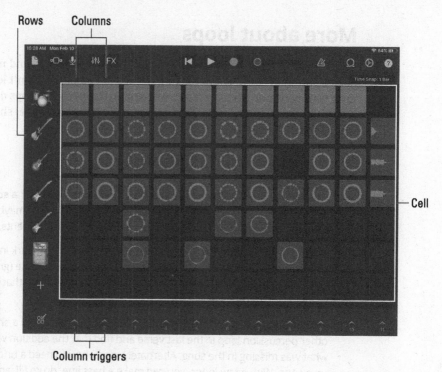

Rows   Columns

Cell

Column triggers

FIGURE 13-1:
Live loops
templates (Rock
is shown here)
are prepopulated
with loops to get
you started.

Here's how the grid works:

>> **Cells:** Cells are arranged in columns and rows; a cell contains a single loop. Play any loop in any cell by tapping it.

>> **Columns:** Columns are vertical groups of cells. Play individual loops by tapping the cell; play all cells in a column by tapping the column trigger at its bottom.

>> **Column triggers:** Tap the little chevron at the bottom of a column (above its column number) to trigger all the loops in that column simultaneously.

>> **Rows:** Rows are horizontal groups of cells. Tap a cell to play it; you can play only one cell at a time in a row.

TIP

To avoid confusion, it's often best to organize rows so they contain related loops using the same instrument. For example, in Figure 13-1 the top row is all drum loops, the next four rows are all guitar loops, and the sixth row has only special amplifier effect loops.

Now, tap any cell or column trigger and listen to the results. Cool, huh?

Now that you know how to tap cells and column triggers, it's a good time to open and play with other templates. Tap the my songs icon on the control bar, tap Live Loops on the My Songs screen, and then tap a template. Tap cells and column triggers to familiarize yourself with them; and then repeat the process with a different template.

Next, let's look at how you work with loops and cells.

Working with Loops

The loop grid is a descendent of Akai MPC (MIDI Production Center, and later Music Production Center). In continuous production since 1988, MPC was the first device to combine sampling, sequencing, and recording with pressure-sensitive pads to trigger sounds.

GarageBand's loop grid takes the MPC concept to new heights on mobile devices, letting you record, sample, sequence, perform, and much more, all from a single screen and all at the tap of a finger.

I'm going to get ahead of myself here by showing you how to add a loop to a cell before you know much about loops and the grid. Why? I believe you'll understand how to use the grid faster if you understand the relationship between loops, the loops browser, and the grid's cells.

Adding Apple loops to cells

Although templates are superb for getting to know the loop grid, you'll probably want to replace some (or all) of a template's loops with loops you prefer. Or you might want to start from scratch with a blank grid instead of a template by tapping New instead of a template on the My Songs screen.

Either way, here's how you add an Apple loop to a cell:

1. **Tap + to add a new row to the grid.**

2. **Tap the loops browser icon on the control bar to open the loops browser.**
   The loops browser is GarageBand's tool for managing the thousands of loops included with GarageBand and downloading additional free content.

3. **Tap the Apple Loops tab to see a list of all installed Apple loops, as shown in Figure 13-2.**

4. **Drag a loop from the list to a cell.**

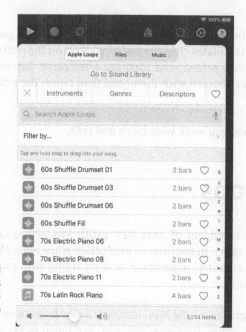

FIGURE 13-2:
The loops browser with the Apple Loops tab selected.

That's all there is to it. Alas, adding a loop to a cell is easy, but finding the right loop is hard, especially when thousands of choices exist.

But Apple has done the heavy lifting for you. To find the right loop, simply tap a button or filter. GarageBand, marvel that it is, does the rest, conveniently hiding loops that don't apply.

By the way, over time, you'll come to know and love certain loops by name. When you do, you can bypass the buttons and filters and merely type your query in the Search Loops field, as I describe shortly.

TIP

If you find a loop that you love and want to keep handy forever, tap its heart icon to add it to your favorites (as described in "Keeping your favorite loops at the ready," later in this chapter).

Finding a loop you love

Here's how you use GarageBand's buttons and filters (see Figure 13-3) to find just the right loop for your song.

FIGURE 13-3:
Filter your loops
by instruments
(left), genres
(middle), or
descriptors
(right).

To winnow down the field, tap the Instruments, Genre, or Descriptors button to filter the loops by instrument, genre, or descriptor, respectively, as shown in Figure 13-3. To clear all three and start over, tap the big X on the left of the buttons.

You can also tap Filter By (on the Apple Loops tab) to filter loops by

>> **Sound pack:** If you've downloaded or purchased one or more sound packs, they'll appear here.

>> **Loop type:** Filter by Audio, Midi, Drummer, or All.

>> **Scale:** Filter by Minor, Major, Neither, Both, or Any.

Another tool you can use for finding the right loop is the search field. If you type a generic term such as *Blues* in the Search Apple Loops field near the top of the loops browser, you see a list of every loop Apple designated as blues-like.

TIP

I don't use the search tool much because I find it unpredictable. Filtering my loop collection with the buttons and filters works for me, so they're my tools of choice when I need to find just the right loop for a project.

Listening to loops

When you find a loop that you think might fit the bill, you'll want to hear it, of course. To listen to a loop, tap it. Note that while a loop is playing, its icon changes to an animated bar chart, as shown in Figure 13-4 for the Bebop Fill loop. Tap the icon a second time to stop the loop playing.

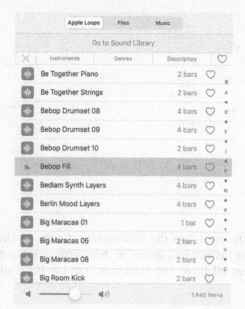

FIGURE 13-4:
Tap a loop
(Bebop Fill) to
listen to it; tap it
again to stop.

Keeping your favorite loops at the ready

Most people have a few specific loops that they really like and want to be able to find quickly. GarageBand's favorites list in the loops browser is just the ticket. It couldn't be easier to use:

>> **Add a loop to your favorites list.** When you find a loop that you like, simply tap the little heart to its right. The heart changes from a white heart with a blue outline to a solid blue heart and the loop is added to your favorites list.

>> **Remove a loop from your favorites list.** Tap the heart again and it reverts to white with a blue outline and the loop is removed from your favorites list.

>> **Use your favorites list.** Tap the heart icon near the top of the loops browser to see the loops you've added to your favorites list.

TIP

To remove a loop from your favorites list, open the list and tap its blue-filled heart. Or use one of the other search methods (buttons, filters, or the search box) to find the loop and then tap its blue-filled heart to remove it.

TIP

The favorites list is particularly handy when you find a loop you like, but it isn't quite right for the current project. By adding the loop to your favorites list, you'll find the loop easily when you're working on another project where it will work perfectly.

Types of loops

GarageBand has three kinds of loops:

>> **Software instrument loops:** Have a green icon and feature synthesized sounds. Software instrument loops let you easily change the tempo, pitch, duration, or timing of individual notes.

>> **Real instrument loops:** Have a blue icon and feature recorded analog sounds, such as electric guitars, basses, horns, wind instruments, and of course, vocals. These loops often sound more realistic than software instrument loops but can't be edited as easily (or at all in some cases).

>> **Drummer loops:** Have a yellow icon and are a special type of real instrument loop. Like real instrument loops, they sound realistic but can't be edited as easily (or at all) as software instrument loops.

TIP

I recommend trying to use software instrument loops first, before you begin to add real instrument loops. That way, if you decide the tempo is too slow or fast, or the pitch is too high or low, you can change the software instrument loops without re-recording them. But if you add real instrument loops and then decide a song is too slow, fast, high, or low, you'll have to find (or record) other real instrument loops.

Some loops are short and others are long, but most are 2, 4, or 8 bars. Don't worry much about length now because, as I explain later in this chapter, loops can be easily looped (repeated indefinitely) or shortened.

Working with Cells

Before you record your masterpiece, let's look at cells and how to make music with 'em.

Editing cells

You can easily cut, copy, paste, move, or delete cells on the grid. To enable cell editing, tap the edit cells icon in the lower-left corner of the live loops grid. The icon is blue when enabled and white when disabled.

With cell editing enabled, tap any cell once, pause for a second, and then tap it a second time. Done properly, this will invoke the Edit menu, as shown in Figure 13-5.

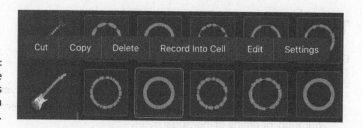

FIGURE 13-5:
Tap a cell twice
(slowly) and its
Edit menu
appears.

WARNING

If you double-tap too quickly, you'll open the settings overlay rather than the Edit menu. If that happens, tap anywhere but on the overlay and try again with a slightly longer delay between taps.

The Edit menu lets you work with the contents of the selected cell or cells as follows:

>> Tap Cut, Copy, or Delete to cut, copy, or delete, respectively, the contents of the selected cell.

>> Tap Paste to paste the clipboard (which contains the last item you cut or copied) into the selected cell. Note that the Paste command appears in the Edit menu only after you've cut or copied a cell.

>> Tap Edit to edit the selected cell in tracks view (as described later in this chapter).

>> Tap Record into Cell to replace the cell's contents with a new recording (as described later in this chapter). Note that Record into Cell doesn't appear in the Edit menu if multiple cells are selected.

>> Tap Settings (or double-tap the cell quickly) to open the cell's settings overlay, as shown in Figure 13-6. Use the settings overlay to alter the settings for the selected cell.

Note that although most cell settings are available for all types of loops, a handful are exclusive to one type (as noted next).

TIP

To hear changes you make in real time, tap the cell while the settings overlay is open.

>> **Gain (blue real instrument and yellow drummer cells only):** Drag the Gain slider left to reduce the cell's volume or right to increase it.

>> **Velocity (green software instrument cells only):** Drag the Velocity slider left to reduce the cell's volume or right to increase it.

FIGURE 13-6:
The settings
overlay for the
Razor Rock
Rhythm Guitar
(real instrument)
loop.

>> **Quantization (green software instrument cells only):** Quantization corrects the timing of notes. Choose Straight for a precise rhythm or choose Triplet or Swing to give the notes a looser feel.

>> **Octaves (green software instruments only):** Transpose this cell one, two, or three octaves up or down.

>> **Time Snap:** Determines how this cell plays in time with other cells. Choose 1 bar, ½ note, ¼ note, 1/8 note, 1/16 note, or turn snapping off completely.

>> **Play Mode:** Determines the mode of play for the cell. Choose Play/Stop to start and stop playback by tapping the cell; choose Play while Pressed to play the cell by pressing and holding down on the cell; or choose Retrigger to restart the cell from the beginning whenever you tap.

>> **Looping:** Enable if you want this cell to play repeatedly. Disable this setting if you want the cell to play only once.

>> **Length:** Tap the arrows to adjust the length of the loop incrementally, or swipe up or down on the numbers to change them by larger values.

>> **Follow Tempo & Pitch (blue real instrument cells only):** Enable this setting to have the cell adopt the song tempo and key.

>> **Semitones:** Tap the plus and minus buttons to raise or lower, respectively, the pitch by one semitone per tap.

>> **Speed:** Drag the Speed slider left to reduce or right to increase this cell's playback speed.

>> **Reverse:** Enable Reverse to play the cell backwards.

>> **Reset All:** Tap Reset All to reset all settings to their default values.

Whew. Now that you know pretty much everything about cells, following are a few tips before you record (or perform live).

Undoing and redoing a loop

If you drop a loop onto a cell that already contains a loop, the loop you dropped replaces the loop in the cell.

That's why GarageBand has an undo icon. I'm not sure how many actions you can undo in GarageBand for iDevices, but it's more than a couple. To redo what you just undid, press and hold down on the undo icon and choose Redo.

TIP

If you're using a Bluetooth or USB keyboard with your iDevice, you can redo things you've undone by typing the Mac keyboard shortcut ⌘+Shift+Z. And, for what it's worth, many of your favorite Mac keyboard shortcuts — including ⌘+X, ⌘+C, and ⌘+V for cut, copy, and paste, respectively — are supported in GarageBand for iDevices as long as you're using an external keyboard. You'll find a list of supported keyboard shortcuts in GarageBand (for iDevices) Help (search for *keyboard shortcuts*).

Finally, you can step forward or backward through your undoes by pressing the undo icon and choosing Undo or Redo, or if you are using an external keyboard, by pressing ⌘+Z to undo or ⌘+Shift+Z to redo. This technique is useful for listening to something the way it sounded before you did whatever you just did, and then the way it sounds after you did it.

WARNING

As with most programs, the Undo and Redo commands are linear, so pay attention lest you undo something you didn't want to undo.

Moving cells

Moving cells is easy once you know the trick: Enable cell editing and then press and drag the cell to its new location.

If the destination cell is empty, you're done. If the destination cell already contains a loop, it will switch places with the cell you're dropping.

Recording into a cell

Last but certainly not least, you don't have to use Apple loops to fill every cell. You can fill cells with your own Smart instrument, vocal, guitar, bass, keyboard, or almost any other type of recording you can think of.

To fill a cell with your own recording, enable cell editing, tap the cell once to select it, and then tap it a second time to invoke its Edit menu (refer to Figure 13-5).

REMEMBER

If you double-tap too fast, the Settings overlay will appear instead of the Edit menu.

Now tap Record into Cell. If the cell is in a touch instrument row, the instrument opens. If the cell is in an empty row, the last-used touch instrument opens and is assigned to that row.

WARNING

If the cell is already filled, the new recording will replace its contents.

Now, to begin recording, tap the red record icon on the control bar and play or sing your part. When you're finished, tap the record icon again and then tap the grid icon to return to the live loops grid.

And that's all there is to recording anything into a cell!

Adding remix FX

Before you record, I'd like to show you one more thing you can do with the grid: Add remix FX to your performance.

With remix FX, you can add scratches and other effects a live DJ might employ. Using them is fun and easy, requiring no skills beyond being able to use your ears and fingers.

To access the remix FX effects, tap the FX icon on the control bar and the remix FX buttons and pads appear at the bottom of the screen, as shown in Figure 13-7.

On the left and right are XY pads, currently assigned to Filter (left) and Repeater (right). To change which effect is assigned to either pad, tap its name and your choices — Filter, Repeater, Wobble, Reverb, Orbit, and Delay — appear, as shown on the left in Figure 13-7.

There's no way to explain what they do in words, so open any live loops template (so you have something to hear), tap the FX icon, and then tap the play icon. Now slide your finger around on either XY pad and listen closely to how it affects the cells playing in the background.

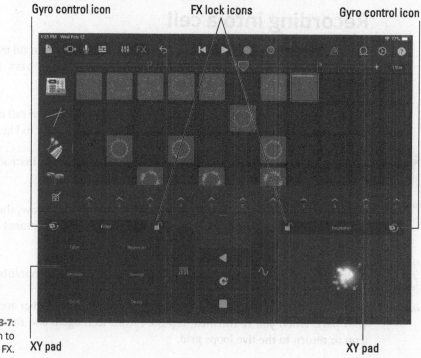

Gyro control icon   FX lock icons   Gyro control icon

FIGURE 13-7:
Tap the FX icon to
see remix FX.   XY pad   XY pad

Now that you know all about rows, columns, triggers, cells, and remix FX, let's move to the meat of the matter — it's time to record your performance!

Recording with the Loop Grid

To record using the loop grid, first make sure all your cells are arranged precisely the way you want them. You're going to trigger cells or columns in time with the beat, so you want to know the sequence of cells or columns you're going to tap before you record. Practice your performance a few times before you record it.

But before you record, you might want to enable count-in and the metronome (if they're not enabled already). Tap the settings icon on the control bar, and then tap Metronome and Count-in.

Now that you've enabled the count-in and metronome and know where you're going to tap, you're ready to record.

Here's how:

1. **Tap the go to beginning icon to make sure all loops are at their beginning.**

2. **Tap the record icon to start recording.**

   After the count-in, the recording starts.

3. **Trigger the first cell or column.**

4. **Before the first cell or column finishes, trigger the second cell or column to cue it up.**

   It will start playing when the first cell or column finishes.

5. **Continue triggering each cell or column in order until your song is complete.**

6. **Tap the stop icon to stop recording.**

You now have a recording of your project. To hear it, tap the tracks icon, where you'll find each instrument or performance on its own track. Tap play to listen to your work.

If you're not happy with your performance and want to re-record your performance, tap the grid icon, tap the undo icon, and then start over at Step 1.

If you're pleased with the performance, you can fine-tune it in tracks mode, which you become acquainted with in the next chapter (and beyond). Or you can tap the my songs icon and share the project as-is. Either way, that's how you record and edit performances you make using the loop grid.

Onward!

» **Controlling software instruments with a MIDI keyboard**

» **Working with software instruments**

» **Working with tracks**

» **Working with regions**

Chapter **14**

Laying Down Software Instrument Tracks

G arageBand is more than just a recording-studio-in-a-box; it also includes an orchestra full of high-quality musical instruments. It's chock-full of pianos, guitars, drums, horns, synthesizers, and even a chorus of heavenly voices, all available to use in your musical compositions for free.

In this chapter, you first learn about MIDI and MIDI controllers, and why they matter. That topic is followed by pretty much all you need to know to play and record using GarageBand's massive collection of software instruments.

What Is MIDI, Anyway?

MIDI stands for Musical Instrument Digital Interface and is pronounced "middy." The term covers a lot of ground, as you can see from this description by the MIDI Manufacturer's Association (www.midi.org):

> *The Musical Instrument Digital Interface (MIDI) enables people to use multimedia computers and electronic musical instruments to create, enjoy and learn about music. There are actually three components to MIDI, which*

are the communications Protocol (language), the Connector (hardware interface) and a distribution format called Standard MIDI Files.

In other words, MIDI is a language, a hardware interface, and a file format. The language of MIDI allows different devices to talk to each other. The hardware interface sends and receives MIDI information between devices that speak MIDI. Music made with MIDI can be saved in a file format that can be understood by other MIDI devices.

The upshot is that many kinds of devices that you may use in audio (or video) production — such as keyboards, computers, mixing boards (control surfaces), and even lighting gear — can talk to each other in a common language called MIDI.

If you're wondering why you might care, it's because, with the proper cable or adapter, you can connect many MIDI controllers to your iDevices!

TIP

Many USB devices that you use with your computer can be used also with your iPhone, iPad, or iPod touch with the Lightning-to-USB camera adapter shown in Figure 14-1 ($29.99).

FIGURE 14-1:
The Lightning-to-USB camera adapter lets you use many USB devices with your iDevices.

The kit converts the standard USB connector on external devices to a Lightning connector you can plug into your iDevice. And, for what it's worth, this trick also connects USB QWERTY keyboards, USB microphones, and other USB peripherals to your iDevices. Although it won't work with devices that require more power than an iDevice supplies (and there's no way to know until you try), it worked with both of my USB MIDI keyboards and most of my USB microphones. It's likely they all would work, but I said "most" because I haven't tested them all with iDevices.

WARNING

You may be tempted to save a few dollars by purchasing a third-party camera adapter knock-off from Amazon or elsewhere. In my experience, half (or more) of the knock-offs don't work at all or don't work properly with certain devices that work with Apple's adapter.

That said, I ordered yet another third-party USB Camera Adapter (sold by Hosal Direct for $12.89 at Amazon.com) as research for this book, and it works (so far — it's been only a couple of months).

Caveat emptor.

Controlling Software Instruments with a MIDI Keyboard

Although MIDI is a multiheaded beast, in the context of using GarageBand, I focus on using a MIDI keyboard to control GarageBand's software instruments.

REMEMBER

Note that word *control*. MIDI keyboards are appropriately referred to as *MIDI controllers* because you're using a device — often a piano-like keyboard connected via USB — to control the software instruments on your Mac.

And, in fact, a pure MIDI keyboard is just that — a controller — incapable of making sounds of its own. All it can do is send MIDI information to a MIDI host (in this case, GarageBand on your Mac or iOS device), which translates the information into sound.

To further complicate things, many MIDI keyboards are *also* synthesizers, which *can* produce sound on their own. For the purposes of this chapter, think of your MIDI keyboard as just a MIDI controller, even if the keyboard can make sounds all by itself.

TECHNICAL STUFF

In the pre-MIDI era, when you played a device such as synthesizer, an electric piano, or an electric organ, the device didn't control anything but its own internal circuitry. So each keyboard device produced only the sounds that its internal circuits knew how to make. For this reason, an Arp synthesizer sounded like an Arp, a Moog sounded like a Moog, and a Prophet 5 sounded like — you guessed it — a Prophet 5. Any artist worth his or her salt had a rack of different synthesizer keyboards for producing different sounds.

We've come a long way since then; that rack of keyboards and much, much more are built right into GarageBand at no extra cost.

By the way, if you have an older sound-making keyboard, it might support MIDI and be usable with GarageBand. If it is, you'll see either a USB port or one or two large round ports, probably labeled MIDI in and MIDI out. If you don't see a USB port, you'll need a MIDI interface — a small, reasonably priced piece of hardware — which converts round MIDI in and MIDI out ports on the device to USB you can connect to your iDevice via the Lightning-to-USB camera adapter mentioned earlier in the chapter.

Here's the bottom line: When you play a MIDI keyboard (controller), the keyboard isn't producing sound. It's noting the keys that you press, and how hard and how long you press them, and then sending that information to your Mac, where GarageBand translates it and plays that sound with a software instrument.

Conversely, when you strike a drum, the sound occurs when the drumstick hits the drumhead. When you play an electric guitar, the sound occurs when the pick or a finger strikes the strings and is captured by your Mac (or an audio interface connected to your Mac as discussed in Chapter 8), or is fed through an amplifier. And, when you play a piano, the sound occurs when the hammers hit the strings.

MIDI controllers can be used also to control other keyboards or anything dedicated to working with the MIDI protocol. For example, *MIDI work surfaces* look like miniature versions of a big-time mixing board, complete with sliding faders, rotating knobs, and VU meters with needles. You use these work surfaces to control audio applications such as Logic, Pro Tools, and even GarageBand. You can also use MIDI drum pads to tap out drum patterns with your fingertips. In addition, you can find MIDI stage lighting controllers and many other types of controllers that speak MIDI. The list of things you can do with MIDI is almost endless, and most USB MIDI controllers work with iDevices (with a USB adapter such as the aforementioned Lightning-to-USB camera adapter).

I highly recommend using a MIDI keyboard if you're even half-serious about recording with GarageBand. For purposes of this chapter, I assume that you're using a USB keyboard such as the M-Audio Keystation 49 MK3 keyboard ($99; www.m-audio.com), shown in Figure 14-2, which is a direct descendant of the MIDI keyboard John Mayer demonstrated when Steve Jobs introduced GarageBand at Macworld San Francisco in 2004. You may be able to find an even cheaper MIDI keyboard, but you can't go wrong with the Keystation 49 MK3 for around $100.

TIP

To avoid confusion, for the rest of the book I refer to the keyboard on which you type letters and numbers as the *QWERTY keyboard*. Keyboards that have black-and-white piano-like keys will be referred to as plain old *keyboards*.

Working with Software Instruments

GarageBand for iDevices offers several types of software instruments. Plain-old *software instruments* are just like their Mac-version counterparts; you play them via onscreen keyboard or external MIDI keyboard.

In addition, *smart instruments* offer unique touch-screen interfaces that make them easier for non-musicians to use.

Finally, there are drummer tracks and drums tracks. *Drummer tracks* are complete, ready-to-use customizable drum parts; *drums tracks* allow you compose the entire drum part by tapping drums on an onscreen drum kit or pressing keys on an external MIDI keyboard.

REMEMBER

A software instrument may contain more than one instrument. Drums, for example, contain 50 or 60 different drum, cymbal, and percussion instrument sounds. If you're using a MIDI keyboard, each drum, cymbal, or other instrument is triggered by a different key. So, for example, playing middle C triggers the sound of a kick drum, D triggers the sound of a snare drum, and D-sharp triggers the sound of a closed hi-hat.

Even though a drum kit contains 50 or 60 different instrument sounds, it's considered a single software instrument and is recorded on a single track. So a track *may* contain the sounds of many instruments, as long as they're all part of the same software instrument like those 50 or 60 different drum sounds.

Creating a new software instrument track

To create a software instrument track, follow these steps:

1. **Create a new empty project (if you haven't already) and tap the my songs icon on the control bar.**

2. **Tap Tracks at the top of the instrument picker and then swipe left or right to see your instrument choices.**

   Your choices are: Strings, Bass, Guitar, World, Drummer, Keyboard, or Drums. The other options — Amp, Audio Recorder, and External — are used for microphone or direct electronic instrument recordings, which you learn about in Chapters 15 and 16.

   What you do next depends on which software instrument you choose because each has different options. For example, the Keyboard offers Smart Piano, Alchemy Synth, Sampler, or More Sounds; the Drummer offers Acoustic, Electronic, Percussion, or More Drummers; and the Guitar, Bass, and Strings instruments all have the same set of options — Smart Instrument, Notes, Scales, or More Sounds.

   I'm sorry to inform you that due to space constraints I'm not going to cover most of these options or instruments; I encourage you to explore them at your leisure. For additional information on these (and almost any other) features, don't forget that wonderful help icon at the bottom of the Settings menu.

3. **Tap an option to place the instrument on the first track of your new project.**

   If you want to follow along at home, choose Smart Guitar (shown in Figure 14-3).

4. **Go ahead and play around.**

   If you chose Smart Guitar, tap a chord at the top of a strip (Em, Am, Dm, and so on in Figure 14-3); swipe up or down on a strip; or tap individual strings. Be sure to check out all four Autoplay options, which fingerpick or strum different patterns.

TIP

You can change the chords in the strips by tapping the settings icon in the control bar and then tapping Edit Chords.

You now have a project with a software instrument track that uses the Smart Guitar (or the instrument you selected). But what if you change your mind and want to record a different instrument?

No worries! GarageBand has hundreds of other instrument choices.

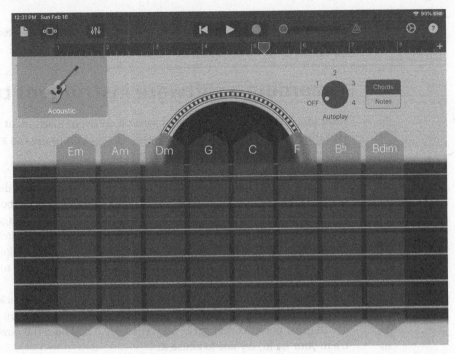

FIGURE 14-3:
Tap a chord or
string or swipe a
strip to play your
Smart guitar.

Selecting a different instrument

Each instrument offers variations. For example, the guitar has the following variations: Acoustic, Classic Clean, Hard Rock, Retro Wah, and Roots Rock. To switch to another variation, tap the instrument button (Roots Rock in Figure 14-4) and then tap a different variation.

Or if you want to select a different instrument completely, tap the browser icon to return to the instrument picker screen.

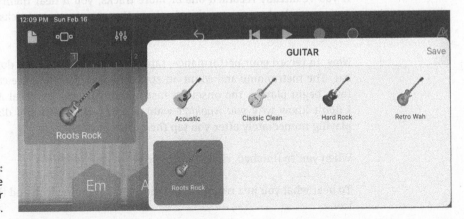

FIGURE 14-4:
Choose from five
different guitar
variations.

You're now ready to record a track with this instrument, as described in the following section.

Recording a software instrument track

After you create a new project and select a software instrument for its first track (see the preceding section), you're ready to move on to the fun stuff — recording some music with that software instrument.

The funny thing is, this is either the hard part or the easy part, depending on your musical chops. If you know your way around a keyboard or fretboard, you'll probably find it easy to record with software instruments in GarageBand. Or if you simply have a bit of theoretical knowledge, the process will likely be a snap. But even if you don't have a shred of musical talent, it won't take long for you to figure out enough to make music, as long as you take the time to experiment.

TIP

GarageBand's software instruments can sound like a million bucks — or a million cats fighting. In the immortal words of Peter Parker (also known as Spider-Man), "With great power comes great responsibility." You hold the power of an orchestra in your hand; try not to abuse it.

REMEMBER

GarageBand offers two features to help you record: the metronome and count-in. With the metronome on, you hear a soft click marking the beat of your song. Note that the sound of the metronome is never recorded. When you have count-in turned on, an additional measure (or two) is counted before GarageBand starts recording. Refer to Chapter 12 to enable or disable either or both.

To practice (before laying down a new track), just tap and swipe the onscreen instrument or play an external MIDI keyboard. To hear the metronome while you practice, tap the metronome icon and then tap the play icon.

If you've already recorded one or more tracks, you'll hear them (along with the metronome) when you tap the play icon. You can mute any tracks you don't want to hear, as described later in the chapter.

Now, to record your performance, tap the record icon (the red dot) in the control bar. The metronome and count-in start (if enabled); when the count-in reaches four, begin playing the onscreen instrument (or your external MIDI keyboard). I don't know why you *wouldn't* want a count-in, but if you disabled it, begin playing immediately after you tap the record button.

When you're finished, click the stop icon.

To hear what you just recorded, tap the go to beginning icon and then tap the play icon.

Working with Tracks

Now that you've recorded a track, you might want to work with it or other tracks you've recorded. To work with tracks, you need to switch to tracks view, which is where you can edit and modify tracks.

 Tap the tracks icon in the control bar to switch to the tracks view, as shown in Figure 14-5.

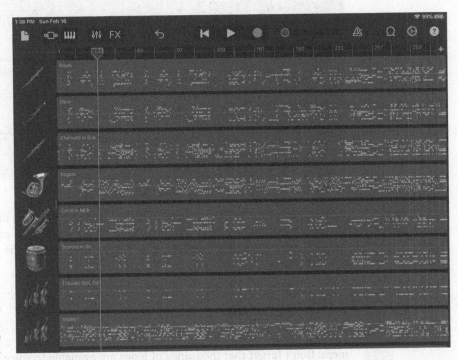

FIGURE 14-5: The tracks view lets you work on tracks you've recorded.

Displaying track headers

The first thing you should do in track view is expose the track headers by dragging any instrument icon (such as the one for the oboe, clarinet, or French horn) to the right. The track headers appear, as shown in Figure 14-6.

Track headers provide three useful controls for working on your project:

>> **Mute icon:** Tap a track's mute icon to silence the track.

>> **Solo icon:** Tap a track's solo icon to silence all tracks except this one.

>> **Track volume slider:** Slide right or left to raise or lower the track's volume.

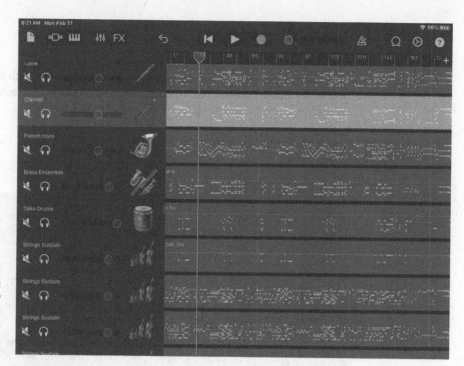

FIGURE 14-6:
Swipe any
instrument icon
to the right to
reveal the track
headers.

You can enable the mute or solo icons on as many tracks as you like, making them super-flexible when you're trying to listen to a single track or record without hearing every track (for example, if you need to hear only the bass and drums while recording a guitar part).

Adding loops

You don't have to perform every part on every track by playing a software instrument. Don't forget that thousands of loops are available to spice up your projects (see Chapter 13). To add a loop to your project, tap the loop browser icon in the control bar and then tap Apple Loops. Search or filter the loops (as you learn in Chapter 13) to find the one you want, and then drag it to the empty space at the bottom of the workspace and drop it. It appears on a new track.

You can also drag a loop to an existing track (of the same color), where it replaces all or part of the region you drop it on. Don't worry about this too much — if you drag a loop onto the wrong type of track, you'll see a descriptive message explaining why you can't do that. For example, in Figure 14-7, I dragged a blue (real instrument) loop onto a green (software instrument) track.

FIGURE 14-7:
Drag a loop onto
the wrong kind of
track and you'll
see a message
explaining why
you can't do that.

If you can't find a loop that works for you, you can add a track (or tracks) and record a performance by tapping the + at the bottom of the track header column. Now swipe left and right on the Browser screen to select an instrument for the new track.

For what it's worth, you can also add electric guitar or bass tracks, vocals, or anything else you can connect to your device or record with a microphone, as I explain in Chapters 15 and 16.

Working with regions

If tracks are the building blocks of songs, regions are the building blocks of tracks. Each time you tap the record icon, a new region is created. GarageBand has three types of regions: Recorded sound regions are blue, software instrument regions are green, and drummer regions are yellow. The good news is they all work pretty much the same.

Selecting, cutting, copying, and pasting regions

To select a region, tap it once.

To select more than one region, touch and hold down on a region and then, without releasing that region, tap additional regions to add them to the selection. Or press and hold down on any empty area in the workspace and drag to select multiple regions.

To select all regions on a track, tap the track header once. To select all regions on all tracks, tap any empty area in the workspace and then tap Select All.

After you've selected a region or regions, tap the selection again to see all available commands, including Cut, Copy, Delete, Loop, Split, Edit, Rename, and Settings, as shown in Figure 14-8. Tap the command you need.

When you cut or copy a region (or anything), the thing you copied remains on the clipboard until you cut or copy another item (or quit GarageBand).

FIGURE 14-8:
Tap once to select
the region, and
then tap again to
reveal its
available
commands.

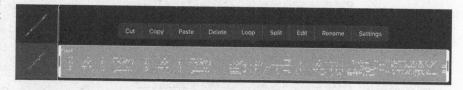

To paste the item that's on the clipboard, tap the destination track and move the playhead (if necessary) to the precise location you want the region to appear. Now tap the track again and tap Paste.

Splitting and joining regions

Sometimes you may want to split or join regions. To split a region, tap the region once to select it, tap it again, and then tap Split. The split marker, which looks like a tiny scissors, appears over the top part of the track, as shown in Figure 14-9. Drag the marker left or right to the proper location and then drag it downward to perform the split.

FIGURE 14-9:
Drag the split
marker to exactly
where you want
the split, then
drag the marker
downward to split
the region at that
spot.

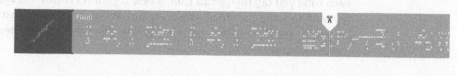

To cancel a split, just tap anywhere outside the region before dragging the split marker downward.

To join regions, they must be on the same track with no other regions between them. Touch and hold down on the first region, and then tap the second region. Tap either of the two selected regions and then tap Join.

You should know two things about joining regions:

>> You can't join blue (recorded audio) regions.

>> If you join yellow (drummer) regions, the second region will inherit the settings of the first region.

Trimming regions

To trim a region — change its start or end point — tap the region to select it, and then drag its left or right edge to change the start or end of the region.

If multiple regions are selected, all are trimmed by the same amount.

Editing your performance in software instrument regions

Now, without further ado, here's how to fine-tune a software instrument region by rearranging the notes.

REMEMBER

Before undertaking any major surgery on your song, it's a good idea to save a copy of the song first by tapping the my songs icon in the control bar and then pressing and holding down on the project until the menu appears. Tap Rename and give the project a new, descriptive name. That way, if you screw things up, you can go back to where you were before you made the changes by opening the original (and un-screwed up) song file.

Also, don't forget that you can tap the undo icon to undo, in reverse chronological order, the things you've done.

To edit a software instrument track, follow these steps:

1. **Tap the green software instrument region you want to edit, tap it again, and then tap Edit.**

The notes in the region are represented by dashes on a grid, as shown in Figure 14-10.

TIP

Tap the play icon to hear the notes on the screen.

The dashes of various lengths displayed in green represent the notes, and each horizontal line in the graph represents a different note on the musical scale or instrument or both, depending on the software instrument.

If you don't see the dashes after you record, swipe up or down to find them.

TIP

To zoom in or out, pinch or unpinch with two fingers. Pinching vertically changes the width of the rows; pinching horizontally changes the length of the dashes.

When you zoom in, you see fewer notes but have finer control over the individual notes that you do see. When you unpinch to zoom out, you see more notes at once, but they're smaller and harder to drag around.

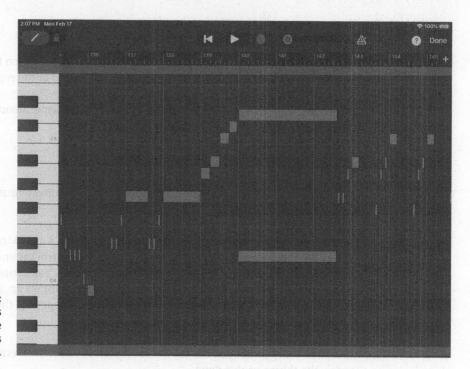

FIGURE 14-10:
The dashes represent the notes in this region.

TIP

If you've recorded higher or lower notes than you see on the screen, swipe up or down to scroll the rows.

2. **To edit a note, select it by tapping the dash that represents it.**

Do you hear that? When you tap a dash, you are "playing" the note that it represents. To select multiple notes, press and hold the first one, and then tap the notes you want to select.

With the note or notes selected, you can start making changes. Here's a quick list of the edits that you can make to the notes:

- **To move a note or notes:** Slide the note to the right or the left on the same horizontal line to change *when* it is played. Slide the note up or down to a different horizontal line to change the *pitch* of the note. It's that simple! When you move a dash, you change when the note is played, the pitch of the note, or both.

- **To change the length of a note:** Tap the note that you want to change to select it. Then grab the beginning or ending edge and drag it to shorten or lengthen the note.

- **To copy and paste a note or notes:** Tap a note to select it (or select multiple notes as just described), and then tap the note again to cut, copy, delete, or change its velocity (loudness).

- **To paste a note you've cut or copied:** Move the playhead to the precise spot where you want to paste the note. Tap the line below the playhead, and then tap Paste.

The note is pasted in the row it was copied or cut from. If that's not where you want it, drag it to a new destination.

When you're satisfied with your edits, tap the Done button in the upper-right corner. When you're absolutely sure you're satisfied, save your changes by tapping the my songs icon to save this version of your project.

Each region has its own settings for Velocity (loudness), Looping, Quantization, Transposition, Speed, and Reverse. To change any or all of these settings, tap the region to select it, tap it again, and then tap Settings to see the overlay (shown in Figure 14-11).

Quantization is particularly useful if you're not a great player because it moves notes to the nearest beat in the grid. If no notes are selected, it affects all notes in the region; if individual notes are selected, it affects only those notes.

Quantization is a great way to perform a quick-and-dirty fix on some tracks. For example, if you have a MIDI drum track with some beats slightly out of time, quantizing the region to the nearest ⅛ or ¹⁄₁₆ note will probably fix the beats that were off.

FIGURE 14-11: The settings overlay for a software instrument track.

Listen to the track, and if the results weren't what you expected, tap the undo icon in the control bar, choose a different value, and try again. Repeat the process until you're satisfied.

TIP

The grid scale affects the amount of correction applied. A scale set to 1/1 Note moves the note a lot farther to fix it than a scale set to 1/32 Note.

TIP

Be careful when using the quantize feature. If you have pickup notes or anything funky or off-beat, you might mess up your track by *fixing* its timing. If you don't like the results, undo the fix immediately, lest you lose your chance by closing the project or quitting GarageBand.

Finally, to change the velocity (loudness) of a note, tap the note (or select multiple notes), tap again, and then tap Velocity. Move the slider left or right to increase or decrease the loudness of the note or notes.

To change the velocity of all notes in a region, tap Done to return to the tracks view. Tap the region, tap it again, and then tap Velocity. Move the slider left or right to increase or decrease the loudness of all the notes.

And that's how you work with regions on your tracks.

Now I have good news for you: Vocal, acoustic instrument, and guitar/bass tracks and regions work pretty much the same as software instrument regions. And altering the sound of what's in a region is mostly the same for all types of regions. You'll learn how to alter what you hear on a track or region in Chapters 15 and 16. And here's more good news — because you already know how to work with tracks and regions, I have more space in Chapters 15 and 16 for other useful features and techniques.

Onward!

Chapter **15**

Recording Vocals and Acoustic Instruments with a Mic

This chapter cuts to the heart of audio recording — using a microphone or microphones to record vocals and instruments. As usual, Apple has done much of the heavy lifting already by including several dozen presets that you can use to change the sound of your recorded vocals and acoustic instruments. You, as the recording engineer, don't have to worry as much about what type of microphone you should use to record which instrument or how much echo to apply to a grand piano, for example. The presets do it for you — and quite nicely I might add.

You'll be surprised at how good your recordings sound even if you use only your iDevice's built-in microphone. However, for better-quality recordings, almost any external microphone you happen to have handy will sound better than the built-in mic. Note, too that some mics work better for vocals and instruments than others. You can find details about choosing a mic in Chapter 2. In this chapter, you find out how to set up and position microphones for recording, as well as advice, tips, and hints for making better recordings with said microphones.

The only thing I'll add here is that if you want to use a third-party microphone with your iDevice, get a microphone that specifically supports iOS/iPadOS. See Chapter 25 for recommendations on where to shop for recording gear.

If you already have a USB microphone, you can probably use an adapter like the Lightning-to-USB camera adapter (see Chapter 14) to connect it to your iDevice. I say "probably" because I tried four USB mics (and two different adapters) and only two worked reliably. I suspect the other two needed more power than an iDevice can provide through its Lightning port, so I ordered a HENKUR USB Camera Adapter with Charging Port for $17 (see Figure 15-1). It has a second Lightning port to connect a power source, and worked properly with all four USB mics.

FIGURE 15-1:
The HENKUR USB Camera Adapter with Charging Port worked with all four of my USB microphones.

Because your device's single Lightning port is the only way to connect wired headphones to your iDevice — and you must use headphones while you record — you need a microphone with a headphone jack that supports monitoring so you can hear other tracks (or the metronome) as you sing or play. Without headphones, you'll encounter dreaded feedback and the sound from the speakers will muddy your recording. If you use the built-in mic, connect headphones to the Lightning port before you record. If you use an external mic, make sure it has a headphone jack so you can hear other tracks or the metronome as you record.

One last thing: It's possible to use multiple microphones to record to separate tracks on your iDevice, but you need a multichannel audio interface for iOS/iPadOS, such as the Focusrite iTrack Solo — Lightning (two microphones or guitars; around $130) or the RME Babyface Pro FS (up to 12 mics; around $900).

Before you start throwing money at the problem, though, remember that recording with microphones is an art, a science, and a skill and you won't master everything at once. Many, many things can affect the sound you record, and understanding how these things interact and alter your recordings will take time. So try the gear you already have before spending any money.

You have a lot to cover, so let's rock.

Getting Ready to Record

I'm going to assume that you are using either the built-in microphone or a third-party mic, are using headphones, and are ready to commence recording. But before you record a single note, you need to attend to a few things if you want to end up with great-sounding tracks.

The two things that you need to master first are microphone placement and level setting. If you nail these two, you'll always get better results.

At this point, I wouldn't recommend spending a lot of time trying to deaden the room (see Chapter 2 for details). Rather, I suggest that you place the microphone and record a test track. Now decide whether you have too much room sound coloring the track and adjust accordingly.

I guarantee that you'll record better-sounding real audio tracks after reading this chapter.

Preparing to record

When your room setup is as good as it's going to get, it's time to set up your mic or mics. Perhaps the most important factor in what ends up being recorded is the position of the microphone during recording. Your job is to position the microphone where it sounds the best to your ear. But to do that, you need to make the microphone live so that you can hear the effect of repositioning it.

To set up your mic so that it's live and then create the track to record on, follow these steps:

1. **Connect headphones to your iDevice. Or if you're using an external mic or audio interface, connect it to your iDevice and then connect your headphones to the audio interface.**

   An alert appears asking you to turn on monitoring (as shown in Figure 15-2).

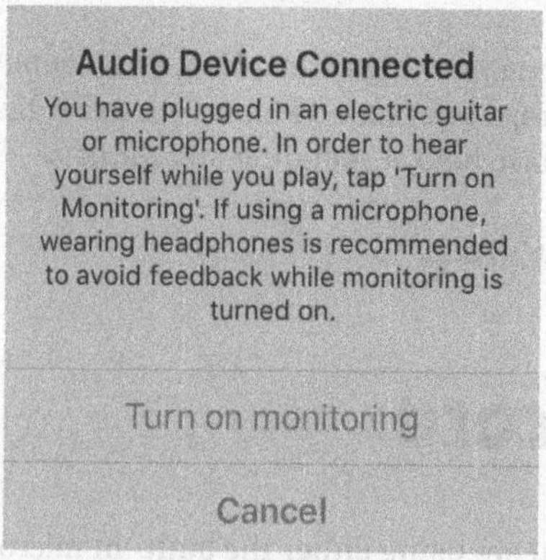

FIGURE 15-2:
Turn on
monitoring to
avoid feedback
and hear yourself
play.

2. **Tap Turn on Monitoring to hear sound from the microphone (and the metronome or other tracks) through your headphones.**

   If you don't see the alert when you plug in your external mic, your iDevice didn't recognize the mic. Disconnect and then reconnect it. If you're using a USB-to-Lightning adapter, disconnect that and reconnect it.

   If your mic (or audio interface) is still not recognized, try a different cable or adapter if you have one.

3. **After your mic or audio interface is recognized by your iDevice, test your setup by putting your headphones on and speaking into the mic.**

   If you hear yourself in the cans, you're golden. If you don't hear yourself (and the track's level-meter LEDs don't light up), consider the following (in no particular order).

   Make sure that

   - All your cables are firmly connected.
   - The proper track is selected (you can't record a track unless it's selected).
   - The track you're recording doesn't have its mute icon illuminated.
   - No other track has its solo icon illuminated.
   - The track's volume slider isn't all the way to the left.
   - The mic is turned on (not all mics have on/off switches).
   - The iDevice's sound is not muted or set too low to hear.
   - If your mic or headphones let you adjust the volume, make sure it's not set too low to hear.

   If none of these solve the problem, try a different mic, cable, or adapter.

4. **Test your headphone connection by tapping the play icon with the metronome enabled.**

If you hear the metronome through anything but your headphones, check your connections and try again. When the only sound you can hear comes out of the headphones, you're good to go.

Should you not follow Steps 1 through 4, you will hear awful high-pitched howling, known as *feedback,* if your speaker and mic are in close proximity.

5. **Tap the my songs icon in the control bar and open an existing GarageBand project or create a new one.**

See Chapter 4 for details on opening and creating projects.

6. **Do one of the following:**

- *If you opened an existing project:* Tap + at the bottom of the track headers to create a new track, and swipe left or right to find and select Audio Recorder.

- *If you created a new project:* Swipe left or right to find and select Audio Recorder.

The audio recorder appears on the screen, as shown in Figure 15-3.

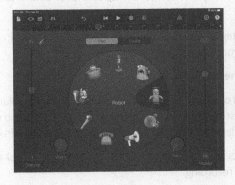 

FIGURE 15-3: The audio recorder's Fun tab (left) and Studio tab (right).

7. **Tap the Fun tab and explore the nine icons that represent its presets.**

Clockwise from 12 o'clock, the icons are Clean, Monster, Robot, Dreamy, Bullhorn, Telephone, Extreme Tuning, Chipmunk, and Alien. Tap a preset to select it and then sing or talk into the mic to hear its effects.

Although the Fun tab is fun, it probably won't provide the sound you seek unless you're recording a novelty song. For serious recording, you are better served by the Studio tab.

8. **Tap the Studio tab so you can look at its presets and controls.**

9. **Tap the current preset (Lead Vocals in Figure 15-3, right) to open the preset picker, as shown in Figure 15-4.**

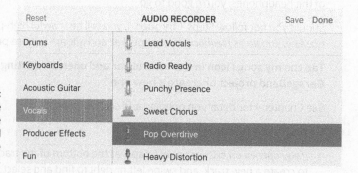

FIGURE 15-4:
Choose the appropriate category and preset for the track.

Reset	AUDIO RECORDER	Save Done
Drums	Lead Vocals	
Keyboards	Radio Ready	
Acoustic Guitar	Punchy Presence	
Vocals	Sweet Chorus	
Producer Effects	Pop Overdrive	
Fun	Heavy Distortion	

10. **Tap a category in the first column.**

    You want to choose the category that best describes the instrument or vocal part you're recording. The categories are self-explanatory: Choose Vocal to record vocals; choose Acoustic Guitar to record acoustic guitars; choose Keyboards to record keyboards (with a mic); or choose Drums to record drums.

    Two additional categories — Producer Effects and Fun — contain presets that you can use with most instruments and vocals.

11. **Tap a preset in the second column.**

    When you select a category, its presets appear in the second column. Tap the preset that best describes the instrument or vocal sound you desire. In Figure 15-4, I selected the Vocals category and the Pop Overdrive preset.

TIP

    To audition presets, play (and pause) your song while you sing or play the instrument you're recording.

    When you're satisfied with your preset choice, tap Done.

12. **Tap the tracks icon in the control bar to return to tracks view.**

13. **Tap the go to beginning icon, make sure the track you want to record is selected, and then click the play icon.**

    You should hear your project — the tracks recorded previously — and your mic should be live with the selected track ready for recording.

Although you may be tempted to tap the record icon now, there are still a few more things to consider.

Positioning the microphone

Assuming that you can hear the input from the microphone in your headphones (as described in Steps 1 and 2 in the preceding list), it's time to adjust the mic's position for optimal recording. Most vocals are recorded using a classic close mic technique, where the microphone is 6 inches or less from the vocalist's lips. For other sound sources, the optimal distance from the sound to the mic can range from 6 inches to 2 feet or more.

Many mics pick up sound in a cardioid pattern (see Chapter 2), which is the preferred pattern for vocals and most single-instrument recordings. The closer you move a cardioid pattern mic to the sound source, the more bass response you hear, which is known as the *proximity effect*. You can really hear this effect in your cans (headphones) as you move the sound source and microphone closer together or farther apart.

Because cardioid-pattern mics pick up sound directly in front of them better than from the back or sides, changing the orientation of the mic can dramatically change what you hear. So don't just move it closer or farther away — change the angle or direction in which the mic is pointed, too.

And by the way, the 6 inches to 2 feet guideline isn't etched in stone. If your oboe sounds fantastic when the mic is exactly 3.75 feet away, fantastic! You can find the sweet spot for a mic only by experimenting with its placement.

After you're happy with your mic's placement, you're ready to set the levels. See the next section for details about how to do this.

CARE AND FEEDING OF MICROPHONES

When you're not using a microphone, store it somewhere cool, clean, and dry. Put it in a pouch or cover it with a piece of cloth or an upside-down plastic bag. (Don't seal the bag; just let it hang over the mic.) If you keep dust and airborne gunk away from your mic, it will perform better and last longer.

Use a pop screen to minimize the amount of saliva that gets onto the mic. Saliva isn't a good thing where delicate electronic devices are concerned, so dry your mic gently with a soft cloth as soon as possible. Do not try to blow a mic dry with a hair dryer or compressed air in a can; either can render the mic inoperable.

Setting levels

When the mic is positioned and sounds its best to you, fine-tune your recording level for the track. Because you're recording real audio (and not a software instrument), you can't change the recording level later. If you record the track too hot (too much level) or too cool (too little level), the track will be distorted or too quiet no matter what you do afterwards.

TIP

If you spike into the red zone once or several times during a performance, don't lose hope. You may be able to use the track volume rubber band to lower the volume during those hot passages. If you don't have too much distortion in the recording (from being too hot) and with other tracks blended in, your track may be fine.

REMEMBER

It's always better to record at the right level, though. If you record a track too hot or too cool, you risk losing a great performance or, at best, having to work extra hard in post-production to salvage it.

So pay close attention to track volume levels (and master levels) while you record and also while you mix and master.

To set the levels before you record a take, play or sing a bit of the song that you want to record and watch the levels on the LED display, which you find in the Mixer column for that track. What should you look for to get a proper recording level? Check out Figure 15-5 to find your answers. The top LED meter shows levels that are too cool (quiet/indistinct); the middle pair of meters represent a good range of recording levels; the bottom meter is too hot (loud/distorted).

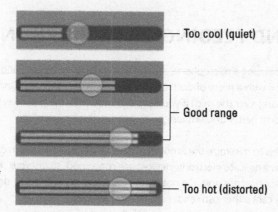

— Too cool (quiet)

— Good range

FIGURE 15-5:
The range of good and bad levels.

— Too hot (distorted)

You want the recording level as green as possible, without much (or any) yellow and little or no red. An occasional spike near the red, as shown in the second image in Figure 15-5, won't hurt, but don't let it stay that hot for long. If both red

LEDs are lit, like they are in the bottom picture in Figure 15-5, your recording will almost certainly be distorted and may be unusable.

If your tracks are too cool or too hot, first try adding a bit of compression, which I discuss in more detail in the next section. Then play a bit of your song again to see whether that puts it in the green. If that doesn't work, try adjusting the level by sliding the level fader to the left. Keep tweaking compression and levels until you find the right amount of level that gives you a useable track. If you're using an audio interface, try increasing its gain (level). You can find more details about adjusting levels in Chapter 4.

Finally, memorize my late, great Uncle Yogi's mantra for recording levels, and things will be fine:

Lots of green, it's sweet and clean;

Too much red, your track is dead.

Adding effects

One way of making a track sound different or better is to add effects to it.

TECHNICAL STUFF

In the past, the rule was to use as few effects as possible during recording. The object was to keep what was on tape as pristine as possible. If you recorded a track with echo and reverb, for example, and later decided that you didn't want echo and reverb or wanted less of it, you were stuck. The track on tape had the echo and reverb in its DNA. Sometimes it was necessary to add some compression or equalization to a track during recording, but most other effects were added later, giving you the option of using them or not.

With GarageBand, you have no such limitation because it uses *nondestructive* effects — meaning that you hear the effects in real-time, but they're not applied to your tracks until you export the project. And that, my friends, is a really good thing.

The upshot is that you no longer have to worry about spoiling a take by adding an effect. If you don't like the effect, you can remove it without affecting your track. No harm, no foul.

If you're a veteran of analog recording, this feature probably seems like a miracle. In the old days, effects were usually outboard hardware devices that were filled with strange DSP chips capable of such real-time shenanigans. Today, our Intel processors are more than powerful enough to add effects such as these on the fly.

It's nice to know that you can add effects at any time. So add 'em or not as you like — you won't hurt anything. Knock yourself out choosing different presets and adjusting the EQ, reverb, and echo — whatever rocks your boat.

That said, with most effects, you don't gain a great advantage adding them before recording. But compression is a special case. Even in the old days, sometimes it was best to add a bit of compression to an instrument or voice before committing it to tape. And the same holds true for GarageBand.

REMEMBER

When you have a track with a few (but not too many) hot spots, you may be able to bring the loudest and softest parts closer together by adding a bit of compression. I almost always add some compression to my vocals, guitar, bass, and drum tracks. There's not much I don't compress at least a small amount. So before you lower the level of the entire track or enable automation and use the track volume control, try adding a small amount of compression, as I describe in a moment.

The *small amount* is key. Although a little compression can make a track that's too hot in some parts and too cool in others sound better, too much compression can make it sound artificial and even robotic.

To add just the right amount of compression for a vocal or acoustic instrument track, follow these steps:

1. **In tracks view, begin playing your song by tapping the play icon.**

2. **Select the track you want to compress by tapping its header.**

3. **Tap the track controls icon in the control bar.**

The track controls appear to the left of the track headers.

4. **In the Plug-ins & EQ section, move the Compressor slider right or left to increase or decrease, respectively, the amount of compression.**

If the slider isn't providing the results you're looking for, try fine-tuning the compressor settings as follows.

5. **Tap the Plug-ins & EQ header to see the effects applied to this track, and then tap the compressor to see its controls, as shown in Figure 15-6.**

6. **Tap the go to beginning icon and then tap the play icon.**

You may want to click the solo icon for the track so you can hear it more clearly.

7. **Slide the Compression Threshold slider until you like what you hear.**

8. **Repeat with the remaining four sliders until you like what you hear.**

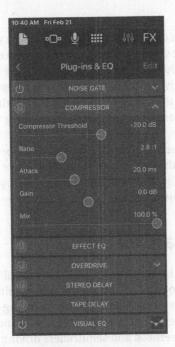

FIGURE 15-6:
The Compressor's
five sliders help
you fine-tune its
settings to
perfection.

9. **Tap the Compressor's power button to disable/enable the compressor, and listen to the track with and without compression.**

10. **Check your levels again.**

For details, see the "Setting levels" section, earlier in this chapter.

You should see less yellow and red in the LED level displays, and you should be able to hear softer passages better than before. A bit of compression can free you from having to "ride the faders" (or "diddle the track volume rubber band controls," in GarageBand parlance) to compensate for loud and soft portions.

TIP

You may have to slide the track's level slider to the left or right by a small amount to achieve the best level for the track after you've added compression or changed your compression settings.

Tweaking the pan to hear vocals better

The *pan settings* control where a sound is coming from in the stereo field — that is, from the left or right. Although it's more effective to wait and fine-tune pan settings for each track when you mix and master, a simple tweak to the pan settings may help you hear vocals better in your headphones.

Here's how it works: Pan a track or more than one track all the way to the left or right and then pan the track that you're recording all the way to the opposite side. This way, you hear the previously recorded instrument or voice tracks in one ear and the track that you're currently recording in the other ear. Some musicians and singers find this less confusing than hearing everything in both ears. Try it and see if it works for you. I find it particularly helpful for recording harmony vocals.

One last thing before we leave track settings: If you want to record multiple takes, tap Track Settings at the top of the pane and enable Multi-Take Recording. Note that multi-take recording is an all-or-nothing proposition — if you enable it, it is enabled for all tracks in your project.

Checking for unwanted noise

I always do one last thing before I start recording: I listen carefully one more time for extraneous noise. Is the air conditioner or refrigerator running? (Better catch it before it runs away.) If you live in the South, listen for ceiling fans; if you're a Northerner, listen for steam pipes or oil heaters clanging; no matter where you live, listen for jet planes flying overhead and semitrailers driving by.

WARNING

If you hear anything in addition to your voice or instrument in the headphones, your take could be spoiled.

TIP

If you're recording vocals, listen carefully and make sure that no sound from your headphones leaks into the mic when you sing. If it does, reduce the headphone output (the better choice) or back away from the mic a little (which may hurt your recording quality and is less likely to work).

See Chapter 2 for a checklist that can help you prevent background noise from showing up on your tracks.

Multitrack Recording

Recording one track at a time with one microphone can be a drag. If you need to record a band live, record several performers simultaneously, or record live drums, you'll want to use a separate microphone and track for each player, instrument, or drum.

I'll use drums as an example of multitrack recording, but the techniques described here work just as well for recording an entire band live, three acoustic guitarists and a singer, or almost any recording scenario you can think of with more than one audio source.

Alas, I am not a drummer and don't even play one on TV, so I asked my friend and colleague Dave Hamilton to help me out. Dave is the drummer for the greatest garage band you never heard, the Macworld All-Star Band; he's also the CEO of BackBeat Media and President of the *Mac Observer*. He's played and toured with members of the Dave Matthews Band, played in the horn section for Phish, and played in David Letterman's CBS Late Night Orchestra. He's the real deal.

Dave is also an underrated writer whose work has appeared in *MacAddict* and the *Mac Observer* as well as other Mac publications (but not often enough, if you ask me).

Now, without further ado, here's Dave's take (pun intended) on recording drums with GarageBand.

Dave Hamilton on multitrack drum recording

The one place where GarageBand falls short is in recording live drums. Garage-Band's limitation of recording one track at a time (without an expensive multi-channel audio interface and enough microphones) leaves many would-be home engineers scratching their respective (drum)heads. Recording drums properly requires a minimum of three microphones (although you can use more if you want), and GarageBand is not built to accept that many mics unless you buy a bunch of additional gear. Don't fret — I have two solutions, depending on your needs.

One track at a time

One option is to let GarageBand dictate the way you record — that being one track at a time. Because you'll be recording one instrument at a time, make sure you have your song mapped out (either in your head or on paper) from start to finish. Choose your first instrument — the hi-hat, for example — and place your microphone accordingly. Then get your song set up in GarageBand, set your tempo (you'll want to record using GarageBand's metronome as a guide), put on a pair of headphones, and fire away. When you have that track the way you want it, move on to the next instrument. Get your bass drum miced the way you want it, put the headphones back on, and go for it. Then do the snare, and so on.

This process is tedious, but the result will be clean and pristine tracks. These tracks can be individually equalized and effected in GarageBand, giving you complete control over the mix. The trade-off is that you may lose some of the feel of having a live drummer playing all the parts at once.

Don't want to make that trade-off, you say? Well, you have two other choices: Use a mixer to record multiple mics to a single track, essentially recording as above, or use a multichannel audio interface to record multiple tracks at once.

Multiple tracks at once

To record multiple tracks at once, you must purchase a iOS-compatible audio interface with enough XLR inputs to match the number of microphones you want to record simultaneously. The Focusrite Scarlett 18i20 allows eight microphones to be connected and is available for less than $500.

After you've procured your audio interface and connected it to your iDevice, you're ready to start. Follow these steps to record with a mixer:

1. **Position your microphones.**

   I prefer a minimum of three mics (one on the bass drum and then two overheads to get a stereo image of the sound) for decent results. You can, of course, move on past that and mic the snare (top and bottom!), toms, and individual cymbals if you're so inclined. Make sure to get a cowbell mic, too.

2. **Connect the microphones to the microphone inputs on the mixer, and head into GarageBand.**

3. **Tap the settings icon in the control bar, tap Advanced, and enable Multitrack Recording.**

   This is the trick that will allow GarageBand to record multiple tracks simultaneously.

4. **Add one audio track for each microphone you've plugged in, and select the input to match.**

   If the bass drum mic is plugged into the first input, choose Input 1 for that track. Then choose Track ⇨ New Track and create the next track, choosing the next input to match.

5. **Tap the newly added record enable icon (red circle) in each drum track (but not your other tracks). Only flashing tracks will be recorded.**

6. **Tap the record icon and bash away, playing the drum track naturally!**

   You may find that you need to adjust the gain levels on the audio interface if one drum is recording too loudly or softly. This process, by its nature, is one of trial and error, so don't record your masterpiece first. Just test it, adjust, and test again until you have a setup that captures your sounds the way you like.

Whichever option you choose, you end up with a decent drum sound that you can tweak to your heart's content with GarageBand's effects.

Happy recording!

To which I say, "Thanks, Dave!"

For what it's worth, Dave sent me an MP3 file of some drumming that he recorded using the three-microphones-and-a-mixer setup described in this section. It sounded just like drums (which is just what it should sound like).

Recording with a MIDI drum controller

You have one more option for recording drums: Use a MIDI drum controller such as the Korg nanoPAD2 Slim-Line USB MIDI Pads to tap out your drum part on 16 velocity-sensitive pads, as shown in Figure 15-7.

FIGURE 15-7:
Korg nanoPAD2
Slim-Line USB
MIDI Pads sends
touch-sensitive
MIDI information
to your Mac.

Remember the MIDI keyboards I've been talking about throughout the book? Think of the Korg nanoPAD2 as serving the same purpose with a twist: Instead of sending MIDI information when you press a key, the nanoPAD2 sends MIDI information when you tap one of the 16 touch-sensitive pads with your finger.

Any drummer will tell you how hard it is to play drums using a piano-style MIDI keyboard. Although I'm not a drummer, I've used nanoPAD2 for many tracks and those tracks sound significantly more realistic than ones I create on a piano-style keyboard.

Priced at around $50, nanoPAD2 is an outstanding value if you need to record drums that sound reasonably realistic on a tight budget.

You can spend more on MIDI drums that look and play like a real drum set, such as the Alesis Drums Nitro Mesh Kit (under $400), shown in Figure 15-8.

FIGURE 15-8:
Alesis Drums Nitro Mesh Kit looks and feels like drums, but it's relatively quiet as it sends its MIDI instructions to your Mac.

Recording the Track

Okay then, now that you have everything ready to record, all that's left is to actually record. No worries — it's a snap.

Here's how:

1. Move the playhead to the point in your song where you want to begin recording, or tap the go to beginning icon to move the playhead to the start of the song.

GarageBand has two features to help you record — a metronome and a count-in.

2. If you want to use the metronome, tap the metronome icon in the control bar.

The metronome is a toggle; it's on when the icon lights up (turns blue), and off when the icon is gray. See Chapter 12 for details on the metronome.

3. If you want to use count-in, tap Settings, tap Metronome and Count-in, and enable Count-in and Visual Count-in.

When count-in is turned on, you get an additional measure counted out before GarageBand starts recording.

4. **Tap the record icon (red dot) and the recording begins.**

    Remember to watch your levels while you record.

5. **When you've finished recording, tap the play/pause icon or press the spacebar to end the recording.**

    Wasn't that simple?

Improving the Sound of Recordings

If you've been paying attention and haven't killed the tracks that you've recorded (remember Uncle Yogi's mantra: *Too much red, your track is dead*), you can tinker with the sound to your heart's content.

Remember the nondestructive feature, described earlier in the chapter? You can add and subtract effects without affecting the quality of your original track — until you export it, that is.

So listen to what you've recorded now, and pay particular attention to both the sound of the instrument or voice and the performance itself. Now add some effects or change some presets, and then listen some more.

Are some parts too loud or too soft? Add a bit of compression, or use the track volume control to reduce the level. As shown in Figure 15-9, I played a chord too loud for this part of the song. The track volume control let me reduce the level smoothly before the loud chord and increase it smoothly after. See Chapter 17 for details on using the track volume control.

FIGURE 15-9:
Changing the
level (riding the
fader) with the
track volume
control.

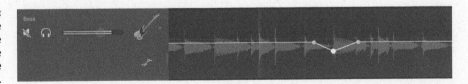

TIP

If you hear other problems on a recording, don't worry yet — small problems can be fixed in several ways without redoing the entire track:

>> **If you hit a wrong note — or even three or four — read the section in Chapter 17 about fixing flubs.** You can find several techniques for editing out mistakes and replacing mistakes with better performances.

>> **To fatten up the sound of almost any instrument or vocal track, try double-tracking, which is an age-old production technique.** GarageBand gives you two ways to do this; each has pros and cons:

- *Way 1:* Duplicate the original guitar track (tap the track header and then tap it again and tap Duplicate). Or copy and paste the original guitar region onto a new track. Either way is fast and easy, but unless you're careful, it will sound mechanical because both tracks will be exactly the same.

  One way to soften the effect is to change one of the tracks by adding effects; try a bit of Chorus and the doubled track sound sounds ethereal. Or choose a preset with lots of distortion for one track and choose a cleaner-sounding preset for the other.

- *Way 2:* Create a new track and record the part a second time, playing or singing along with the original track. You want to repeat your performance as precisely as you can, but because you're only human, the second recording will have small differences from the original track. Although this technique can take you more time, the differences between the two takes can make this sound better than copying and pasting the same performance.

Chapter 16

Recording Guitars and Basses without Mics or Amps

I n Chapters 14 and 15, I explain how to record software instruments and vocal and acoustic instrument tracks. In this chapter, I explain how to record another type of instrument: an amplified instrument, most notably an electric guitar.

REMEMBER

Throughout this chapter, I use the electric guitar as an example because that's the instrument I happen to own and play. However, the electric guitar is just one of many electronic or amplified instruments you might record directly. So, if you play another electronic instrument, such as an electric piano, synthesizer, violin, bass, or whatever, merely substitute the name of your instrument wherever you see the word *guitar*.

For the most part, electric instrument tracks are the same as vocal and acoustic instrument tracks (discussed in Chapter 15). The big difference is that you can record electronic instruments without a mic by plugging the instrument directly into your iDevice (or audio interface) instead of placing a microphone in front of the instrument's amplifier.

For those who prefer recording the old-school way, I also include a section on recording guitars and other electronic instruments with a mic in front of their amplifiers.

Finally, I show you how to customize the sound of your electronic instrument track to make it sound even better.

Overview from the Top: Direct or Live Recording

Recording an electronic instrument with GarageBand is easier than with some other recording software because, once again, Apple did the heavy lifting for you. This time Apple has included built-in guitar amplifier and stomp box emulations with presets designed by professional guitarists and recording engineers. By merely choosing a different preset, you can give your guitar a vintage British Invasion sound, the overdriven distortion of Chord Burner, the dulcet tones of Cool Jazz Combo, and other guitar and bass presets too numerous to mention. Just pick a preset and record your masterpiece.

Recording electronic instruments with GarageBand is easy also because Garage-Band doesn't require you use an amplifier. Instead, you plug the instrument into your iDevice (or into an audio interface connected to your iDevice), and Garage-Band emulates the sound of the amplifier and stomp box effects. The result sounds like an amp and stomp boxes. It's slick.

TIP

Even if you're not a guitarist, if you have a guitar available — even if it's a crummy one that sounds like garbage through an amplifier — try some of GarageBand's guitar presets. I think you'll be pleasantly surprised.

In the recording industry, plugging an electric guitar (or other electronic instrument) directly into your computer is called *direct recording*. I recommend direct recording if possible. Unless you have a lot of time to experiment with amplifier and microphone placement, you'll almost always get better results this way — and it's faster.

However, I realize that some purists, pros, recording engineers, and producers prefer to capture the unique interplay of guitar and amplifier by recording the guitar and amplifier *live*, using a microphone or microphones. If you want to record your guitar live, I cover most of what you need to know about setting up and recording with microphones in Chapter 15. Amplifiers are notoriously difficult to record well, so I have a few tips and hints for those of you who insist on recording with an amp and microphone(s).

When I worked in recording studios in the 1970s, the technology wasn't advanced enough to record directly and have it sound good. Back then, the only way to record electric guitar and bass tracks was with a mic and an amp.

Today, amp-modeling and sound-shaping software is so spectacular sounding that many popular artists play through modeled amps on stage and in recording. A few years ago, I played two sets with the Macworld All-Star Band sans amplifier, using GarageBand for all amp and effects sounds, with my MacBook connected directly into the house sound system! It sounded great and, as a pleasant side effect, the sound level onstage was lower than usual, which meant we could hear ourselves playing and singing better.

TIP

I show you how to use GarageBand to play live without an amplifier in Chapter 20.

My Marshall amp died a few years ago and I didn't bother to replace it. These days, if I want to play, I just open GarageBand and use one of its fine guitar presets (without recording) instead of an amp and stomp boxes.

Direct Recording with GarageBand's Virtual Amplifiers

When you record directly, you bypass amplification and plug your instrument directly into your iDevice (or an audio interface connected to your iDevice). When you play, the sound comes out of your iDevice speakers or headphones. You can change your instrument sounds by selecting a different instrument (guitar or bass) or preset.

Setting up to record

Before you begin, you need two things: your instrument and the appropriate cable or cables to connect it to your iDevice or audio interface. (See Chapter 2 if you're wondering what an audio interface is.)

TIP

If you have a USB audio interface for your Mac, you may be able to use it with your iDevice with a USB-to-Lightning adapter as described in Chapter 15. Or you can get an iOS-compatible guitar interface such as the $100 iRig HD 2 from IK Multimedia (shown in Figure 16-1).

FIGURE 16-1:
IK Multimedia's
iRig HD 2 lets you
connect a guitar
and headphones
to your iDevice
for recording.

It's probably worth having a ¼-inch-to-Lightning adapter or cable even if you have an audio interface for your iDevice. I keep one in my backpack so I can plug in and record a guitar without lugging around yet another device and cables.

Now that your instrument is plugged into your iDevice, follow these steps to record your guitar (or another instrument) directly into a new GarageBand project:

1. **Tap the my songs icon in the control bar, and then tap Create Song to create a new project.**

2. **Tap Tracks at the top of the screen, and then swipe left or right until you see the amp.**

3. **Tap Clean or Distorted for guitar; tap Bass for (d'oh) bass guitar.**

The Amp screen appears, as shown in Figure 16-2. Swipe left or right to see other amps; strum your guitar to listen to the current amp.

4. **Tap the name of the current preset (Glam Rock in Figure 16-2; Bell Bottom Rock in Figure 16-3) to switch to another preset.**

Tap a preset category on the left (Clean, Crunchy, Distorted, or Processed) and then tap a preset on the right.

To use presets for bass guitar, tap Main Categories and then tap Bass.

5. **Strike a chord or play a riff (or do whatever it is you like to do with your instrument).**

Did you hear what you played from your output source (usually your iDevice's built-in speakers or headphones)? And did you see activity in the track's level meter and the master level meters?

If you heard your instrument loud and clear and answered both questions with a resounding "yes," you're good to go. Feel free to skip ahead to the "Setting levels" section." If you answered "no" to either question, see the next section, "Troubleshooting your setup."

FIGURE 16-2:
Fine-tune your guitar sound using the onscreen amp.

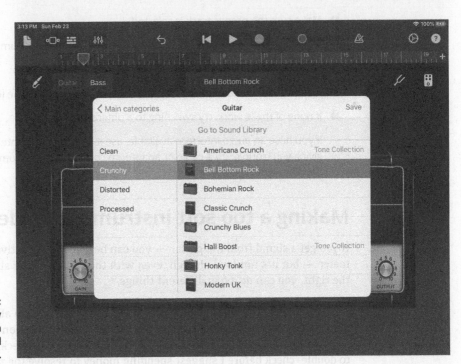

FIGURE 16-3:
Tap a category (Crunchy) and a preset (Bell Bottom Rock).

Troubleshooting your setup

If you followed the steps in the preceding section and the setup didn't work quite right, here are some quick fixes (in no particular order):

>> Make sure all your cables are connected firmly.

 Tap the set input options icon (which looks like a ¼-inch guitar cable and is shown in the margin) and enable the Monitor switch (if it's not enabled already).

>> If you're using an audio interface with multiple channels, tap the set input options icon, tap Channel, and then tap the channel your instrument is on.

>> Make sure the volume control on your guitar is turned up.

>> Make sure your iDevice's speakers aren't muted or set too low.

>> If you're using an audio interface, make sure its level control is set high enough.

If you still don't hear yourself when you play, tap the tracks view icon in the control bar to switch to tracks view and

>> Make sure the proper track is selected.

>> Make sure the mute icon for the track you're recording isn't illuminated.

>> Make sure the solo icon for another track is not illuminated.

>> Make sure the volume slider for the track isn't all the way to the left.

>> If none of these work, try switching to a different input.

If you have an audio interface available, use it. If it's an audio interface that's giving you trouble, try a cable or adapter to connect your instrument to your iDevice's Lightning port instead.

Making a too soft instrument louder

If you get a signal from the guitar — you can hear it and see activity in its volume meter — but it's not loud enough, even with the volume slider slid all the way to the right, you can do a few different things.

First, make sure the volume knob on your guitar is cranked up all the way. Temporarily use the same cable to plug into an amp or a headphone amp to check. I know I just mentioned this earlier, in the list of things to check, but I want you to double-check before I suggest spending money to resolve the problem.

If checking the volume didn't do the trick, an audio interface can make your instrument louder without adding noise (hissing, buzzing, crackling, and the like). If your guitar still doesn't put out a loud enough signal and you've turned up the input levels everyplace you can, you need an audio interface — but not just any audio interface. Get one with preamps to give your guitar more signal.

My Scarlett Solo USB audio interface (shown in Figure 16-4), for example, has two inputs with preamps and suits my needs perfectly at a reasonable price (around $150).

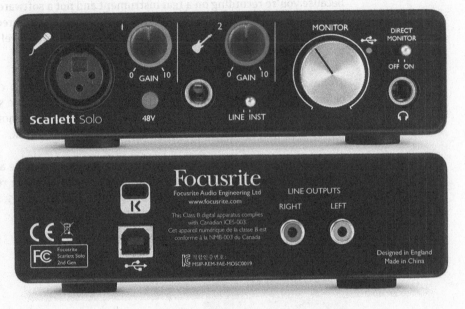

FIGURE 16-4:
Scarlett Solo USB (front and back) is an audio interface and preamp, which makes instruments and microphones louder without adding unwanted noise.

In addition to a pair of ¼-inch guitar inputs, the Scarlett Solo also offers an XLR port, which can supply phantom power to microphones. The interface is super quiet (it doesn't add noise) and boosts the level of my guitars and microphones quite nicely for GarageBand.

An audio interface with preamps can be used with almost any instrument or microphone you use to record — electric guitars and basses, acoustic guitars, microphones with XLR connectors, or other electronic instruments that require additional amplification to provide a sufficient signal to GarageBand.

TIP

Most audio interfaces include at least one input with a preamp. Many also offer one or more XLR inputs with phantom power. Read the specifications carefully to make sure your choice has the features you need before you buy, and buy this kind of stuff from a trusted vendor with a reasonable return policy.

I mention a few of my go-to online audio gear vendors in Chapter 26.

Finally, the Scarlett Solo USB draws more power than my USB microphones, so it doesn't work with a regular USB-to-Lightning adapter. It works only with an adapter that includes a charging port, like the HENKUR USB Camera Adapter I mention in Chapter 15.

Setting levels

Because you're recording on a real instrument and not a software instrument, you won't be able to change the recording level after a track is recorded. So if you record the track *too hot* (too much level) or *too cool* (too little level), that's the track you're stuck with.

To ensure that you're making a useable track, remember to check your levels before you begin recording. You do this by playing a bit of the song you want to record and watching the LEDs next to the track. So, if you're not already in track view, tap the track view icon in the control bar and take a look.

What should you look for? Take a gander at Figure 16-5 for the answer. You want to see as much green as possible without much or any yellow or red. An occasional spike near the red, as shown in the third picture in Figure 16-5, is fine as long as there aren't too many and they don't last too long.

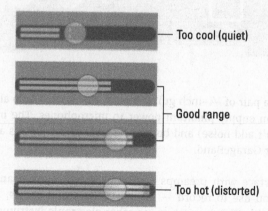

FIGURE 16-5:
The top picture is too cool, the two middle pictures are in the just-right range, and the bottom picture is too hot.

— Too cool (quiet)

Good range

— Too hot (distorted)

WARNING

If *both* red LEDs light up at once, as shown in the bottom picture in Figure 16-4, your recording will almost certainly be distorted and is likely to be unusable.

For more on checking and adjusting levels before you record, see Chapter 12.

By the way, if Figure 16-5 looks familiar, that's because it's also in Chapters 7 and 8. But it's so important that I felt obliged to include it here, too, for your convenience.

That's pretty much it. Just remember this mantra when you record guitars (or anything else, for that matter): *Lots of green and it's sweet and clean. Too much red and your track is dead.*

Recording the track

There's really not much to recording a track after GarageBand (and you) hear your guitar and you've set the levels. Because you've already created the track, all that's left to do now is to turn on the metronome and enable count-in (if you want them), and then record. (See Chapter 15 for the specific steps.)

  One last thing before you tap the record icon. If your instrument is tunable, you should tune it before you tap record. To use the built-in tuner, tap the amp icon in the control bar (shown in the margin)to return to amp view, and then tap the tuning fork icon (shown in the margin) to display the tuner. Pluck a string and tune it until its name and the dash below its name are dead center and blue (as shown on the left in Figure 16-6). If the dash is left of center, the string is flat; if it's right of center, the string is sharp.

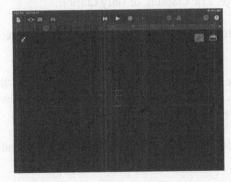 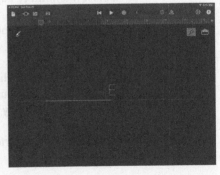

FIGURE 16-6:
In tune (left) and out of tune (right).

One more thing: Even if you checked the levels twice or thrice before recording, you still need to pay careful attention to levels while you record.

TIP

If only one or two brief passages were recorded too hot or too cool (as opposed to a track that's too hot or too cool from start to finish), you can try lowering or raising the level of the hotter or cooler passages using the track volume control. (See Chapter 15 for details.) If the recording doesn't have too much distortion (from being too hot) and you have other tracks playing simultaneously, you can often make the recording good enough to get by. Still, it's better to record at a proper level in the first place.

Let your ears be your guide. If it sounds good, it's a keeper. If it doesn't sound good, re-record it.

Recording Live with an Amplifier and Microphones

As I mention earlier in the chapter, recording an electric guitar (or other electronic instrument) *live* means that you hook your guitar up to a traditional guitar amp and record the amp (and room sound) with a mic, rather than plugging your guitar directly into your iDevice and using GarageBand's amp simulators.

The key to a good amplified electric guitar recording is patience. You need to experiment with mic positions, amp positions, microphones, rooms, and surfaces before you begin to understand how to achieve just the sound you want. If you think you're just going to simply plug in a mic, hang it near an amplifier, and get a great guitar sound, you've got another think coming 'cause it ain't that easy. But if you're not averse to a bit of work, the results can be outstanding, just like (well, almost like) Jimmy Page, Eric Clapton, or Gary Clark Jr.

All the details in Chapter 15 apply to recording an amplified electric guitar with a microphone.

TIP

I recommend using the audio recorder (not the amp) to record live guitar with a mic, but it's up to you. If you're not getting the sound you desire from the audio recorder's presets, try some of the amp's presets.

Here are additional tricks and tips to help you capture the sound you desire as it leaves the amplifier:

>> **Mic placement is key.** You need to experiment and find the best location for the mic you're using. No single right way exists; you have to find the sweet spot for your combination of microphone, guitar, and amp. Start with the mic about an inch from one of the amp's speaker cones. Move it off-axis, to the left and right. Swivel it at different angles. Move it away from the speaker cabinet in small increments. If your amp has an open back design, try micing the back of the cabinet instead of the front. Move the mic around as before.

Microphone stands are a must in situations like this where precise positioning of the mic is necessary.

>> **Loud isn't always good.** If you're trying to get an overdriven or distorted guitar sound, set the levels of your amp and guitar as low as you can and still achieve the effect you desire. Playing louder will just muddy the recording (make it sound distorted and buzzy). This effect may be the one you're looking for, but you'll usually get a better recording if you play at the lowest level you can.

>> **A small practice amp is often better than a big old Marshall double stack for home recording.** If you have both, try your little amp — you'll be surprised at how nice it sounds when recorded.

>> **Consider room acoustics.** If you're going for that reverb/echo/distortion sound, a lively room with many hard surfaces will add natural echo and reverb. For a more jazz-like passage, you might prefer that the room add as little color as possible, with soft surfaces to absorb reflected sound waves before they leak back into the mic.

If you play too loudly, you'll end up with echo-and-reverb-laden mud instead of a sweet rock-and-roll guitar sound.

Try this experiment: Record something three times with the amp set to three different levels — quieter than usual, normal, and louder than heck. You'll find that the louder-than-heck version rarely sounds as good as either of the others.

Many engineers like to record guitar amps in the bathroom. All you need is a long enough mic cord and guitar cable. The effect is interesting, to say the least.

If you try the bathroom trick, remember to experiment with mic position. It's a time-consuming chore but worth it if you want the best sound. I've heard more than one recording engineer say that setting up guitar mics (or drum mics) properly often takes longer than the recording session itself.

Conversely, if you're getting too much room sound in the track, try using pillows or blankets in front of the amp to reduce reflected sound. Move the amp around the room, too, and point it in different directions if you think that will help.

Finally, if you're trying to record an acoustic guitar, you may have more luck with an electrified acoustic guitar, such as the J.R. Beck 9861EQ acoustic/electric guitar shown in Figure 16-7. It's a standard acoustic guitar with three additions: a pickup inside (think little baby microphone), a hole to plug a guitar cable into, and a 4-band equalizer and volume controller. It plays and sounds like an acoustic guitar, but you can plug it into an amplifier, an audio interface, or an iDevice and record it without a microphone.

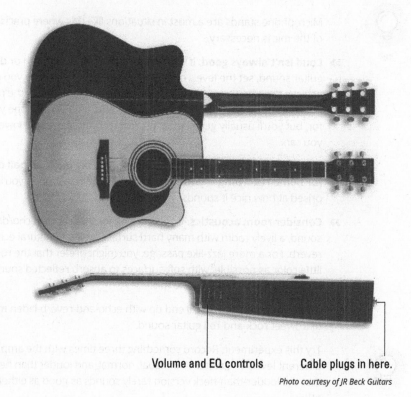

FIGURE 16-7:
This acoustic guitar can be recorded as though it were an electric guitar!

Volume and EQ controls   Cable plugs in here.

I can't tell you how much easier it is to record my J.R. Beck 9861 than it is to record my older Yamaha acoustic with a microphone. Also, the sound is much better, with less unwanted noise and other crud. If you plan to record a lot of acoustic guitar tracks, an electric/acoustic will save you hours of setup and microphone placement and adjustment. It will also almost certainly sound better.

TIP

J.R. Beck was a small guitar manufacturer that used the Dell model to offer great guitars at amazingly low prices on the web. The 9861 in Figure 16-7, for example, cost me around $200 but still plays and sounds better 20 years later than some electric and acoustic guitars costing more. Sadly, J.R. Beck went out of business.

Customizing the Sound of Your Guitar Tracks

Now that your guitar track is in the can, you can do many things to it to make it sound different if not better.

Changing presets and amp simulators

The first and easiest task is to choose a different amp model.

Tap the track controls icon in the control bar and then tap the current preset's name at the top of the Track Settings pane (Industrial Overdrive in Figure 16-8). Tap a category on the left and then choose a preset on the right.

FIGURE 16-8:
The Vintage Drive effect (left) and choosing a second stomp box effect (right).

When I changed from the Crunchy category's Bell Bottom Rock preset to the Distorted category's Industrial Overdrive preset, I heard an entirely different guitar sound than before.

TIP

If you're looking for an unusual sound, try some of the bass presets, which may sound great laid on your guitar track. Don't be afraid to try different presets; you can always undo if you don't like it.

Changing and modifying stomp box effects

You can change the stomp boxes associated with a preset. If you're in tracks view, tap the amp icon in the control bar to return to amp view, and then tap the stomp box icon (shown in the margin) to reveal the stomp box effects for the current preset (Vintage Drive in Figure 16-8).

Each preset can have up to two stomp box effects. I tapped the empty stomp box outline in Figure 16-8 to choose a second effect for the Industrial Overdrive amp.

For each stomp box, tap the silver stomp button at the bottom to turn the effect on or off. Then twist the knobs and flip the switches to change the effect's effects (ha).

To change a stomp box to a different stomp box, tap it and your choices will appear below (as shown for the empty slot on the right in Figure 16-8). Tap any stomp box to switch to it.

Editing presets

If you still haven't found the sound you want among the guitar or bass presets, find the one that's the closest to the sound you desire and edit it to your specifications.

Each preset includes an amplifier, stomp boxes, and plug-in effects, as shown in Figure 16-9 for three presets.

Note that each of the three presets has unique controls.

REMEMBER

1. **Adjust the knobs on the amp until you like what you hear.**

   You can play (or record) while you're adjusting these controls. That way, you can try a bunch of settings before settling on the ones you want to record.

2. **If you're still not satisfied with what you hear, tap the track settings icon in the control bar, tap Plug-ins & EQ, and then tap one of the plug-ins and tweak its settings.**

3. **Repeat Step 2 (if necessary) for the other plug-ins.**

4. **Tweak the master effects sliders for Echo and Reverb.**

TIP

   Don't forget that occasionally turning off a plug-in (by tapping the power button to its left) is more effective and faster than trying to tweak it.

5. **If you like the sound enough to want to reuse it someday, tap the preset's name (Industrial Overdrive in Figure 16-10), tap Save, and type a name.**

WARNING

   Choose a name other than the preset's original name. If you reuse the original name when you save, you run the risk of confusing your preset with the Apple-configured version, which is never a good thing. Although your modified preset appears in the Custom category rather than Clean, Crunchy, Distorted, or Processed category, if it has the same name as the original, it's harder to know which is which. At the very least I add the word *my* before the name, so when I modified the Industrial Overdrive preset, I saved it as My Industrial Overdrive, as shown in Figure 16-10.

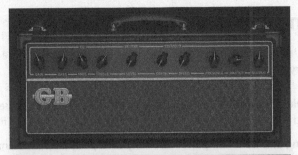

FIGURE 16-9: Controls for the Brit Pop (top), Sunshine Drive (middle), and Modern Metal (bottom) amp presets.

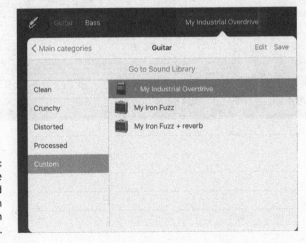

FIGURE 16-10: Presets you've modified and saved appear in the Custom category.

Making other changes

When you're satisfied with the sound of your guitar track, here are some more tricks to try:

» **Double tracking:** Double tracking is an age-old technique to fatten up the sound of a guitar (or voice or other instrument). See Chapter 18 for details.

» **Finding additional amp models:** Many third-party amp modeling plug-ins are available on iDevices, but my favorite is IK Multimedia's AmpliTube (see Figure 16-11). Its assortment of amps, speakers, preamps, stomp box effects, and presets is virtually endless. Even a mediocre guitar sounds better when you play it through an AmpliTube amp.

FIGURE 16-11:
AmpliTube for iPad offers dozens of realistic amp models, plus stomp boxes and myriad presets.

5

Postproduction: Finishing Songs on an iDevice

Learn how to edit tracks (and fix your mistakes) quickly and easily.

Marvel at the magic of mixing — that alchemistic undertaking where you tweak the level and tonal characteristics of each individual track so that they all blend together blissfully.

Uncover the secrets of mastering. (Hint: If you want to master your masterpiece properly, you'll have to do it on a Mac — the iDevice version of GarageBand doesn't include the same fabulous mastering tools as the Mac version.)

» **Editing software instrument versus real instrument tracks**

» **Fixing mistakes**

» **Rearranging regions**

» **Sweetening**

Chapter **17**

Editing and Polishing Tracks

This chapter covers the details of editing tracks, which is your last sanity check before you mix and master your song. Here, I ask you to think about editing, arranging, and sweetening your song — all the things you do to give it that little something extra that makes some songs more special than others.

First, I explain some basics: the best time to edit and the important differences between editing software instrument tracks and real instrument tracks. Then, I cover easy ways to fix mistakes without re-recording the entire track. You also discover all-purpose editing techniques that can be used to improve an imperfect track as well as things that you may (or may not) want to add to the song before you mix.

TIP

If you plan to do heavy experimentation on a song, save a copy of it first. To do so, tap the my songs icon to close the project and then press on the song in the My Songs window and tap Duplicate in the shortcut menu. Now press on the song again, but this time tap Rename, give the project you're about to experiment upon a descriptive name, and then tap Done. Finally, tap the renamed project to open it for experimentation. Now, if your experiment goes awry, you can delete this version and open the original, even if you've tapped the my songs icon (which automatically saves the project) while you experimented.

"When Should I Edit Tracks?"

The acts of editing and sweetening aren't time sensitive and can take place at almost any point in production or postproduction. In other words, you don't have to wait until the tracks are in the can to edit, arrange, or sweeten them.

You can do anything any time you like. I prefer to do my editing, arranging, and sweetening (hand claps, tambourines, shakers, and so on) after all (or most) tracks are in the can.

REMEMBER

It's okay to edit or sweeten at any point in the process, even after you've mixed and mastered once or twice. But it's better if you do as much as possible of the track editing and new track creation (that is, sweetening) *before* mixing and mastering.

If you edit or sweeten a song after you mix and master it, you'll have to go through at least one more cycle of remixing, listening, remastering, and listening again. Remixing and remastering can be a huge time sucker, so I try to avoid these extra steps whenever possible by doing as much editing and sweetening as I think the song needs before I even attempt a rough mix.

Editing Software Instrument versus Real Instrument Tracks

Not too surprisingly, software instruments offer you the greatest control when it comes to changing almost anything, including individual notes. As you've read before, real instrument tracks contain recorded sounds but software instrument tracks contain information about the note you played. Because software instrument tracks contain information rather than recorded sound, you can do things to them that you can't easily do to a real instrument recording, such as changing the intensity, pitch, duration, and sustain of any note or notes, or changing the song's tempo — a little or a lot — without affecting sound quality.

You can't do most of those things to real instrument tracks.

When editing software instruments (green regions) you have a variety of options. For example, you can

>> **Change the tempo.** If you feel the song is too fast or too slow, you can change the tempo a little or a lot and your software instrument tracks will adapt to the new tempo instantly and sound wonderful most of the time.

>> **Change the pitch.** If you attempt to sing the song but can't reach the highest notes, you can transpose the song into a lower key as long as it doesn't yet contain real instrument tracks.

TECHNICAL STUFF

You can try to correct the pitch of real instrument tracks without third-party plug-ins (with the Vocal Transformer plug-in). But I've never been pleased with the results. Even if you use a high-quality plug-in such as AutoTune (GarageBand for Mac only), many (if not most) real instrument tracks will sound lousy if you try to correct or change their pitch.

>> **Rearrange notes.** You can get away with some drastic edits in a software instrument track. For example, moving a note to the left or right changes when it is played, and moving a note up or down changes which note (or, in the case of some instruments including drums, which instrument) is played.

>> **Change the duration of notes.** Change the duration of a note or notes by grabbing its left or right edge and dragging to extend or shorten the note.

>> **Cut, copy, and paste notes.** To cut or copy a single note to the clipboard, tap it once and then tap Cut or Copy. To cut or copy multiple notes to the clipboard, press on the first note and continue pressing as you tap additional notes to add them to the selection. When you've added the last note, tap any selected note, and then tap Cut or Copy.

To paste the note or notes on the clipboard, move the playhead to the spot where you want the notes to appear, tap an empty spot on the grid, and then tap Paste.

TIP

Lay down as many software instrument tracks as you can before you start recording real instrument tracks. That way you'll have the option of changing the tempo or key for the project. After you add real instrument tracks, you're locked into the key and tempo unless you re-record the real instrument tracks in the new key or tempo.

I explain all the details of editing tempo, pitch, and individual notes in the "Editing Software Instrument Tracks" section, later in this chapter.

You have less control over fixing boo-boos in a real instrument track (including vocal tracks). Although you can't change sour notes or make them play longer, you still have options. You can do what the pros call a punch-in and punch-out. A *punch-in* and *punch-out* is the act of recording over a section of a track, without touching the rest of the track. So, if you have a mistake in your bass line, guitar line, or even your vocals, you can punch-in over the mistake and fix it.

I made it sound easy to punch-in and -out, but the process is often hard to do properly. When you have a recorded session and try to replace part of that session at a different time or location, the ambient sounds are likely to be different. Or the track might have a particular room sound that would make replacing part of it difficult or impossible anywhere but in the same room with the same microphones — and even then it might not sound quite right.

WARNING

If you have a mistake of that magnitude, you may have to re-record the entire track.

Arranging and Rearranging

It's important to remember that with digital recording, you can easily move anything to anywhere. You can take any region and drag it anywhere on the timeline, even to a different track. And you can copy and paste regions anywhere on any track.

REMEMBER

All of these tasks come with one proviso: Software instrument regions can go only on software instrument tracks, and real instrument regions can go only on real instrument tracks.

Song sections

Just as GarageBand on the Mac offers an *arrangement track* and *arrangement markers* to denote different sections, such as an intro, verse, or chorus, GarageBand for iDevices offers song sections that serve a similar purpose. After you define the sections in your song, you can move them around, duplicate them, or delete them with ease.

By default, a new song contains one 8-bar section named Section A. To open the song section controls and add sections, tap + at the right end of the ruler.

To create a new section, tap Add; to duplicate a section, tap to select it and then tap Duplicate. Either way, the section is created after Section A and is named Section B. If you add or duplicate another section, it'll go after Section B and be named Section C, and so on.

As far as I can tell there's no way to edit section names. If you find a way, please let me know.

Moving right along, to change the length of a section, tap the Inspector icon (*i*-in-a-circle) next to its name. If the Automatic switch is enabled, tap it to disable it and then tap the up or down arrow or swipe up or down to increase or decrease, respectively, the number of bars for this section.

To change the order of sections, tap the edit icon in the song section controls, and then move the section up or down in the list by pressing and dragging the handle on its right edge. When you change the order of sections, all regions on all tracks in the section move with it. Think about that for a moment. In my experience, moving regions often requires tweaking every track to make the transition sound decent.

WARNING

Pay close attention when you change the order of, duplicate, or delete sections, and remember to use undo if you make a mess of things. And, as I say at the beginning of this chapter, it would behoove you to make a copy of the song before you start rearranging its sections.

To work on a specific section (and have it fill the workspace), tap the section in the song section controls list. Tracks view changes to show only that section. Tap anywhere on the workspace to close the song section controls.

TIP

To switch between adjacent sections without opening the song section controls again, swipe left or right on the workspace until the adjacent section slides into view.

One last thing: It's a good idea to add your sections as you build the song, not at the end. Trying to divide a finished song into sections is harder and more likely to cause you pain. That said, having sections makes fixing flubs a lot faster and easier.

Fixing Flubs and Faux Pas

GarageBand lets you disguise and fix mistakes in tracks in a number of different ways. I'm a terrible musician and a worse singer, so fixing and disguising mistakes after the fact is almost always faster and easier than re-recording the entire track, at least for me. So the next time you lay down a track that's almost perfect (or even just pretty good) or find a flaw that you hadn't noticed before in a track, don't delete the track until you've tried some or all of the following techniques.

TIP

Every so often a track has problems that can't be fixed or disguised. In the beginning, you won't know until you try, so check out some of the techniques discussed in this chapter before you press Delete. After a while, you'll have a sixth sense about whether a mistake is fixable the moment that you make it.

Punching in and out to replace part of a track

If you make a mistake when you record a track, you can sometimes fix the mistake by re-recording the part with the mistake. In recording parlance, this process is called *punching in* and *punching out*.

In the olden days, punching in and out was an exotic process that was done only in the best studios using the highest of high-end audio gear. If you were recording at home, your gear was too noisy to get away with punching in much if at all. So if there was a mistake in a track, you either masked it as best you could with the available tools or re-recorded it. As time marched onward, the technique trickled down to consumer recording equipment; today, punching in and out has become a checklist item, available in almost every audio program.

REMEMBER

Punching in using GarageBand is easy; doing it well enough to fool your ears is challenging.

When you punch-in and -out in GarageBand, you use the song section controls to designate the part of the track you want to re-record. I find punching in and out far easier on a Mac using the cycle area than on an iDevice using song sections. See Chapter 19 for tips on working with one file on both platforms (Mac and iDevice).

Assuming you've created sections for your song, you can record multiple takes in a row quickly without stopping by enabling multi-take recording. The alternative is to move the playhead to where you want to start recording, tap Record, play or sing the part, tap Stop, and then listen to the take.

To enable multi-take recording, do the following:

1. **Tap the track header to select the track you want to re-record, and then tap the track settings icon in the control bar.**

   The Track Settings pane opens.

2. **Tap Track Settings at the top of the pane, and then tap Recording.**

3. **If the button says "Multi-Take Recording: Off" in white letters, tap the button once.**

   The text now says "Multi-Take Recording: On" in blue letters.

4. **Tap the track settings icon to hide the Track Settings pane.**

TIP

Now, when you tap the record icon, you can lay down as many takes as you care to. Keep playing it until you get it right. I often find that it takes a few tries before I find the groove, and then a few more tries after that to nail it. But my skills are meager at best, so you may be able to nail it on the first or second take.

To punch-in and -out on a track, follow these steps:

1. **Tap + on the right side of the ruler to open the song section controls.**

2. **Tap the section you want to re-record.**

3. **Tap anywhere on the workspace to close the song section controls.**

4. **Tap the track you want to re-record to select it.**

5. **Tap the record icon.**

   The section will play over and over so you can record as many takes as you like.

6. **When you finally nail it, tap the stop icon.**

7. **To select a take, tap the region you just recorded, tap it again, and then tap Takes.**

   A menu appears listing all the takes you recorded. The little 8 in the upper-left corner of the region in Figure 17-1 tells you that the region contains 8 takes.

FIGURE 17-1:
The takes menu with take #8 selected.

8. Tap a take to select it, and then tap the play icon.

9. Use the solo or mute icons, if necessary, to listen critically to your takes with and without other tracks.

10. Select the take you like best or record additional takes.

Just undo it . . . and then redo it

With GarageBand, it's easy to undo many mistakes immediately. You can undo the last thing that you did. But did you know that you can undo the next-to-last thing you did, and the thing before that one, and the thing before that, and so on?

The first time you use the undo feature, it reverses the last change that you made. But tell GarageBand to undo a second time, and it undoes the action before that. You can continue to use undo as needed.

Here's a quick list of undo and redo commands:

>> **To undo the previous action:** Tap the undo icon in the control bar or press the undo icon and then tap Undo *previous action name.*

>> **To redo what you just undid:** Press and hold down on the undo icon in the control bar and choose Redo *previous action name.*

>> **To get the ultimate undo:** The iDevice rendition of GarageBand automatically saves your project while you work on it, and when you close it, there is no Revert to Original command (as there is on the Mac). To achieve the same effect, duplicate the project in my songs and rename the duplicate Working Copy of *project name* before you begin. Then, work on the working copy. If you are happy with the results, delete the original (or save it with a different name) and rename the former working copy something like Finished or Final.

REMEMBER

The undo and redo features are linear, so pay close attention. It's easy to undo something good — something that you *didn't* want to have undone — if you just keep pressing the undo icon without taking note of what happens each time you press.

TIP

A better technique is to press and hold down on the undo icon, which reveals the action(s) you can redo or undo, as shown in Figure 17-2.

Don't rely too heavily on undo and redo. I recommend that you always duplicate your song before you begin editing, sweetening, or mixing, and then work on the duplicate.

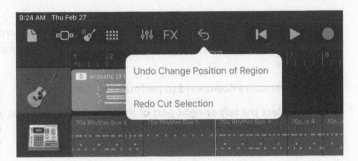

FIGURE 17-2:
Press and hold down on the undo icon to see what you can undo or redo.

Splitting and joining regions

You can take any region on any type of track and divide it into two or more parts. This technique has many practical uses, but the one you'll probably use most is deleting part of a region.

From a cough to a sour note, splitting a region is the most direct, easiest, and often the best way to edit out a part of a track that you no longer need.

TIP

If you trim out dead space in live instrument tracks, your songs will have a brighter, cleaner sound. For example, if you start recording 12 seconds before the guitar plays the first note, you should trim out those 12 seconds of dead space. The same goes for vocals — if you recorded dead air before the singing starts, trim it out because that dead air has noise in it. Deleting the dead space lowers the overall noise level for your song. So if you want the cleanest, brightest mix possible, delete dead space longer than 2–3 seconds on any real instrument track. It's a hassle, but your song will sound better for your trouble.

To split a region, follow these steps:

1. **Move the playhead to the precise point where you want the split to occur.**

2. **Tap the region once to select it, then tap it again to reveal the available commands.**

   To split multiple regions on different tracks, press and hold down on the first region and then, without releasing the first region, tap each region you want to add. The selected regions change color (to a lighter shade of green, blue, or orange) to indicate that they're selected.

3. **Tap Split.**

   The split marker, which looks like a scissors, appears over the top part of the track, as shown in Figure 17-3.

You can drag the split marker left or right if necessary, to position it precisely. And, don't forget you can always zoom in or out by pinching or unpinching the workspace.

4. **Drag the scissors downward to perform the split.**

5. **Tap to select the left or right part of the region (the part that you want to delete), tap it again, and then tap Delete.**

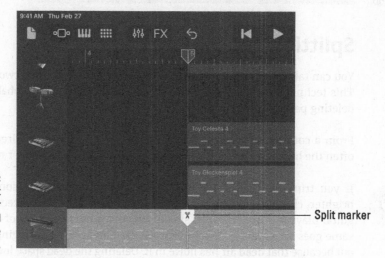

FIGURE 17-3:
Drag the split marker downward to split the region.

Split marker

You can split a region into as many regions as you want. If you're cutting out part of a track, you may need to add a second split to isolate the section that you want to delete. After you do that, select the middle section of the region that needs to go and delete it.

Silencing mistakes with automation curves

Some tracks just can't be fixed. If nothing else so far in this chapter has helped, you can try one more tool: automation curves, which you use to make the mistake fade out gradually so that no one knows that the mistake was ever there.

If this feature sounds like the *track volume automation controls* you use in the Mac version, you're right — it's the same feature but with a different name. Why would Apple do that? Who knows.

Here's how to use automation curves (the feature known as track volume automation controls on the Mac) to erase a mistake:

1. **Listen to the track and find the mistake.**

2. **Tap any track header, and then tap it again to reveal the available commands.**

3. **Tap Automation.**

   All tracks expand to reveal their track automation curves, as shown in Figure 17-4.

4. **Slide the pencil on the left edge of the control bar to the right to unlock the automation curves so you can add control points.**

5. **Tap the track's automation curve (which I still call a rubber band) to create a control point one or two seconds before the mistake.**

6. **Tap to create three more control points — two in the middle of the mistake and one after the mistake, as shown in Figure 17-4.**

7. **Drag the two middle control points downward to reduce or eliminate the mistake, as shown in Figure 17-4.**

TIP

To adjust precisely when this adjustment begins and ends, drag the first or fourth control point to the left or right. To make the adjustment louder, drag the two middle control points upward; to make it quieter, drag the two middle points downward. To delete a control point, tap it once.

FIGURE 17-4:
Part of my vocal was too loud, so I used the automation curve to make the loud part quieter.

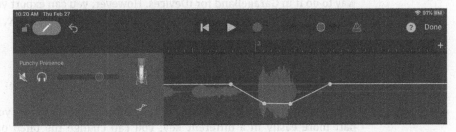

This trick won't work every time, but if your song has enough other stuff going on, you can usually fade a mistake right out of the mix, with no one (except yourself) the wiser.

Editing Software Instrument Tracks

Software instrument (green) tracks offer the greatest flexibility for editing. You can, of course, choose a different instrument, but you can also change the pitch or tempo (and not just by a little), without ill effect. You can't do those things to real instrument tracks. If you alter their tempo or pitch very much, they'll sound unnatural — or worse.

REMEMBER

As I've said before, I recommend laying down software instrument tracks before you begin recording real instrument tracks. That way, if you decide the tempo is too slow or too fast, or the pitch is too high or too low, you can make the appropriate changes to the software instrument tracks without re-recording them. If you record real instrument tracks first and then decide that a song is too slow, fast, high, or low, you will have to re-record all the real instrument tracks.

Changing the tempo of a song

GarageBand lets you change the tempo of an entire song but not the tempo of an individual track. If you change the tempo of one track, you have to change the tempo of all tracks.

If that's what you want to do — change the tempo of the song — tap the settings icon in the control bar, tap Tempo, and then either tap the up or down arrows or swipe upward or downward on the number to increase the tempo or decrease it, respectively.

If you want to change the tempo for just part (or parts) of your song, there's no way to do it in GarageBand for iDevices. However, you can export your project and change the tempo for part of your song with GarageBand for Mac, as described in Chapter 9.

Changing the pitch

If you can't sing the highest notes or, as often happens to me, you can play the part more easily in a different key, you can change the pitch of any software instrument track at any time and it won't affect the rest of your tracks.

But as I mention earlier in this chapter, changing pitch works well only with software instrument tracks.

If you want to change the key of the entire song, you have to do the following for each software instrument (except drums and percussion instruments). To change the pitch of a software instrument track:

1. Tap the region for which you want to change the pitch, tap it again, and then tap Settings.

The Settings overlay appears.

2. **Under Transposition, tap + or – to change the pitch of the region.**

You can change the pitch by full octaves or by semitones (1/12 of an octave), as shown in Figure 17-5.

TIP

You may want to change the pitch by a little or a lot, depending on your intent. If you can't quite hit the highest note in a song, dropping the song's pitch by one, two, or three semitones ought to do the trick.

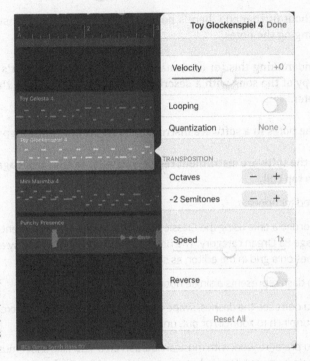

FIGURE 17-5:
Tap the + or – to increase or decrease the pitch by octaves or semitones.

TIP

I often make my software instrument tracks sound differently by transposing them up or down one full octave, which is 12 semitones. Sometimes when I double-track an instrument, I'll transpose one of the tracks up or down an octave for a fuller sound. A benefit of transposing by a factor of 12 is that you don't have to change the pitch of any other instrument tracks.

3. **Listen to the region by moving the playhead to its start and tapping the play icon.**

Click the solo icon, if necessary, to listen to only the transposed track.

4. **Adjust the Octaves or Semitones setting again if necessary.**

5. **Tap Done.**

Be careful if you change the pitch of just one loop or region. The new pitch needs to be in the same key as other loops and regions, or it will sound icky. Without getting into a bunch of musical theory that is beyond the scope of this book (plus, I couldn't explain it to you, anyway), just remember to listen and confirm that the transposed region sounds right after you adjust its pitch.

Rearranging notes in a region

Now, without further ado, here's how to fine-tune a software instrument region by rearranging the notes.

Before undertaking this (or any) major surgery on your song, it's a good idea to save a copy of the song with a descriptive name, as described at the beginning of this chapter.

To edit the notes in a software instrument track, follow these steps:

1. **Tap the software instrument region you want to edit, tap it again, and then tap Edit.**

   The editor appears.

   I recorded a take using the Classic Rock Organ software instrument from the Vintage B3 Organ category. The notes I played are represented by a series of dashes on a grid in the editor, as shown in Figure 17-6.

   Each dash represents a single note in your region.

   If you don't see the dashes, swipe up and down in the editor to scroll, or pinch and unpinch to zoom in or out, until you find them.

   If you prefer to work with musical notation on a staff (like sheet music), you can't do it on your iDevice but you can on your Mac. So if you're comfortable working with notes on a staff, you might want to export your project and use GarageBand for macOS's score mode as described in Chapter 9.

2. **Change the zoom in the editor so that you can see the notes that you want to edit (refer to Figure 17-6, bottom).**

   The size of each dash grows when you zoom in. The top picture is zoomed out to show 14 measures; the bottom picture is zoomed in to show 2 measures.

   If your region contains many high or low notes, you might have to scroll up or down in the editor (or zoom out farther) to see them all.

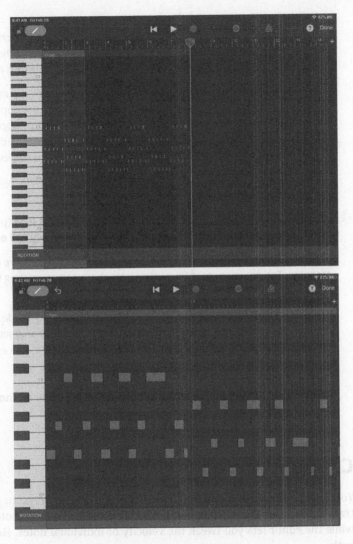

FIGURE 17-6: Editing the software instrument region zoomed out (top) and zoomed in (bottom).

3. **To edit existing notes in the editor, tap a dash.**

   Do you hear that? When you tap a dash, you're playing the note that it represents. To select multiple notes, press and hold down on one dash and then tap the dashes you want to add to the section. With the note or notes selected, you can start making changes.

   Here's a quick list of edits you can make to notes:

   - *To move a note or notes:* Slide the note to the right or the left on the same horizontal line, and you change *when* it is played. Slide the note up or down to a different horizontal line and you change the *pitch* of the note. It's that simple! When you move a dash, you change when the note is played, the pitch of the note, or both.

- *To change the length of a note:* Tap the note that you want to change; then grab the right edge and drag it to the right or left. Dragging the edge to the right lengthens the note while dragging it to the left shortens it.

- *To duplicate a note:* Tap the note or notes to select them, tap again, and then tap Copy. Move the playhead to where you want the duplicate note, and then tap the grid (not a dash) and tap Paste. The note appears on the same line (that is, the same pitch/note) as the note you copied. Drag it up or down to change its pitch, or drag it left or right to change its timing.

- *To delete a note:* Tap to select the note and then tap Delete. Again, you can select multiple notes the same way as before.

4. **To create a new note, press and hold down on the edit icon (pencil) on the left edge of the control bar, and then tap any empty cell on the grid.**

   As long as you're pressing the edit icon, you can create or remove notes by tapping. Tap an empty spot to create a note there; tap an existing note to delete it.

   You can also slide the edit icon to the right to unlock editing mode. When you do, you won't have to keep pressing the edit icon to create or delete notes. When you're finished editing, slide the edit icon to the left to lock editing mode.

   As always, listen to your changes by tapping the play icon.

5. **When you're satisfied, close the editor by clicking Done on the right edge of the control bar.**

Changing a note's velocity

You can change the velocity (loudness) of a note in two ways: in the editor or in tracks view. The difference is that tracks view applies to every note in the region, while the editor lets you tweak the velocity of individual notes. Here's how to do both:

>> **In the editor:** Tap the note to select it, tap it again, and then tap Velocity. A slider appears above the note, as shown in Figure 17-7. Slide it to the left to make the note quieter or to the right to make the note louder.

>> **In tracks view:** Tap the region to select it, tap it again, and then tap Settings. Slide the Velocity slider to the left to make all notes in the region quieter or to the right to make all the notes louder.

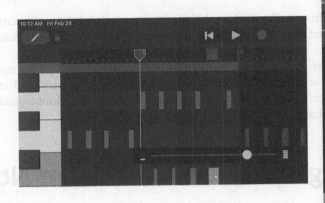
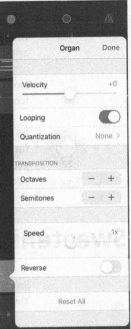

FIGURE 17-7:
The slider in the
editor (left) and in
tracks view
(right).

To quantize or not

Use the quantize feature to correct the timing of notes played too early or late by automatically sliding all notes in a region to the nearest vertical line on the grid.

Quantization is a great way to perform a quick-and-dirty fix on some tracks. For example, if you have a MIDI drum track with some beats slightly out of time, quantizing the region to the nearest ⅛ or ¹⁄₁₆ note may fix the beats that were off.

To enable quantization, tap the track you want to quantize to select it. Now, tap the track settings icon in the control bar, tap Track Settings, and then tap Quantization.

WARNING

When quantization is enabled for a track, the track's regions are all quantized. If you add new regions to this track, they too will be quantized.

Now tap Straight, Triplet, or Swing to see your quantization options. I almost always get the results I want from Straight, which provides a more precise rhythm than either of the other choices. Your mileage may vary.

Next, tap the note value you want to apply to this track. If you tapped Straight, those values are 1/4, 1/8, 1/16, 1/32, or 1/64 note. The values for Triplet and Swing are different but work the same; tap the one you want to apply to the track.

Now listen to the track, and if the results aren't what you expected, tap the undo icon and try a different value. Repeat the process until you're satisfied.

TIP

Be careful when using the quantize feature. If you have pickup notes or anything funky or off-beat (but cool), you may mess up your track by *fixing* its timing. If you don't like the results of quantization, undo the fix immediately, lest you lose your chance by saving or crashing before you do (undo).

Sweetening: Add New Material or Not?

Sweetening is a concept, not a technique, so it doesn't matter if you're using a Mac or an iDevice.

In the interest of saving trees, and because I said what I have to say about sweetening in Chapter 9, please read (or reread) the last section, a delightful little ditty that contains everything you need to know to sweeten (or not sweeten) your song on a Mac or iDevice.

IN THIS CHAPTER

» **Finding out what mixing is**

» **Setting levels**

» **Panning tracks left or right**

» **Adding effects**

» **Doubling tracks**

Chapter **18**

Mixing Tracks into Songs

T
he tracks are in the can. You've edited, tweaked, and cleaned each track until it's the best it can be, and added a few more to sweeten your project. Now you're ready to convert that pile of individual tracks into a song. I'm talking, of course, about mixing.

In this chapter, you learn what mixing is, and then you discover how to mix a song. You conclude with an age-old studio trick that can make your mix better with little effort.

What Is Mixing?

When you've done all you can with individual tracks, it is time to blend them harmoniously by mixing the tracks together to create a stereo track you can master and then export, listen to, and share with others.

Here's how mixing works. Play each track and do the following:

1. Set its level (volume) so it blends harmoniously with the others.

2. Set its pan (left/right) to place this instrument (or vocal) in its place in the imaginary stereo sound field.

3. Add effects, such as echo, reverb, and compression (if needed).

TIP

Not every track needs effects. In fact, adding too many effects is a common mistake, particularly when the producer is new to multitrack recording. Forewarned is forearmed; don't overdo it. Remember your mantra: "Look for a reason to leave it alone."

I mix my songs in the same order as the preceding steps — set the levels, set the pan, and then add effects. But that order isn't ironclad; if you want to add effects before you set your pan positions, go for it. The point is that three fairly discrete components make up the mixing process. You need to pay attention to all three if you want the final song to sound its very best.

REMEMBER

When you master your song (which you explore in the next chapter), you pretty much repeat the mixing process. But rather than tweaking individual tracks, you set levels, add fade-ins and fade-outs, and include effects such as echo or reverb to all the tracks mixed together.

TIP

Take your time mixing your songs. Experiment and try different combinations of levels, pan, EQ, and effects. The mix is where the magic occurs; I often spend more time on mixing than recording.

You don't need a degree in musicology or even audio engineering to mix. All you really need are ears. There is no right or wrong mix; the perfect mix is the one that sounds right to you.

To me, mixing is the most creative part of the production and postproduction process — and the most fun. Mixing is where you add that special something that makes your song "music" and not just a collection of recorded tracks.

Now relax, get comfortable, and let's mix.

Creating a Level Playing Field

In general, you're shooting for a mix in which no instrument or voice overpowers the others, and each instrument or vocal can be heard clearly. So, the first step in mixing is usually to create a rough mix, where you set the level of each track relative to the other tracks. Then you can fine-tune the levels of each track. All the while, keep an eye on both individual track levels and the master level to make sure they all stay out of the red.

The following sections have the details.

Roughing it with a rough mix

Before you do anything else — before you touch the pan control or add effects — you create a rough mix, adjusting each track so that no instrument or vocal track is dominant and all the tracks can be heard clearly. Create your rough mix by following these steps:

1. **Play your song by tapping the play icon, and then listen closely to the levels.**

   Is any instrument or vocal far too loud or soft? Are you hearing every instrument and vocal track?

2. **Drag any track icon to the right to reveal the track headers.**

3. **Adjust the level of each track that seems too soft or too loud by moving its slider control to the left or right in the track header.**

   TIP

   Keep an eye on the master level meter in the control bar; it represents the level of your stereo mix. If you make a track too hot, you'll probably overload the master level meter and start seeing red. If you keep an eye on the meter now, you won't have to readjust your levels later to prevent clipping.

   Your goal is to keep track levels set so that you see little or no red on the master level meter.

4. **Listen to the song again to see how adjusting the level affected the rough mix. If the levels still aren't quite right, keep tweaking using the volume sliders.**

   I usually spend a few minutes adjusting level controls for any tracks that are too loud or soft. I then listen and adjust any tracks that are still too loud or soft. When I have a reasonably good balance and nothing is horribly loud or soft, I move on to the next step, knowing that I can always make additional adjustments later if necessary.

   And that's all there is to the first step in the process. You now have a rough mix of your song.

TIP

You can use the mute and solo icons in the track header to enable or disable tracks when you're working on your rough mix. I usually mute the vocal tracks until I have a rough mix of the instrument tracks. Then I unmute the vocal tracks and mix them in.

When you're satisfied with your rough mix, it's time to begin mixing in earnest by fine-tuning your levels, which it what the next section is all about.

A fine tune

Now you'll give your song a more critical listening, this time searching for *parts* of tracks that are too loud or too soft. If you have a wonderful vocal that sounds perfect during the verses but overloads the level meters during the louder choruses, you can fine-tune the track so that its level is perfect all the way through.

The track volume automation control is the key. You use it to lower the level of the vocal during those overly loud choruses so that the entire track plays without seeing red in the meters.

TIP

You can use this technique also to emphasize a solo or disguise a flubbed part.

Figure 18-1 shows a mix that's been fine-tuned by using the track volume control on two of the four tracks. The acoustic guitar (Acoustic) is louder during the introduction and quieter during the verse; the electric guitar (Crunchy Blues) is softer during the intro and louder during the verse. Note how the chorus begins at measure 5, with the acoustic guitar getting louder and the electric guitar getting softer.

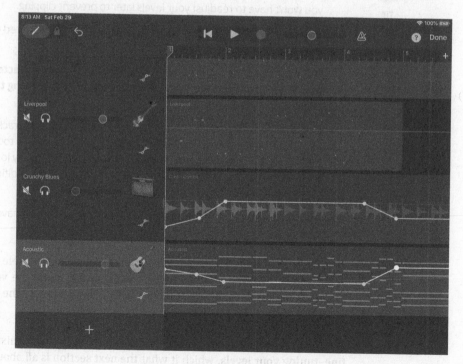

FIGURE 18-1:
A fine-tuned mix, with the acoustic and electric guitar part levels automated.

TIP

I almost always mix drums and bass (the rhythm section) first, and I rarely use the track volume control for either. The rhythm section usually remains at a constant level throughout the entire song — except when it doesn't. (Every rule has exceptions.)

To use the track volume automation control for a track, see the section on silencing mistakes with automation curves in Chapter 17.

TIP

After tweaking the volume on tracks that need it, if your song doesn't sound smooth and natural, try dragging the control points around a little — up or down to change the level, or left or right to change the duration.

Level meters: Red = dead

Each track has a pair of level meters for its left and right channels. Be sure and pay attention to them as you mix your song. If the level of any track is too hot (that is, too high), you'll introduce distortion and other undesirable crud to your song — something you should avoid at all costs.

If a track's level is too hot, you'll see red LEDs on the right side of its level meters. In a nutshell, no track should be red for more than a second, and it's better if you see no red at all.

The most important level meters of all are the master level meters near the upper-right corner. These indicate the level for the left and right channel of the stereo mix. If *they* go into the red, you risk ruining the entre song. So although it's important to keep individual tracks out of the red, it's even more important that the master levels aren't too hot.

TIP

The master levels reflect the combined levels of all the tracks. If your master levels are hot, reduce the level of one or more tracks. Ideally, you want to see as much green and yellow as possible and little or no red.

Panning Tracks Left or Right

When you're satisfied with your levels, it's time to look at panning your tracks. *Pan* determines how much of each track is sent to the left and right speaker. The object of panning is to create an imaginary stereo sound field and to place instruments on the virtual stage.

For example, suppose that the singer and drummer are smack dab in the middle, the bass player is just to the right of the drummer, the acoustic guitar player is on the far right side of the stage, and the electric guitarist is on the far left side. Figure 18-2 shows tracks that are panned to create the illusion that I just described. From left to right, drums (SoCal) and vocals (Lead Vocal) are panned dead center; bass (Liverpool Bass) is panned soft right; and the electric and acoustic guitars (Crunchy Blues and Acoustic) are panned hard left and hard right respectively.

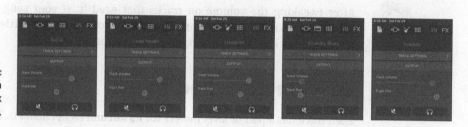

FIGURE 18-2:
Pan settings for a song might look like this.

You can even create the illusion that one instrument is closer to the front of the stage than others with effects such as delay, reverb, and echo. For more on these terms, see "The Effects of Adding Effects," later in this chapter.

The ear is less sensitive to the direction of low frequencies such as a bass guitar or kick drum, so bass and drums are usually panned dead center. All other instruments and voices, though, are candidates for panning.

REMEMBER

Another objective in mixing is to separate different but similar-sounding instruments so that you can hear that they're two different instruments. To that end, you should avoid panning instruments in the same frequency range to the same side. Here's an example: If your song has guitar and harmonica tracks (both occupy the midrange), you should pan one to the left and the other to the right. If you panned them both the same way, they blend, and neither will sound as clear and distinct as when they're panned to opposite sides.

Pan positions range from no pan, or dead center, to all the way to the left or right, known as panning the track hard left or hard right, respectively.

As I said earlier, mixing is not an exact science. However, if you're trying to create a song that sounds like what you hear on the radio, here are some suggestions for panning particular instruments and vocal parts:

>> **Drums:** If the drums are a loop and contained on a single track, I pan them dead center. But if I have separate drum tracks for different drum parts, I may pan the kick drum and snare dead center and the tom-toms and cymbals a little off-center, say to 11 o'clock and 1 o'clock, respectively.

>> **Bass:** Remember what I said earlier about low frequencies being less directional? I usually pan the bass dead center or slightly off-center, as shown in Figure 18-2.

>> **Guitar:** There's no hard and fast rule here. I sometimes pan the lead guitar hard left or hard right and the rhythm guitar hard to the opposite side. Other times, I pan the lead guitar a little to one side and the rhythm guitar a little to the opposite side — say, 2 o'clock and 10 o'clock.

>> **Keyboards/organs/pianos/synths:** Again, there's no set rule about where keyboard instruments sound best in a mix, so they might go left or right or even center if the drums and bass aren't completely filling the center of the mix. If you have guitar parts and keyboard parts, it's usually best to pan guitars one way and keyboards the other. In this case, the lead guitar might be panned left slightly, the rhythm guitar panned hard left, and the keyboard panned somewhere on the right.

>> **Lead vocal:** This vocal is usually panned dead center or slightly off-center. If I double a vocal track, I pan one track slightly left and the doubled vocal slightly right.

>> **Background vocals:** I almost always double background vocals and usually pan one track hard left and the second track hard right. If I want an even thicker harmony vocal sound, I sometimes add a third instance of the track panned dead center but with a lower level than the left and right ones. This gives a kind of Beach Boys effect to the background vocals.

Be careful: The middle of the sound field gets mighty crowded in most songs, so adding more tracks panned dead center can muddy the mix rather than make it clearer.

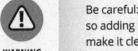

WARNING

>> **Handheld percussion (tambourine, shakers, washboards, and so on):** Pan it anywhere you think it sounds good. If you have cymbals panned left or right, you might want to pan the percussion instrument the opposite way.

Let these suggestions be your guide, but remember that there are no absolute rules for setting a track's pan. If you pan each track where it sounds best to you, regardless of what anyone (including me) suggests, your songs will come out sounding just fine.

The Effects of Adding Effects

Using effects in the studio could be the subject of a book even bigger than this one. Not only are there so many different effects, but you can use them in so many different ways. In this section, I offer you a quick glimpse of a few of the effects that you'll likely be using the most.

Using effects on your tracks isn't mysterious or technical: You basically turn the effect on, twiddle with the settings, listen to the track, and decide whether the effect helps or hurts the song.

Turn on an effect and listen to the difference. Tweak its settings, and listen to what happens. After a while, you'll know what each effect does and what it sounds like when applied to a track. It won't be long before you find yourself listening to a song on the radio and thinking, "I love the chorus effect on that guitar."

I'll say it one more time: "Just trust your ears."

TIP

To modify or add effects, first select the track, and then tap the track controls icon in the control bar. The track settings for the selected track appear on the left side of the screen (as shown in Figure 18-3).

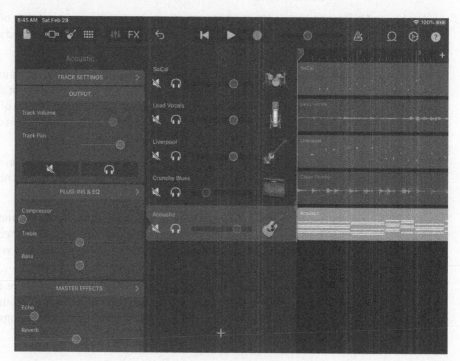

FIGURE 18-3:
Track settings for the Acoustic Guitar track.

Here's the good news: After you know how to enable and use one plug-in effect, you know how to enable all the effects. So here's how to enable any of the effects in the rest of this section (and many others):

1. **Tap the track controls icon in the control bar.**

2. **Tap Plug-ins & EQ.**

3. Tap Edit.

A track can have up to six plug-ins, and most instrument presets have two plug-ins enabled — usually compressor and visual EQ. In Figure 18-4, I'm about to add an effect to the first of the four empty plug-in slots.

4. Tap + on the left side of any empty slot to choose an effect.

Choose an effect in the Effects tab (shown in Figure 18-4) or the Audio Unit Extensions tab.

FIGURE 18-4: Four of this drummer track's six plug-in slots are open.

In the next section, I introduce you to a few of the effects that come into play (pun intended) most often.

Equalization or not?

Equalization (also known as *EQ*) lets you control specific frequencies within a track (or song) and increase or decrease the volume for those frequencies to impart different sound characteristics to a track. Want to brighten an acoustic guitar? EQ can do that. Want to make a cymbal sound less hissy? That's another issue you can fix using EQ.

Words aren't the best way to understand the effect of EQ, so let's try a little experiment:

1. **Open GarageBand, and create a new song project with a software instrument track.**

   Choose a piano for the track if one isn't already assigned to it.

2. **Record a few measures of piano.**

3. **Tap Plug-ins & EQ in Track Settings, and then tap Visual EQ.**

   The Visual EQ editor appears, as shown in Figure 18-5.

TIP

To work in full-screen mode, tap the little arrows in the lower-right corner of the Visual EQ overlay.

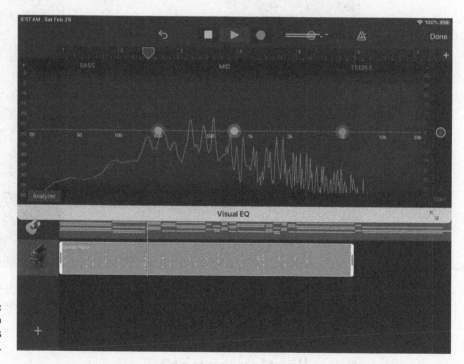

FIGURE 18-5:
Tap Visual EQ to tweak a track's equalization.

4. **To see the frequencies in your song in real time, tap the Analyzer button in the lower-left corner of the Visual EQ overlay.**

   In Figure 18-5, most of the frequencies are clustered in the midrange and treble bands.

5. **In the control bar, tap the go to beginning icon and then tap the play icon.**

   Listen once or twice to get a feel for what it sounds like before you add any EQ.

6. **Adjust the EQ.**

   See Chapter 6 for details on adjusting the EQ.

7. **When you're satisfied with what you hear, tap Done to return to the tracks view.**

8. **Tap the go to beginning icon and then tap the play icon.**

9. **To compare the track with and without EQ, tap the on/off icon to the left of the Visual EQ button in Plug-ins & EQ (in Track Settings).**

   When the on/off icon is lit, EQ is being applied (Figure 18-6, left); when it's dark, EQ is off (Figure 18-6, right).

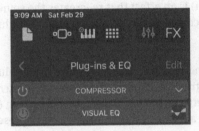 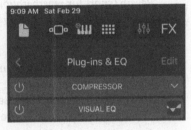

FIGURE 18-6:
Visual EQ on (left)
and off (right).

And that's how you add EQ to (or remove EQ from) a track.

TIP

My advice is to adjust EQ in very small increments.

Finally, if visual EQ and analyzer are too complicated for your tastes, you can achieve a similar effect using the treble and bass sliders in track settings. You won't have as much control over which frequencies you're boosting or cutting, but the treble and bass sliders might be all you need for a quick fix.

Compressor

The *compressor* effect decreases the difference between the loudest and the softest parts of a song or track. Compression adds punch and focus to a song and can make it sound better when played on a cheap audio system or on the radio. Many hit songs have a bit of compression applied to compensate for the limited frequency response of most radio speakers.

See Chapter 6 for additional info on applying compression to tracks. Although that chapter is about GarageBand for Mac, I'd say the same things about compression here.

TIP

If you don't use the compressor on a track or tracks, you can still apply compression to your entire song as part of the mastering process, which I cover in Chapter 19.

The following sections give brief descriptions of several more frequently used plug-in effects.

Echo and reverb

Echo (also known as *delay*) copies the original sound and plays it back later in time, with enough of a time lapse to be heard distinctly from the original.

Reverb (short for *reverberation*) is an effect that re-creates the sound of an acoustic space by playing back many copies of the original signal, at slightly varied times and volume levels.

You have two types of echo and reverb. *Track reverb and echo* are plug-ins you enable and use for on a specific track, as described previously. *Master echo and reverb* are applied from the Track Settings pane's Master Effects section (at the bottom). Tap Master Effects to choose a master echo or master reverb preset.

It's hard to explain when and how to use these effects, so just turn them on, crank them up, and listen to the results. Some tracks sound much better with a little echo or reverb or both; other tracks sound better with none. Once again, trust your ears. See Chapter 6 for additional info on applying echo and reverb to tracks.

Chorus

The *chorus* effect plays copies of the original sound later than the original, with each copy slightly out of tune, so one voice or instrument sounds like several voices or instruments playing in unison. (Actually, the instruments or voices play *close to* unison, which is not quite *in* unison.)

To use the chorus effect, tap + in one of the open plug-in slots and then tap Chorus. Try the chorus effect on vocals or instruments, but only use a little bit. Too much chorus will sound dorky.

Doubling Tracks

Doubling tracks is one of my favorite pro mixing tips. When a track sounds wimpy, try *doubling* it to thicken the sound a bit. This means you have two copies of the same track, which you can create by copying and pasting or by re-recording the same part on a new track.

The copy-and-paste method

The copy-and-paste technique is fast and easy. Those are its pros. The con is that unless you're careful the result will sound mechanical because both tracks are *exactly* the same.

Following is the copy-and-paste method:

1. **Duplicate the track: Tap its track header icon to select the track, tap it again to reveal options, and then tap Duplicate.**

You now have a new track with the same settings as the original.

2. **Tap to select the region you want to double-track, tap it again to reveal the options, and then tap Copy.**

3. **Tap the duplicate track's header icon to select the track, tap it again to reveal options, and then tap Paste.**

Applying a different instrument or preset to the doubled guitar track can work wonders, making it sound like a wall of guitars rather than a single wimpy one.

Now, here's how to make a doubled track sound even better:

1. **Turn off GarageBand's snap-to-grid feature, which is enabled by default.**

Here's the secret gesture shortcut to turn off snap-to-grid. Pinch-zoom in as much as you are can, and then lift your fingers. Now, pinch-zoom in again. The text *Snap to Grid Off* appears at the top of the workspace, as shown in Figure 18-7. To reenable snap-to-grid, just pinch-zoom out.

2. **Slide the duplicated region to the right by the tiniest amount you can slide.**

Now the duplicated track starts a fraction of a second after the original track. In Figure 18-7, I transformed a single thin-sounding acoustic guitar track into a pair of guitar tracks that sound much richer and fuller.

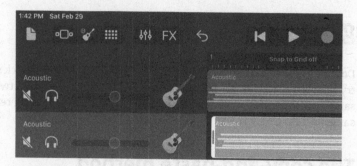

FIGURE 18-7:
Use the secret double-zoom gesture to disable snap-to-grid.

You can use this technique to make one guitar track sound like a pair of blazing-hot guitarists. Or transform a thin-sounding vocal into a lush, warm croon. Try it — you'll like it!

TIP

You'll get a richer, fuller sound if you pan one of the doubled tracks left and pan the other track right by an equal amount. Try different combinations of panning and offsetting the doubled tracks until you find the combo that's perfect for your song.

The re-recording method

Alternatively, you can double the track by creating a new track and recording the part a second time, playing or singing along with the original track. You want to try to duplicate your original performance as precisely as you can, but because you're only human, the second recording is guaranteed to have small differences from the original track.

Although this technique can take you more time, the differences between the two takes can result in a better sound than copying and pasting the same performance. If you're a consistent enough player or singer, the minor differences between the two performances may sound spectacular when played together; just ask the Beatles.

REMEMBER

To achieve a different kind of depth, offset one of the tracks just a bit by turning off the grid, zooming all the way in on the timeline, and sliding one of the tracks slightly to the left or right, as described in the preceding section (and shown in Figure 18-7).

On the next track you record that could use a little more oomph, you should absolutely, positively try double-tracking.

Chapter **19**

Mastering Mastering

There's no mystery about mastering — you already know how to do it; you just don't know that you know yet. You see, mastering is nothing more than applying familiar effects, such as EQ, echo, reverb, and compression, to your entire song instead of individual tracks.

Mastering is the final step in the multitrack recording process; it's the last thing you do before you distribute your work for others to hear. In big-time major-label music production, mastering is a specialized art performed by a handful of highly paid mastering engineers with state-of-the-art mastering studios and the highest-of-high-quality audio-processing hardware and software.

Fortunately, you don't have to go to that trouble or expense: GarageBand's built-in mastering presets harness the knowledge of a roomful of mastering engineers.

I'm only half-kidding. The GarageBand mastering presets are excellent and can give most people the results they want and expect most of the time. However, if you plan to have your song professionally duplicated in quantity, you might want to enlist a good mastering engineer to ensure that what ends up on the discs (or digital files) sounds exactly the way you want it to — or, perhaps more importantly, the way that radio programmers expect it to.

Mastering your masterpiece in GarageBand can be as easy as choosing a preset. If you're not sure what your song needs, let that room full of experienced mastering engineers do the mastering for you, and don't touch those dials. Or, if you prefer the hands-on-the-knobs approach, start with the preset that sounds closest to your ideal and then tweak its individual settings until your fingers bleed. Either way, you'll end up with a song that sounds darned good to most people most of the time.

Before You Master

Mixing and mastering are different sides of the same coin, so GarageBand makes it easy to switch between these two chores. This is a good thing because everything you do to the master track affects the mix.

REMEMBER

You can always go back and change anything you like in the mix, but it's best to have your mixing as close to complete as possible before you master. If not, you may end up spending more time than necessary remixing and remastering.

Before you begin mastering, double-check that you are happy with the following:

>> Relative loudness (level) of each track

>> Ronal characteristics (equalization) of each track

>> Spatial positioning (pan) of each track

You did all these things when you mixed, which I cover in great detail in Chapter 18.

TIP

You should also trim noise or extraneous sound at the head or tail of any or all tracks (if you haven't done so already); your final product will sound better for it. The easiest way to get rid of dead space is to create a split where you want the song to begin and then delete the dead space after it's split from the song. Check out Chapter 17 for details.

Having checked and double-checked your mix and ensured that it's as good as it's going to get, it's time to master it — and (I hope) make it sound even better.

Now for the bad news: GarageBand on iDevices doesn't include the excellent mastering features and presets of the Mac version. You can add a fade-out and apply master echo and reverb to a song, but that's about the extent of it. The sad reality is that if you want your recording to sparkle and sound more professional, you'll have to export the project from your iDevice and master it on your Mac.

If you don't have a Mac, are thrilled with the sound of your project already, or don't care if it sounds better and more professional, you are pretty much finished. Feel free to skip the next section, "Exporting to a Mac for Mastering."

WARNING

Skip the next section if you like, but do not skip the "Sharing Songs" section — at least not if you care to get songs off your iDevice for others to enjoy or to use as a ringtone.

Now, without further ado, here's how you export your project so you can master your masterpiece on a Mac.

Exporting to a Mac for Mastering

If you want your song to sound the best it can, you're doing the right thing by mastering it on a Mac. So let's get to it.

To export your almost finished song to a Mac, start by doing the following on your iDevice:

1. **Tap the my songs icon in the control bar, tap the Select button, and then tap the song you want to export.**

2. **Tap Share at the bottom of the screen, and then tap Project on the Share Song sheet to export an editable song file for your Mac.**

3. **Tap the option you prefer on the Share Sheet to access the file on your Mac.**

   I typically use AirDrop to send the file to my Mac wirelessly, but feel free to send the file via Messages, Mail, Dropbox, Google Drive, or whatever other means you like as long as it gets the file from your iDevice to your Mac.

Now, open the file you just transferred on your Mac and follow the instructions in Chapter 11 for mastering your song on the Mac.

Sharing Songs

If you don't care to export and master your project, you may still want to send it to friends, post it online, or transform it into a ringtone.

To share your song with others, tap the my songs icon in the control bar, and then long-press on the song you want to share. Tap Share to see your three sharing options: Song, Ringtone, or Project.

Tap Song. Then tap the audio quality level you desire and edit the song info if you care to, as shown in Figure 19-1.

‹ Share Song	Share Song	Share
AUDIO QUALITY		
Low Quality		64 kBit/s
Medium Quality		128 kBit/s
High Quality		192 kBit/s
✓ Highest Quality (iTunes Plus)		256 kBit/s
Apple Lossless		44.1kHz/16-bit
Uncompressed (AIFF)		44.1kHz/16-bit
Uncompressed (WAV)		44.1kHz/16-bit
MY INFO		
Artist	Bob "Dr. Mac" LeVitus	
Composer	Bob "Dr. Mac" LeVitus	
Album	Smell the Glove	

FIGURE 19-1: Choose the audio quality you desire and edit the song info if you care to.

TIP

Scroll down in the Share Song dialog if you want to add a cover image, as shown in Figure 19-2.

After you've tapped a quality level and edited the song info (or not), tap Share.

TIP

The higher the quality you choose, the better the song will sound. But higher quality also means larger files. So, check out Figure 19-3, which shows the same song (around 8 minutes long) at each available quality level.

Moving right along, if you want to turn your song into a ringtone or text tone, remember that ringtones (and text tones) have to be 30 seconds or less. If your song is longer, GarageBand will warn you first and then export the first 30 seconds as your ringtone. If that's not what you want, shorten the song before you continue.

Now, to share your song as a ringtone, tap the my songs icon in the control bar, and then long-press on the song. Tap Share and then tap Ringtone.

FIGURE 19-2:
Scroll down to add a cover image to your song (if you care to).

Apple Lossless		44.1kHz/16-bit
Uncompressed (AIFF)		44.1kHz/16-bit
Uncompressed (WAV)		44.1kHz/16-bit

MY INFO

Artist	Bob "Dr. Mac" LeVitus
Composer	Bob "Dr. Mac" LeVitus
Album	Smell the Glove

GarageBand will use this information to identify your songs in iTunes (not available for AIFF and WAV).

COVER IMAGE

Choose Photo...

For best results, convert images to 1:1 (square, not available for AIFF and WAV).

FIGURE 19-3:
Note the file sizes for the same song shared with different quality settings.

Downloads

7 items, 578.78 GB available

Name	Size ^	Kind
Beethoven's 5th Low.m4a	4.3 MB	Apple MPEG-4 audio
Beethoven's 5th Medium.m4a	8.5 MB	Apple MPEG-4 audio
Beethoven's 5th High.m4a	14.7 MB	Apple MPEG-4 audio
Beethoven's 5th Highest.m4a	16.3 MB	Apple MPEG-4 audio
Beethoven's 5th Apple Lossless.m4a	45.9 MB	Apple MPEG-4 audio
Beethoven's 5th (Uncompressed WAV).wav	91 MB	Waveform audio
Beethoven's 5th (Uncompressed AIFF).aiff	91 MB	AIFF-C audio

The Export Ringtone dialog appears. Rename the ringtone (if you like) and then tap Export. The Ringtone Export Successful dialog appears with two options:

>> **Use Sound As** lets you choose the sound for your standard ringtone or text tone or assign it to a contact.

>> **OK** saves the ringtone without activating it, so you can choose it as a standard ringtone or text tone or assign it to a contact in the future.

And that's how to create ringtones and text tones for free!

6

Everything Else You Might Need to Know

Play live using GarageBand's amps and stomp boxes to tailor the sound of your guitar, bass, or keyboard.

Jam with your friends over Wi-Fi — a treat for iDevice users.

Create AAC, MP3, or uncompressed files from your recordings, and understand what compression means in regards to sound quality and file sizes.

Burn audio CDs so your friends can enjoy your songs on their home or car stereo or computer (assuming said computer has an optical drive).

Chapter **20**

Playing Live with GarageBand Amps and Effects

I rarely play live these days, but I play in my office/studio almost every day. And since I have had a GarageBand-capable device nearby for decades, I no longer own a guitar amp or effects pedals. I rely entirely on GarageBand (or MainStage, which you hear more about later in the chapter) to provide the amp tones and effects I need.

When I feel like playing, I plug my guitar into whichever device is close at hand, launch GarageBand, create a real instrument track for my guitar, and then choose the guitar preset I need.

Easy peasy. My guitar sounds fantastic, and as a bonus, it's quieter and more reliable than any amp and pedal board combination I've owned.

I have played close to a dozen two-hour live sets with The Macworld All-Star Band playing through GarageBand with physical amp or effects. The process worked great, and I show you how to do it in this chapter. Which is to say, this chapter details the ins and outs of playing your guitar or bass without an amp or stomp boxes.

One last thing: I realize that some of you love the sound of your amp and stomp boxes. I get it. I felt that way for a long time. That said, give stomp boxes a try before you shun them.

The rest of this section should sound familiar if you read Chapters 8 or 16. The procedure for using GarageBand's guitar or bass settings live is pretty much the same as the procedure for recording guitars or basses in the studio. The only difference is that you won't click or tap the record icon (unless you feel like recording your performance).

Now, are you ready to plug in your instrument and rock (or hip-hop, or jazz, or country, or whatever type of music floats your boat)?

Great. Start by launching GarageBand (d'oh).

Playing at Home

Here are the steps to prepare your Mac or iDevice to serve as your guitar amp and stomp boxes (which appear on the pedalboard):

1. **Create a new GarageBand project with one real instrument track.**

2. **Choose a guitar or an amp preset for that track.**

3. **Plug your guitar into your audio interface (which is connected to your Mac or iDevice, of course) and strum a chord or two.**

   If you don't hear anything, make sure you have the correct input and output selected in the Audio/MIDI pane of GarageBand's Preferences. If you're connected via an audio interface with more than one input, make sure the proper input is selected in Recording Settings (Mac) or Input Settings (iDevices).

4. **Tune your instrument using GarageBand's built-in tuner (or your tuner of choice).**

   TIP

   If your instrument isn't in tune it's going to sound terrible mixed with software instrument tracks, which always have perfect pitch.

5. **Fine-tune your guitar or amp preset.**

   Don't fret (ha-ha) if the preset isn't exactly what you want to hear. The next step is to tweak amp and effects settings until you find the precise tone you desire.

6. **Adjust the amp controls, plug-in effects, and stomp boxes until you love what you hear.**

7. **Adjust the track's level so there's no red in the meter.**

8. **If the sound you've created is truly a masterpiece and you want to use it again in this or other projects, rename it something meaningful when you save it.**

   On a Mac, click Save at the bottom of the library. On an iDevice, tap the track controls icon in the control bar, tap the preset name near the top of the Track Controls pane, and then tap Save.

TIP

You'll find your custom presets in the User Patches (Mac) or Custom (iDevice) category, which are created after you save your first custom preset.

Believe it or not, that's all there is to it. You now know how to play your guitar or bass without an amp or effects and still have it sound pretty darn good.

That's a good start, but wait — there's more! I've been playing without an amp or effects for more than a decade. I'd like to think I've learned a thing or two you might find helpful if you choose to become an ampless and effectless guitarist or bassist like me.

General Tips for Guitarists and Bassists

If you intend to play amp-free more than occasionally, it will behoove you to create a practice file with a handful of starter tones. Why? The steps in the preceding section are too time-consuming when you want to play right away.

Create a practice file

When I want to play, I want to play right now, so I created a GarageBand file called Guitar Practice with six tracks preconfigured with guitar tones I created and love.

If I want to play, I launch this file (shown in Figure 20-1), plug in my guitar, click the track with the tone I want, and play. I often open windows for one or more plug-ins while I play (Amp Designer and Pedalboard in Figure 20-1) so I can make tweaks if necessary.

I love that I can change from one tone to another with a press or click of the up- or down-arrow keys.

Take the time to create a practice file now. Then the next time you feel like picking up your guitar and playing, you can do just that without delay.

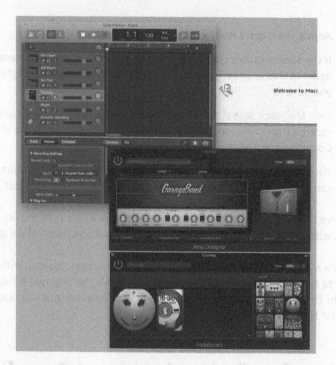

FIGURE 20-1:
My GarageBand
practice setup.

Get to know your amps, pedals, and other plug-ins

Another thing I recommend is that you spend some quality time with plug-ins. Pick a guitar or amp preset, then open a plug-in and twist its knobs and slide its sliders while listening closely.

You have more than 50 plug-ins by default, and if you know what they all do, you can use them appropriately going forward. If you're going to play only with a few, I suggest you start with Amp Designer and Pedalboard. To be honest, those two alone could keep you occupied for days. But try as many as you can — knowledge is power (chords).

Expand your palette with third-party plug-ins

If you find that you like playing without an amp or pedals, consider investing in one of the many third-party guitar emulation plug-ins and take GarageBand's tonal palette to the next level.

My favorite is IK Multimedia's AmpliTube, as I mention in Chapter 8. Others emulations are good and some are probably better, but I've created so many AmpliTube presets that I have no real interest in creating them again in a different plug-in.

That said, if you have a favorite guitar plug-in, let me know what it is and why you love it at GarageBandForDummies@boblevitus.com. **Thanks!**

Playing on Stage

Playing live in front of an audience, especially at a venue with a real stage, house sound, and floor monitors, is a different kettle of fish than playing at home alone in your room.

The stakes are higher when people are watching, so here are a few precautions I suggest for preventing embarrassing snafus:

» **Bring spares.** Murphy's law states that anything that can go wrong will go wrong. Dr. Mac's law states that when you're in front of an audience, anything that can go wrong probably will.

So, prepare for the worst by bringing all the spare gear you can. Bring spare strings, ¼-inch guitar cables, USB cables, power adapters, wall chargers, extra batteries, and so on. If you have a spare guitar, bring it.

If you already have a spare of something you'll use on stage, always bring the spare to the gig. If you don't have a spare, consider what would happen if the original died. Then, buy a spare or don't.

» **Test and test again.** Nothing is worse than getting everything set up at a gig and discovering that something doesn't work. It's wise to test your entire setup — every device, cable, power source, and instrument you'll be using on stage — before you leave the house.

» **Create a checklist.** Remember all those spares I told you to bring? Make a list of everything you need on stage and every spare you might need. Before a gig, use the list to confirm you're not forgetting something.

» **Create a set list in GarageBand.** Remember the guitar practice file I created for practicing at home? I create something like it for each live set I'm going to play, creating a track for the guitar sound (or sounds) I'll need for each song in the order we'll play them, as shown in Figure 20-2.

» **Be nice to the sound guy.** D'oh.

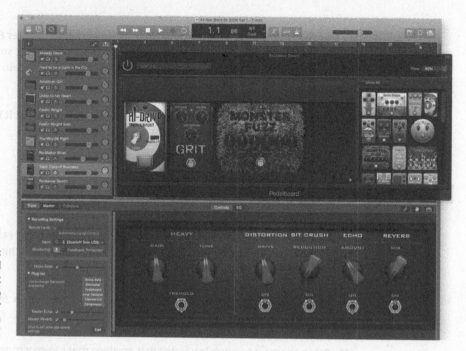

FIGURE 20-2:
My GarageBand setup for the first set at the 2006 Macworld All-Star Band show in San Francisco.

Finally, Apple makes a companion app to GarageBand for the Mac called Main-Stage ($29.99 in the Mac App Store), which it bills as a "Live rig for musicians."

"MainStage 3 lets you take your Mac to the stage with a full-screen interface optimized for live performance, flexible hardware control, and a massive collection of plug-ins and sounds that are fully compatible with Logic Pro X."

To which I would add "and compatible with GarageBand, too."

Although MainStage (shown in Figure 20-3 and 20-4) is purpose-built for live performance, I'm more comfortable using GarageBand. I know more than one professional musician who prefers MainStage (and at least one pro who uses GarageBand live on stage every night).

If playing live is your thing, try it — you might like it better than GarageBand. Or not. But you'll never know if you don't try.

One last thing: All the advice in this chapter is based on my many years of experience performing infrequently. Take it with however many grains of salt you like.

Now go out and knock 'em dead!

FIGURE 20-3:
MainStage's
full-screen
performance
interface.

FIGURE 20-4:
MainStage's
editing interface.

» Becoming a member of a jam

» Playing in a jam session

Chapter **21**

Jamming with Others over Wi-Fi

Did you know you can jam with other GarageBand users over Wi-Fi? Playback and recording is synchronized among all connected devices, which means you can play and record together as a duo or even a whole band. In this chapter, you discover how to set up a jam session, how to control playback and recording of your session, and anything else you might need to know in order to jam with friends.

You should know three things before you get too excited. The first is that the Mac version of GarageBand isn't invited to this jam session — only iOS and iPadOS users can play. The second is that jam sessions work only with touch instruments and tracks view. In other words, the live loops grid is off-limits for jam sessions (although that would be a hoot). Finally, a jam session can have no more than eight tracks. I talk about this again later in the chapter, but for now, that's all you need to know.

Let's dive right in.

Becoming the Bandleader

A jam session's creator is called the *bandleader*. I'm going to assume that's you for the rest of this chapter to avoid confusion.

After the bandleader creates a jam session, other members can join as long as they're on iDevices connected to the same Wi-Fi network.

To demonstrate, I used my iPad Pro as the bandleader and my iPhone X as the member, as shown in Figure 21-1.

As members join, the song settings you created as bandleader for this project are copied to their devices. These settings include tempo, key, time signature, sections, master effects, custom chords, fade-outs, and count-in.

The bandleader is the only one who can change these settings unless he or she disables the Bandleader Control switch in Jam Session Settings.

To create a jam session as bandleader, open the Jam Session controls by tapping the settings icon in the control bar and then tapping Create Session, which then changes to Stop Session, as shown in Figure 21-1.

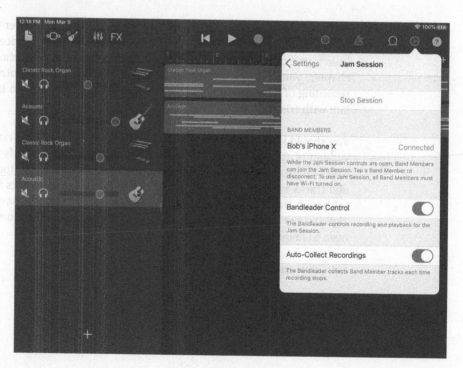

FIGURE 21-1:
My iPad Pro is the bandleader and created this jam session.

As the bandleader, you're responsible for settings such as tempo, key, time signature, and the others mentioned previously, so make any of those changes first.

And if you want to choose custom chords for your jam — which I almost always do — switch to the smart instrument view, tap the settings icon in the control bar, and tap Edit Chords. Then assign the chords you want as described in Chapter 14.

Your session is now ready for members to join.

To start recording a take, the bandleader taps the record icon and the count-in appears on everyone's screen simultaneously (assuming the bandleader has count-in enabled) before recording begins.

When you (bandleader) tap the stop icon, all takes from members are automatically collected on your device unless Auto-Collect Recordings or Bandleader Control is enabled.

TIP

The Auto-Collect Recordings switch in Jam Session Settings is enabled by default for a reason. If you disable it, members' recordings will not be automatically copied to your device after each take.

You might want to disable this switch when you simply want to jam with friends. When Auto-Collect Recordings is enabled, all members (and the bandleader) have to wait after each take for the recording to be collected on the bandleader's device. This process can take anywhere from a few seconds to a few minutes, depending on the length of the take and the number of players. If you don't care about preserving a recording of every (or any) take, disable Auto-Collect Recordings and save some time after each take.

TIP

If you disabled Auto-Collect Recordings and wish you hadn't, you can still collect members' recordings. Open Jam Session Settings and tap Collect Recordings. Note that you won't see Collect Recordings when either the Auto-Collect Recordings or Bandleader Control switch is disabled. Put another way, if both switches are blue, you won't see a Collect Recordings button.

Finally, you can end a jam session in two ways. Either tap the settings icon in the control bar, tap Jam Session, and then tap Stop Session, or tap the my songs icon in the control bar.

Becoming a Member

To join the session a bandleader has created, members tap the settings icon, tap Jam Session, and then tap the name of the session they want to join (iPad Pro in Figure 21-2).

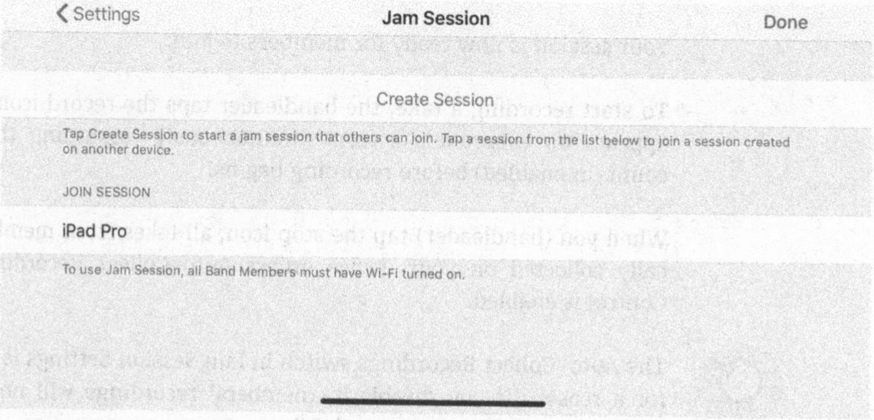

‹ Settings	Jam Session	Done

Create Session

Tap Create Session to start a jam session that others can join. Tap a session from the list below to join a session created on another device.

JOIN SESSION

iPad Pro

FIGURE 21-2:
My iPhone X (member) joining my iPad Pro (bandleader) jam session.

To use Jam Session, all Band Members must have Wi-Fi turned on.

When the bandleader taps the record icon on his or her iPad Pro to start the jam session, the count-in appears on both devices and then the recording begins.

When the bandleader ends the take by tapping the stop icon, member recordings are automatically collected on the bandleader's device. When the collection process is complete, the bandleader can tap the record icon again to lay down additional tracks (until the bandleader reaches the limit of eight tracks for jam sessions, as discussed in the next section).

A member can leave a jam session voluntarily by tapping the settings icon in the control bar, tapping Jam Session, and then tapping Leave Session, or by tapping the my songs icon in the control bar.

A member can also leave a jam session involuntarily due to network issues.

If you're disconnected from a jam session involuntarily, you should be able to rejoin the jam session the same way you joined it before.

All remaining jammers receive a message when a member leaves, but as long as two or more remain, they can continue the jam session.

Working with Jam Sessions

As mentioned, you're limited to eight tracks in a jam session. When a jam session grows to eight tracks (on the bandleader's device) you can't collect or auto-collect additional tracks. If this happens, a bandleader has several choices:

» Delete a track or tracks from the jam session on his or her device.

» Ask members to delete a track or tracks from the jam session on their devices.

» Ask members to mute a track or tracks (muted tracks are never collected).

After reducing the track count one of these ways, tap Collect Recordings again.

I discovered a way to increase the number of tracks in a jam session based on an old-time technique used when recording to tape: bouncing tracks. In the old days, if you were in danger of running out of tracks, you would *bounce* (move) two or more existing tracks onto the last remaining empty track. Then you could erase the two or more tracks you just bounced and reuse them.

So, when you have eight tracks in your jam session, tell the other players to take a break while you do the following:

1. **Save the song by tapping the my songs icon.**

2. **On the My Songs screen, press the song and share it with your Mac as a project.**

   For details on sharing a song as a project, see Chapter 19.

3. **Open the project on your Mac.**

   Your song will have eight tracks, as shown in Figure 21-3. GarageBand asks you to save it and suggests the same name with a numeral after it.

4. **Save the song using the name GarageBand suggests.**

   I shared a jam named My Jam and GarageBand suggested I save it as My Jam1.

   You may feel like renaming the file, but don't. Keep the name GarageBand suggests or you'll break the connection that makes the magic in the next step happen.

   WARNING

5. **Share the project with iOS and open it on your iDevice (as detailed in Chapter 19).**

   When you open the project on your iDevice, you'll find that GarageBand (for Mac) has magically mixed (bounced) the eight tracks on the Mac into a single track on iOS, as shown in Figure 21-4.

FIGURE 21-3:
Sharing my
eight-track song
with iOS.

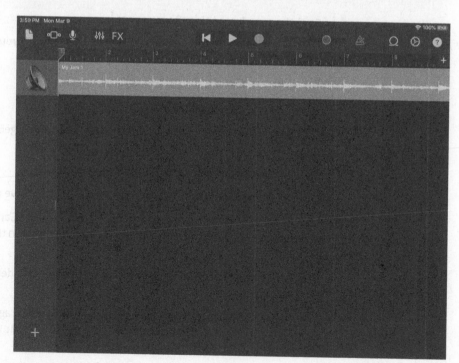

FIGURE 21-4:
The shared
eight-track song
becomes a
one-track song
when shared
to iOS.

This single track contains a mix of the eight tracks from your jam session. You'll hear all eight of the old tracks (playing from the first track) as you record the next seven tracks!

When you've finished recording those seven tracks, follow the same steps as before.

When you reach Step 3, you'll be surprised to see that the file has 15 tracks: 7 new ones plus 8 original tracks.

If you're wondering where the 16th track went, GarageBand (Mac) created it from the first 8 tracks before sharing it to the iPad. GarageBand was then smart enough to delete it when the file was reshared to the Mac.

Now, when you share this 15-track song back to your iDevice, its 15 tracks will be mixed down onto 1 track so you can add 7 more tracks before doing the share dance again.

WARNING

Finally, and this is very important: If your goal to end up with a GarageBand file that contains more than eight tracks, *do not rename the file* on either device after you've shared it to your Mac the first time.

And that's pretty much all there is to jamming with your friends using iDevices.

Have fun!

» **Making AAC and MP3 files**

» **Distributing your music**

Chapter 22

File Compression and Your Music

The first release of GarageBand exported exactly one file format — the Audio Interchange File Format (AIF or AIFF). Today, GarageBand on the Mac can export your song in pretty much all popular file formats — AAC, MP3, AIF, and even the Windows standard for audio, WAV (or WAVE).

You can't export an MP3 from GarageBand on an iDevice, but you can export AAC, AIFF, and WAV files, as well as Apple Lossless files, which aren't an option on the Mac. AIF and WAV files are, by definition, uncompressed. Files compressed with MP3 or AAC are much smaller — 50 percent to 95 percent — than an uncompressed AIF or WAV file of the same song.

Compression, by its nature, removes part of the sound in the file. In theory, it's the part that people can't hear, but some people notice a big difference between uncompressed audio and compressed audio, even on cheap stereo systems. Many others can't tell the difference. It's a matter of degrees. Some people notice the difference between compressed audio files encoded (*ripped*) at bit rates of 160 versus 192 Kbps. Others hear no difference.

The bottom line is that smaller, compressed audio files sound good enough to most people most of the time. And for what it's worth, almost all streamed music today is compressed, which is probably why compressed music has become a de facto standard.

iPhones (and most other personal music players) and the Music app (or iTunes), along with most other personal music-playing software on most devices, can play both uncompressed and compressed files. But most people store most of their music as compressed audio files, so they can have five to ten times as many songs in the same amount of storage space.

Compression is all about choices, so this chapter looks at those choices and describes how to compress an audio file to send via email or iMessage or listen to on your iDevice (or other digital audio device).

Let's look at the big picture before I talk about which option to use and what to use it for.

Understanding Compression

The quality of an AIF or a WAV file is top of the heap because it, by definition, contains 100 percent *uncompressed* audio. Nothing has been added or removed; every note, breath, harmonic, overtone, string noise, buzz, hiss, and other sound in the master recording is in an AIF or WAV file.

About uncompressed audio files

AIF (and WAV) files are uncompressed audio — the real deal. AIFF (or AIF) is the Mac standard for uncompressed audio; WAVE (or WAV) is the Windows standard.

Songs on your store-bought audio CDs appear as AIF files in Finder, as you can see in Figure 22-1.

Technically, the files on an audio CD are Red Book Audio files, which are slightly different from AIF files. The technical aspects aren't important; the important part is that when you shove an audio CD into your Mac, it sees Red Book Audio files and automatically thinks of them as AIF files, as shown in Figure 22-1. No conversion or translation is needed — to your Mac, Red Book Audio files are AIF files and vice versa, even if the rest of the world says that Red Book and AIF are different.

FIGURE 22-1:
Insert an audio
CD, and your Mac
sees AIFF files.

WARNING

Although uncompressed audio may be the right format for shiny silver discs, it's not the right format for email, streaming, texting, or the web because uncompressed audio files are gargantuan.

About compressed audio files

MP3 and AAC are the two most common compressed audio file formats on the Mac. MP3 came first and has essentially been the compressed audio standard for many years. Then, when Apple introduced the iTunes Music Store, it also introduced the AAC file format, which is used for music purchased from the iTunes Music Store as well as songs streamed through Apple Music.

Figure 22-2 is worth a couple of thousand words — I shared (saved) a one-minute song in each file format, at each available quality level. The exported files are sorted by size from biggest (top) to smallest. Note how one minute of uncompressed audio (16.9 megabytes) is an order of magnitude bigger than the same minute compressed at the lowest setting (under 600 kilobytes).

Table 22-1 is a handy reference to the file types and the common ways in which each type is used. You find out how to save your own songs in those formats in the next section.

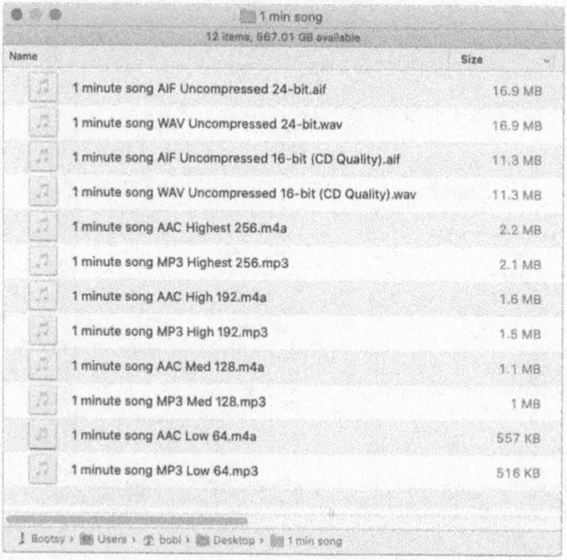

FIGURE 22-2:
Compare the file size of the same song saved in four different file formats.

TABLE 22-1 ## File Types Large and Small

File Type	Compressed?	What's It Good For?
AIF	No	Burning Audio CDs, listening, and archiving music in a file format that retains all available audio information. Can be used with iDevices, but files are 5–10 times the size of compressed formats.
WAV	No	This Windows file format is the equivalent of an uncompressed AIF file on a Mac. Use it for sharing files with Windows users. File sizes are 5–10 times the size of MP3 files, which is the compressed file format of choice among Windows users. (AAC is the compressed format of choice on the Mac.)
Apple lossless	Compressed, but lossless	Music app or iTunes, or for archiving music in a file format is smaller than an uncompressed file. In theory it sounds the same as AIF or WAV in a significantly smaller file. Can be used with iDevices but files are 3–7 times the size of compressed formats.
MP3	Yes	iTunes, email, the web, and sharing with Windows users. Files are much smaller than any uncompressed or lossless format, making MP3s ideal for almost all uses.
AAC	Yes	Same as MP3 but is Mac-centric. Slightly smaller files than MP3 with slightly better sound quality. Alas, some Windows users can't play AAC files.

Sharing Your Masterpiece

As I mention in the preceding section, different file types work better for different purposes, whether that is playing a song on your iDevice, emailing a song to a friend, or making sure that as many people as possible can listen to your song however they want to.

Each compressed file format can encode your song at four different bit rates — the higher the bit rate, the higher the quality. Alas, the higher the bit rate, the bigger the file.

Because the procedure for exporting (sharing) finished songs differs on iDevices and Macs, you explore them one at a time.

Sharing your songs from a Mac

Now that your song is finished, you probably want to share it with others so they can listen to it on their favorite device. The solution is GarageBand's Share menu.

Following is a brief description of the Share menu options:

>> **Song to Music:** Choose this option to share a song to the Music app (macOS Catalina or later) or iTunes. This option allows you to sync the song to mobile devices. Songs can be shared to Music in any compressed or uncompressed file format at any quality level.

When you choose this option, the Share to Music dialog appears, as shown in Figure 22-3.

The dialog is prepopulated with the information you provide in the My Info tab of GarageBand's Preferences.

TIP

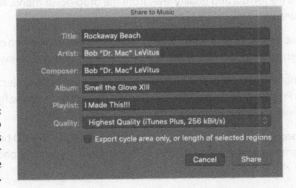

FIGURE 22-3:
The Share to Music dialog lets you edit your song info before sharing.

Choose the quality level you prefer from the Quality pop-up menu and then click Share. The whole song is then shared, with any silence at its beginning or end automatically trimmed.

To export part of your song, enable the Export Cycle Area Only, or Length of Selected Regions check box and set the cycle area or select a region or regions.

When you click Share, the song appears in the Music app (or the iTunes library in macOS Mojave or earlier). Now you can add the song to a playlist, burn it to a CD (as described in Chapter 23), or sync it with your iDevices.

>> **Song to Media Browser:** Choose this option to share audio files to Media Browser, where you can view and open them from other Apple applications, including Mail, iMovie, Notes, and Final Cut Pro X.

The entire project is saved as an audio file with the same name as the project, with any silence at the beginning or end trimmed automatically before the file appears in Media Browser.

If cycle mode is enabled, only the part of the project between the start and end of the cycle area will be shared.

>> **Song to SoundCloud:** SoundCloud is a popular music website used by bands and other musical artists to share their music. You need a SoundCloud account to use this option. When the Share to SoundCloud dialog appears, tap Change and enter your login and password.

To share a file from your disk, select the File radio button; to share the current song, select the Bounce radio button. Now fill in the information for the song and choose a quality level and visibility and permission levels for SoundCloud. When everything is just as you want it, click Share. Within a few minutes your song will be available on SoundCloud.

>> **AirDrop:** Choose this option to use the macOS/iOS AirDrop feature to share your song or GarageBand project wirelessly with a nearby Mac or iDevice (within about 6 feet). Choose Project or Song; edit the title (if you care to), choose a file format and quality level from the drop-down menu, and then click Share.

Note that to use AirDrop, both devices must have AirDrop turned on and Bluetooth enabled, and must be connected to the same Wi-Fi network.

>> **Mail:** Choose this option to share your song or GarageBand project via email. Choose Project or Song, edit the title (if you care to), choose a file format and quality level from the drop-down menu, and then click Share.

>> **Burn Song to CD:** This option is enabled only on Macs with a CD burner or other compatible optical drive (internal or external). If you have one, you can

choose this option to burn the current song onto an audio CD that you can listen to in most CD audio players or computers with optical drives.

To burn a song on a CD, choose this option and then insert a blank CD disc in your drive. Soon thereafter you'll have an audio CD with one song that can be played on most (but not all) home, portable, automobile, and computer CD audio players.

>> **Export Song to Disk:** Choose this option to create a compressed or uncompressed audio file on your local disk. When you do, you'll see a standard Save file sheet like the one in Figure 22-4.

First choose a file format (AAC, MP3, AIFF, or WAVE), and then choose a quality level from the drop-down menu. Navigate to the folder you want to save the file into and then click Export.

>> **Project to GarageBand for iOS:** Refer to Chapters 19 and 21 for information on sharing projects to and from iOS.

FIGURE 22-4: GarageBand's Save sheet lets you choose a file format and quality level for your exported file.

And those are your options for exporting a song from GarageBand on your Mac for others to enjoy.

Sharing your songs from an iDevice

Exporting a project from an iDevice works pretty much the same as on a Mac. However, the steps are slightly different, so this section gives you the scoop on sharing songs and projects from iDevices:

1. **Tap the my songs icon in the control bar, tap the Select button, and then tap the project you want to export.**

2. **Tap Share at the bottom of the screen, and then tap Song on the Share Song sheet to export the file as a song.**

    The other sharing options — Ringtone and Project — are discussed in Chapter 19.

3. **Tap the file format you prefer — Low, Medium, High, or Highest AAC, Apple Lossless, or Uncompressed AIFF or WAV.**

4. **(Optional) Edit the Artist, Composer, and Album fields if necessary.**

5. **(Optional) Choose a photo as the cover image for this song.**

    Note that this option is not available if you're exporting an AIFF or a WAV file.

6. **Tap Share.**

7. **Tap the option you prefer on the Share Sheet to share the file.**

    I typically use AirDrop to send the song to my Mac or other iDevices wirelessly, but feel free to use Messages, Mail, Dropbox, Google Drive, or whatever floats your boat (as long as it gets the song from your iDevice to where you want it).

And that's how you share a song from your iDevice.

If you're wondering how much compression is the right amount for your ears, check out the next section.

How Much Compression Can You Stand?

Some ears are more sensitive or discerning than others. So how much different do songs ripped (*compressed* or *encoded*) at different bit rates sound to you? Here's an easy way to find out:

The trick is to create a playlist in the Music app (or iTunes) with two or three songs in pristine, uncompressed AIF (or WAV) format, plus MP3 or AAC versions (or both) compressed at different bit rates.

With such a playlist on your Mac or iDevice, you can listen to the same passage with different amounts of compression applied and determine which one you prefer.

You'll need AIF or WAV files for the songs you want to test. If you don't happen to have them, you can copy them to your Mac from store-bought CDs. To get started, choose two or three songs you know well.

TIP

Choose songs with wide dynamic ranges — both loud and soft passages — which will help you evaluate the effects of compression.

When you have your songs selected, use the uncompressed AIF or WAV version as the master to export versions in the compressed formats you want to test, adding the file format and bit rate to the filename when you export, as shown in Figure 22-5.

Compression Testing Playlist

Compression Testing Playlist
9 SONGS · 19 MINUTES
▶ Play   ⤭ Shuffle

Three songs with wide dynamic ranges at three settings—uncompressed (AIFF), AAC 256, and AAC 64.

Day After Day AIFF	
Day After Day AAC 256	
Day After Day AAC 64	
I Want You (She's So Heavy) AIFF	
I Want You (She's So Heavy) AAC 256	
I Want You (She's So Heavy) AAC 64	
Stairway to Heaven AIFF	
Stairway to Heaven AAC 256	
Stairway to Heaven AAC 64	

9 of 9 songs, 19 minutes, 111.5 MB

FIGURE 22-5: My compression testing playlist with the file format and bit rate appended to each song.

You may want to make a playlist with more versions of each song. I like to try to hear the difference between three settings — Lowest (64), Highest (256), and Uncompressed, which are three of the most common bit rates.

I've performed this test many times and ultimately decided that AAC at 160 Kbps was good enough for me. I couldn't hear much (or any) difference between 160 Kbps and 192 Kbps. Even if there was a difference, it wasn't enough to justify the bigger (192 Kbps) files.

One last thing: Feel free to put additional songs or bit-rate variations on your playlist if you have enough space for them.

Distributing Your Music

You may want to send the song you made in GarageBand and compressed in iTunes to your friend via email, or you may want to post the compressed version on a web page. You know where that song is located in the Music app or iTunes library, right? But where is the actual file stored on your hard drive?

Finding the song file on your Mac

TIP

The easy way to find the file for any song in your Music or iTunes library is to select the song (click it) and then choose File ⇨ Show in Finder or press ⌘+R. Thinking of this command as "Reveal in Finder" helped me memorize the shortcut quickly.

Finder becomes active, the appropriate window opens, and the song file is selected. That's where it is on your hard drive.

Of course, you can also use Spotlight to find your song, but the Music app's Show in Finder command is faster, especially if the Music app is already open. (If it's not open, a Spotlight search may be faster.)

Sending AAC or MP3 files via Mail or Messages

There's nothing special about compressed audio files (AAC or MP3). Well, there's something special — they sound almost as good as files ten times their size — but there's nothing special about enclosing an MP3 or AAC file in an email message.

If you're sharing from your device, use the Share sheet to choose Mail or Messages (or AirDrop).

If you've exported the file previously, you can attach it to an email or iMessage the same way you'd attach any other type of file. An even faster way is to right- (or Control-) click the file, choose Share, and then choose Mail, Messages, or AirDrop.

REMEMBER

If you're sending the file to PC users, an MP3 file is more likely to work for them than an AAC file. See the "Understanding Compression" section, earlier in this chapter, for details about the different file types and the ways you can use them.

TIP

Some Windows users can play AAC files, especially ones who have iTunes for Windows, which is a free download. For those Windows users, feel free to send an AAC file, which provides better sound in a smaller package than MP3.

If you have any doubt, just send an MP3.

iTunes

» **Creating the final CD**

» **Distributing your CDs**

Chapter **23**

CD Recording, Reproduction, and Distribution

'm going to go out on a limb here and assume you'd like to share your marvel-ous music with other people. Although sending a file via email or iMessage is easy, sometimes it's more professional to send something physical, such as an audio CD.

When you burn a CD, you don't have to even think about file formats, compatibil-ity, or compression, because the songs on your audio CD are uncompressed by default. Plus, an audio CD is likely to work in almost any CD player — car, home, or pocket.

By the way, though it might be possible in theory to burn a CD from your iDevice, it's not a supported feature and isn't covered in this chapter. If you want to burn a song you created on an iDevice to a CD, share the file to your Mac and burn it there.

The Benefits of Burning CDs

If you haven't already burned CDs on your Mac, you really should become familiar with the process because it's useful for more than just GarageBand. But for the purposes of this chapter, I'm assuming that you want your friends to hear these great tunes you're making with GarageBand.

Of course, CDs aren't the only way to share your songs. You can put songs on the web or send a song file with the Mail or Messages app or AirDrop (see Chapter 22 for details). But because not everyone has a broadband Internet connection to download your music, and not everyone has a player compatible with every file format you might send electronically, handing out CDs to your friends and family can be a good thing indeed.

TIP

One of the things I like to do when I'm getting close to finishing a song is to take it for a ride in my car. In addition to the benefit of having no distractions — such as other people in the house, incoming instant messages and emails, or those bills I have to pay — listening to a song in the car has another benefit, too. We all grew up listening to music in the car, which is effectively a lifetime of training. Put that training to use in listening to *your* music, too. The advantage is that you're listening to an uncompressed version of the song, which in theory should sound better than any compressed version.

If you have an iDevice and can play it through your car stereo, listening to songs that way is even better and quicker than burning a disc. Save an uncompressed version if you prefer. Either way, listening to your newly created masterpiece in your car helps you determine if it needs additional mixing or mastering (or sweetening) before you unleash it on the world.

Relax. CD burning on your Mac is a piece of pie. (I don't like cake.)

Getting Ready to Burn Songs on CDs

Burning a CD of your GarageBand song is fairly straightforward, but it requires a few steps. First, you need to make sure that you have all the hardware. Then, you need to check the cycle area and export your song to the Music app (or iTunes).

Gathering what you need to burn CDs

To start, here's a list of what you need:

- ❯❯ Completed song
- ❯❯ Music app or iTunes
- ❯❯ Blank CD-R disc (the *R* stands for *recordable*)
- ❯❯ Compatible CD burner or Apple SuperDrive

WARNING

If you're making an audio CD, you must burn it to a CD-R disc. You can use any type of burner: CD-R, CD-RW, or SuperDrive, but the disc you burn must be a CD-R disc, and not a CD-RW (rewritable) or DVD-R or DVD-RW disc.

Put another way, if you burn anything other than a CD-R disc, it is unlikely to work properly in an audio CD player.

TIP

If your Mac doesn't have a burner or SuperDrive, you can buy Apple 's external USB SuperDrive for $79. It's what I'm using and a good value if you like to burn CDs or DVDs.

And that's all you need — a Mac with a CD burner, a blank CD-R disc, and the Music (or iTunes) app.

Setting the cycle area

Although you generally use the cycle area to loop a song during recording or rehearsal, it serves a different purpose during exporting. When you export, the *cycle area* defines the portion of the song to be exported. To export the entire song, stretch the cycle area to include all of the song's regions or disable the cycle area. Either way, the entire song will be exported.

So, before you go near the Share menu, make sure that the cycle area in your GarageBand project is turned off, covers the entire song, or covers the part of the song that you want to export and burn to disc.

If you've left the cycle area turned on and it's shorter than the full length of the song, only that short portion is exported, which may not be what you want (but sometimes it is, as I explain in this section).

When the cycle area is on, it appears in yellow, just below the tempo ruler at the top of the timeline, as shown in Figure 23-1. (Because you can't see the yellow in a grayscale figure, the yellow area is marked in the figure.)

Enable/disable cycle area   Cycle area

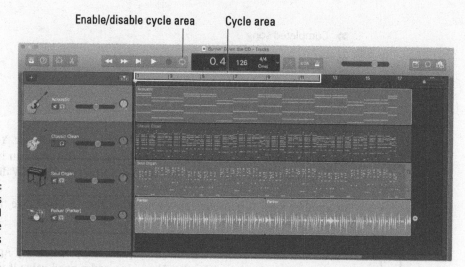

FIGURE 23-1:
The cycle area is
enabled and
covering the
first two-thirds
of this song.

TIP

Using the cycle area is a great way to control how much of your song is exported. Just set the cycle area for the portion of the song that you want, and then export normally. GarageBand exports only the portion of the song that's defined by the cycle area. The length of the song, number of tracks, and speed of your Mac's processor determine how long an export will take, so if you're in a hurry and just need part of a song, the cycle area can help you do the job faster.

Here's how to tweak the cycle area so that you get the song (or portion of the song) that you want:

>> **To toggle the cycle area on or off:** Click the circular arrow icon to the right of the record icon (and shown in the margin), or press C.

>> **To move the whole cycle area to the left or right:** Click in the middle of the cycle area and drag it left or right.

>> **To extend or shorten the cycle area:** Click the right or left edge of the cycle area, and then drag to extend or shorten it.

After you have the cycle area set up the way that you want, export the song as I describe in the next section.

Burning Songs to CDs

If you merely need to burn one song or part of one song to a CD-R disc, all you need is GarageBand, as I show you in the next section.

However, if you want to burn multiple songs to a disc (with control over the order in which the songs appear), you'll need to share the songs to the Music app (or iTunes) first, create a playlist, and then burn a disc from that playlist.

You explore burning a single song from GarageBand in the next section, then burning multiple songs in the section after next.

Burning a song to a CD with GarageBand

Burning a song or part of a song to a CD from GarageBand is as easy as pie. (Remember, I don't like cake.)

After setting up the cycle area (or not), as described earlier in the chapter, choose Share➪ Burn Song to CD. The Please Insert Blank Media dialog appears; insert your blank CD-R disc and click OK.

After a few minutes of clicking and whirring, your song will be magically transferred to the disc, which will work in most CD players.

TIP

It would behoove you to test the disc in your favorite CD player before bestowing it upon anyone. Although the technology is mature and usually works, sometimes it doesn't. It's better to find that out now than to have the producer you sent the disc to inform you it doesn't work.

You may think testing the disc on your Mac is good enough, but discs you burn will occasionally work on your Mac but not in third-party CD players. Conversely, discs you burn can sometimes work on third-party CD players but won't play on your Mac. For what it's worth, one of my test discs for this chapter worked in my car and my wife's car but not in my Mac. That's strange considering the disc was burned on the same SuperDrive that no longer recognizes the disc.

My point is that burning CDs on a Mac usually works properly but can fail occasionally.

TIP

One last thing: If two or more discs in a row fail, I suggest trying a different brand of blank CD-R. In my experience, when you buy a spindle of blank CD-R discs (25 or 50) and more than a couple of them fail, the rest of the discs are likely to have a high failure rate. Return them if you can, and try a different brand. I have no direct evidence, but my gut feeling is that the cheapest blank discs — usually a store brand or a brand you've never heard of — seem to fail more frequently than those from national brands. Even so, I've had spindles of CD-R discs with high failure rates from most (if not all) manufacturers over the years.

Burning songs to a CD with the Music app or iTunes

To burn a CD with more than a single song, you need to first share your song from GarageBand to the Music app (or iTunes).

Step-by-step instructions appear next, but in a nutshell you export the songs from GarageBand to the Music app (or iTunes) as uncompressed files, create a playlist and put your songs in the order you want them to appear on the disc, and then burn the playlist to a CD-R disc.

Now, without further ado, here's how to create a multi-song CD.

Part I: In GarageBand

Here's the procedure for creating multi-song CDs in GarageBand, followed by the procedure for doing the same in the Music app (or iTunes):

1. **If you want to export only part of a song from GarageBand, enable the cycle area and define the part as described earlier in the chapter, and then select the Export Cycle Area Only check box.**

2. **Choose Share ⇨ Song to Music (or iTunes).**

   The Share to Music dialog appears, as shown in Figure 23-2.

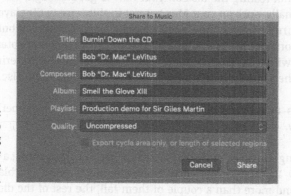

FIGURE 23-2:
The Share to Music dialog ready to share my song to the Music app.

> Title: Burnin' Down the CD
> Artist: Bob "Dr. Mac" LeVitus
> Composer: Bob "Dr. Mac" LeVitus
> Album: Smell the Glove XIII
> Playlist: Production demo for Sir Giles Martin
> Quality: Uncompressed
>
> Export cycle area only, or length of selected regions
>
> Cancel   Share

3. **(Optional) Edit the title, artist, composer, and album and specify a playlist for the burned song.**

4. **In the Quality drop-down menu, select Uncompressed.**

5. **Click Share.**

   GarageBand creates a stereo mix of the song, generates an AIFF file from that mix, exports that AIFF file to the Music app (or iTunes), and then opens the Music app (or iTunes) — all without you lifting a finger (after choosing Share ⇨ Song to Music, of course).

And that's the end of the GarageBand part.

Part II: In the Music app (or iTunes)

If the Music app (or iTunes) didn't open automatically when you shared the song (which it's supposed to but occasionally doesn't), open the Music app (or iTunes) now.

In the Music app (or iTunes), here are the steps to burn multiple songs to a CD-R disc:

1. **Find the playlist you specified in the Share to Music dialog. If you didn't specify a playlist, create a playlist (File ⇨ New Playlist or ⌘+N).**

2. **(Optional) Right-click the playlist and choose Open in New Window.**

   You don't have to perform this step, but it makes it easier to work with the playlist, especially if you have songs in your library you want to include on this playlist.

3. **If you specified the playlist in the Share to Music dialog, all the songs you want to burn will be in it already. If you didn't specify a playlist or all the songs don't appear, locate the other songs in your library and drag them to the playlist, as shown in Figure 23-3.**

4. **Drag the songs up or down in the list to put them in the order you want them to play on the CD.**

5. **Choose File ⇨ Burn Playlist to Disc.**

   The Burn Settings dialog appears, as shown in Figure 23-4.

6. **In the Preferred Speed pop-up menu, choose Maximum Possible.**

7. **In the Gap Between Songs pop-up menu, choose how much silence you want between songs.**

   I like a two-second gap but you can choose zero to five seconds here.

TIP

8. **Insert a blank CD-R disc and then click Burn.**

   iTunes will try to burn the entire playlist. If the content of your playlist exceeds 700MB or 80 minutes of playtime, the Music app (or iTunes) will burn as many of the playlist's songs as can fit on the disc.

Drag from here...

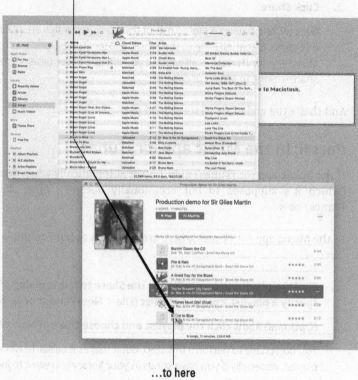

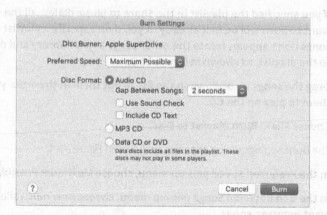

FIGURE 23-3:
Drag songs
from your library
to the playlist
if necessary.

...to here

FIGURE 23-4:
Configure the
burn settings and
then click Burn.

TIP

The number of tracks, total playing time of the tracks, and total size of the tracks appear at the bottom of the playlist window. As you can at the bottom of the playlist window (Production Demo for Sir Giles Martin) in Figure 23-3, those numbers are 6 songs, 11 minutes, and 224.6 MB.

That's it. After you click that Burn button, you can stick a fork in your CD — it's as good as done.

Wasn't that easy?

Making multiple copies of the same CD

At some point, you will want to make multiple copies of the same CD. You can do it two ways. Each method has advantages and disadvantages, depending on your needs.

Burn 'em yourself with a CD duplicator

iTunes allows you to burn the playlist onto as many CDs as you like. Repeat the preceding instructions as many times as necessary.

Obviously, this method works best if you only need a few copies. A diligent person could burn a gross of CDs one at a time (a gross is 12 dozen — 144 discs). If you need larger quantities, consider buying a CD duplicator that connects to your Mac or buying a stand-alone CD duplicator that can burn discs in batches of 25, 100, or more.

These devices automatically produce multiple CDs, one after another. Some print and affix a label to the CD at the same time; others print the label directly onto the CD. Some need to be connected to a Mac to be used; others are stand-alone devices that don't require a computer.

CD-duplicating equipment used to cost tens or even hundreds of thousands of dollars. Today, CD duplicators can be found for less than $150, an amazing reduction in the barrier to entry for do-it-yourself CD production.

Using one of these devices is far beyond the scope of this book; suffice it to say that many brands and models of CD duplicators are on the market.

I haven't tested any duplicators, so do your research before you buy. Many reviews are available on the Internet, so the information shouldn't be too hard to find.

Have someone else do it for you

Consider one other option: If you need a lot of CDs — 100 or more — consider having the work done by a company that specializes in duplicating media. This option will cost more than burning them yourself, but it has the following big benefits:

>> **The CD will be a real pressed CD as opposed to a burned CD-R.** People in the know will be more impressed with the former than the latter. Having a

pressed CD can add enormous perceived value to your CD. Think about it: When was the last time you cared about a burned CD, even if it came with a label? CD-R discs have become so common that people tend to treat them with disdain. A pressed CD, on the other hand, is something you buy from a store, and people will treat it accordingly.

>> **If you send your CDs out to be pressed, you save a ton of time compared to burning them yourself.** The question is, how much is your time worth?

As with CD-duplicating equipment, the details of CD manufacturers fall beyond the purview of this book.

Lovely labels for your CDs

TIP

If you're trying to make a good impression, make a label for your CD. A variety of label-making kits, including some that work with your printer, and dedicated label makers are available.

For a quick and easy label with a list of tracks, select your playlist in the Music app (or iTunes) and choose File ⇨ Print (or press ⌘+P) and select CD Jewel Case Insert.

Your playlist will be printed as a jewel case insert like the one shown in Figure 23-5.

Production demo for Sir Giles Martin

1. Burnin' Down the CD / Bob "Dr. Mac" LeVitus   0:34
2. Fire & Rain / Dr. Mac & His All Garageband B...   3:03
3. A Good Day for the Blues / Dr. Mac & His All...   0:56
4. You're Breakin' My Heart / Dr. Mac & His All...   0:44
5. *iTunes Must Die! (final) / Dr. Mac & His All... 2:39
6. Brown to Blue / Dr. Mac & His All Garageban...   2:12

Smell the Glove XIII

DoctorMac
And His All-Garage Band

Printed with iTunes

FIGURE 23-5:
You can print a jewel case insert like this from the Music app (or iTunes).

If you plan to make a lot of copies, you may prefer to buy one of the dedicated CD duplicators mentioned earlier in this chapter. These units can burn and label 25, 50, or more copies of a CD without human intervention.

REMEMBER

If you have someone duplicate your discs, chances are the price you pay per disc includes labeling and jewel cases.

Distributing Your Music

As Steve Jobs is famous for saying, "There is one last thing," and that one thing is distribution for your CD.

Now if all you care to do is to send one CD to Aunt Edna, distribution isn't an issue. But if you want the whole world to hear your music, you're going to want some type of distribution for your music.

Two popular companies that provide distribution services are CD Baby and TuneCore. Read on to take a quick look at both.

CD Baby and TuneCore

CD Baby (https://cdbaby.com) and TuneCore (www.tunecore.com) are a couple of popular independent music distributors. You can have CDs manufactured and shipped for you; you can sell your music online through the Apple, Amazon, and Google stores; you can offer your music to streaming services; you can have your song pressed on vinyl; and much more. Check out both for myriad ways to get your song out to more people.

More distribution ideas

I want to mention one last thing about distribution: You may want to look around your hometown for local record shops that can sell your CD. If you can find one, it'll probably offer you a consignment deal. So if the record shop doesn't sell any copies of your CD, you won't make any money.

Most of the record stores that make such deals are independently owned and operated — not the big names like Best Buy or Fry's. But don't let that stop you from pitching your CD to any local store. One never knows, do one? (Apologies to Archie McNally for stealing his phrase.)

Be careful if you do get your CD in a local record store. You may experience a rapid rise in heartbeat the first time you see your CD between The Beastie Boys and The Beatles or between Emerson, Lake, and Palmer and Eminem.

7

The Part of Tens

IN THIS PART . . .

Tackle troubleshooting performance issues, otherwise known as "ten things to do if GarageBand screeches to a halt."

Get ten superb suggestions for taking your recordings to the next level.

Discover ten terrific online resources for budding music producers.

» Checking out FileVault

» Paying attention to CPU activity

» Checking memory usage

» Recording at 16-bits versus 24-bits

» Minimizing the GarageBand window

» Getting more RAM

» Obtaining faster storage

» Resetting MIDI drivers

» Turning off Wi-Fi

Chapter **24**

Ten Ways to Improve GarageBand's Performance

I must say that GarageBand is relatively stable. For an application that does so much computing, it rarely crashes or freezes on any platform. Still, it is an app, which means it may occasionally cause you trouble. And most of that trouble involves performance, which is why this chapter offers ten ways to shoot that trouble right between its beady little eyes and get your GarageBand rocking again.

TIP

I don't have much advice for iDevice users — I've had no performance issues using GarageBand on any of my relatively new iDevices (an iPhone X and iPad Pro 9.7-inch). In general, the older your Mac or iDevice (which is to say, the slower its processor), the more likely you'll encounter performance issues. That said, no device is truly immune. If you add enough tracks to your project and add enough effects to your tracks, you'll bring your Mac (or iDevice) to its knees.

If you 've never (or almost never) seen the ugly warning dialog box in Figure 24-1, you're either lucky or fortunate to use a Mac booting from an SSD (and not an old-school hard disk) and with a fast multicore processor and 8GB of RAM (or preferably more).

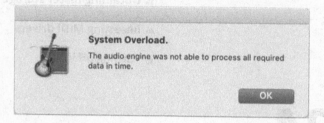

FIGURE 24-1:
No! I hate when it
says that!

In the next few pages, I show you tips, techniques, and work-arounds to help you keep making music based on my nearly 20 years of infatuation with digital recording.

Starting with the Basics

Because this is a Part of Tens chapter and I only get ten shots, I'm going to cheat a little and start with a quick set of things to try *before* you try anything else in this chapter:

1. **Close every open application except GarageBand.**

TIP

If you have other applications open while you're using GarageBand, they're using up RAM and processing power that can be put to better use. It's a good idea to close all other programs to give GarageBand more RAM and processor time to work with.

2. **Check all your cable connections.**

3. Save your file, quit GarageBand, and then reopen it.

4. Delete the GarageBand preference file (com.apple.garageband.plist) from your Home/Library/Preferences folder.

5. Log out of your macOS user account and then log back in.

6. Restart your Mac.

WARNING

If you've deleted your GarageBand preferences, every setting you modified in GarageBand Preferences has been reset to the defaults — as they were the first time you ever used GarageBand. Open GarageBand Preferences (choose Garage-Band ➪ Preferences or press ⌘+?) to reset the preferences to the way they were.

Checking on FileVault

Another possible performance-robber is macOS FileVault, which can cause excessive reading and writing to your hard drive. If your startup disk is an SSD, File-Vault probably isn't a problem for you. But for those who boot from a hard disk (and not a solid-state drive), FileVault may be the cause of performance hiccups and slowdowns.

To turn off FileVault (or determine if it's enabled), follow these steps:

1. Launch the System Preferences application.

2. Click the Security & Privacy icon.

3. Click the FileVault tab.

4. Do one of the following:

   • If the text reads, "FileVault is turned on for the disk" followed by your disk's name, and the button to the right of the text says Turn Off FileVault, click the Lock icon in the lower left and provide your user account password, and then click the button to turn off FileVault.

   • If the text reads, "FileVault is turned off for the disk" followed by your disk's name, and the button to the right of the text says Turn On FileVault, you're golden.

5. Quit System Preferences and continue your recording session.

TIP

If you can't live without FileVault (and you're certain FileVault is responsible for your issue), store your project files on an external disk: hard or solid-state (though an SSD will deliver better performance when recording).

Okay, now let's get serious. The following sections give you some other things to try when GarageBand goes sour.

Paying Attention to CPU and RAM Usage

Keep an eye on your Mac's CPU load and memory usage if GarageBand is throwing up error messages or complaining it can't do something. Chances are your processor is being swamped by requests from GarageBand, or GarageBand (or something else) is chewing up all memory (RAM).

Adding tracks and effects increases the load on your Mac's processor, and some complex effects, such as the Amp models, use more processor time than others. So I recommend turning off effects or muting some of your tracks if you need to reduce the strain on your processor.

WARNING

If you don't fix a heavy processor load or an out-of-memory condition before it happens, a dialog box or an audio dropout will likely wreck the take. So try the techniques that follow if GarageBand is acting wonky and your processor load or memory is in the danger zone.

What's that you say? How do you determine that your Mac's processor (CPU) load or memory (RAM) is in the danger zone?

Glad you asked. Apple provides a handy tool for just such determinations. It's called Activity Monitor and it's in your Utilities folder (which is inside your Applications folder).

If I have a project with a lot of software instruments, amp models, or effects laid onto tracks and GarageBand bogs down, the first thing I do is launch Activity Monitor and arrange its windows on my screen so I can see it alongside my project, as shown in Figure 24-2.

FIGURE 24-2:
GarageBand is
consuming
roughly 44
percent of my
CPU's cycles.

Checking Out Activity Monitor's CPU and Memory Tabs

With your project playing in GarageBand, take a look at Activity Monitor's main window and its CPU tab (bottom left in Figure 24-2) and Memory tab (Figure 24-3).

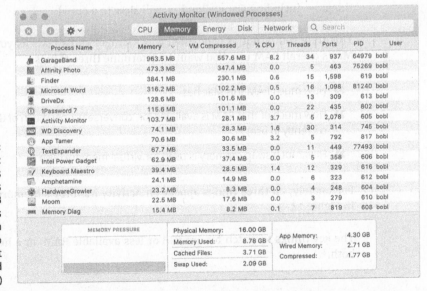

FIGURE 24-3:
Do the math:
16.00GB minus
8.78GB equals
7.22GB. (7.22GB
available RAM is
more than
enough to
complete most
GarageBand
projects.)

The first thing you're interested in is the % CPU column. If GarageBand is using more than 70 to 80 percent of your CPU cycles and GarageBand is stuttering or throwing up error messages, try muting some tracks and turning off effects.

TIP

This is probably the quickest, easiest fix for performance problems: If you don't need the track or effect for whatever you're doing right now, mute tracks or disable effects or both.

The same issues can arise if another app is consuming a large percentage of CPU cycles, which can leave too few cycles for GarageBand. In that case, quit the other program (or programs).

TIP

Activity Monitor displays All Processes by default. So you'll see items such as kernel_task or launchserviced in Figure 24-2, which are part of the system software and can't be quit. I like to see them, so if anything — including system software — is chewing up a ton of my CPU, I will see which app or process is responsible. If you don't care about such minutiae, choose View⇨Windowed Processes and you'll see only applications that are currently open and can be quit in the usual fashion.

To display the CPU History window (top left) and CPU Usage window (middle left) above the main Activity Monitor window in Figure 24-2, choose Window⇨CPU History (or press ⌘ + 3) and Window⇨CPU Usage (or press ⌘ + 2). Note that my window has eight bars because my CPU has eight cores. Your mileage may vary.

The other thing of interest is the Memory tab at the top of the main Activity Monitor window. The thing you're most interested in is how much of your total RAM (memory) is free. The closer the available RAM gets to 0, the more things — including GarageBand — will slow to a crawl.

This time you're not as concerned with GarageBand's stats as you are with your Mac's overall RAM use. You want to determine three things:

>> How much RAM this Mac has

>> How much of that RAM is available (or, conversely, how much of that RAM is currently in use)

>> How much swap memory is used for virtual memory (VM)

Fortunately, all three things appear on Activity Monitor's Memory tab, as shown in Figure 24-3.

The key things to watch for are 1GB or less available RAM, or a huge swap file or both.

The first — less than a gigabyte of free RAM — is easy. Just do the math: Physical memory minus memory used equals available memory.

The second — a huge swap file — is a little mushier. The Swap Used amount is how much of your SSD (or hard disk) is being used (swapped) for RAM (known as virtual memory) because not enough physical RAM is available.

If your RAM isn't all being used, the swap file will vary from 0 to a few gigabytes; the more RAM you have installed, the bigger your normal swap file. Take a look at the Memory tab occasionally and note what Swap Used looks like when things are going well on your Mac. Then, if you notice the swap file swelling beyond what is normal on your Mac, quit one or more apps to free up memory.

When do you need to worry? After you know what normal looks like on your Mac, any time you see your swap file grow by 3 times or more, your Mac is likely to run sluggishly. On my MacBook Pro, with 16GB of RAM and a normal swap size of around 2GB, I start getting concerned if I see my Swap Used grow beyond 8GB.

Note that the Swap Used is dynamic. If you free up some memory by quitting one or more apps, the swap size should go down (although not instantly).

Finally, restarting your Mac often cleans up memory-related issues and speeds things back up without doing anything else.

Alas, at certain times, most notably mixing or mastering, muting tracks, disabling effects, or reducing RAM usage isn't possible. Keep reading for more tricks to try if things bog down.

Recording: 16-bits versus 24-bits

One thing that can affect performance is the resolution you're using for recording. GarageBand records at 16 bits by default, but as I mention in Chapter 4, you have the option of recording at 24 bits.

The good news is that 24-bit recordings are higher quality because you're capturing roughly 33 percent more data than a 16-bit recording. The bad news is that GarageBand is working with 33 percent more data, which uses more CPU cycles and memory.

So if you're having performance issues, check the resolution at which you're recording by choosing GarageBand➪ Preferences (or pressing its shortcut, ⌘+comma) and then clicking the Advanced icon.

If the 24-bit Audio Recording Resolution check box is selected, deselect it and then close the Preferences window.

With the recording resolution reduced to 16 bits, GarageBand will be more responsive and less prone to errors.

Minimizing the GarageBand Window While Playing or Recording

Minimizing the GarageBand window — by choosing Window ⇨ Minimize, pressing ⌘+M, or clicking the yellow gumdrop in the upper-left corner of the GarageBand window — provides some respite for your processor.

When you minimize the window, GarageBand doesn't have to draw to the screen, reducing the demand on the processor. It is, alas, somewhat less convenient than some of the other remedies.

Why is it less convenient? First, you have to remember to begin your recording (or playback) and then minimize the window. Then, before you can stop recording (or do anything else), you have to maximize the window again by clicking its icon in the dock.

TIP

The Count In feature (Record ⇨ Count In) gives you four beats before recording begins, which should be plenty of time to minimize the window.

The bottom line is that this solution might provide some relief if your Mac is bogging down, and it's easy. And you don't need to see the window while you record as long as you've adjusted the track level properly before you started recording.

If you're still having trouble building the kind of songs that you want to build because your processor or hard drive is too slow or you keep getting error messages, check out the following sections to find some more things that can help.

Getting More RAM

Most Macs today ship with 8GB of RAM, which is enough to run GarageBand acceptably but may not be enough to record the kinds of songs you want to record. Even if your Mac has 8GB of RAM, GarageBand will almost certainly perform better after you add more.

Some Macs have their Mac soldered in so it can't be replaced or upgraded. Other Macs make it easy to install additional RAM — anyone can do it in 15 minutes or less. For under $100, you can buy a 16GB upgrade kit for many Mac models. (RAM prices are volatile. That was the price as of spring 2020. By the time you read this, prices might be noticeably higher or lower. I'm just sayin'.)

If you bump up your RAM to 16 gigabytes or more, GarageBand will run even better — and allow you to have more tracks, instruments, effects, and notes in your songs before those dreaded warning dialog boxes start to appear.

Getting Faster Storage

Your internal disk drive may not be fast enough for GarageBand, especially if it's an old-school rotational hard drive or even a hybrid drive. When it comes to recording music, nothing comes close to using a solid-state drive.

TIP

Most USB 3 external hard drives (and all external SSDs) run at higher speeds than internal hard drives or hybrid drives from Apple. If you have a USB 3 external hard drive, it's faster than the internal disk or hybrid drive in your Mac. If your Mac has a hard or hybrid drive inside it, and you have a faster external drive available, it would behoove you to save your projects on the faster external drive instead of your slower boot disk.

For years, pro audio programs recommended saving your projects on any hard drive *except* the boot disk (that is, the disk with macOS and GarageBand on it). If you save your projects on the fastest drive you have, you are likely to see fewer error messages.

If you're considering an external drive, look for hard drives that run at 7,200 rpm or higher rather than the cheaper — and easier to find — 5,400-rpm drives. Most drive vendors display the speed of a drive in the product description; if you don't see it, ask about it.

If your Mac has Thunderbolt, as many do today, a Thunderbolt disk drive running at 7,200 rpm moves data faster than a USB 3 drive at 7,200. But Thunderbolt drives are less common and cost significantly more than USB 3 drives. Still, Thunderbolt may be worthwhile if you record multiple tracks at once or create complex projects with dozens and dozens of tracks and effects.

Finally, if your boot disk is a hard or hybrid disk, you may be able to replace it with an SSD. This option will be more expensive than buying an external SSD but may be more convenient if you have a laptop.

Resetting MIDI Drivers

I saved this tip for last because it's only likely to cure a single symptom — a MIDI device that doesn't become available in GarageBand when you connect it to your Mac. If this happens (and it does every so often), open GarageBand Preferences (GarageBand⇨ Preferences), click the Audio/MIDI tab, and then click the Reset MIDI Drivers button.

If that didn't fix it, make sure the cable you're using is good. If it is and the problem persists, try restarting your Mac.

Turn Off Wi-Fi Before Recording or Performing

If you're still having performance issues after trying other suggestions in this chapter, you can try one more thing: Turn off Wi-Fi. Doing so will reduce the load on your processor and free up a bit of memory, which should improve Garage-Band's performance.

And, although I've mentioned it before, I'll say it again here: Don't forget to quit all other applications before you begin recording or performing with GarageBand.

Chapter 25

Ten Ways to Take Your Recordings to the Next Level

Okay, now that you understand how to work with GarageBand, here are some ways that you can make your songs even better. Alas, most of the suggestions in this chapter cost money, but each one will contribute to making your GarageBand compositions sound even better than before.

Getting a Better Microphone

If you record acoustic instruments or vocals, an easy way to make your recordings sound better is to use a better microphone. You can find details about getting a microphone to suit your needs in Chapter 2. Audio magazines and websites are also good sources of more detailed information about mics; these sources review recording equipment all the time, and they may be your best bet for learning more about specific mics and models.

That said, here are a few general tips about microphones:

>> You don't have to spend a lot of money to get a decent mic. Don't spend more than $200 on a mic unless you're extremely serious about recording. Many excellent microphones are available for $200 or less.

>> AKG, Audio-Technica, Blue, Rode, Sennheiser, and Shure have been in the microphone business for as long as I've been recording. And all of them have products at a wide variety of prices.

>> Wind screens and pop filters can make a big difference in your vocals. If you don't own one of these screens (described in Chapter 2), consider buying one or both of them.

>> Good recordings require proper microphone placement, which is hard to do without good mic stands. Boom-style stands are more flexible than the pole-type units, but the boom types are inherently less stable — particularly cheap ones. If you use boom mic stands, be careful not to knock them over to avoid damage to the microphone, stand, or both.

Making Sure Your Speakers Reproduce Sound Decently

Nothing compares to hearing music that's reproduced accurately. Unfortunately, the speakers built into computers are mostly junk — they don't even come close to producing sound accurately.

Most multimedia computer speakers — especially ones with subwoofers — will work in a pinch, but if you're serious about hearing every little nuance, you should buy a set of good desktop speakers. Such speaker systems, called *reference monitors*, can cost anywhere from a few hundred dollars a set to thousands of dollars per speaker.

I have two pairs of speakers on my desk with an A/B switch, so when I'm mixing or mastering, I can listen on consumer speakers or reference monitors with a flick of the A/B switch.

The consumer speakers are the Audioengine A2+ (www.audioengine.com) speakers I mention in Chapter 2. For around $250 a pair, they sound great. They're crisp and crystal clear with a surprisingly tight and punchy bottom end for such small speakers. I recommended them highly.

Better still, spend a bit more for some reference monitors such as the (now discontinued) Tapco's S-5 Active Studio Monitors I mention in Chapter 2.

One last thing: If you're going to get only one pair of speakers, think long and hard about whether you'd be happier with speakers that sound great or that reproduce sound accurately. Reference monitors generally reproduce music more accurately than regular speakers, but that doesn't mean they sound better for everyday listening. I prefer the smaller Audioengine A2+ speakers for almost everything I do at my Mac *except* mixing and mastering. On the other hand, switching between two sets of speakers — even if neither pair are reference monitors — almost always highlights a flaw I might not have noticed with one set of speakers.

As always, your mileage may vary. And as I mention in Chapter 11, you need to listen to your almost-finished songs on as many different devices and through as many types of speakers as possible. I consider this step one of the most important in creating great-sounding songs. After you're happy with what you're hearing at your desk, export (share) the song and listen to it in your car, on your home stereo, on a boom box, in the shower, on Bluetooth speakers, on an iDevice — with and without earphones — and on every other device you can find.

TIP

I always carry a notebook to write down anything that sounds funky as well as the audio system I was listening to. After listening to a semi-finished track on five or six different sound systems, I go back to GarageBand and try to fix the funkiness. Then I export a new version and listen on five or six different devices again. If I still hear flaws, I repeat the process until all the funkiness has been removed and I don't have notes from any of the sound systems. When that happens, the last version I exported becomes the golden master and is the version I share with the world.

Getting Better Headphones

As I mention in Chapter 2, you should use sealed headphones — ones that leak as little sound as possible — when you record. If you're using cheap headphones with porous foam ear cups when you sing, some of the music you're hearing in the headphones is likely to bleed onto your track.

Good sealed headphones not only prevent such noises from leaking onto your track but also reproduce sound more accurately than cheaper models.

Don't underestimate the importance of a good set of cans. You'll almost certainly improve your vocal and acoustic instrument tracks when you can hear the other instruments and voices clearly. And you'll have fewer takes spoiled by sound leaking from your cans.

Fine-Tuning Mic Placement

The location of your microphone makes all the difference when you're recording. I've heard many recording engineers tell me that setting up mics correctly can take longer than the actual recording.

Don't be afraid to experiment. If that acoustic guitar isn't sounding quite right, move the mic to the left or the right, or point it up or down a bit, or move it farther from the sound hole.

Each small move changes the sound that ends up on your track. If you take the time to discover the mic placement that sounds best to you, the resulting tracks will sound that much better.

Improving Room Acoustics

Also consider the room you're recording in. Hard surfaces and parallel walls in your studio can resonate, reflect, and reverberate sounds; these issues are undesirable when you're recording. The more hard surfaces (and parallel walls) in the room, the more reflected yuck you hear on the track.

If you're not getting the sound you want from a mic, try throwing some blankets or pillows over hard surfaces, or moving the mic to a different part of the room (or a different room) with fewer reflective surfaces.

TIP

I've been known to make a tent out of old quilts and record hand-held percussion instruments by holding the instrument (usually a tambourine or maracas) and the mic under the quilt tent. It may not be pretty, but it's cheap and it works.

Using Quality Cables

Most computer peripherals and audio devices include a cable or two. Isn't that nice? The problem is, many manufacturers throw in the cheapest, crummiest cable they can buy. As a result, the quality may be lacking, and the cable may become nonfunctional sooner than you expect.

I'm not suggesting that you replace your existing cables with high-end cables, but if you're buying cables, it's best to avoid the cheapest ones. They won't last as long, and because they use the cheapest available components, they may introduce unwanted noise and interference.

I get most of my cables at Amazon.com and Monoprice.com, reading the reviews and ratings before I click Buy. For what it's worth, I like Monoprice a lot. It specializes in cables, and engineers and manufactures most of its offerings. Monoprice often has cables in more lengths, colors, thicknesses, and qualities than Amazon. Monoprice is often a little more expensive than Amazon, but I know I'm getting the exact cable I need, and it's likely to last longer than a cheapie on Amazon.

Adding an Audio Interface (and, Optionally, a Mixing Board)

Sometimes you'll need to record more than one track at a time. For example, a standard drum set needs as many as seven microphones to be recorded well. This requirement is a no-brainer for big-time audio recordings. Simply set up the microphones and then record each one on a different track. But unless you have an audio interface with at least seven microphone inputs, you're out of luck.

Another example: You're recording a large vocal group, and the group is too large to all sing into a single microphone.

In these cases, the answer is a multi-input audio interface or a small mixing board (which includes an audio interface). Like an audio interface, mixing boards have inputs and outputs so you can connect as many mics as the board has inputs. Then you can adjust their level, equalization, tone, pan, effects, and so on from a physical device with knobs and faders, all before it's passed to GarageBand and recorded on its own track.

You know the big sound board you see in the middle of the floor at a rock concert? That's a big, expensive mixing board that obtains input from all the microphones on stage and then sends the output to the giant speakers facing the audience.

TIP

Guitar Center and Sweetwater sell a wide variety of mixing boards compatible with GarageBand. Search for *USB mixer for GarageBand* and you'll find mixers ranging from 4-channel mixers under $100 to 24-channel mixers that cost thousands.

I don't have any room for a mixing board, so I bought a Korg nanoKONTROL2 ($75), as shown in Figure 25-1.

FIGURE 25-1: It is cheaply made but does what it's supposed to and takes up little space.

With nanoKontrol2, I can tap a physical button to start or stop recording, slide a physical fader to raise or lower levels, or press physical buttons to solo, mute, or record.

Switch to More Powerful Software

If the preceding section sounded good to you — and you're interested in recording multiple instruments or vocals on multiple tracks, all at the same time — you might be happier with more powerful software than GarageBand.

Pro audio-recording applications include GarageBand's sibling from Apple, Logic Pro ($299), and DigiDesign Pro Tools.

The software expense will be the least of your worries if you decide to assemble a semipro or pro-quality home studio. For starters, you'll need a multichannel audio interface or mixing board. Then you'll want at least one microphone for each channel on your interface or board. You'll also need a very fast Mac with very fast drives used only for recording.

But I digress.

Logic Pro

In addition to GarageBand, Apple makes an excellent professional-quality music creation program called Logic Pro. When I got it, it cost $999, but it is now available for a much more reasonable $199.

Logic Pro has two big advantages over other professional audio editors. One, it will open GarageBand files. Sadly, it's one-way, and you can't (easily) open a Logic Pro file in GarageBand. The second advantage is that unlike most other DAW (digital audio workstations) such as Pro Tools, Logic Pro includes free upgrades for life.

The interfaces are quite similar, as shown in Figure 25-2. And most of Garage-Band's features work the same way in Logic Pro. Because you already know how to use GarageBand, it won't be long before you're comfortable with Logic Pro.

There are many reasons why you might want (or need) to use Logic Pro to finish a project you started in GarageBand, such as the following:

>> **Your project has more tracks than GarageBand can handle.** Instead of using the tricks in the preceding chapter to eke out the last drop of performance from GarageBand, you could just open the project in Logic Pro, which is more efficient and uses less of the processor and memory than GarageBand. Because Logic Pro is designed for pros, it supports projects with track and effects counts that would bring GarageBand to its knees.

>> **You want to use a Logic Pro instrument or effect not included in GarageBand.** Logic Pro has more of almost everything GarageBand has, including more instruments (1,000+), more instrument and effect patches (2,800+), more drummers (28), as well as more guitar and bass amps, stomp boxes, custom pedalboards, and more.

>> **You want to create a project in the 5.1 or 7.1 surround sound format.** GarageBand does not support either surround sound format.

The truth is that either program will produce radio-quality music. Still, unless you absolutely know you need a feature that's exclusive to Logic Pro, I recommend you stick to GarageBand, since it's less complicated and you know how to use it.

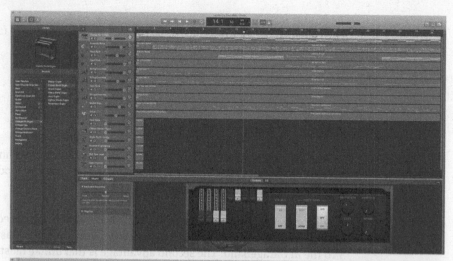

FIGURE 25-2:
If you don't look closely it's hard to tell GarageBand (top) and Logic Pro (bottom) apart.

Pro Tools

Pro Tools from Avid is worthy of consideration, primarily because there are so many different versions of it at a bewildering array of price points, as shown in Figure 25-3.

The good news is that all versions are compatible with each other and you can work on the same file with any version.

FIGURE 25-3:
With prices from $299 ($99 for students) to $2,599, there's a version of Pro Tools to fit every budget.

Pro Tools is the most common software you'll find in commercial recording studios. That point is worth considering if you intend to record in a studio. With Pro Tools, you can take the project file you recorded with a $100,000+ Pro Tools hardware/software system and later work on that file with the $299 version of Pro Tools on your MacBook Pro.

One last thing: Pro Tools is more difficult to learn and master than either Garage-Band or Logic Pro. If you decide Pro Tools is the right tool for you, block out a big chunk of time before your first session to become familiar with the software.

Chapter **26**

Ten Useful Websites

I f you're producing songs, you can find a handful of extremely useful sites on the web for obtaining anything from cables to microphones and MIDI files to song lyrics. In no particular order, here are the URLs and brief descriptions of some websites that you may find useful.

Learn Songs on Guitar or Bass

You can learn a song in many ways, but my favorite method is to download a chord chart or tablature for the song and then try to play it.

Search for free chord charts or tablature

Using your favorite search engine, enter the name of the song you want to sing or play, appending *free guitar chords* or *free guitar tablature.* For example, when I searched for *Wasted Time free guitar chords* and *Wasted Time free guitar tablature,* I found hundreds of files with the song's chords and tablature.

A *chord chart* displays the chords above the lyrics, so you can strum the song immediately (as long as you know how to play its chords).

Tablature, or *tab*, is a special form of musical notation used for guitar parts. Designed to be typed on a computer, it's usually displayed in a monospaced font such as Courier so everything lines up properly.

Figure 26-1 is a guitar riff in tablature notation played on the second and third strings from the top (for a right-handed guitarist). You read the tablature from left to right. The numbers tell you what fret to play, and the line that the number is on tells you which string to play it on.

```
                 Riff
High  E    [------------------------------[
      B    [------------------------------[
      G    [------------------------------[
      D    [--------3-2--------\7-6-5------[
      A    [---5-5--------3-5----------3---[
Low   E    [------------------------------[
```

FIGURE 26-1:
The tablature for
a guitar riff.

Sometimes tablature includes chords (Figure 26-1 does not), and some chord charts include tablature. The bottom line is that if you want to learn a new song, you'll learn it faster from a chord chart or tablature than by ear.

My advice is to try both.

Ultimate-Guitar

The Ultimate-Guitar website (www.ultimate-guitar.com) is, for lack of a better term, a community resource for guitarists and bassists. You can find guitar tablature and chords for over a million popular songs; search by artist or song title.

In addition to being a great place to find chords or tabs for songs, Ultimate Guitar offers a native app on most devices (Mac, Windows, iDevices, and Android). And for a few bucks a month, you can get a Pro subscription with higher-quality tablature, lessons, and more.

GarageBand Karaoke (free MIDI files)

To listen to a MIDI file, first use your favorite search engine to find the song you want to sing or play, appending *free MIDI* to its name. You can then listen to the downloaded MIDI file with QuickTime Player or open it with GarageBand, which is more fun. When you use GarageBand, the MIDI file becomes a GarageBand project you can play (or sing) along with immediately or modify to your heart's content.

For example, I felt like singing "Wasted Time," but there's no way I could learn to play all the parts. I searched for *Wasted Time free MIDI* and downloaded several versions (not every MIDI file sounds the way you want it to sound). I previewed them using QuickTime Player and opened the best one with GarageBand. The result is shown in Figure 26-2.

FIGURE 26-2:
The Wasted Time
MIDI file opened
in GarageBand.

Note that tracks sometimes get assigned to the wrong instrument. If something sounds funky, try changing the instrument. The regions on the track often contain clues. For example, the Bassoon Solo region is labeled Lead Vocal. That told me that the bassoon will play the melody of the lead vocal. Because I wanted to sing it (and know the tune by heart), I muted the bassoon track.

The guitar track below the bassoon didn't sound right with the instrument assigned to it, so I changed it from Rock Guitar to Acoustic Guitar and it sounded almost perfect. I added a vocal track and had a ball singing (and wishing I sang like Don Henley).

I could never have recorded all those tracks from scratch. By starting with a free MIDI file, I was singing a few minutes after I had the urge.

If you're trying to learn a favorite song and can find a decent a MIDI rendition of it, this trick, which I call GarageBand Karaoke, is the fastest way to get from a blank screen to playing or singing along.

Mix Magazine

Mixonline (www.mixonline.com) is the online home of *Mix* magazine, the magazine of "Professional Audio and Music Production." The site is chock-full of useful information, including reviews of products for your studio and tutorials on many aspects of recording. You will find little (or no) GarageBand-specific information here, but the products and tutorials apply to GarageBand users as well as pros.

Some articles may be too technical for some readers, but if you're interested in knowing more about how the pros do it and the tools that they use, Mix can give you the dish.

MusicRadar

MusicRadar (www.musicradar.com) claims to be "the Number 1 Website for Musicians." I don't know how it determined it was number 1, but with news, reviews, lessons, buyers' guides, advice, and more, it's probably true.

With sections dedicated to guitars, amps, pedals, drums, synths, software, controllers, and more, there's something for everyone.

It's also a good place to find deals. For example, the day I wrote this, MusicRadar had a deal on AmpliTube Brian May (guitarist for Queen), with emulations of Brian's amps, cabinets, and stomp boxes plus presets for many of his most iconic guitar tones, including clean, rhythm, and solo tones (presets) for "We Are the Champions," riff and solo tones for "Bohemian Rhapsody," "Under Pressure," "Keep Yourself Alive," and many more. If I sound enthusiastic, I am — I love AmpliTube and I really love the Brian May pack.

I almost forgot — the reason I brought up AmpliTube was the deal I saw on Music-Radar: Buy it for $83.99 and save $16 (it's regularly $99.99).

For the latest info on gear and musicians, you can't beat MusicRadar.

Sweetwater Sound

Sweetwater Sound (www.sweetwater.com) is more than just an online audio dealer. It's also a huge state-of-the-art commercial recording studio. The salespeople put the gear into use in a real studio and can tell you whether something does or doesn't work. The site is full of excellent information about the products the company sells, its selection is second to none, and it has a very reasonable return policy. The site offers downloadable gear guides and informative, free e-newsletters.

Sweetwater Sound is the first site I go to when I'm shopping for something — and it's the site where I usually end up making my purchase.

Finally, its customer service is superb. When I bought my Scarlett Solo interface from Sweetwater, my salesperson called me a few weeks later just to ask how it was working and if I had any questions. Called me on the phone, mind you, not to sell me anything but to make sure I was a happy customer. Who does that anymore?

Musician's Friend

If Sweetwater is number one, Musician's Friend (www.musiciansfriend.com) is surely a strong number two. With a fantastic selection of instruments and recording gear, and lots of closeouts and other killer deals, this is another site that you should not miss if you're shopping for gear.

TIP

Look at both sites before you buy. One time I wanted an M-Audio Oxygen 8 keyboard. It was the same price at both sites, but Sweetwater was throwing in a carrying bag at no additional cost. I've seen the same thing happen with Musician's Friend, where it was bundling an item that Sweetwater wasn't.

TIP

It pays to visit at least two or three vendor sites before you reach for your wallet.

Monoprice

Monoprice (www.monoprice.com) is my first stop for cables and other accessories for both recording and general computing. I've purchased two large-screen displays and dozens of small gadgets and cables from Monoprice over the past decade and have never been disappointed with the quality or the price.

Monoprice specializes in cables and offers USB cables with every connector ever invented. It also has Thunderbolt, Lightning, and Ethernet cables as well as guitar (¼ inch) and microphone (XLR) cables. The best part is that most of its cables come in a plethora of lengths and colors.

Other stuff it makes includes home automation gear (cameras, security, and so on), cable adapters, docks, hubs, power banks (batteries), and more HDMI cables than I could count. All Monoprice cables are reasonably priced, and its HDMI cables are higher quality and cost less than BestBuy's mediocre house brand HDMI cables (for example).

One last thing: I recently noticed that Monoprice has its own house brand guitars, amps, and reasonably priced MIDI keyboard controllers. Although I haven't tried any of them yet, I would absolutely consider Monoprice the next time I need a new guitar, amp, or MIDI controller.

Apple GarageBand Discussion Board

If you have a question about how to do something in GarageBand, Apple's Garage-Band discussion board is the place to get an answer:

>> **For Macs:** https://discussions.apple.com/community/ilife/garageband

>> **For iDevices:** https://discussions.apple.com/community/ios_apps/garageband_for_ios

It's hosted by Apple and is full of questions and answers by both Apple staffers and other GarageBand users like you and me. Here are some recent topics:

>> Frequently asked questions (FAQs)

>> GarageBand compatibility list

>> Recording multiple tracks in GarageBand

>> Making new instruments

>> Exporting tracks to Logic Pro

You can find hundreds of other GarageBand-related topics, and the boards seem to get a lot of traffic, so many questions are answered the same day they're posted. If you post a message, don't forget to come back to the site the next day (or every day for a few days) to read the replies and thank the helpful posters.

TIP

You may want to bookmark the page that contains your message so you can find it quickly when you return.

Index

A

AAC file, 365, 367–368, 374–375

accessing remix FX effects, 253

accessories, for GarageBand, 12–14

acoustic instruments
  recording with mics on iDevices, 273–290
  recording with mics on Macs, 137–155

acoustics, room, 166, 404

Activity Monitor, 11, 395–397

adding
  Apple loops to cells, 245–246
  audio interfaces, 42–44
  chorus effect
    on iDevices, 338
    on Macs, 210
  compression
    on iDevices, 282–283
    on Macs, 146
  compressor effect
    on iDevices, 337–338
    on Macs, 209–210
  echo
    on iDevices, 338
    on Macs, 209
  effects
    on iDevices, 281–283, 333–338
    on Macs, 145–146, 206–210, 215
  equalization (EQ), 207–209
  fade-in/fade-outs, 216
  loops
    to favorites list, 102, 248
    on iDevices, 266–267
    on Macs, 104–109
  MIDI keyboards, 37–39
  plug-in effects, 125–129
  remix FX, 253–254
  reverb
    on iDevices, 338
    on Macs, 209

third-party loops to loop browser, 102–103

adjusting
  amp simulators, 168
  compressor effects, 219–221
  duration of notes on iDevices, 311
  effects
    on iDevices, 334
    on Macs, 206, 217–221
  equalization (EQ)
    on iDevices, 218
    on Macs, 125
  global settings, 228–229
  length of notes, 194
  levels, 51, 65–67, 216
  loop tempo, 104
  master echo, 218–219
  master effects, 219–221
  master EQ, 218
  master reverb, 218–219
  pan
    on iDevices, 283–284
    on Macs, 142
  pitch
    on iDevices, 311, 320–322
    on Macs, 176–177, 189–190
  plug-in effects, 125–129
  presets
    on iDevices, 303
    on Macs, 168
  settings for tracks, 62–63
  Smart controls, 120
  sound of software instruments, 119–134
  start/end points of cycle area, 81
  stomp box effects on iDevices, 303–304
  tempo
    on iDevices, 311, 320
    on Macs, 176, 232–233
  tonal characteristics, 215

adjusting (continued)
  track instruments, 64
  velocity
    on iDevices, 324–325
    on Macs, 195
  volume of parts of song, 216
Advanced pane
  about, 89
  Audio Recording Resolution setting, 89–90
  Auto Normalize setting, 90
  Movie Thumbnail Resolution setting, 90
Advanced setting, 235
The Age of Monaural Music, 50
The Age of Recorded Music, 50
The Age of Stereo, 50
AIF/AIFF (Audio Interchange File Format), 365, 366–367, 367–368
AirDrop option (Share menu), 370
Akai MPC (MIDI Production Center), 245
Alesis Drums Nitro Mesh Kit, 152
amp icon, 303
amplifiers
  changing simulators, 168
  live recording
    on iDevices with microphones and, 300–302
    on Macs with microphones and, 165–167
  playing live with effects and, 349–355
  virtual, 159–165
AmpliTube, 170–171, 209
angle bracket (>), 21, 23
Antares Auto-tune, 155
Apple GarageBand discussion board, 416
Apple loops, 93, 245–246
Apple lossless files, 368
Apple's Lightning-to-3.5mm headphone jack adapter, 40
Apple's Lightning-to-USB camera adapter, 39, 40
applying effects/presets to master track, 216–217
Arpeggiator button, 124
arrangement markers, 185–187, 312
arrangement track, 185–187, 312
arranging, on iDevices, 312–313
Audio Interchange File Format (AIF/AIFF), 365, 366–367, 367–368
audio interfaces
  adding, 42–44
  tips for, 405–406

Audio Recording Resolution setting (Advanced pane), 89–90
Audioengine A2+ speaker system, 35
audio-in port, 40
Audio/MIDI Preferences pane
  about, 82
  Devices section, 80–84
  Effects section, 84
  MIDI section, 84
audio-out port, 40
Aurora Bell, 122–123
Auto Normalize setting (Advanced pane), 90
Auto-Collect Recordings switch, 359
automation curves, silencing mistakes with, 318–319
Auto-Tune EFX+, 209

B
background noise, preventing, 28
background vocals
  panning
    on iDevices, 333
    on Macs, 206
  sweetening with, 196–197
bandleader, 358–359
bass
  panning
    on iDevices, 333
    on Macs, 205
  recording on iDevices, 291–306
  tips for, 351–353
  websites for learning, 411–413
bi-directional (figure-8) microphones, 32, 33
Biting Distortion Heavy preset, 132–133
Blue Compass, 46
Blue Yeti Pro, 33
Bluetooth MIDI Devices setting, 235
Bluetooth setting, GarageBand access and, 228
boom, 45–46
bounce, 361
Browser icon, 236, 237
Burn Song to CD option (Share menu), 370–371
burning CDs. See CD recording
button view
  searching for loops in, 97–99
  viewing loops in, 94–96
buttons, for Smart controls, 124

C

cables, 39–42, 405
cardioid mics, 32, 33
CD Baby, 387
CD duplicator, 385
CD recording
  about, 377
  benefits of, 378
  burning songs, 380–387
  labels for, 386–387
  making multiple copies, 385–386
  preparing for, 378–380
CD-R/-RW, 379, 381
cells (loop grid)
  about, 244
  adding Apple loops to, 245–246
  editing, 249–252
  moving, 252
  recording into, 253
  working with, 249–254
Chaffin, Bryan (tech editor), 28
changes, testing, 136
Cheat Sheet (website), 4
checking
  on FileVault, 393–394
  levels, 64–65
  for noise
    on iDevices, 284
    on Macs, 146–148
  system requirements, 10–12
Choose a Project dialog, 18–19
chord chart, 411
chorus effect
  adding on iDevices, 338
  adding on Macs, 210
click track, 84, 118, 230
column triggers (loop grid), 244
column view
  searching for loops in, 99–100
  viewing loops in, 94–96
columns (loop grid), 244
Compare button, 124
compressed audio files, 367–368
compression
  about, 365–366
  adding

    on iDevices, 282–283
    on Macs, 146
  amounts of, 372–374
  compressed audio files, 367–368
  distributing music, 374–375
  sharing songs
    from iDevices, 372
    from Macs, 369–371
  uncompressed audio files, 366–367
compressor effects
  adding
    on iDevices, 337–338
    on Macs, 209–210
  adjusting, 219–221
compressors, 129–131
computers, connecting MIDI keyboards to, 39
condenser microphones, 31–32
connecting MIDI keyboards to computers, 39
connectors, 39–42
control bar, 236–239
controlling
  software instruments with MIDI keyboard, 112–114, 259–261
  song files, 73–75
Controls button, 124
copy and paste method
  on iDevices, 339–340
  on Macs, 210–211
copying notes on iDevices, 311
cost, of microphones, 30
Count In feature, 118–119, 254, 264, 398
Count-in setting, 231–232
CPU tab (Activity Monitor), 395–397
CPU usage, 394–395
creating
  drummer tracks, 134
  fade-outs, 221
  jam sessions, 358–359
  new projects, 19–20, 22
  practice files, 351–352
  rough mix on iDevices, 329
  software instrument tracks on iDevices, 262–263
  tempo curves, 188
Crosstalk Protection setting, 229
customizing
  guitar tracks on iDevices, 302–306
  guitar tracks on Macs, 168–171

cutting
  notes on iDevices, 311
  tracks, 53–69
cycle area
  adjusting start/end points of, 81
  enabling, 80
  setting, 379–380
Cycle Off/On pop-up menu, 81

D

dashes, 192
deadening sound, 27–28
delay. *See* echo
deleting
  loops from favorites list, 102, 248
  notes, 194
  tempo points, 189
Devices section (Audio/MIDI Preferences pane), 80–84
DigiDesign Pro Tools, 406, 408–409
direct recording
  about, 158–159
  on iDevices, 292–300
  with virtual amplifiers
    on iDevices, 293–300
    on Macs, 159–165
displaying
  CPU History window, 396
  instruments in loop browser, 96–97
  master track, 215
  track headers on iDevices, 265–266
distortion effect, 221
distribution
  about, 377, 387
  CD Baby, 387
  music, 374–375
  TuneCore, 387
Document Storage setting, GarageBand access and, 229
double tracking
  about, 170, 210
  on iDevices, 306, 339–340
  on Macs, 210–212
dragging and dropping loops, 105–106
drum kits, 115, 135
drum/drummer tracks, 134–136, 261

drummer loops, 249
drums
  panning on iDevices, 332
  panning on Macs, 205
duplicating notes, 194
duration of notes, changing on iDevices, 311
dynamic microphones, 31–32

E

earbuds, 36–37
echo
  about, 127–129
  adding
    on iDevices, 338
    on Macs, 209
  master, 218–219
Edit Chords setting, 233, 234
Edit menu, 249–252
editing
  cells, 249–252
  changing
    pitch, 189–190
    tempo, 188–189
  loops, 108–109
  performance in software instrument regions, 269–272
  presets
    on iDevices, 304–305
    on Macs, 169–170
  real instrument tracks on iDevices, 310–312
  rearranging notes in regions, 190–195
  software instrument tracks
    on iDevices, 310–312, 319–326
    on Macs, 188–195
  software instrument *versus* real instrument tracks, 176–177
  tracks
    on iDevices, 309–326
    on Macs, 175–198
  when to use, 176
editor, changing velocity of notes on iDevices with, 324
effects. *See also specific effects*
  adding
    on iDevices, 281–283, 333–338
    on Macs, 145–146, 206–210, 215

applying to master track, 216–217

enabling on iDevices, 334–335

modifying

on Macs, 206, 217–221

on iDevices, 334

nondestructive, 147–148

playing live with amps and, 349–355

Effects section (Audio/MIDI Preferences pane), 84

electric guitars, recording, 157–171

electronic instruments, recording, 157–171

Enable the Force Touch Trackpad check box (General Preferences pane), 82

enabling

cell editing, 249, 252, 253

count-in, 254

cycle area, 80

effects on iDevices, 334–335

EQ, 125

metronome, 254

multi-take recording on iDevices, 314

mute icon, 266

quantization, 325

solo icon, 266

end points, adjusting for cycle area, 81

EQ button, 124

equalization (EQ)

adjusting, 218

on iDevices, 335–337

on Macs, 207–209

equalizer effect, 125–127

equipment, for recording studio, 28–29

errors. See mistakes

Export Song to Disk option (Share menu), 371

exporting to Macs, from iDevices for mastering, 343

extending

cycle area, 380

loops, 107–108

F

Fade Out setting, 233

fade-ins/fade-outs, 216, 221

fader control, 65–66

favorites list, for loops, 102, 248

features, of microphones, 30

feedback, 277

figure-8 (bi-directional) mics, 32, 33

file compression

about, 365–366

adding

on iDevices, 282–283

on Macs, 146

amounts of, 372–374

compressed audio files, 367–368

distributing music, 374–375

sharing songs

from iDevices, 372

from Macs, 369–371

uncompressed audio files, 366–367

FileVault, 393–394

filtering

by loop type, 101

loops, 246–247

finding

keyboards, 37–38

loops, 92–103, 242, 246–247

loops with loop browser, 94–103

song files on Macs, 374

fixing

errors, 178–185

mistakes on iDevices, 313–319

Focusrite iTrack Solo - Lightning, 274

Focusrite Scarlett Solo, 44, 160, 162–163

Follow Tempo & Pitch setting, 251

FX icon, 237

G

Gain setting, 250

GarageBand. See also specific topics

about, 8

accessories for, 12–14

allowing access, 228–229

burning songs to CDs using, 381

for iDevices, 20–23

for Mac, 18–20

origins of, 7–8

settings, 229–236

uses for, 9–10

GarageBand Karaoke, 412–413

General Preferences pane

  about, 80

  Enable the Force Touch Trackpad check box, 82

  Reset Warnings button, 82

  Software Instrument Recordings section, 80–81

getting started

  about, 79, 227

  Advanced pane, 89–90

  Audio/MIDI Preferences pane, 82–84

  control bar, 236–239

  GarageBand settings, 229–236

  General Preferences pane, 80–82

  global settings, 228–229

  Loops Preferences pane, 86–88

  Metronome Preferences pane, 84–86

  My Info pane, 88–89

  sharing projects with Macs, 239–240

global settings, adjusting, 228–229

Go to beginning icon, 238

Grado SR-60 headphones, 36

Greek chorus, sweetening with, 197

Grid icon, 237

grid scale, 195, 272

Guitar Center, 406

guitarists

  tips for, 351–353

guitars

  panning

    on iDevices, 333

    on Macs, 205

  recording on iDevices, 291–306

  websites for learning, 411–413

H

Hamilton, Dave (drummer), 149, 285

handheld percussion instruments

  panning on iDevices, 333

  panning on Macs, 206

hard drives

  improving space on, 47–48

  recording with, 14

harmony vocals, sweetening with, 197

headphones

  tips for, 403–404

  using, 36–37

Help setting, 235–236

HENKUR USB Camera Adapter with Charging Port, 274

hiding master tracks, 215

horns, sweetening with, 198

I

icons

  +, 243

  amp, 303

  Browser, 236, 237

  explained, 3

  FX, 237

  Go to beginning, 238

  Grid, 237

  Info, 238, 239

  library, 168

  loop browser, 94, 238

  Master volume slider, 238

  Metronome, 238

  mute, 61, 201, 265, 266, 329

  My Songs, 236

  Play, 238

  Quick Help, 21

  record, 238, 299

  set input options, 295

  Settings, 238

  solo, 61, 201, 265, 266, 329

  speaker, 101

  Track controls, 237

  tracks, 265

  Tracks view, 236

  undo, 238, 252

iDevices

  adding

    chorus effect on, 338

    compression on, 282–283

    compressor effect on, 337–338

    echo on, 338

    effects on, 281–283, 333–338

    loops on, 266–267

    reverb on, 338

  adjusting

    duration of notes on, 311

    effects on, 334

    equalization (EQ) on, 218

    pan on, 283–284

pitch on, 311, 320–322
presets on, 303
stomp box effects on, 303–304
tempo on, 311, 320
velocity on, 324–325
Apple GarageBand discussion board for, 416
arranging on, 312–313
checking for noise on, 284
choosing instruments on, 263–264
copy and paste method on, 339–340
copying notes on, 311
creating
rough mix on, 329
software instrument tracks on, 262–263
customizing guitar tracks on, 302–306
cutting notes on, 311
direct recording on, 292–300
displaying track headers on, 265–266
double tracking on, 306, 339–340
duration of notes, changing on, 311
editing
presets on, 304–305
real instrument tracks on, 310–312
software instrument tracks on, 310–312, 319–326
tracks on, 309–326
enabling
effects on, 334–335
multi-take recording on, 314
exporting to Macs from, 343
fixing mistakes on, 313–319
GarageBand for, 20–23
improving sound of recordings on, 289–290
increasing volume of instruments on, 296–298
joining regions on, 268, 317–318
level meters on, 331
live recording on, 292–293, 300–302
mastering
exporting to Macs from, 343
preparing for on, 342–343
mixing tracks on, 327–340
multi-take recording, enabling on, 314
multitrack recording on, 57–59, 284–288
panning
adjusting on, 283–284
background vocals on, 333

bass on, 333
drums on, 332
guitar on, 333
handheld percussion instruments
on, 333
keyboards on, 333
lead vocals on, 333
pianos on, 333
shakers on, 333
synths on, 333
tracks on, 331–333
washboards on, 333
pasting notes on, 311
playing live with amps and effects, 349–355
positioning microphones for, 279
preparing
for mastering on, 342–343
for recording on, 275–284
quantize feature on, 271–272, 325–326
rearranging
notes in regions on, 322–324
notes on, 311–313
recording
with acoustic instruments and mics on,
273–290
basses on, 291–306
guitars on, 291–306
preparing for on, 275–284
software instrument tracks on, 264
tracks on, 57–59, 288–289, 299–300
vocals with mics on, 273–290
re-recording method on, 340
setting levels on, 280–281, 298–299
setup
for recording on, 293–295
troubleshooting on, 295
sharing
projects from Macs to, 240
songs from, 343–345, 372
splitting regions on, 268, 317–318
sweetening on, 326
system requirements for, 12
track volume automation control on, 330–331
trimming regions on, 269
troubleshooting setup on, 295

improving
  hard drive space, 47–48
  performance, 391–400
  recordings, 401–409
  sound of recordings
    on iDevices, 289–290
    on Macs, 153–155
  vocals, 142
in the can, 53
increasing
  volume of instruments on iDevices, 296–298
  volume of instruments on Macs, 162–163
Info icon, 238, 239
inserting loops into tracks, 105
instruments
  displaying in loop browser, 96–97
  increasing volume for, 162–163
  selecting on iDevices, 263–264
iOS, changing track settings on, 62–63
iTunes, burning songs to CDs using, 382–384

J

Jam Session setting, 235
jam sessions
  about, 357
  bandleader, 358–359
  member, 360
  working with, 361–363
Jobs, Steve (Apple CEO), 7
joining
  regions on iDevices, 268, 317–318
  regions on Macs, 182–184
J.R. Beck 9861EQ acoustic/electric guitar, 166–167, 301–302

K

key signature, setting, 233, 234
Keyboard Browsing setting (Loops Preferences pane), 86–87
Keyboard Layout setting (Loops Preferences pane), 87–88
keyboard shortcuts, 252
keyboards
  finding, 37–38
  on-screen, 12, 13

panning
  on iDevices, 333
  on Macs, 205
Knob Gestures setting, 229

L

laying down software instrument tracks, 257–272
lead vocals
  panning on iDevices, 333
  panning on Macs, 205
Learn from this app setting, 228
length, changing for notes, 194
Length setting, 251
level meters
  on iDevices, 331
  on Macs, 203–204
levels
  adjusting, 51, 65–67, 216
  checking, 64–65
  setting
    on iDevices, 280–281, 298–299
    on Macs, 143–144, 163–164
Levine, Steve (producer), 209
library, opening, 168
library icon, 168
Lightning audio interfaces, 43
Lightning-to-USB camera adapter, 258, 274
line level, 34
listening
  to loops, 247–248
  to tracks, 59–62
live loops, 249. *See also* loops
live recording
  with amplifiers and microphones
    on iDevices, 300–302
    on Macs, 165–167
  on iDevices, 292–293
  on Macs, 158–159
locating
  keyboards, 37–38
  loops, 92–103, 242, 246–247
  loops with loop browser, 94–103
  song files on Macs, 374
location, for microphones, 165–166
Logic Pro, 406, 407–408

loop browser
  adding third-party loops to, 102–103
  displaying instruments in, 96–97
  finding loops with, 94–103
loop browser icon, 94, 238
Loop Browser setting (Loops Preferences pane), 88
loop grid, 243–245, 254–255
looping, 242
Looping setting, 251
loops
  about, 91–92, 241–242, 243
  adding
    Apple loops to cells, 245–246
    on iDevices, 266–267
    on Macs, 104–109
  dragging and dropping, 105–106
  editing, 108–109
  extending, 107–108
  favorites list, 248
  filtering
    on iDevices, 246–247
    on Macs, 101
  finding, 92–103, 242, 246–247
  finding with loop browser, 94–103
  listening to, 247–248
  loop grid, 243–245
  previewing, 101–102
  recording with loop grid, 254–255
  redoing, 106–107, 252
  repeating, 107–108
  reusing, 109
  saving, 102
  searching for, 97–100
  setting tempo for, 103–104
  shortening, 107–108
  tracks and, 58–59
  types of, 249
  undoing, 106–107, 252
  using, 93
  viewing in button/column view, 94–96
  working with, 245–249
Loops Preferences pane
  about, 86
  Keyboard Browsing setting, 86–87
  Keyboard Layout setting, 87–88
  Loop Browser setting, 88

M

Macs
  adding
    chorus effect on, 210
    compression on, 146
    compressor effect on, 209–210
    echo on, 209
    effects on, 145–146, 206–210, 215
    loops on, 104–109
    reverb on, 209
  adjusting
    effects on, 206, 217–221, 334
    equalization (EQ) on, 125
    pan on, 142
    pitch on, 176–177, 189–190
    presets on, 168
    tempo on, 176, 232–233
    track settings on, 62–63
    velocity on, 195
  Apple GarageBand discussion board for, 416
  checking for noise on, 146–148
  customizing guitar tracks on, 168–171
  direct recording with virtual amplifiers on, 159–165
  double tracking on, 210–212
  editing
    presets on, 169–170
    software instrument tracks on, 188–195
    tracks on, 175–198
  exporting to from iDevices, 343
  finding song files on, 374
  GarageBand for, 18–20
  improving sound of recordings on, 153–155
  increasing volume of instruments on, 162–163
  joining regions on, 182–184
  live recording on, 158–159, 165–167
  mastering
    exporting to, 343
    preparing for on, 214–215
  mixing tracks on, 199–212
  multitrack recording
    with MIDI drum on, 151–152
    multiple tracks at once on, 150–151
    one track at a time on, 149–150
    recording tracks on, 54–57

Macs (continued)

panning
  adjusting on, 142
  background vocals on, 206
  bass on, 205
  drums on, 205
  guitar on, 205
  handheld percussion instruments on, 206
  keyboards on, 205
  lead vocals on, 205
  pianos on, 205
  shakers on, 206
  synths on, 205
  tracks on, 204–206
  washboards on, 206
playing live with amps and effects, 349–355
positioning microphones for, 142–143
preparing for mastering on, 214–215
quantize feature on, 194–195
rearranging
  notes in regions on, 190–195
  notes on, 177
recording
  acoustic instruments with mics on, 137–155
  guitars on, 157–171
  software instrument tracks on, 111–136
  tracks on, 54–57, 152–153, 164–165
  vocals with mics on, 137–155
recording tracks on, 54–57
Redo command, 107
re-recording method on, 211–212
setting levels on, 143–144, 163–164
sharing
  projects with, 239–240
  songs from, 369–371
splitting regions on, 182–184
system requirements for, 10–12
track volume automation control on, 202–203
troubleshooting setup on, 161–162
Undo command, 107
Mail, sending AAC/MP3 files via, 374–375
Mail option (Share menu), 370
MainStage app, 354
Master button, 124
master echo, 127–129, 218–219, 338
master effects, 219–221

master EQ, 218
master reverb, 218–219, 338
master tracks, 215–217
master volume, setting, 221–222
Master volume slider icon, 238
mastering
  about, 71–73, 213–214, 341–342
  applying presets/effects to master track, 216–217
  defined, 16
  exporting to Macs from iDevices for, 343
  finalizing after, 222–223
  master track, 215–222
  preparing for
    on iDevices, 342–343
    on Macs, 214–215
  setting master volume, 221–222
  tweaking effects, 217–221
M-Audio Keystation 49 MK3 keyboard, 37, 114
May, Brian (guitarist), 209, 414
MDR-7506 Sony headphones, 36
member, 360
Memory tab (Activity Monitor), 395–397
Messages, sending AAC/MP3 files via, 374–375
metronome
  about, 84, 264
  enabling, 254
  settings for, 230–232
  using, 118
Metronome icon, 238
Metronome Level slider, 231–232
Metronome Preferences pane, 84–86
mic stands, 45–46
microphones
  about, 12
  choosing, 29–34
  condenser, 31–32
  dynamic, 31–32
  live recording
    on iDevices with amplifiers and, 300–302
    on Macs with amplifiers and, 165–167
  placing, 165–166
  polarity patterns, 32–33
  positioning
    for iDevices, 279
    on Macs, 142–143
  preamps, 33–34

recording
    acoustic instruments on iDevices on, 273–290
    acoustic instruments on Macs with, 137–155
    vocals on iDevices with, 273–290
    vocals on Macs with, 137–155
    ribbon, 31
    setting up, 34, 138–142
    storing, 143, 279
    third-party, 274
    tips for, 401–402, 404
MIDI
    about, 39, 112, 257–259
    recording with, 111–136
    work surfaces, 113
MIDI controllers, 112, 113, 259
MIDI drivers, resetting, 400
MIDI drum, recording with a, 151–152
MIDI drum controllers, multitrack recording on iDevices with, 287–288
MIDI keyboards
    adding, 37–39
    controlling software instruments with, 112–114, 259–261
MIDI Manufacturer's Association (website), 112
MIDI section (Audio/MIDI Preferences pane), 84
minimizing GarageBand window, 398
Miracle Piano, 37
mistakes
    fixing
        on iDevices, 313–319
        on Macs, 178–185
    silencing
        with automation curves, 318–319
        on Macs, 184–185
Mix (magazine), 413–414
mixing
    about, 69–70, 199–200, 327–328
    adding effects, 206–210
    doubling tracks, 210–212
    level meters, 203–204
    panning tracks, 204–206
    rough mix, 201
    setting the pan, 70–71
    track volume automation control, 202–203
    tracks
        on iDevices, 327–340
        on Macs, 199–212

Mixonline, 413–414
modifying
    amp simulators, 168
    compressor effects, 219–221
    duration of notes on iDevices, 311
    effects
        on iDevices, 334
        on Macs, 206, 217–221
    equalization (EQ)
        on iDevices, 218
        on Macs, 125
    global settings, 228–229
    length of notes, 194
    levels, 51, 65–67, 216
    loop tempo, 104
    master echo, 218–219
    master effects, 219–221
    master EQ, 218
    master reverb, 218–219
    pan
        on iDevices, 283–284
        on Macs, 142
    pitch
        on iDevices, 311, 320–322
        on Macs, 176–177, 189–190
    plug-in effects, 125–129
    presets
        on iDevices, 303
        on Macs, 168
    settings for tracks, 62–63
    Smart controls, 120
    sound of software instruments, 119–134
    start/end points of cycle area, 81
    stomp box effects on iDevices, 303–304
    tempo
        on iDevices, 311, 320
        on Macs, 176, 232–233
    tonal characteristics, 215
    track instruments, 64
    velocity
        on iDevices, 324–325
        on Macs, 195
    volume of parts of song, 216
mono, stereo *vs.*, 51
mono connection, 40
mono plugs, 40

Monoprice, 415–416

Move Tempo Curve Automation Point, 188–189

Movie Thumbnail Resolution setting (Advanced pane), 90

moving

  cells, 252

  cycle area, 380

  loops within/between tracks, 105

  notes, 194

MP3 files, 365, 368, 374–375

multiple takes, 68

multi-take recording, enabling on iDevices, 314

multitrack drum recording, 285–287

multitrack recording

  about, 49–50, 149

  adjusting

    instruments on tracks, 64

    levels, 65–67

    settings for tracks, 62–63

  checking levels, 64–65

  cutting tracks, 53–69

  defined, 8

  on iDevices, 284–288

  listening to tracks, 59–62

  loops and tracks, 58–59

  managing song files, 73–75

  mastering, 71–73

  with MIDI drum

    on iDevices, 287–288

    on Macs, 151–152

  mixing, 69–71

  multiple takes, 68

  multiple tracks at once

    on iDevices, 286–287

    on Macs, 150–151

  one track at a time

    on iDevices, 285–286

    on Macs, 149–150

  overdubbing, 68

  polishing tracks, 67

  process of, 52–53

  quadraphonic, 51

  recording tracks

    on iDevices, 57–59

    on Macs, 54–57

  role of stereo in, 50–52

Save/Save As command, 74–75

  setting the pan, 70–71

  stereo *vs.* mono, 51

  sweetening, 69

Multitrack Recording setting, 235

Music app, burning songs to CDs using, 382–384

Musical Instrument Digital Interface (MIDI). *See* MIDI

Musician's Friend, 29, 32, 415

MusicRadar, 414

mute icon, 61, 201, 265, 266, 329

My Info pane, 88–89

My Songs icon, 236

N

nanoPAD2, 152

near-field reference monitors, 35

noise

  checking for on iDevices, 284

  checking for on Macs, 146–148

nondestructive effects, 147–148

Note Pad setting, 234

notes

  changing velocity of on iDevices, 324–325

  copying on iDevices, 311

  cutting on iDevices, 311

  moving, 194

  pasting on iDevices, 311

  rearranging

    on iDevices, 311

    on Macs, 177

  rearranging in regions

    on iDevices, 322–324

    on Macs, 190–195

Notifications setting, GarageBand access and, 229

O

Octaves setting, 251

omni-directional mics, 32, 33

on-screen keyboard, 12, 13

opening

  Audio/MIDI Preferences pane, 82

  existing projects, 18–19, 22

  General Preferences pane, 80

  library, 168

organs
  panning on iDevices, 333
  panning on Macs, 205
overdrive effect, 221
overdubbing, 68

P

package, 17–18
pan, setting the, 70–71
pan settings control, 283
panning
  adjusting
    on iDevices, 283–284
    on Macs, 142
  background vocals
    on iDevices, 333
    on Macs, 206
  bass
    on iDevices, 333
    on Macs, 205
  drums
    on iDevices, 332
    on Macs, 205
  guitar
    on iDevices, 333
    on Macs, 205
  handheld percussion instruments
    on iDevices, 333
    on Macs, 206
  keyboards
    on iDevices, 333
    on Macs, 205
  lead vocals
    on iDevices, 333
    on Macs, 205
  organs, 205
  pianos
    on iDevices, 333
    on Macs, 205
  shakers
    on iDevices, 333
    on Macs, 206

synths
  on iDevices, 333
  on Macs, 205
tambourines, 206
tracks
  on iDevices, 331–333
  on Macs, 204–206
washboards
  on iDevices, 333
  on Macs, 206
pasting notes on iDevices, 311
percussion, sweetening with, 196
performance
  Activity Monitor, 395–397
  basic troubleshooting steps, 392–393
  checking on FileVault, 393–394
  CPU usage, 394–395
  drummer tracks and, 135
  editing in software instrument regions, 269–272
  improving, 391–400
  minimizing GarageBand window, 398
  RAM, 394–395, 398–399
  recording resolution, 397–398
  resetting MIDI drivers, 400
  storage speed, 399
  turning off Wi-Fi, 400
pianos
  panning on iDevices, 333
  panning on Macs, 205
pitch
  changing on iDevices, 311, 320–322
  changing on Macs, 176–177, 189–190
placing
  loops on tracks, 105
  microphones, 165–166
Play icon, 238
Play Mode setting, 251
playing live
  with amps and effects, 349–355
  at home, 350–351
  on stage, 353–355
plug-in effects, adding/changing, 125–129
polarity patterns, for microphones, 32–33

pop filters, 47
ports, 39–42
positioning
  microphones for iDevices, 279
  microphones for Macs, 142–143
practice files, creating, 351–352
preamps, 33–34
preparing
  for CD recording, 378–380
  for mastering
    on iDevices, 342–343
    on Macs, 214–215
  for recording on iDevices, 275–284
presets
  applying to master track, 216–217
  changing
    on iDevices, 303
    on Macs, 168
  choosing, 216
  editing
    on iDevices, 304–305
    on Macs, 169–170
preventing background noise, 28
previewing loops, 101–102
Pro Tools, 406, 408–409
Project to GarageBand for iOS option (Share menu), 371
projects
  creating new, 19–20, 22
  opening existing, 18–19, 22
  sharing with Macs, 239–240
proximity effect, 142, 279
punching in/out, 178–181, 311–312, 314–316

Q

quadraphonic sound, 51
quantizate feature
  on iDevices, 271–272, 325–326
  on Macs, 194–195
Quantization setting, 251
Quick Help icon, 21

R

Radio Shack, 42
RAM

about, 11
  upgrading, 398–399
  usage of, 394–395
RCA connection, 40
RCA jacks, 42
real instrument loops, 58–59, 92, 249
real instrument tracks
  editing on iDevices, 310–312
  software instrument tracks vs., 176–177
rearranging
  notes
    on iDevices, 311–313
    on Macs, 177
  notes in regions
    on iDevices, 322–324
    on Macs, 190–195
  regions, 185–187
record icon, 238, 299
recording
  acoustic instruments with mics
    on iDevices, 273–290
    on Macs, 137–155
  basses on iDevices, 291–306
  CD
    about, 377
    benefits of, 378
    burning songs, 380–387
    labels for, 386–387
    making multiple copies, 385–386
    preparing for, 378–380
  into cells, 253
  direct, 158–165, 292–300
  electronic instruments, 157–171
  guitars
    on iDevices, 291–306
    on Macs, 157–171
  improving, 153–155, 401–409
  live, 158–167, 292–293, 300–302
  with loop grid, 254–255
  with MIDI, 111–136
  with a MIDI drum, 151–152
  multitrack
    about, 49–50, 149
    adjusting instruments on tracks, 64
    adjusting levels, 65–67

adjusting settings for tracks, 62–63

checking levels, 64–65

cutting tracks, 53–69

defined, 8

on iDevices, 284–288

listening to tracks, 59–62

loops and tracks, 58–59

managing song files, 73–75

mastering, 71–73

with MIDI drum, 151–152, 287–288

mixing, 69–71

multiple takes, 68

multiple tracks at once, 150–151, 286–287

one track at a time, 149–150, 285–286

overdubbing, 68

polishing tracks, 67

process of, 52–53

quadraphonic, 51

recording tracks, 54–57, 57–59

role of stereo in, 50–52

Save/Save As command, 74–75

setting the pan, 70–71

stereo vs. mono, 51

sweetening, 69

preparing for on iDevices, 275–284

resolution for, 397–398

sequence for, 15–18

setting up for, 159–161

software instrument tracks

on iDevices, 264

on Macs, 111–136

tape vs. hard drive, 14

tracks

on iDevices, 57–59, 288–289, 299–300

on Macs, 54–57, 152–153, 164–165

vocals with mics

on iDevices, 273–290

on Macs, 137–155

recording space

about, 25

adding

audio interfaces, 42–44

MIDI keyboards, 37–39

budget-friendly, 26–27

cables, 39–42

choosing

mic stands, 45–46

microphones, 29–34

speakers, 34–35

connectors, 39–42

equipment for, 28–29

improving hard drive space, 47–48

pop filters, 47

ports, 39–42

tips for, 27–28

tuning devices, 48

using headphones, 36–37

wind screens, 47

Red Book Audio files, 366–367

Redo command, 107, 181–182, 252, 316–317

redo features, 181–182

redoing loops, 106–107, 252

reducing crosstalk, 229

reference monitors, 35

reflected sound, 27

regions

joining

on iDevices, 268, 317–318

on Macs, 182–184

rearranging

on iDevices, 322–324

on Macs, 185–187, 190–195

splitting

on iDevices, 268, 317–318

on Macs, 182–184

trimming on iDevices, 269

working with on iDevices, 267–272

Remember icon, 3

remix FX, adding, 253–254

repeating loops, 107–108

reproduction, 377

re-recording method

on iDevices, 340

on Macs, 211–212

Reset All setting, 252

Reset Warnings button (General Preferences pane), 82

resetting

MIDI drivers, 400

volume slider, 221

resolution, for recording, 397–398

Restore Purchase setting, 235
reusing
  loops, 109
  saved settings, 131
reverb
  about, 127–129
  adding
    on iDevices, 338
    on Macs, 209
  master, 218–219
Reverse setting, 252
ribbon microphone, 31
ripping, 365
RME Babyface Pro FS, 274
room acoustics, 166
rough mix
  creating on iDevices, 329
  creating on Macs, 201
rows (loop grid), 244
Run in Background setting, 235

S

Save/Save As command, 17, 74–75
saving loops, 102
scale, filtering loops by, 247
Scarlett Solo USB audio interface, 297–298
search field, 100, 247
searching for loops, 97–100
selecting
  instruments on iDevices, 263–264
  mic stands, 45–46
  microphones, 29–34
  presets, 216
  software instruments, 114–117
  speakers, 34–35
  tracks to hear, 61
Semitones setting, 251
Send MIDI Clock setting, 235
sending files via Mail or Messages, 374–375
set input options icon, 295
set list, 353
setting the pan, 70–71
setting(s)
  Advanced, 235
  Bluetooth MIDI Devices, 235

changing for tracks, 62–63
cycle area, 379–380
Edit Chords, 233, 234
Fade Out, 233
Follow Tempo & Pitch, 251
Gain, 250
GarageBand, 229–236
global, 228–229
Help, 235–236
Jam Session, 235
key signature, 233, 234
Length, 251
levels
  on iDevices, 280–281, 298–299
  on Macs, 143–144, 163–164
Looping, 251
master volume, 221–222
for metronome, 230–232
Multitrack Recording, 235
Note Pad, 234
Octaves, 251
Play Mode, 251
Quantization, 251
Reset All, 252
Restore Purchase, 235
Reverse, 252
Run in Background, 235
Semitones, 251
Send MIDI Clock, 235
Speed, 252
Tempo, 232–233
tempo for loops, 103–104
time signature, 233
Time Snap, 251
24-bit Audio Resolution, 235
Velocity, 250
Settings app, 228
Settings icon, 238
setup
  microphones, 34, 138–142
  for recording
    on iDevices, 293–295
    on Macs, 159–161
  recording track, 138–142
  software instrument track for recording, 115–116

troubleshooting
   on iDevices, 295
   on Macs, 161–162
shakers
   panning on iDevices, 333
   panning on Macs, 206
Share menu, 369–371
sharing
   projects with Macs, 239–240
   songs from iDevices, 343–345, 372
   songs from Macs, 369–371
shortening
   cycle area, 380
   loops, 107–108
Show in Search setting, 228
Show Siri Suggestions setting, 229
silencing mistakes, 184–185, 318–319
Siri & Search setting, GarageBand access and, 228–229
16-bit recording, 397–398
Smart controls
   adding plug-in effects, 125–129
   adjusting, 120
   adjusting plug-in effects, 125–129
   buttons for, 124
   using, 120–124
Smart instruments, 12, 13, 261
software instrument loops, 58–59, 92, 249
Software Instrument Recordings section (General
   Preferences pane), 80–81
software instrument regions, editing performance in,
   269–272
software instrument tracks
   about, 257
   adding loops, 266–267
   controlling software instruments with MIDI keyboards,
    259–261
   copying regions, 267–268
   creating
    on iDevices, 262–263
    on Macs, 262–263
   cutting regions, 267–268
   displaying track headers, 265–266
   editing
    on iDevices, 269–272, 310–312, 319–326
    on Macs, 188–195
   joining regions, 268

laying down, 257–272
MIDI, 257–259
pasting regions, 267–268
real instrument tracks vs., 176–177
recording
   on iDevices, 264
   on Macs, 264
selecting
   instruments, 263–264
   regions, 267–268
splitting regions, 268
trimming regions, 269
working with, 265–272
software instruments
   choosing, 114–117
   controlling with MIDI keyboard, 112–114, 259–261
   recording with, 111–136
   working with on iDevices, 261–264
software tips, 406–409
solo icon, 61, 201, 265, 266, 329
Song to Media Browser option (Share menu), 370
Song to Music option (Share menu), 369–370
Song to SoundCloud option (Share menu), 370
songs
   finding files on Macs, 374
   managing, 73–75
   mixing tracks into on iDevices, 327–340
   sections of on iDevices, 312–313
   sharing
    from iDevices, 343–345, 372
    from Macs, 369–371
sound
   deadening, 27–28
   improving for recordings
    on iDevices, 289–290
    on Macs, 153–155
   reflected, 27
sound field, 51
sound pack, filtering loops by, 247
sound stage, 51
speaker icon, 101
speakers
   choosing, 34–35
   tips for, 402–403
special effects, sweetening with, 198

speed, of storage, 399
Speed setting, 252
splitting
  regions on iDevices, 268, 317–318
  regions on Macs, 182–184
stage, playing live on, 353–355
start points, adjusting for cycle area, 81
stereo
  mono vs., 51
  role of in multitrack recording, 50–52
stereo connection, 40
stereo plugs, 40
stomp box effects, changing on iDevices, 303–304
storing
  microphones, 143, 279
  speed of, 399
strings, sweetening with, 198
Suggest Shortcuts setting, 229
SuperDrive, 379
sweetening
  about, 69, 195–196
  backing vocals, 196–197
  horns, 198
  on iDevices, 326
  percussion, 196
  special effects, 198
  strings, 198
  woodwinds, 198
Sweetwater, 406
Sweetwater Sound, 29, 32, 414–415
synths
  panning on iDevices, 333
  panning on Macs, 205
system requirements, checking, 10–12

T
tablature, 412
tambourines
  panning on iDevices, 333
  panning on Macs, 206
Tapco's S-5 Active Studio Monitors, 35
tape, recording with, 14
Technical Stuff icon, 3

tempo
  adjusting
    on iDevices, 311, 320
    on Macs, 176, 232–233
  setting for loops, 103–104
tempo curve, 188
tempo points, 189
Tempo setting, 232–233
testing changes, 136
third-party amp modeling plug-ins, 170, 306
third-party loops, 102–103
third-party microphones, 274
third-party plug-ins, 352–353
Thunderbolt audio interfaces, 43
Thunderbolt disk drive, 399
Time Quantize drop-down menu, 194
time signature, setting, 233
Time Snap setting, 251
timeline, 56
Tip icon, 3
toggling
  cycle area on/off, 380
  between loop views, 96
  metronome on/off, 85, 231
tonal characteristics, adjusting, 215
Tone slider (Metronome Preferences pane), 86
too hot/too cool, 163–165
Track button, 124
Track controls icon, 237
track echo, 338
track headers, displaying on iDevices, 265–266
track reverb, 338
track volume automation control
  about, 66–67
  on iDevices, 330–331
  on Macs, 202–203
track volume control, 184–185
Track volume slider, 265
tracks
  adding loops to, 104–109
  changing
    instruments for, 64
    settings for, 62–63
  cutting, 53–69

editing
  on iDevices, 309–326
  on Macs, 175–198
listening to, 59–62
loops and, 58–59
mixing
  on iDevices, 327–340
  on Macs, 199–212
panning
  on iDevices, 331–333
  on Macs, 204–206
polishing, 67–69
punching in/out, 178–181
recording
  on iDevices, 57–59, 288–289, 299–300
  on Macs, 54–57, 152–153, 164–165
  with software instruments, 117–119
working with on iDevices, 265–272
tracks icon, 265
tracks view, changing velocity of notes on iDevices with, 324–325
Tracks view icon, 236
transport controls, 59
trimming regions on iDevices, 269
troubleshooting
  basic steps for, 392–393
  setup
    on iDevices, 295
    on Macs, 161–162
TuneCore, 387
tuning devices, 48
turning off
  analyzer, 126
  FileVault, 393
  Wi-Fi, 400
tutorial (website), 4
24-bit Audio Resolution setting, 235
24-bit recording, 397–398

U

Ultimate-Guitar (website), 412
uncompressed audio files, 366–367
Undo command, 107, 181–182, 252, 316–317
undo feature, 59, 106, 181–182
undo icon, 238, 252

undoing loops, 106–107, 252
upgrading RAM, 398–399
USB audio interfaces, 43
USB SuperDrive, 379
USB-to-Lightning adapter, 293

V

velocity
  changing on iDevices, 324–325
  changing on Macs, 195
Velocity setting, 250
verifying
  on FileVault, 393–394
  levels, 64–65
  for noise
    on iDevices, 284
    on Macs, 146–148
  system requirements, 10–12
viewing loops in button/column view, 94–96
virtual amplifiers
  direct recording on iDevices with, 293–300
  direct recording on Macs with, 159–165
Visual Count-in setting, 231–232
vocals
  improving, 142
  recording with mics
    on iDevices, 273–290
    on Macs, 137–155
volume
  adjusting for parts of songs, 216
  increasing for instruments
    on iDevices, 296–298
    on Macs, 162–163
  master, 221–222
volume slider, 86, 221

W

"wall of egg cartons" technique, 28
warning dialog, 121–122
Warning icon, 3
washboards
  panning on iDevices, 333
  panning on Macs, 206
WAV file, 365, 366–367, 368

websites
AmpliTube, 209
Apple GarageBand discussion board, 416
Audioengine A2+ speaker system, 35
Auto-Tune EFX+, 209
Cheat Sheet, 4
GarageBand Karaoke, 412–413
M-Audio Keystation 49 MK3 keyboard, 114
MIDI Manufacturer's Association, 112
Mixonline, 413–414
Monoprice, 415–416
Musician's Friend, 29, 32, 415
MusicRadar, 414
Radio Shack, 42
recommended, 411–416

Sweetwater Sound, 29, 32, 414–415
tutorial, 4
Ultimate-Guitar, 412
Wi-Fi, turning off, 400
Wi-Fi collaboration. *See* jam sessions
wind screens, 47
woodwinds, sweetening with, 198
workspace, 56

X

XLR cables, 41
XLR connection, 40, 41
XLR port, 297
XY pad, drummer tracks and, 134–135

About the Author

Bob LeVitus, often referred to as "Dr. Mac," is considered one of the world's leading authorities on the Macintosh, its operating systems, and GarageBand. A prolific author, he has written 88 popular computer books, selling millions worldwide.

His most recent titles include *macOS Catalina For Dummies* and *iPhone For Dummies,* 13th Edition.

Bob is known for his expertise, trademark humorous style, and ability to translate techie jargon into usable and fun advice for regular folks.

Bob is a huge GarageBand fan, but one with real-world audio production experience. Long before becoming a Mac geek, he studied audio engineering with Grammy award-winning producer Bill Lazerus in Los Angeles while playing guitar and singing in bands as well as producing artists and bands.

Dedication

For my family: Lisa, Allison, and Jacob.

I missed you guys so much, but now that this book is finished you know what happens next.

I'll be back!

Can't wait!

Love,

Dad (a.k.a. Bob "Dr. Mac" LeVitus)
Spring 2020 (during the great zombie apocalypse)

Author's Acknowledgments

First and foremost: Thank you for buying my book.

This book was a team effort. Although my name appears on the cover, it wouldn't exist without the extraordinary efforts of that team. And so, before we go any further, I'd like to take this opportunity to express my heartfelt gratitude to all of them.

Major thanks to Steve Hayes at Wiley, for believing in this project and giving me the green light.

Big time thanks to my project editor, Susan Pink, who not only minded my Ps and Qs, but managed to keep me from using the word *stuff* on every page.

And thanks to all the folks in production for their efforts in putting together the book you hold in your hands.

My super-duper literary agent, Carole "Swifty" Jelen at Waterside Productions, deserves a double helping o' praise for putting up with me for more than 25 years. Thanks again. (And, for what it's worth, you'll always be "Swifty" to me.)

A heaping helping of thank-you to my tech editor and all-around good influence, Matthew Fecher. This book wouldn't be the same without his contributions.

To my wife, Lisa, and my kids, Allison and Jacob, thanks again for putting up with my all-too-frequent hibernations and for giving me the space I needed to do what I do. I love you guys.

Whew. I'm almost done, but I'd be remiss if I didn't thank some of the nice folks at Apple who helped this book along in some way, including the Czarina of Product Loans, Keri Walker. Thanks y'all.

Last but definitely not least: Thanks to Apple for creating GarageBand and pricing it right (free).

Publisher's Acknowledgments

Executive Editor: Steve Hayes

Project Editor: Susan Pink

Copy Editor: Susan Pink

Technical Editor: Matthew Fecher

Proofreader: Debbye Butler

Sr. Editorial Assistant: Cherie Case

Production Editor: Mohammed Zafar Ali

Cover Image: © Andersen Ross Photography Inc/ Getty Images

Leverage the power

Dummies is the global leader in the reference category and one of the most trusted and highly regarded brands in the world. No longer just focused on books, customers now have access to the dummies content they need in the format they want. Together we'll craft a solution that engages your customers, stands out from the competition, and helps you meet your goals.

Advertising & Sponsorships

Connect with an engaged audience on a powerful multimedia site, and position your message alongside expert how-to content. Dummies.com is a one-stop shop for free, online information and know-how curated by a team of experts.

- Targeted ads
- Video
- Email Marketing

- Microsites
- Sweepstakes sponsorship

20 MILLION PAGE VIEWS **EVERY SINGLE MONTH**

15 MILLION UNIQUE VISITORS PER MONTH

43% OF ALL VISITORS ACCESS THE SITE VIA THEIR MOBILE DEVICES

700,000 NEWSLETTER SUBSCRIPTIONS TO THE INBOXES OF *300,000* UNIQUE **INDIVIDUALS EVERY WEEK**

# of dummies

Custom Publishing

Reach a global audience in any language by creating a solution that will differentiate you from competitors, amplify your message, and encourage customers to make a buying decision.

- Apps
- Books
- eBooks
- Video
- Audio
- Webinars

Brand Licensing & Content

Leverage the strength of the world's most popular reference brand to reach new audiences and channels of distribution.

For more information, visit **dummies.com/biz**

PERSONAL ENRICHMENT

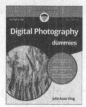

9781119187790	9781119179030	9781119293354	9781119293347	9781119310068	9781119235606
USA $26.00	USA $21.99	USA $24.99	USA $22.99	USA $22.99	USA $24.99
CAN $31.99	CAN $25.99	CAN $29.99	CAN $27.99	CAN $27.99	CAN $29.99
UK £19.99	UK £16.99	UK £17.99	UK £16.99	UK £16.99	UK £17.99

9781119251163	9781119235491	9781119279952	9781119283133	9781119287117	9781119130246
USA $24.99	USA $26.99	USA $24.99	USA $24.99	USA $24.99	USA $22.99
CAN $29.99	CAN $31.99	CAN $29.99	CAN $29.99	CAN $29.99	CAN $27.99
UK £17.99	UK £19.99	UK £17.99	UK £17.99	UK £16.99	UK £16.99

PROFESSIONAL DEVELOPMENT

9781119311041	9781119255796	9781119293439	9781119281467	9781119280651	9781119251132	9781119310563
USA $24.99	USA $39.99	USA $26.99	USA $26.99	USA $29.99	USA $24.99	USA $34.00
CAN $29.99	CAN $47.99	CAN $31.99	CAN $31.99	CAN $35.99	CAN $29.99	CAN $41.99
UK £17.99	UK £27.99	UK £19.99	UK £19.99	UK £17.99	UK £17.99	UK £24.99

9781119181705	9781119263593	9781119257769	9781119293477	9781119265313	9781119239314	9781119293323
USA $29.99	USA $26.99	USA $29.99	USA $26.99	USA $24.99	USA $29.99	USA $29.99
CAN $35.99	CAN $31.99	CAN $35.99	CAN $31.99	CAN $29.99	CAN $35.99	CAN $35.99
UK £21.99	UK £19.99	UK £21.99	UK £19.99	UK £17.99	UK £21.99	UK £21.99

dummies.com

dummies
A Wiley Brand

Learning Made E...

ACADEMIC

Algebra I

9781119293576
USA $19.99
CAN $23.99
UK £15.99

Basic Math & Pre-Algebra

9781119293637
USA $19.99
CAN $23.99
UK £15.99

Calculus

9781119293491
USA $19.99
CAN $23.99
UK £15.99

Chemistry

9781119293460
USA $19.99
CAN $23.99
UK £15.99

Physics I

9781119293590
USA $19.99
CAN $23.99
UK £15.99

1,001 Practice Questions SAT

9781119215844
USA $26.99
CAN $31.99
UK £19.99

Organic Chemistry I

9781119293378
USA $22.99
CAN $27.99
UK £16.99

Statistics

9781119293521
USA $19.99
CAN $23.99
UK £15.99

2016/2017 ASVAB

9781119239178
USA $18.99
CAN $22.99
UK £14.99

1,001 Practice Questions Praxis Core

9781119263883
USA $26.99
CAN $31.99
UK £19.99

Available Everywhere Books Are Sold

dummies.com

dummies
A Wiley Brand

easy books for big imaginations